CORPOR

GOVERNA

and Financial Reform
in China's
Transition Economy

To

Michael J. Trebilcock

— without whom this book could not have been possible

CORPORATE GOVERNANCE

and Financial Reform

in China's

Transition Economy

LENG Jing

香港大學出版社
HONG KONG UNIVERSITY PRESS

Hong Kong University Press
14/F Hing Wai Centre
7 Tin Wan Praya Road
Aberdeen
Hong Kong

© Hong Kong University Press 2009

Hardback ISBN 978-962-209-931-9
Paperback ISBN 978-962-209-932-6

Secure On-line Ordering
http://www.hkupress.org

British Library Cataloguing-in-Publication Data
A catalogue record for this book is available from the British Library.

Printed and bound by Kings Time Printing Press Co. Ltd., Hong Kong, China

Contents

Preface

This book provides a comprehensive and up to date review of corporate governance reforms and related financial reforms in China during the country's transition to a market economy. The discussions in this book cover China's enterprise, banking and securities sectors and take China's participation in economic globalization as a critical background to its domestic reform agenda.

By exploring the dynamics of China's evolving corporate governance regime, this book presents an important country study of corporate governance reforms in developing and post-communist transition economies to show the possibility of alternative paths to the market. As revealed in this book, China's experience illustrates the benefits of a gradualist transition strategy which emphasizes proper sequencing and pacing of reforms at different stages of economic development and the merits of transitional corporate governance institutions. Set as a counter-example is the radical privatization approach adopted by Russia, known as "shock therapy," which this book regards as a less successful case of building a vibrant corporate sector and a well functioning corporate governance system in a transition economy.

Drawing on the comparison between China and Russia, this book argues that for transition economies there is no universal path to a market economy; alternative approaches are possible. In moving toward the market, distinct social, political and cultural contexts that are peculiar to individual economies can create path dependence phenomena in country-specific reforms and should be carefully digested in reformers' policy making and strategy design processes.

International best practices may not work at a particular stage of development in a particular economy, often due to a lack of supporting and complementary institutions.

The book emphasizes that corporate governance reforms in China have proceeded under various constraints imposed by the country's limited political liberalization, underdeveloped legal environment and inadequate institutional, regulatory and human capital. These practical constraints have themselves been undergoing changes and adjustments over the course of China's economic development. These factors illustrate that in building a market-oriented corporate governance regime, it is sensible economics, as well as politics, for China to adopt a gradualist strategy in initiating and stepping up reforms to corporate ownership, control and financing mechanisms in both state and non-state sectors. Under this gradualist strategy, what has played a key role in discovering a better road to the market is a number of institutional innovations suitable to the particular social, political, economic and institutional conditions at a given stage of China's transition. These institutional innovations have generated sustained outcomes of economic efficiency, which in turn have created stimuli for the further expansion and deepening of reforms at later stages. While such innovative yet transitional institutions have shown the benefits of sequencing and pacing in corporate governance reforms in China, they have not fully complied with a full market economy — they instead have served as "stepping stones" to it.

Three features of the book

At a more specific and technical level, this book has three features in its coverage and analysis.

Firstly, the book articulates a dynamic theory of corporate governance and applies it to China's transition. This theory brings together two burgeoning fields of studies in legal scholarship: corporate governance and law and development. The book draws on the rapidly growing literature in these two fields to analyze the specific question of the evolution of corporate governance in China as the country is moving from central planning to a market economy. The analysis and reasoning in this book are grounded in legal, economic and political theories, in an effort to make a fresh cross-disciplinary contribution to contemporary research on post-communist transition.

Secondly, the book presents abundant empirical evidence reported in a vast volume of previous studies on both the Chinese and international experiences in corporate governance reforms — especially, evidence from other transition economies, particularly Russia — and makes necessary comparisons. The empirical and comparative perspectives of this book make it an informative and useful source of reference to those interested in not only the progress made in

China's transition, but also the broader dimensions of post-communist transition in a global context.

Thirdly, to relate academic inquiries to practical policy concerns on the part of national governments, especially of China's reformers, the topics discussed in this book display a wide range of issues that have received serious attention from the Chinese government at its various attempts to reform the country's enterprise and financial sectors. Corporate governance reforms in China have in recent years closely targeted two goals: improving the efficiency and global competitiveness of domestic enterprises; repairing and upgrading the financial system which funds the enterprises. Accordingly, the following topics are closely addressed in this book:

- History and development of China's corporate governance reforms at state-owned enterprises (SOEs), township and village enterprises (TVEs), private enterprises and listed companies
- Interactions between capital market development and corporate governance reforms in China
- Role of banking reform in China's corporate governance reform agenda
- Constraints of China's underdeveloped legal and institutional environments on corporate governance improvements
- Broad implications of China's experience for international debates on comparative corporate governance

Structural framework of the book

By way of introduction, Chapter 1 discusses the relevance of corporate governance to China as an economy in transition to the market and the impact of economic globalization on China's corporate governance reforms. Meanwhile, a dynamic theory of corporate governance is proposed as an analytical tool to interpret China's corporate governance reforms.

Chapter 2 locates the Chinese corporate governance regime in international and historical contexts. Section I introduces basic concepts of corporate governance and important mechanisms impacting on corporate governance. Section II reviews the new waves of global corporate governance reforms, particularly in the wake of a series of corporate scandals in both the U.S. and Europe. Section III discusses the latest trends in contemporary corporate governance research.

Chapter 3 reviews the history of China's enterprise reforms and the emergence of corporate governance issues since the country started to pursue market-oriented reforms and an "open door" policy for trade and investment in the late 1970's and early 1980's.

Chapter 4 provides a general review of corporate governance practices of major types of Chinese enterprises during the transition, including large state-owned enterprises (SOEs), small and medium enterprises (SMEs), listed companies, township and village enterprises (TVEs), and private enterprises. Chapter 4 also points out the constraints of China's underdeveloped legal and institutional environments on corporate governance improvements.

Chapter 5 analyzes the interaction between capital markets and corporate governance of Chinese listed companies and proposes future reform strategies for enhancing China's capital markets.

Chapter 6 addresses the issue of China's banking reform as both a necessary complement to the SOE reform and a critical component of the overall agenda of corporate governance reforms in China.

Chapter 7 explores the potential of China's experience to inform major debates in contemporary corporate governance literature.

Chapter 8 concludes by highlighting the merits of China's gradualist strategy for corporate governance reforms and suggests broad implications of China's experience for other developing and transition economies in their pursuit of market-building and economic development.

Acknowledgments

The completion of this book marked a milestone in my academic career. This is my first monograph, which is heavily built upon research done during the four years of my doctoral studies at the University of Toronto Faculty of Law from 2001 to 2005. My years in Toronto had been incredibly rewarding. In this intellectually enriching, emotionally engaging, and at times physically overcharging process, I had been transformed from a curious young student from China with a preliminary exposure to academic training, to a fully committed academic.

It is fair to say that when I look back, I realized that the path that I have followed to reach today's destination has been filled with many surprises. These surprises, with their strong effects on me both professionally and personally, not only have made my life in Toronto by far the most exciting experience in my still unfolding journey of searching for individual fulfillment, but also have permanently changed my character and my perspective on thinking about the world.

The first surprise was that I met two fabulous doctoral thesis supervisors who had provided me with the most vigorous academic training that one can ever dream of. Professors Michael Trebilcock and Edward Iacobucci of the University of Toronto Faculty of Law succeeded in an otherwise difficult, if not impossible, task of turning an international student with substantial initial difficulties in mastering both the English language and the knowledge of related research fields, to an independent researcher. I owe tremendous gratitude to them. Without their generous input and never fading encouragement, I could never have been able to proceed this far. Of particular significance to the visible advances in my research was the tireless push and always prompt feedback from Michael. As an intellectual giant with an exceedingly impressive academic profile, he treated me with unusual patience and generosity. Although he was not flattering when I lagged in keeping up with my work schedule, he was always an insightful observer and delightful commentator when I did make progress and showed signs of improvement. After I took up an appointment with the University of Hong Kong in 2005, Michael has continued his role as an unwavering mentor and a reliable confidant and friend, and at times also a loving fatherlike figure. I am fortunate to have this abundant source of support and inspiration in life.

The second surprise was that I was fortunate to work with Doug Harris, now Vice-President and Associate General Counsel of Investment Industry Regulatory Organization of Canada. Doug is an extremely conscientious individual with an almost flawless personality. Having him sit on my thesis advisory committee had brought me fruitful rewards. Doug has been, in many ways, a role model to me, whose sense of responsibility and warm style have always impressed me.

Another surprise came from my good friend in the SJD program at the University of Toronto, Russ Brown, now teaching at the University of Alberta Faculty of Law. Russ is an enthusiastic and well-rounded academic. His invaluable friendship, not least reflected by his help with the proofreading of my SJD thesis, a tremendous favor that I was initially embarrassed to ask him, has infused me with so much comfort and encouragement over the past several years. His genuine interest in China and unreserved support for my academic endeavors will always remain the most precious part of my impression of Canada, where I had harvested so much of what life has to offer to those it favors most.

I had also had an extensive exposure to the broad academic community at the University of Toronto, which contributed positively to my research for this book. I met a number of wonderful people who had become my advisors or friends. Dean Ron Daniels, Professors David Beatty, Brian Langille, David Dyzenhaus, Kent Roach, Darlene Johnson, Jon Putnam, Lorne Sossin, Jean-François Gaudreault-DesBiens, Noah Novogrodsky, Frédéric Mégret, Sujit Choudhry, Richard Owens, Jim Phillips, Ernest Weinrib at the Faculty of Law, as well as Christina Kramer at the Department of Slavic Languages and Literatures, are among those to whom I am grateful for their efforts in helping me grow intellectually. My colleagues in the SJD program — Cam Hutchison and Michael Plaxton, as well as close friends in Toronto — Tim Wu and Onil Bhattacharyya, with whom I had had great experience in learning about law and Canada, also deserve my sincere thanks.

My gratitude goes to Professor Stéphane Rousseau of Université de Montréal as well, who in his capacity as the external reviewer of my doctoral thesis offerred thoughtful comments which greatly benefited the revisions of this book from its earlier drafts.

I also thank Professors Ben Liebman, Katharina Pistor and Curtis Milhaupt at Columbia Law School for giving me the opportunity to present parts of this book at CLS and to receive their valuable feedback on improving my work.

During the process of revising earlier drafts of this book, my colleagues Albert Chen and Douglas Arner at the University of Hong Kong Faculty of Law have been extremely generous in mentoring their young colleague on managing various fronts of a demanding job as I tumbled through the first few years of my academic career. Dennis Cheung, managing editor of Hong Kong University Press, has shown wonderful support, as well as remarkable patience, in making the publication of this book possible. My husband and colleague Zheng Ge, my long-time supporter in both academic pursuit and personal development, has always stood firm in giving any assistance and encouragement I need. His deep understanding of the value of my work, especially in times of difficulty, has been one of the most important sources of my courage and strength in moving forward.

Earlier drafts of two chapters have been published elsewhere. Chapter 5 appears in "The Interaction between Domestic and Overseas Capital Markets and Corporate Governance of Chinese Listed Companies", in Joseph J. Norton & Jonathan Rickford (eds.), *Corporate Governance Post-Enron: Comparative and International Perspectives* 273 (London: BIICL, 2006). Chapter 6 appears in "China's Banking Reform in the Context of Globalization and Transition", 17:5 *European Business Law Review* 1271 (2006). I am grateful for permission to include their updated versions here.

Jing Leng
March 2009
Hong Kong

1

Introduction

Chapter 1 presents an introduction to the domestic and international backgrounds to China's corporate governance reform. Section 1.1 discusses the relevance of corporate governance to China as an economy in transition from central planning to the market in an age of rapid integration of the world economy.[1] Section 1.2 briefly examines China's motivation in joining the World Trade Organization (WTO) as well as the implications of China's accession to this multinational trading system for the country's corporate governance reform. In particular, Section 1.2 reviews China's commitments to financial liberalization under the WTO agreements and highlights their impact on China's enterprise and financial sectors, most importantly the banking and securities industries, both of which are closely associated with China's ongoing corporate governance reform. Section 1.3 proposes a dynamic theory of corporate governance as an analytical tool adopted in this book to interpret China's experience. Finally, Section 1.4 clarifies the major subjects of investigation in this book and explains the reasons for their selection.

---

1. There are competing definitions and understandings of "corporate governance," which are generally reviewed in Chapter 2. This book adopts a relatively broad understanding of corporate governance when applying this concept to China. In China, the state (as both the owner and regulator of enterprises), managers and employees of state enterprises, banks (as the primary creditors to state enterprises), private entrepreneurs and their employees, and public investors of listed companies are all relevant parties or stakeholders in the context of corporate governance reform in China.

1.1 The Relevance of Corporate Governance to China

1.1.1 Corporate governance reform as part of a broader agenda for China's economic liberalization and structural reforms at a new stage of transition

In recent years, the topic of enterprise and corporate governance reforms in China has attracted extensive attention from academics in contemporary research on transition economies. This is primarily because corporate governance has significant relevance to China's transition to a market economy at the new stage of economic development since the late-1990s, especially after China's accession to the WTO in 2001.

As China's transition from a command economy to a market economy proceeds, corporate governance has been identified as the core element of a "modern enterprise system" (*xiandai qiye zhidu*) toward which China's lagging state sector has been striving. To the extent that China's corporate governance reform is aimed at transforming its traditional state-owned enterprises (SOEs) to modern competitive firms operating on market basics, they can be seen as part of a broader agenda for China's continuing economic liberalization and structural reforms.

Since China joined the WTO, structural reforms of the SOE and financial sectors have increasingly proved a bottleneck to the country's transition to a full market economy. While China's growth has been driven by the non-state sector in which collectively owned township and village enterprises (TVEs), foreign-invested enterprises (FIEs) and private enterprises dominate and outperform SOEs, the state sector, still of a considerable size, remains an inefficient component of the national economy. In the meantime, China's banking sector has increased its exposure to the likelihood of a potential systemic financial risk due to years of policy lending to loss-making SOEs, embodying the dangerous consequence of an accumulation of massive non-performing loans (NPLs).

Early attempts at state enterprise reforms had obtained limited results in solving the persistent problem of SOE inefficiency, largely because these programs had only focused on managerial incentive building and autonomy expansion without seriously addressing the ownership issue. Having realized the limitations of previous reform programs, the Chinese government started to implement a shareholding experiment in the early 1990s as an alternative approach to SOE reform, which marked the first serious attempt by the government at tackling ownership reform in the SOE sector. The shareholding reform has been aimed at diversifying the ownership structure of SOEs and transforming them into shareholding companies with a set of Western-style corporate governance structures spelled out in the Company Law. It was expected that good corporate governance practices would change managerial behavior and provide effective solutions to the agency problem of SOEs. Increasingly, the importance of corporate governance reform has been recognized by Chinese policy makers.

Scholars interested in emerging markets and transition economies often find China's corporate governance reform a fascinating topic because the reform has been conducted in a weak legal and institutional environment. This unfavorable condition raises the need for developing necessary complementary market-supporting institutions, such as a strong securities market and an efficient banking system that would ensure the success of corporate governance reform in a transition economy. In addition, legal and judicial reforms that provide investors with better protections are also widely considered an important condition for the establishment of a functioning corporate governance regime in a transition economy like China. It is now widely shared by researchers that to better understand the overall dynamics of China's transition to a market economy under legal and institutional constraints, it is highly necessary to investigate corporate governance reform in China.

1.1.2 Corporate governance matters for firm performance and financial stability in emerging markets

On the relationship between corporate governance and firm performance, empirical findings seem to diverge. A number of studies on corporate governance in developed market economies have suggested that a positive link usually exists between good corporate governance and superior firm performance.[2] However, other less positive studies have pointed out that firm-specific corporate governance initiatives have little or no effect on market value in developed countries.[3] By comparison, for transition economies and emerging markets the correlation between corporate governance and firm performance seems unequivocally significant: a number of empirical studies have demonstrated that corporate governance does matter in these less

---

2.   These studies are discussed in more detail in Chapter 2.
3.   See, for example, Bernard Black, "Does Corporate Governance Matter? A Crude Test Using Russian Data," 149 *U. Pa. L. Rev.* 2131 (2001); Bernard Black, "The Non-Correlation between Board Independence and Long-Term Firm Performance," 27 *J. Corp. L.* 231 (2002); Sanjai Bhagat & Bernard Black, "Board Composition and Firm Performance: the Uneasy Case for Majority-Independent Boards," 1053 *PLI/Corp* 95 (1998); Benjamin E. Hermalin & Michael S. Weisbach, "Boards of Directors as An Endogenously Determined Institution: A Survey of the Economic Literature," 9:1 *FRBNY Economic Policy Review* 20 (2003); Anup Agrawal & Charles R. Knoeber, "Firm Performance and Mechanisms to Control Agency Problems between Managers and Shareholders," 31:3 *Journal of Financial and Quantitative Analysis* 377 (1996), p. 394; Anup Agrawal & Charles R. Knoeber, "Do Some Outside Directors Play A Political Role?", XLIV *Journal of Law and Economics* 179 (2001).

developed economies, in the sense that a firm's corporate governance practices can have a huge effect on its market value in a country where other constraints on corporate behavior are weak.[4]

For example, two recent empirical studies confirm that in China, there does exist a positive correlation between corporate governance quality and firm performance. One study finds that better-governed companies are associated with (a) higher profitability as measured by ROA (return on assets) and ROE (return on equity), (b) higher stock market valuation as measured by the ratio of market value and book value of the net assets, and (c) lower market turnover ratio.[5] The results indicate that good corporate governance matters greatly in China's emerging stockmarket. The other study constructs a corporate governance index for Chinese listed companies and finds that the index has a statistically and economically significant effect on firms' market valuation, indicating that investors indeed pay a considerable premium for well-governed firms in China.[6]

As international institutional investors have started to realize the growing importance of portfolio equity flows to emerging markets, including the Chinese market, corporate governance in these economies has attracted growing attention from the global equity investing community. For example, the Institute of International Finance (IIF), a financial organization of a group of international portfolio management firms, recently released a Code of Corporate Governance that it hoped to promote in major emerging markets, such as China, Brazil, Mexico, Poland, Russia, South Africa and South Korea.[7] No doubt, from the perspective of attracting international investors, China needs to improve its corporate governance regime.

Despite the increasing awareness of the importance of good corporate governance among domestic companies, the general business environment in China does not look encouraging, and has raised concerns among international investors. A 2001 PricewaterhouseCoopers survey on global business opacity in 35 countries ranked China the lowest (Russia the second lowest), pointing to corruption and lagging legal, tax, banking, property rights and accounting reforms as major problems.[8] Moreover, according to a 2001 Credit Lyonnais

---

4.   See, for example, Leora F. Klapper & Inessa Love, "Corporate Governance, Investor Protection, and Performance in Emerging Markets," World Bank Research Working Paper, No. WPS 2818 (2002).

5.   Chong-En Bai *et al.*, "Corporate Governance and Protection of the Rights of Minority Shareholders in China," Working Paper, Centre for China Financial Research (CCFR) at the University of Hong Kong (2002).

6.   Chong-En Bai *et al.*, "Corporate Governance and Market Valuation in China," 32 *Journal of Comparative Economics* 599 (2004).

7.   The Institute of International Finance, Inc. (IIF), "Corporate Governance in China: An Investor Perspective" (April 2004), p. 1.

8.   Art Haigh, "We Look into Russia's Future with Optimism," *Kommerstant-Daily* (January 26, 2001), online <http://www.pwcglobal.com/ru/eng/ins-sol/issues/01-02-26_ah.

Securities Asia (CLSA) survey on corporate governance in emerging markets, many countries in the lower half of the rankings had seen their indexes fell 50 percent or more over the preceding three or five years. The two biggest transition economies, China and Russia, were both among the falling capital markets.[9] The CLSA survey warns that the consequence of lagging corporate governance is that investors are moving away from poorly governed markets.

More recently, a 2004 survey by *The Economist* magazine attributes the difficulties encountered by foreign investors doing business in China to the "eccentric nature" of the country's business environment, characterized as "a disorderly heaven" where the "rulebook, business-school texts and western management theory" have not been found in much use.[10] It is said that the "non-rational" business practices of Chinese domestic companies have largely contributed to this disappointing investment environment, which can be summed up under three headings — "bureaucracy," "rule of man rather than rule of law," and a "cultural aversion to business logic."[11] Although such an unflattering assessment may well be exaggerated as more balanced remarks — particularly by development economists — suggest that China's active involvement in economic globalization has resulted in considerable improvement of its domestic investment environment, the urgent need to reform its corporate governance regime as a response to expectations of international portfolio investors interested in emerging markets should not be underestimated.[12]

For emerging markets, corporate governance is associated not only with the availability of external finance, but also with the health of their financial sectors in general. One of the lessons from the East Asian financial crisis in the late 1990s is that weak corporate governance can lead to excessive corporate debt and that the lack of transparency and monitoring in corporate decision-making can result in more expropriation by managers and a large fall in asset prices.[13]

---

html>. "Business opacity" is measured against such standards as levels of transparency of legal rules and regulations, corruption among state agencies and officials, red-tape for businesses, the effectiveness of contract enforcement, and the culture of commercial credit.

9. CLSA Emerging Markets, "Saints or Sinners: Who's Got Religion?", [survey report on corporate governance in emerging markets], April 2001, p. 7.

10. "A Disorderly Heaven," in "Behind the Mask: A Survey of Business in China," *The Economist*, March 18, 2004, pp. 10–13.

11. *Ibid.*

12. For example, Deepak Bhattasali, former lead economist for China at the World Bank, remarked recently that globalization boosts China's economic growth and stimulates the improvement of its domestic investment environment. See "Globalization Boosts China's Economic Growth: WB Expert," *People's Daily Online*, March 21, 2004, online < http://english.peopledaily.com.cn/200403/20/print20040320_138047.html >.

13. Simon Johnson *et al.*, "Corporate Governance in the Asian Financial Crisis," 58 *Journal of Financial Economics* 141 (2000).

The negative effect of weak corporate governance can become acutely severe when local firms are exposed to global markets. Seen from this perspective, the need for corporate governance reforms in China has now become ever more urgent, especially at a time when its entry into the WTO exposes Chinese companies to increasing global competition.

1.1.3   Corporate governance and related institution-building are crucial for a successful transition to the market: Lessons from Russia's privatization

Russia's mass and rapid privatization in the 1990s was not a success story. Despite the original enthusiasm about the gains that mass and rapid privatization was anticipated to generate, a decade later the well-intentioned but not equally well-conceived privatization programs implemented under a "shock therapy" strategy seemed to have frustrated the expectations of many. Mass privatization through voucher and the infamous loans-for-shares (LFS) programs had caused devastating consequences in Russia. It did not succeed in bringing prosperity to the country. Instead, the reverse seemed to be true: Russia had seen severe economic decline, intensified social and economic inequalities, and increased poverty through the first decade of transition. According to Joseph Stiglitz, a Noble Laureate in economics, Russia had suffered greatly from flawed privatization: over the first decade of transition, it had experienced constant stagnation and its economy declined sharply. He bitterly points out, "GDP in post-1989 Russia fell, year after year. The loss was even greater than Russia had suffered in World War II: in the period 1940–46 the Soviet Union industrial production fell 24 percent; in the period 1990–99, Russian industrial production fell by almost 60 percent."[14]

In searching for the reasons of Russia's privatization failure, researchers have pointed out a series of causal links to explain why performance of Russian privatized firms has generally lagged. First, it has been suggested that there was a causal link between the method of privatization ("insider privatization") and the prevailing feature of management control in Russia's privatized firms. Second, the insider control corporate governance structure has been found to create incentives to loot. Third, massive self-dealing and asset stripping resulting from distorted incentives of insiders have ultimately led to the "fiascoes" among Russian firms.[15] Thus not long after privatization was completed, Russia

---

14. Joseph E. Stiglitz, *Globalization and Its Discontents* (New York: W. W. Norton & Company, 2002), p. 10.
15. Merritt B. Fox & Michael A. Heller, "Corporate Governance Lessons from Russian Enterprise Fiascoes," 75 *New York University Law Review* 1720 (2000).

quickly earned a reputation for poor corporate governance.[16] In the absence of institutional constraints on insider opportunism, what has been induced is wealth destruction. Given the generally poor corporate governance of Russian privatized firms (with some exceptions), it is not surprising that short-term activities and asset stripping have become common practices for managers.

The primary lesson from Russia's privatization is clear: in an institutional vacuum, privatization "can lead and has led to stagnation and decapitalization rather than to better financial results and increased efficiency."[17] Many Russian economists have concluded that the "mass and rapid privatization approach was wrong," that it "should have been preceded (not accompanied) by institution-building" such as corporate governance reform, prudent regulation for financial markets, and effective insolvency or bankruptcy regimes, which are all too weak or simply lacking in Russia.[18]

Russia's experience with privatization illustrates that when market-supporting institutions were weak or non-existent and privatized firms did not adhere to good corporate governance practices to curb managerial abuses, privatization was bound to fail. This lesson should be learned by China to avoid similar mistakes in its own privatization experiments, corporate governance reform and related institution-building.

1.2 The Impact of Economic Globalization on China's Corporate Governance Reform

Section 1.2 reviews the impact of economic globalization on China's corporate governance reform, which is primarily reflected by China's WTO commitments to the liberalization of its financial system, including the banking sector and capital markets.

1.2.1 The debate on globalization and how China features in this debate

As a highly complex and controversial phenomenon in contemporary human history, globalization has yielded mixed outcomes. On the one hand,

---

16. Galina G. Preobragenskaya & Robert W. McGee, "Corporate Governance in A Transition Economy: A Case Study of Russia," paper presented at the Annual Conference of Academy of International Business, Clearwater, Florida, November 13–14, 2003 [unpublished].

17. John Nellis, "Time to Rethink Privatization in Transition Economies," IFC Discussion Paper No.38 (1999), p. 17. According to Nellis, the most needed legal and administrative institutions are those that create and enforce property rights, and those that regulate both capital markets and the network and natural monopoly elements of infrastructure firms.

18. *Ibid.*, p. 9 and pp. 6–17.

globalization "has spread knowledge, information and technology across nations and has led to renewed attention to long-established intergovernmental institutions," such as the United Nations (UN), the International Labor Organization (ILO), the World Health Organization (WHO) and more recently, to the WTO.[19] On the other hand, globalization also seems to have created losers in both developing and developed countries as its benefits are not evenly shared by a wider range of the world's population. This disparity has resulted in a long-standing debate on globalization that has reached a level of passionate intensity over the past few years.[20]

The critics insist that globalization is a conspiracy of money and politics in the rich West and a damaging process primarily serving the interest of profit-thirsty western multinationals eager to exploit poor people in the developing countries. They allege that the impact of globalization on living conditions in poor countries too often proves negative as the environment in these countries deteriorates and the gap between the poor and the rich becomes even wider. Other sins of which globalization is accused include encouraging child labor, harming women, threatening democracy, lowering wages and eroding labor standards.[21]

Faced with a slate of charges against globalization, the pro-globalization camp replies with counter-arguments. Recently there have been two influential efforts to defend globalization. One comes from Jagdish Bhagwati, the world's "number one free trader," who wrote a new book, *In Defense of Globalization*,[22] as a response to Joseph Stiglitz's *Globalization and Its Discontents*.[23] In this book, Bhagwati takes a very positive view of globalization. By taking on globalization's critics, he argues that economic globalization is "an unambiguously good thing," with a few downsides that can be mitigated through proper management and regulation. He shows that, contrary to the exaggerated claim by antiglobalists that globalization has done little good for poor countries, it does have "a human face," and what the world needs to do is to make this face "more agreeable."[24]

---

19. Stiglitz, *supra* note 14. It is noticeable that Stiglitz seems to particularly emphasize the economic aspect of globalization in his book.
20. For an excellent review of the winners and losers during the past two "global centuries," the first of which ended with World War I and the second of which started at the end of World War II, see Jeffrey G. Williamson, "Winners and Losers Over Two Centuries of Globalization," NBER Working Paper, No. 9161 (2002).
21. See, for example, Naomi Klein, *No Logo: Taking Aim at the Brand Bullies* (New York: Picador USA, 2001, c1999).
22. Jagdish Bhagwati, *In Defense of Globalization* (New York: Oxford University Press, 2004).
23. Joseph Stiglitz's *Globalization and Its Discontents* was a bestseller in 2002. According to Jagdish Bhagwati, the title of Stiglitz's book does not closely correspond to its contents, which are basically about the International Monetary Fund (IMF), rather than a "balanced look" at globalization. See Edward Nawotka, "Globalization 101: PW Talks with Jagdish Bhagwati," 251:4 *Publishers Weekly* 244 (2004).
24. "In Defense of Globalization," Book review of *In Defense of Globalization* by Jagdish Bhagwati, 251:4 *Publishers Weekly* 244 (2004).

Bhagwati's favorite examples of the beneficiaries of globalization's "human face" are India and China, which have realized remarkable poverty reductions over the past two decades by opening up to foreign trade and investment. For example, India has obtained an average 5 percent growth rate in the two decades since it adopted more liberalizing trade and investment policies. By 2000, India's poverty rate had dropped to 26 percent, compared to 55 percent thirty years ago. China is an even bigger success: as a result of trade liberalization and economic reforms, poverty declined from 28 to 9 percent between 1978 and 1998.[25]

The other defense is made by Martin Wolf, the associate editor and chief economics commentator of the *Financial Times* who published a book titled *Why Globalization Works* to explain how globalization brings about positive results. He claims that the biggest obstacles to global economic prosperity have been the failures "not of the market, but of politics and policies" and that the world's poorest countries suffer "not from globalization but from the absence of it."[26] China and other emerging markets in Southeast Asia are the good examples he praises for actively pursuing integration into the world markets and consequently having achieved remarkable growth rates.

In both books, China features prominently as a "good globalizer" or one of the most commendable beneficiaries of globalization. This partly explains China's motivation in joining the WTO in 2001 as a historical step toward greater integration into the world economy in anticipation of expanded benefits and opportunities provided by globalization. There are also challenges from globalization, which are largely reflected by the deep impact that China's WTO membership has brought to its structural reforms in the state enterprise and financial sectors, of which corporate governance reform is a key element.

1.2.2 China's motivation in joining the WTO and its "WTO-plus" commitments

Perhaps the most remarkable achievement of economic globalization in recent years has been the establishment of the WTO. Founded in 1995 as a successor to the General Agreement on Tariffs and Trade (GATT) of 1947, the WTO now has more than 150 members accounting for over 97 percent of world trade.[27] As a multilateral trading system that provides the ground rules for international commerce, the WTO has greatly contributed to the promotion of a more open and liberal global trade order. China became a member of the WTO in 2001 after a 15-year long arduous negotiation process.

---

25. See Richard N. Cooper, "Bhagwati Review Essay: In Defense of Globalization," 83:1 *Foreign Affairs* 152 (2004).

26. Martin Wolf, *Why Globalization Works* (New Haven: Yale University Press, 2004).

27. Source: WTO website < http://www.wto.org/english/thewto_e/whatis_e/tif_e/org6_e.htm >.

China's motivation in joining the WTO

The primary reason for China's accession to the WTO was a strategic and pragmatic consideration among the reformist leaders that the WTO membership could serve as a powerful lever to push forward China's structural reforms and to facilitate its transition to a full market economy. In other words, China's WTO accession could be seen as an attempt by the reformers at locking economic policies into internationalization and a market-oriented course that are costly to reverse (i.e., a "credible commitment" to the market).[28]

In practice, China's WTO membership has been used by the government as an external impetus to overcome domestic obstacles to further reforms and to protect its trade interests.[29] For example, as noted by Nicholas Lardy of the Brookings Institute, a revered long-time western observer of China's economic reform, before China's WTO accession, the increased international competition faced by domestic firms had both stimulated efficiency improvement and generated social costs, such as growing unemployment.[30] He reasons, accordingly, that to constrain its policy options, the Chinese government needs a lever provided by the WTO membership to maintain and deepen its market-oriented reform efforts in the face of internal resistance to the adoption of more painful reform measures in the state enterprise and banking sectors.[31]

China's "WTO-plus" commitments

China's accession to the WTO has been widely regarded as a landmark event both for the country and in the history of the international trading system. This significance is reflected in two aspects.

First, China has emerged as a major player in the global economy over the past two decades, and its accession to the WTO is unique for the world trading system. By 2002 China had become one of the four largest trading countries in the world, and it seems likely that within a decade China will surpass Japan and Germany to become the world's second largest trader.[32] Indeed, by December 2006, five years after China's accession to the WTO, it had already become the world's third largest trader by volume of both exports and imports.[33] Although

---

28. Wing Thye Woo, "Recent Claims of China's Economic Exceptionalism: Reflections Inspired by WTO Accession," 12 *China Economic Review* 107 (2001), p. 133; Harry G. Broadman, "The Business(es) of the Chinese State," 24:7 *World Economy* 851 (2001), p. 873.
29. Ramesh Adhikari & Yongzheng Yang, "What Will WTO Membership Mean for China and Its Trading Partners?", 39:3 *Finance & Development* 22 (2002).
30. Nicholas R. Lardy, *Integrating China into the Global Economy* (Washington DC: Brookings Institute Press, 2002), p. 28.
31. *Ibid.*
32. *Ibid.*, p. 176.
33. Hu Shuli, "WTO: Five Years On (WTO wunian)," *Caijing*, December 9, 2006, online < http://www.caijing.com.cn/newcn/home/editorial/2006-12-09/14361.shtml >.

the technological content of its exports is limited and most of the goods China sells to the world markets are labor-intensive, its participation in the WTO trading system has the promise of bringing 1.3 billion people into the mainstream of the world economy, which is undoubtedly a remarkable step toward greater economic globalization.[34] The effectiveness of the WTO would be essentially enhanced if China can play a constructive role in facilitating further multilateral trade negotiations, particularly in the ongoing Doha round, and behave responsibly as a rule-abiding trading giant.

Second, China's WTO commitments are sweeping, especially with respect to market access. For example, China made the commitment to allow international investors to enter telecommunications, financial services and distributional services sectors, which is "genuinely revolutionary" in view of some trade experts.[35] Not only has China agreed to abide by the whole package of the WTO agreements, in some important areas China's commitments even exceed normal WTO standards, which are usually called "WTO-plus commitments."[36] Of strong relevance to China's corporate governance reform are those commitments with regard to financial services liberalization, involving its banking, securities and insurance sectors.

1.2.3 The impact of China's accession to the WTO on domestic economy

The estimated overall impact on China's economy

As China's entry into the WTO marked a historic achievement during the country's long quest for integration into the world economy, the Chinese government views it not only as an economic event, but as a symbolic political success as well. The very fact that the Chinese government is willing to abide by international trading rules is remarkable. Optimism notwithstanding, there are also reasons to be cautious about the overall impact of China's accession to the WTO on its domestic economy.

According to a number of welfare studies, WTO membership will exert overall positive impacts on the economic, legal and political institutions in China.[37] There will be substantial efficiency gains, which are most likely to be

---

34. Jeffrey D. Sachs, "The Historical Significance of China's Entry to the WTO," *Project Syndicate*, May 2000, online < http://www.project-syndicate.org/commentary/299/1 >.
35. Supra note 30, p. 176.
36. *Ibid.*, p. 2.
37. Some commentators have estimated that the short-term losers will be in the agricultural and services sectors, since these sectors will be the hardest hit by increased international competition.

reflected in the emergence of more domestic non-state enterprises that are successful in competing with foreign rivals. However, concerned commentators point out that the efficiency gains in the enterprise sector under the WTO are not likely to be realized unless the reform of China's banking sector is accelerated. As argued by Nicholas Lardy, if banks continue to channel funds to inefficient SOEs and restrict capital access of non-state enterprises, the resources necessary for production expansion and research and development will be insufficient for those genuinely competitive firms.[38]

While expecting the overall positive impacts of China's participation in the WTO, some economists have also pointed out that these impacts will likely be small and gradual. According to an excellent review of China's entry into the WTO, there are several reasons to remain cautious: (a) the terms of membership are introduced in steps, (b) there is inertia in existing institutions that makes them difficult to change, at least in the short run, (c) the central government's concern with possible social instability will make it particularly cautious in monitoring the speed of changes to avoid social unrest, and (d) local governments and lower-level state sectors will slow down effective implementation of the WTO commitments made by the central government to protect local interests and cushion the pains of reallocation of social and economic resources.[39]

The impact on China's financial and enterprise sectors

It is commonly believed among Chinese economists and policy makers that there will be both benefits and risks to domestic financial institutions as foreign players enter China's financial markets. Benefits would derive from the high quality services, sophisticated professional skills and additional capital that foreign financial institutions will bring into China's markets. However, since major players in China's financial industry, including those in the banking and securities sectors, are all state-owned and with few competitive advantages against their foreign rivals, the opening up of China's financial markets entails potential risks and costs. This is particularly true for the state banks, given their burdens of huge amounts of non-performing loans and weak capital bases. Therefore, establishing an effective corporate governance structure at state banks is essential for the success of China's ongoing banking reform centered on transforming major state banks from quasi-government agencies into genuine commercial lenders.

---

38. Supra note 30, pp. 132–133.
39. Gregory C. Chow, *China's Economic Transformation* (Blackwell, 2002), p. 83.

*The relationship between banking reform and the overall agenda of corporate governance
reform under China's WTO commitments*

The banking sector is in particular likely to encounter tremendous challenges
after China's WTO accession. China's "big four" state banks are widely known
for having accumulated a mountain of non-performing loans from years of
policy lending to favored state enterprises.[40] Therefore, they are in a poor
position in the face of imminent competition from foreign banks that operate
on a commercial basis and have a much healthier capital base. The challenge
from competition brought by foreign banks with advanced technology, sound
risk management and rich experience in conducting commercial lending
is tremendous. To catch up with foreign rivals after the 5-year grace periods
expired by the end of 2006, Chinese banks have an extraordinarily difficult task
to accomplish.

Regardless of how difficult it is, China's banking reform cannot be delayed.
If banking reform is delayed and banks continue to channel funds to loss-
making SOEs on non-commercial terms, the expected efficiency gains under
the WTO will be largely lost. Consequently, China's ongoing enterprise and
corporate governance reforms will yield limited results because easy bank loans
destroy the financial incentives of SOEs to improve performance. If banking
reform is delayed, the budget constraints from banks on SOEs will still remain
soft and banks will remain unqualified candidates to participate in the corporate
governance of SOEs as prudent creditors. In this sense, banking reform aimed
at transforming state banks into modern commercial lenders is critical to the
ultimate success of enterprise and corporate governance reforms in China.

By the same token, enterprise and corporate governance reforms are also
critical to achieving meaningful advances in banking reform because the soft
budget constraints faced by SOEs are the primary cause of non-performing
loans at state banks. Chinese state banks had until recently been in a very bad
state of solvency precisely because inefficient and loss-making SOEs have had
a poor record on loan repayment.[41] Therefore, the structural reforms in both
China's banking and enterprise sectors are closely intertwined and should
proceed simultaneously.

The government has recently taken new moves to address banking reform
through capital injections and the adoption of shareholding and corporate
governance reforms at the "big four" state banks. The purpose of recapitalization

40. The "big four" state-owned commercial banks are Industrial and Commercial Bank of
China (ICBC), Bank of China (BoC), China Construction Bank (CCB), and Agricultural
Bank of China (ABC). They in combination control 60 percent of all banking assets in
China.
41. The capital adequacy of BoC, CCB and ICBC has been improved in the latest round of
banking reform, largely through capital injections by the Chinese government in 2004–
05.

and restructuring is to bolster the capital base of the "big four" and prepare them for domestic and overseas public listings. It is widely realized that among a series of reform measures recently adopted at state banks, corporate governance reform, as compared to overseas listing, is the most important part of the overall reform agenda for the banking sector.

The interaction between the opening up of China's securities markets and the introduction of new standards of corporate governance

Although the opening up of China's securities markets has been gradual and cautious, it is widely believed that this process will be greatly enhanced as the Chinese government has realized that allowing foreign institutions into China would be beneficial for the country's economy in a number of ways.[42] For example, their participation in the domestic A-share market through a "qualified foreign institutional investor (QFII)" framework would increase the capital available to domestic listed companies and introduce international expertise, technology and portfolio management skills into the Chinese market. Moreover, international investment banks would help China's enterprises with overseas listing and expansion. Finally, allowing the subsidiaries of foreign companies to list in China's stockmarket would provide new standards of corporate governance in the market.[43]

1.3   China and a Dynamic Theory of Corporate Governance

As a major analytical tool adopted in this book, Section 1.3 proposes a dynamic theory of corporate governance that stresses proper sequencing and pacing of reform at different stages of development in an economy in transition. At the centre of this theory is the emphasis on the importance of legal and institutional reforms aimed at ensuring the proper functioning of basic market mechanisms, which should proceed prior to, or alongside, privatization. This book applies this dynamic theory to interpret China's corporate governance reform.

1.3.1   Key concepts under the dynamic theory of corporate governance

Alternative approaches to the market

In the dynamic theory of corporate governance, it is suggested that for transition economies there is no universal path to a market economy, such as mass and

---

42.   Stephen Green, *China's Stockmarket: A Guide to Its Progress, Players and Prospects* (London: Profile Books, 2003).
43.   *Ibid.*

rapid privatization adopted in Russia. Alternative approaches are possible. For example, while privatization in Russia has transformed thousands of former SOEs to private enterprises in a rapid manner, China provides an example of a gradualist strategy for privatization whereby the government has insisted on the maintenance of state ownership and control in many transformed SOEs and had not started to seriously consider relinquishing state control in non-strategic industries until recently. This makes China an interesting subject in comparative corporate governance research, as has been demonstrated in the long standing debate between the shock therapists and the gradualists over the merits of alternative transition strategies.

Institutional innovations

Institutional innovations refer to the experiments with local solutions to transitional problems that have emerged at different stages of development during the evolving process of reform in an economy in transition. These experiments may not be in conformity with mainstream economics or "global best practices," but nevertheless can work effectively under the legal and institutional constraints at a particular stage of transition if designed to accommodate the existing social, economic and institutional conditions and to correspond to proper sequencing and pacing of reform.

There are four examples of institutional innovations in China's enterprise and corporate governance reforms.

The first is the "dual-track" approach to enterprise reform at an early stage of development that encouraged the growth of the non-state sector alongside the state sector and the introduction of competition by the non-state sector with the state sector.

The second example is local government ownership and control in the township and village enterprises (TVEs) as a second best solution to the agency problem at an early stage of economic reform whereby the local governments provided effective protection of enterprise property rights, facilitated financing and the use of factors of production such as land, as well as imposed less predatory taxations and fees. As an innovative but transitional institution, Chinese TVEs started to experience widespread privatization since the mid-1990s as an adjustment to previous practices.

The third example is the corporatization and shareholding reforms (including public listings) of partially privatized SOEs, which are aimed at ownership diversification and the establishment of a western-type corporate governance system without full privatization, in particular with respect to large SOEs.

The fourth example is the decentralized privatization of small and medium SOEs controlled by local governments, which can be understood as "privatization, Chinese style" partly determined by "federalism, Chinese style." The primary feature of "federalism, Chinese style" is the fiscal contracting system, which is an arrangement between the central and local governments regarding revenue sharing under fixed terms. The fiscal contracting system offers local governments strong financial incentives to pursue market-oriented reform because they can benefit from the improvement of firm performance through collecting more taxes and fees. Faced with hard budget constraints, local governments have actively encouraged the development of non-state enterprises and greater reform in SOEs within their jurisdictions to generate more revenues.[44] Their fiscal incentives to reform enterprises have largely shaped the decentralized feature of privatization in China.[45] Local governments have also played a very important role in corporate governance of local enterprises. For example, in local government-controlled enterprises (usually the TVEs), managers have been given partial or total residual shares by the local governments in order to induce them to pursue higher efficiency and profits.[46]

Transitional institutions or second best solutions

Transitional institutions can be seen as second best solutions to problems and challenges of market-oriented reform in an economy in transition under legal and institutional constraints at early stages of development. In other words, transitional institutions are best understood as an outcome of constrained optimization of institutional choice. The thrust of this concept is the qualified validity of the sub-optimal institutional choice: the efficiency of such choice is limited to early stages of development and may be lost at the next stages when the institutional environment evolves and the political economy of transition changes. One such example was local government control of TVEs or state-owned small and medium enterprises (SMEs) at early stages of China's reform, which served as a second best solution to the agency problem when there did not exist a conducive environment to the prosperity of private ownership.[47] For example, to the benefits of these local government-controlled firms, the governments provided relatively effective protection of enterprise

---

44. Hehui Jin, Yingyi Qian & Barry R. Weingast, "Regional Decentralization and Fiscal Incentives: Federalism, Chinese Style," Working Paper, Center for Research on Economic Development and Policy Reform at Stanford University (2001), pp. 36–37.
45. Michael Burawoy, "The State and Economic Involution: Russia through a China Lens," 24:6 *World Development* 1105 (1996).
46. Shaomin Li, Shuhe Li & Weiying Zhang, "The Road to Capitalism: Competition and Institutional Change in China," 28 *Journal of Comparative Economics* 269 (2000).
47. Yingyi Qian, "The Institutional Foundation of China's Market Transition," in Boris Pleskovic & Joseph Stiglitz (eds.), *Annual World Bank Conference on Development Economics* (World Bank, 2000), p. 394; Jiahua Che, "From the Grabbing Hand to the Helping Hand: A Rent Seeking Model of China's Township-Village Enterprises," United Nations University Discussion Paper No. 2002/13 (2002), p 1.

property rights by levying much less predatory taxations and fees, imposed less burdensome requirements on firms in facilitating their finance and use of factors of production such as land, and at times provided technological support to help firms grow and expand.

The concept of transitional institutions distinguishes between political economy constraints (such as those created by a rigid, authoritarian political regime with slow constitutional reform) and technical constraints (such as those resulting from limited human capital, scarce financial resources and inadequate regulatory capacity) on reform and institution-building. Consequently, in practice institutional choices need to take into account the viability of specific reform strategies in a particular political environment, in order to avoid politically unrealistic solutions.

1.3.2　The central claim under the dynamic theory of corporate governance

The dynamic theory of corporate governance crystallizes the merits of staged corporate governance reform that emphasizes the importance of proper sequencing and pacing at different stages of development, as opposed to the radical privatization approach adopted by Russia. At the centre of this theory is the claim that mutually supporting or complementary legal and institutional reforms aimed at ensuring the proper functioning of basic market mechanisms, such as banking and stockmarket reforms, should proceed prior to, or alongside, privatization in an economy in transition.

Applying the dynamic theory of corporate governance, this book argues that for transition economies, there is no universal path to a market economy and the radical approach of mass and rapid privatization that had been endorsed by neoclassical economists but regrettably failed in Russia compares unfavorably with the gradualist strategy adopted by China.

Under existing constraints on China's economic reforms, which are imposed by the country's limited political liberalization, underdeveloped legal environment and inadequate institutional, regulatory and human capital, it is sensible for China to adopt a gradualist strategy for corporate governance reform that can generate visible initial outcomes as stimuli for the further expansion and deepening of reform. Under this strategy, what has played a significant role in discovering a better road to the market is a number of institutional innovations suitable to the particular social, political, economic and institutional conditions at a given stage of China's transition. Although such transitional institutions may not fully comply with a full market economy, they nevertheless have served as "stepping stones" to it. In other words, an institutional vacuum should be avoided in the process of a country's transition from a command economy to a market economy. Meanwhile, mutually supporting and complementary structural reforms of China's enterprises, banks, and stockmarket should proceed simultaneously in order to achieve synergies and sustained results.

1.3.3   Three aspects of sequencing and pacing in China's corporate governance reforms

In terms of sequencing and pacing, the gradualist strategy for corporate governance reforms in China requires special attention be paid to the following three aspects.

The first aspect is that ownership reform of SOEs cannot produce competitive private firms without the accompanying implementation of necessary legal and institutional reforms to ensure the proper functioning of basic market mechanisms, the protection of private property rights and the establishment of a social safety net. For a transition economy at its early stages of development, wide-scale privatization should not be a policy priority until necessary legal and institutional reforms — such as the banking and stockmarket reforms — have achieved preliminary results.

The second aspect is that in searching for optimal solutions to the emerging corporate governance problems during China's transition, it is not always workable to import "global best practices" from developed market economies that do not yet have their operating foundations in China. Instead, some local solutions, or local "institutional innovations," many of which were transitional and imperfect but nevertheless efficient at a particular stage of transition, have played a positive role in promoting China's economic growth over the past three decades. This is not to deny, however, that these transitional solutions may become no longer efficient and should be adjusted or abandoned as China's transition proceeds to the next stage. In this sense, institutional innovations, which compromise with "Chinese characteristics" but do not conform to market basics, may have higher marginal benefits at the early stages of development and should properly move toward market basics as China enters a new stage of transition.

The third aspect of sequencing and pacing concerns the adjustment of corporate governance reform strategy as China enters a new and more advanced stage of transition, in which the country is faced with not only the opportunity for development created by globalization, but also the internal and external challenges to the preservation and strengthening of its market-oriented reform policy. At this new stage, institutional innovations under the constraints of China's political regime cannot by themselves generate strong enough motivation and determination on the part of the government to deepen and speed up structural reforms in the enterprise and financial sectors, which have been regarded as the bottleneck to China's transformation to a full market economy.

Accordingly, the adjustment of sequencing and pacing at this new stage needs fresh catalytic inputs for more extensive ownership reform in the state sector and more comprehensive legal and institutional reforms to support further development of the private sector. In this context, China's accession to the WTO can be viewed as a strategic and pragmatic move by the reformist elements in the Chinese leadership to obtain an external lever to constrain the policy options of the government and to push forward China's market-oriented reforms. In particular, China's WTO accession has precipitated further corporate governance reforms of SOEs and state banks through shareholding restructuring and public listing in both domestic and overseas markets.

1.3.4 Major applications of the dynamic theory of corporate governance to China

In this book, there are three major applications of the dynamic theory of corporate governance to China as an economy in transition at a new stage of economic development.

The first application is corporate governance reforms of major types of Chinese enterprises, including the following schemes:

(a) The corporatization and shareholding reforms of Chinese SOEs, in particular, the decentralized privatization of state-owned small and medium enterprises at local levels, and efforts to establish an effective state asset management system.

(b) The adoption of the TVEs as a transitional but efficient institution at the early stages of China's transition, as well as subsequent widespread privatization of these firms since the mid-1990s.

(c) The emergence and growth of Chinese private enterprises, first under a "dual track" system at the early stages of transition, whereby private enterprises were allowed to develop alongside state enterprises, and at the later stages under the "grasp the large, release the small" (*zhuada fangxiao*) strategy, whereby competitive industries in the national economy have been undergoing expanded privatization since the late 1990s.

The second application is the examination of the interaction between both domestic and overseas capital markets and corporate governance of Chinese listed companies.

The third application is the discussion of China's ongoing banking reform as an overriding policy priority of structural reforms at the new stage of the transition after China's accession to the WTO, and the interaction between the banking reform and enterprise reform.

1.3.5 **Three perspectives of the dynamic theory of corporate governance**

There are three perspectives of analyses employed in this book that are largely inspired by recent advances in contemporary economic and development studies.

The comparative perspective

Although this book is primarily a country-specific study examining the dynamics of China's transition in a particular aspect (corporate governance), the role of comparative study in this book is prominent. The comparative perspective is informed by the "New Comparative Economics (NCE)" school and the "Comparative Institutional Analysis (CIA)" school; both schools emphasize the impacts of globalization and post-communist transition on national economic performance.[48] The NCE scholarship argues for the centrality of institutional reforms to national economic performance and recognizes institutional diversity within capitalist economies, with an emphasis on the "politics" of countries' institutional choices. Similarly, the CIA scholarship endorses the merits of institutional diversity and complementarities and suggests a path-dependent and evolutionary pattern of institutional development in a particular country. A salient contribution of the CIA scholarship to inter-disciplinary research on development is its attempt at theorizing about the likely interactions between different patterns of institutional development in individual countries through regional and global economic integration.

In this book, the comparative perspective is employed to analyze alternative transition paths to the market. Specifically, Russia's mass and rapid privatization guided by the "shock therapy" strategy is closely examined in comparison with China's gradualist approach toward the market. Also, China's corporate governance reform is discussed in comparison with Russia's (so far unsuccessful) experience in establishing an efficient corporate governance regime for privatized firms. There are several similarities between these two countries with respect to corporate governance reform. One is that both China and Russia have turned to international best practices, primarily the OECD (Organization for Economic Co-operation and Development) Principles of Corporate Governance, for guidance. In addition, both China and Russia have enacted extensive laws and regulations on corporate governance issues in recent years. Moreover, corporate governance failures and pathologies have been rampant in both countries.

---

48.   The NCE is systematically articulated in Simeon Djankov *et al.*, "The New Comparative Economics," 31 *Journal of Comparative Economics* 595 (2003). The CIA scholarship has been advanced largely by Masahiko Aoki, and is well theorized in his book, *Toward a Comparative Institutional Analysis* (Cambridge MA: MIT Press, 2001).

Another dimension of comparison in this book is associated with experiences of mature market economies in corporate governance reforms and is reflected selectively where it is necessary to highlight the contrast between overseas and Chinese approaches to same or similar corporate governance concerns. For example, when alternative choices of corporate governance arrangements in China are discussed, international practices, including some "international best practices," are reviewed critically, with an emphasis on their relevance and applicability to China.

The institutional perspective

To a large extent, firms' internal corporate governance practices are influenced or motivated by the external environment in which they operate, which is in turn shaped by the combined influence of a set of institutional infrastructures, including legal infrastructure, regulatory regime, information infrastructure, market infrastructure and political infrastructure.[49] In transition economies, it is often the case that both the internal corporate governance structures of firms and the external institutional environment in which firms operate are under transformation at the same time. Therefore, corporate governance reform in transition economies is not an economic agenda associated only with organizational improvements at the firm level, but is often situated in a broader backdrop of social and institutional transformation. An institutional perspective, which goes beyond the mechanical organizational perspective, is necessary in this context.

The development perspective

As the book will reveal, from China's experience in corporate governance reform, some general lessons for developing economies with respect to the sequencing and pacing of market expansion and institution-building may be drawn. Most importantly, there is a need for a re-evaluation of the "convergence temptation" commonly observed across the developing world, which emphasizes legal and institutional transplantation from the developed world to build national economic strength. In addition to (or instead of) "institutional convergence," new thinking on "institutional innovations" may be more relevant to discovering alternative choices of development strategies.

1.4 Subjects of Investigation

In this book, major subjects of investigation are China's SOEs — including large SOEs and small and medium SOEs, listed companies, TVEs, private enterprises

---

49. Standard & Poor's Governance Services, *Standard & Poor's Corporate Governance Scores: Criteria, Methodology and Definitions* (New York: McGraw-Hill, 2002), p. 12.

and state-owned commercial banks (the "big four" banks). Foreign-invested enterprises (FIEs) are not covered in this book due to their still moderate impact on China's corporate governance regime.

1.4.1 The ownership forms of enterprises in China

Broadly speaking, there are six major types of enterprises that currently operate in China:
(1) SOEs, including small and medium SOEs and large SOEs
(2) Collectively-owned enterprises, including urban collectives and rural TVEs
(3) Privately-owned enterprises, defined as private firms with more than seven employees
(4) Individually-owned enterprises, defined as private firms with no more than seven employees
(5) Foreign-invested enterprises
(6) Other firms not included in the above five categories

As revealed in the above categories, there is a distinction between the "non-state sector" and the "private sector" in China, which are not identical concepts in the Chinese context. In Chinese statistical terminology, "non-state" enterprises include all ownership forms *other* than SOEs, which encompass firms in groups (2) to (6). The "private sector" in China, on the other hand, usually covers firms in groups (3) to (6), because most collectively-owned enterprises in group (2) are also public enterprises, with ownership structures generally dominated by local government stakes.

1.4.2 Reasons for selection

There are several reasons why particular types of China's enterprises, as well as banks, are selected as the main subjects of analysis in this book.

First, while the private sector has grown rapidly in recent years, the importance of SOEs in the Chinese economy is still significant and whether their reform can succeed will have a tremendous impact on the future prospect of China's transition to a market economy and its growth potential. Despite the decline in importance of SOEs to the growth of the national economy, they are still a huge burden on the government.

Some statistical facts can illustrate the relevant importance of SOEs to the Chinese economy. As of December 2003, there were about 150,000 SOEs in China, most of which now take the form of shareholding companies through corporatization.[50] Although the number of SOEs now accounts for only a quarter

---

50. Source: SASAC, "Insisting on the Direction of SOE Reform and Orderly Pushing Forward SOE Reform with Regulation (jianchi guoqi gaige fangxiang, guifan tuijin

of all enterprises in China, according to official estimates they still produce about half of the country's industrial output (that they produce this much at higher costs than non-state enterprises would is another matter). Not only do SOEs receive half of all bank loans and a large amount of government subsidies, they also dominate strategic industries and still employ 35 percent of urban workforces. Virtually all of China's heavy industry and much of its technology are in state hands.[51] In addition, publicly listed former SOEs also dominate China's stock exchanges. As of June 2007, there were 1,477 listed companies in China,[52] the majority of which were state-controlled or state-held. The state alone owns two-thirds of equity in all listed companies, which, for the purpose of retaining control, had been non-tradable before a share structure reform (*gu gai*) was launched very recently to make these shares ultimately tradable. Since SOEs (especially large ones) are so crucial to China's economy and social stability, corporate governance reform in China must first address the problem of their inefficiency.

Second, current corporate governance discourse in China focuses almost exclusively on two types of firms: SOEs, particularly after their transformation to shareholding companies through corporatization, and listed companies. These two types of firms not only attract a great deal of attention from academics and business practitioners, but are also the major subjects of existing corporate governance laws, regulations and institutions in China.[53] Accordingly, SOEs and listed companies on both domestic and overseas stock exchanges are the most discussed topics in the contemporary research on corporate governance in China.

Third, corporate governance practices of TVEs help explain China's economic growth at the early stage of development. China's non-state sector, which consists of TVEs, foreign-invested enterprises and private enterprises, has been the main driving force for China's export expansion and economic growth over the last three decades. These firms have generally outperformed SOEs and have been the major contributors to job creation and capital investment. Of the non-state enterprises, Chinese TVEs had been the most significant players in productivity growth and employment enhancement at the early stage of China's transition, particularly by the mid-1990s. Accordingly, studying corporate governance of the TVEs is helpful to understanding the dynamics of China's economic reform.

Fourth, reforms of China's banking sector and stockmarket are critical complements to China's enterprise reforms. In China, the "big four" state banks

guoqi gaizhi)," *People's Daily*, September 29, 2004, online < http://news.xinhuanet.com/fortune/2004-09/29/content_2036001.htm >.

51. "The Other China: Parts That The Bulldozers Have Not Yet Reached," *The Economist*, January 8, 2004, pp. 59–61.

52. Source: China Securities Regulation Commission (CSRC), < http://211.154.210.238/cn/tongjiku/report/200706/c/8070101M200706_1.htm >.

53. Donald C. Clarke, "Corporate Governance in China: An Overview," 14 *China Economic Review* 494 (2003), p. 494.

are the primary lenders to SOEs. Plagued by both non-performing loans and widespread corruption, the banking sector is in an urgent need of reform to clean up its practices in the wake of much broader financial liberalization under China's WTO commitments. In the meantime, the government has to date failed to establish an efficient stockmarket to facilitate efficiency-enhancing finances in both the state and non-state sectors. Because corporate governance reform in the enterprise sector cannot obtain effective and sustained results if the reforms of the banking sector and stockmarket continue to lag behind China's pace of economic growth and integration into the global economy, structural reforms in all sectors concerned — SOEs, banks and the stockmarket — should proceed simultaneously to achieve synergies. Therefore, the banking sector and the stockmarket are also important subjects of investigation in this book.

2

Basic Concepts of Corporate Governance and Global Movements in Corporate Governance Reforms

Chapter 2 locates the Chinese corporate governance regime in international and historical contexts. Section 2.1 introduces basic concepts of corporate governance through an analysis of various definitions of corporate governance and a brief description of different mechanisms impacting on corporate governance. Section 2.2 reviews new waves of global corporate governance reforms in the early 21st century, particularly in the wake of a series of corporate scandals in both the U. S. and Europe. Section 2.3 discusses some notable trends in contemporary research on comparative corporate governance.

2.1 Basic Concepts of Corporate Governance

Of basic concepts associated with corporate governance, the most relevant to the discussions in this book are the diverse definitions of corporate governance, various mechanisms impacting on corporate governance, and the relationship between corporate governance and firm performance.

2.1.1 Definitions of corporate governance

There are various definitions of corporate governance. One of the relatively narrow definitions regards corporate governance as "dealing with the ways in which suppliers of finance to corporations assure themselves of getting a return on their investment."[1] Broader definitions extend the scope of corporate constituencies to include stakeholders other than capital investors, such as employees, customers, suppliers, the community within which the corporation operates, and national governments. These broader definitions are generally described as taking a "stakeholder approach" to corporate governance.

In early years, discussions in the U.S. and U.K. jurisdictions about protecting stakeholders' interests mainly derived from emerging public concern over the relatively weak contracting position of corporate constituencies in the face of the increasingly effective control of management over large public corporations.[2] Later propositions for the stakeholder approach have been voiced largely in the Japanese and German contexts of corporate governance discourse, where employees' welfare and representative power are traditionally emphasized. However, as a result of globalization and international convergence of corporate governance principles, recently there have been discussions about a possible shift of focus in the German corporate governance system toward the primacy of shareholder value. Moreover, the Corporate Social Responsibility (CSR) movement advocates the priority of advancing community welfare on corporate agendas. The CSR movement is the latest manifestation of the stakeholder approach to corporate governance issues but has been subject to debates.

The rationale of some commentators in adopting the broad stakeholder approach to defining corporate governance is the following argument: all actors who have an economic or financial stake in a firm or are likely to be affected by the firm's actions should be considered relevant players in the corporate governance structure of the firm. According to these commentators, the purpose of corporate governance is to hold the balance between economic and social goals and between individual and communal goals. Other commentators disagree, arguing that the stakeholder approach is inherently flawed and should be firmly rejected because it blurs the boundary of managerial accountability, resulting in no effective accountability at all.[3]

2.1.2   Mechanisms impacting on corporate governance

Based on different definitions of corporate governance, scholars over the past two decades have proposed several approaches to the understanding

---

1.   Andrei Shleifer & Robert W. Vishny, "A Survey of Corporate Governance," 52:2 *The Journal of Finance* 737 (1997).
2.   Oliver Williamson, "Corporate Governance," 93 *Yale Law Journal* 1197 (1984), pp. 1199–1200.
3.   Oliver Williamson, *ibid.*; Elaine Sternberg, "The Defects of Stakeholder Theory," 5:1 *Corporate Governance* 9 (1997).

of corporate governance structures. These alternative approaches put their emphasis on different mechanisms that impact on corporate governance, including economic, political, cultural, regulatory, legal and institutional mechanisms. Of these approaches, the most widely discussed are the following:

(a) the economic model (agency/contracting model) of corporate governance,
(b) political and historical determinants of corporate governance,
(c) social and cultural factors influencing corporate governance, and
(d) legal and institutional perspectives on corporate governance.

Chapter 7 will explore in detail these different approaches in the context of global corporate governance debates and discuss whether, and to what extent, these approaches have relevance to China.

2.1.3 The relationship between corporate governance and firm performance

According to the World Bank, institutions which affect the governance of firms are important for determining how resources are allocated, and who has rights over resources, both within countries and between countries.[4] Therefore, corporate governance institutions affect growth and poverty reduction.[5] According to the World Bank's empirical studies, weak governance in large firms has been associated with financial and economic crises, which can have severe consequences for poor people. This is because large firms, although few in number relative to small firms, on average account for a significant proportion of value added and employment across countries.[6] When these large firms perform well as a result of good corporate governance, they contribute significantly to growth and poverty reduction.[7] Despite this affirming claim on a link between weak corporate governance of large firms and negative economic consequences, cross-country empirical findings on the general relationship between corporate governance and firm performance, in particular financial performance in capital markets, seem to diverge and present inconsistent results.

Mixed or equivocal evidence on the link between corporate governance and firm performance

Researchers have found mixed or equivocal results regarding the empirical link between corporate governance and firm performance. For example, some

---

4. World Bank, *World Development Report 2002: Building Institutions for Markets* (Oxford University Press, 2002), p. 73.
5. *Ibid.*
6. *Ibid.*
7. *Ibid.*

researchers have found that it is difficult to establish a positive link between outside directors and better financial performance, such as firms' market valuation.[8] According to other researchers, however, while the causality between the quality of corporate governance and the level of financial performance is difficult to prove, there does seem to have emerged some strong evidence in support of a close correlation between good corporate governance and firms' long-term performance.

In a literature review published in 2005, researchers at Hermes, a well-known institutional investor in the U.K. that has been active in promoting corporate governance among its investee companies, reached the following conclusion[9]:

> ...[W]e believe the active promotion of good corporate governance in investee companies increases shareholder value in the long term. In this paper we review the evidence for a link between corporate governance and performance and conclude that the research we have found supports the proposition that underlies our corporate governance work...[10]

Country characteristics, such as levels of economic development, have a strong impact on the link between corporate governance and firm performance

It is particularly important to note that for countries at different levels of economic development, the results of empirical investigation of the relationship between corporate governance and firm performance vary significantly. In developed economies, such as the U.S., researchers have found that there usually exists a positive link between better corporate governance and better financial performance, measured by shareholder returns and firm value. For example, it has been reported that among a set

---

8. See, for example, Anup Agrawal & Charles R. Knoeber, "Do Some Outside Directors Play a Political Role?", XLIV *Journal of Law and Economics* 179 (2001); Bernard Black, "The Non-Correlation between Board Independence and Long-Term Firm Performance," 27 *The Journal of Corporation Law* 231 (2002); Sanjai Bhagat & Bernard Black, "Board Composition and Firm Performance: the Uneasy Case for Majority-Independent Boards," 1053 PLI/Corp 95 (1998); Benjamin E. Hermalin & Michael S. Weisbach, "Boards of Directors as An Endogenously Determined Institution: A Survey of the Economic Literature," 9:1 FRBNY *Economic Policy Review* 20 (2003).

9. Hermes is an institutional fund manager independent of any broader financial services group. It invests funds on behalf of over 200 clients, including pension funds, insurance companies, government entities and financial institutions, as well as charities and endowments. See Hermes, online < http://www.hermes.co.uk/ >.

10. Hermes, "Corporate Governance and Performance: A Brief Review and Assessment of the Evidence for a Link between Corporate Governance and Performance" (2005), online < http://www.hermes.co.uk/pdf/corporate_governance/corporate_governance_and_performance_060105.pdf >.

of 24 governance provisions followed by the Institutional Investors Research Centre (IRRC) in the U.S., increases in the level of an "entrenchment index" (which consists of six provisions favorable to management but unfavorable to shareholders) are "monotonically associated with economically significant reductions in firm valuation, as measured by Tobin's Q."[11] These six provisions are aimed at preventing a majority of shareholders from having their will prevail over that of the management, and allowing boards to adopt anti-takeover measures such as poison pills and golden parachutes.[12]

By comparison, with regard to transition economies and emerging markets such as Russia, China and South Korea, researchers have found that corporate governance, particularly at firm-level, does matter for firm performance, especially when the general legal and institutional environments are not well developed to afford investors strong protection. To better understand this general assessment, it is helpful to note three recent empirical findings by researchers at the World Bank regarding the link between corporate governance and firm performance in emerging markets.[13] The first finding is that the determinants of firm-level corporate governance in emerging markets include the extent of asymmetric information and contracting imperfections that firms face, which are influenced by the legal environments in which firms operate. Second, better corporate governance is highly correlated with better operating performance and market valuation. Third, comparing with more developed economies where legal environments are sound, firm-level corporate governance provisions matter more in countries with weak legal environments.[14]

In addition, researchers have also found that in transition economies like Russia and China, the quality of corporate governance has a significant impact on both investor confidence and securities market development, thus affecting firms' financial performance in the securities markets.[15] Moreover,

---

11. Bebchuk, Alma Cohen & Allen Ferrell, "What Matters in Corporate Governance?", John M. Olin Centre for Law, Economics, and Business at Harvard Law School, Discussion Paper No. 491 (2004).

12. *Ibid.*

13. Leora F. Klapper & Inessa Love, "Corporate Governance, Investor Protection, and Performance in Emerging Markets," World Bank Research Working Paper, No. WPS 2818 (2002).

14. *Ibid.*

15. See, for example, Bernard Black, Reinier Kraakman & Anna Tarassova, "Russian Privatization and Corporate Governance: What Went Wong?", 52 *Stanford Law Review* 1780 (2000); Bernard Black, "Does Corporate Governance Matter? A Crude Test Using Russian Data," 149 *U. Pa. L. Rev.* 2131 (2001); CLSA Emerging Markets, "Saints or Sinners: Who's Got Religion?" (survey report on corporate governance in emerging markets), April 2001, p. 7; Chong-En Bai *et al.*, "Corporate Governance and Protection of the Rights of Minority Shareholders in China," Working Paper, Centre for China Financial Research (CCFR) at the University of Hong Kong (2002); Chong-En Bai *et al.*, "Corporate Governance and Market Valuation in China," 32 *Journal of Comparative Economics* 599 (2004).

recent evidence from South Korea also provides some preliminary empirical support for the proposition that there exists a positive and causal link between corporate governance institutions, such as outside directors, and better financial performance, such as higher share prices.[16]

Recent studies suggesting a reverse link between economic growth and corporate governance institutions

While some researchers have found a positive link between corporate governance on one hand and firm performance and financial market development on the other hand, by contrast, other researchers have found a reverse causal link between economic growth and better corporate governance institutions.

For example, in a recent study, some scholars point out that almost all of the variation in corporate governance ratings across firms in less developed countries is attributable to country characteristics, such as a country's financial and economic development, rather than to firm characteristics.[17] What is more, according to these researchers, financial globalization and "piggy-backing" can sharpen firms' incentives for better corporate governance, but also decrease the importance of home-country legal protection of minority shareholders.[18] In other words, law matters less in these countries where domestic firms seek overseas listings in mature and better regulated capital markets. Recently, some researchers have also found a general reverse link between the level of economic growth and the quality of institutions in less developed countries.[19]

2.2   Recent Corporate Governance Failures in the West and New Waves of Global Corporate Governance Reforms

Good corporate governance seems to be a precious commodity today, hard to acquire but easy to break. Recent high-profile corporate governance failures in both the U.S. and Europe, involving firms such as Enron and Parmalat, have put degraded business ethics, executive greed and gatekeepers' oversight on display, thus triggering a new round of corporate governance reforms in both the U.S. and Europe.

---

16. Bernard S. Black, Hasung Jang & Woochan Kim, "Does Corporate Governance Predict Firms' Market Values? Evidence from Korea," University of Texas Law School Law and Economics Working Paper, No. 26 (2004).
17. Craig Doidge, G. Andrew Karolyi & René M. Stulz, "Why Do Countries Matter So Much for Corporate Governance?", ECGI (European Corporate Governance Institute) Working Paper, No. 50/2004 (2004).
18. *Ibid.*
19. Edward L. Glaeser *et al.*, "Do Institutions Cause Growth?", NBER Working Paper, No. 10568 (2004).

2.2.1 **Recent corporate governance failures in the West**

The dramatic fall of Enron in December 2001 and the financial disaster which erupted in July 2003 at Italy's Parmalat, one of the world's largest dairy firms, represented two of the most spectacular corporate failures in recent years in the U.S. and Europe, respectively. Other high-profile corporate scandals on both sides of the Atlantic have been witnessed worldwide in the collapse of WorldCom in June 2002, executive trials connected with financial fraud at Tyco, Credit Suisse First Boston and Credit Lyonnais in 2003, and the exposure of accounting problems in February 2003 at Royal Ahold, a Dutch company and the world's third-largest food retailer. Ahold was later labeled "Europe's Enron."[20]

In Germany, the controversy over the hostile takeover in February 2000 of Mannesmann, a German conglomerate, by Vodafone, a British mobile-phone manufacturer, had led to a criminal charge in 2003 against the CEO of Deutsche Bank and five other individuals for breach of trust while sitting on Mannesmann's supervisory board.[21] Recently, Royal Dutch/Shell, one of the world's largest oil companies, had been accused of "recklessly violating accounting rules and guidelines," which resulted in an "enormous and shocking overstatement of oil and gas reserves" and had been followed by a number of shareholder class-action lawsuits.[22]

Another recent corporate scandal in North America was the Hollinger scandal. Starting from July 2003, a special committee at Hollinger International, a newspaper company headquartered in Chicago, had been working for 14 months on a report about how Conrad Black, its majority shareholder, allegedly looted the company. The result was a report titled "The Hollinger Chronicles" which was released in September 2004 and was "as remarkable a tale of alleged excess as any in the history of joint-stock companies." As a result, shareholders filed lawsuits against Hollinger International's directors for failing to fulfill their fiduciary duties.[23]

---

20. See, "The Rise and Fall of Parma's First Family," *The New York Times*, January 11, 2004; "Ahold: Europe's Enron," *The Economist*, February 27, 2003.
21. See, "German's Fat Cats on Trial," *The Economist*, September 27, 2003, p. 68. The six men were first acquitted by a German criminal court in 2004, but had to go through a retrial ordered by the country's Federal Supreme Court in which the proceedings were ended in November 2006 on the condition that the defendants agreed to making public and charitable payments out of their own pockets. See "V for Victory," *The Economist*, November 30, 2006.
22. See, "Royal Dutch/Shell: Another Enron?", *The Economist*, March 11, 2004.
23. See, "The Chronicles of Greed," *The Economist*, September 2, 2004. Conrad Black was later found guilty of fraud by a Chicago court in July 2007, along with three of his former employees, and could face as many as 35 years in prison. See, "Conrad Black, Ex-Press Baron, Guilty of Fraud," *The New York Times*, July 14, 2007.

2.2.2 **New waves of corporate governance reforms around the world**

Following public outcry over Enron, WorldCom and other corporate accounting scandals, the U.S. quickly — even "hastily" according to critics — enacted the Sarbanes-Oxley Act of 2002 (the "SOX") to clean up the American corporate sector, a remarkable move that was claimed to be "one of the most far-reaching reforms of American business practices since the time of FDR."[24] The SOX, however, is now considered by some commentators as an "ill conceived" piece of legislation driven largely by political imperatives rather than by economic considerations and has been under sharp criticism from both academics and practitioners.[25]

Within the European Union (EU), new initiatives in corporate governance reform aimed at providing investors with stronger protection have also been introduced by several member states, such as Germany, France, Italy and the U.K.. These measures are widely regarded as both an immediate reaction to recent corporate governance failures in Europe, and a coordinated effort within the EU to push forward the ongoing movement of global harmonization of corporate governance principles. Calls for closer convergence of national corporate governance practices have become increasingly strong within the EU, where its member states' divergent codes of corporate governance are considered "an obstacle to the creation of a single capital market."[26]

Moreover, in order to strengthen its business sector to meet the challenge of globalization, Japan has also experienced a "sea change decade" of corporate law reform in the past years.[27] According to some observers, as a result of massive legal change in Japan, a formal institutional framework conducive to good corporate governance is now in place, which has reduced the transaction costs of basic corporate activities, such as mergers and acquisitions.[28] However, Japanese corporate governance reform is still incomplete, as other complementary institutions outside formal corporate law are yet to be developed in the Japanese corporate sector.[29] Of these complementary institutions, the most needed are

---

24. Elisabeth Bumiller, "Bush Signs Bill Aimed at Fraud in Corporations," *The New York Times,* July 31, 2002, A2.
25. For a forceful critique of recent corporate governance reform in the United States, see Roberto Romano, "The Sarbanes-Oxley Act and the Making of Quack Corporate Governance," 114 *Yale Law Journal* 1521 (2005).
26. "Special Report: Europe's Corporate Governance," *The Economist,* January 17, 2004, p. 61.
27. Curtis J. Milhaupt, "A Lost Decade for Japanese Corporate Governance Reform?: What's Changed, What Hasn't, and Why," chapter prepared for Magnus Blomstrom & Sumner La Croix (eds.), *Institutional Change in Japan: Why It Happens, Why It Doesn't* (New York: Oxford University Press, 2004), pp. 31–32.
28. *Ibid.*
29. *Ibid.*

managerial incentive structures, active institutional investors, and a flexible labor regime further deviating from the "lifetime employment" practice.[30]

More recently, there has been a program of "choice-driven" corporate governance reform in Japan since April 2003 that allows big Japanese firms to switch from "Japanese boards" identified with statutory audits to "American boards" characterized by a committee structure.[31] However, because this reform lacks the complementary institutions that enhance the functionality of the committee system in the U.S., in particular judicial review of directorial independence that serves as a crucial complement to the committee structure, its degree of effectiveness still remains to be seen.[32]

While the world's major developed market economies have been active in reviewing their corporate governance systems and reshaping (for some, thoroughly overhauling) their corporate sectors, transition economies in the former Soviet bloc have also experienced corporate governance reforms both during and after mass privatization. However, largely because legal and institutional reforms did not receive adequate attention while privatization claimed policy priority, these countries have encountered an array of serious challenges and disappointments in their corporate governance reforms. For example, Russia's mass and rapid privatization has not resulted in a vibrant and competitive private sector, partly because corporate governance institutions that would prevent or reduce self-dealing and asset stripping in Russian privatized firms have been weak or were simply non-existent.[33]

As the primary subject of this book, China, one of the star performers among emerging markets for the last two decades, has accelerated its enterprise and corporate governance reforms through corporatization and partial privatization (or "ownership diversification" in the Chinese terminology) since the mid-1990s, with the ultimate goal of establishing a "modern enterprise system" (*xiandai qiye zhidu*) in China. China has seen some improvements in this aspect, especially after its accession to the WTO in 2001 that opened a wider window of competition from abroad. However, because of the insistence on maintaining state ownership in "strategic sectors" by the government in the ongoing enterprise reform, China's inefficient SOE sector still remains a huge burden on the national economy.[34] Recently, discussions about a new approach

---

30. *Ibid.*
31. See Ronald J. Gilson & Curtis J. Milhaupt, "Choice as Regulatory Reform: The Case of Japanese Corporate Governance," paper presented at the Law and Economics Workshop at the University of Toronto Faculty of Law, No. WS 2004-2005 (1) (2005), p. 14 [unpublished, archived at the University of Toronto Faculty of Law Bora Laskin Library].
32. *Ibid.*, p. 37.
33. Bernard Black, Reinier Kraakman & Anna Tarassova, "Russian Privatization and Corporate Governance: What Went Wong?", 52 *Stanford Law Review* 1780 (2000).
34. In December 2006, the Chinese government announced, through the State-owned Assets Supervision and Administration Commission (SASAC), a regulatory body at the

to corporate governance reform, which would emphasize large reductions of state control and ownership concentration and encourage broader participation by private and foreign investors in the restructuring of state enterprises, have become intense within China's policy-making circles.

2.3 New Trends in Contemporary Corporate Governance Research

The current waves of corporate governance reforms across the globe offer new opportunities for academic research on comparative corporate governance to yield new insights into the relationship between institutional quality and development outcomes. The following text aims to sketch a general picture of the current state of comparative corporate governance research and to point out some notable advances made over the past two decades.

2.3.1 The growing interest in comparative corporate governance research

In recent years, corporate governance has attracted increasing public attention in both developed and developing countries. A subject of intense interest in both business and academic circles, corporate governance has stimulated an explosion of international debate over the last two decades.[35] In particular, legal academics and economists, equipped with sophisticated analytical tools due to advances in inter-disciplinary research, have been extensively involved in corporate governance studies and produced a number of seminal contributions to the theory of the firm, institutional economics and financial economics. Given its prominence today as an important research frontier with profound

---

central government level to oversee the largest SOEs in China, that the state will still retain absolute control in seven "strategically important sectors" that are crucial to the country's "national economic security," including armaments, power generation and distribution, oil and petrochemicals, telecommunications, coal, aviation and shipping. See Zhao Huanxin, "China names key industries for absolute state control," *China Daily*, December 19, 2006, p. 1, online < http://www.chinadaily.com.cn/china/2006-12/19/content_762056.htm. >

35. The first attempt at academic inquiry into "corporate governance" issues can be traced back to the 1980s. As early as 1982, the American Law Institute (ALI) started to launch its Corporate Governance Project and published a draft "Principles of Corporate Governance and Structure: Restatement and Recommendations" for comments. In 1984, Oliver Williamson, a leading scholar in the New Institutional Economics (NIE) school, published an article on corporate governance in the Yale Law Journal, proposing a law and economics perspective on corporate governance structure, and arguing for a contractual approach toward the understanding of corporate control. See Oliver Williamson, "Corporate Governance," 93 *Yale Law Journal* 1197 (1984).

implications for real economies, corporate governance has been constantly drawing vigorous intellectual investigation.

Recent research on comparative corporate governance indicates several major reasons why corporate governance has become a prominent topic in the past two decades, including the following:

(a) the worldwide wave of privatization of the past two decades, which has been dramatic in Western Europe, Latin America, Asia, as well as Central and East Europe;

(b) pension fund reform and the rise of active institutional investors in major industrialized countries;

(c) the rapid growth in direct and indirect (through mutual funds) equity ownership by individuals, especially in North America;

(d) the takeover wave in the U.S. in the 1980s and 1990s and in Europe in the 1990s, together with a new round of cross-border merger transactions over the past two decades on both sides of the Atlantic;

(e) deregulation on, and the integration of, capital markets worldwide;

(f) the eruption of a series of financial crises in Russia, East Asia and Latin America in 1997–98, which have intensified the discussion of corporate governance in emerging markets; and

(g) the exposure of recent corporate governance failures in both the U.S. and Europe.[36]

2.3.2 Corporate governance and the changing dynamics of the global economy

The context for corporate governance discourse in the 21st century is changing. Today, the trend of economic globalization has become increasingly strong, with its consequences for the internationalization of industrial production, the integration of global capital markets, and the contagious nature of financial crises. As the domestic business environments in many countries have to various degrees undergone adjustments or transformations in response to the impact of globalization on their national economies, the challenge faced by indigenous firms to adapt to a new pattern of the dynamics of the global economy in order to compete and survive has become urgent. As a result, corporate governance is now being addressed with unprecedented intensity in public discourse not only in developed market economies, where, unfortunately, a series of corporate scandals on both sides of the Atlantic have been exposed over the last few years, but also in developing and transition economies that are looking for a better road to economic growth and market-building.

---

36. See Macro Becht, Patrick Bolton & Ailsa Roell, "Corporate Governance and Control," ECGI Working Paper, No. 02/2002 (2002), pp. 10–14.

The changing dynamics of the global economy has inspired new perspectives on the current thinking on development, which has started to incorporate the dimension of institutional diversity and institutional innovation in searching for better development strategies. China can serve as an example to illustrate the merits of institutional innovation during its transition from a command economy to a market economy with respect to enterprise and corporate governance reforms. One notable example is to allow local government ownership and control in the TVEs, which had been a second-best solution to the agency problem in local firms at an early stage of economic reform.

Accordingly, the primary task of corporate governance research in an era of globalization and post-communist transition is to provide theoretical explanations and empirical testing of the effectiveness of alternative institutional arrangements and governance structures adopted by firms and financial institutions, such as banks, in both public and private sectors across nations. At the center of this task is a straightforward question: Which model of corporate governance system can better serve a firm to achieve long-term growth and competitiveness in a rapidly integrating world economy? Certainly, this is a critical issue of interest not only to managers who naturally have a high stake in running their firms successfully, but to national governments as well, as they compete for international investment and try to build or reinvigorate national economic strength. Broadly speaking, the global race for institutional excellence in relation to better economic performance has made corporate governance a focal issue in domestic reforms of many countries.

2.3.3 Comparative corporate governance research: from "first generation" to "second generation"

According to some scholars, comparative corporate governance research is currently in its "second generation." The first generation of research on comparative corporate governance had mainly focused on the examination of individual governance mechanisms — particularly board composition and equity ownership — in individual countries. In other words, corporate governance research at this stage had generally employed an "organizational perspective" at the firm level while the role of comparative studies across nations was not yet prominent.

The second generation of research, by comparison, tends to emphasize the possible impact of differing legal systems and institutional environments on the structure and effectiveness of corporate governance regimes and compare systems across countries. Accordingly, corporate governance research at this stage has made prominent the institutional and comparative perspectives. The focus of corporate governance debates has thus shifted from organizational and national studies to legal and institutional analyses as well as to cross-country comparisons. At the center of the ongoing corporate governance debate are two issues: (a) the role of mandatory laws and regulations in protecting investors' rights and promoting capital market development; and (b) the prospects for international convergence of national corporate governance systems toward shareholder primacy. These issues will be revisited in Chapter 7.

3

The History of China's Enterprise Reform and Emerging Corporate Governance Issues

Chapter 3 reviews the history of China's SOE reform and the emergence of corporate governance issues during the country's transition from a centrally planned economy to a market economy over the past three decades. The historical background, objectives, strategies, designs and actual effects of alternative reform initiatives at different stages of China's economic development are discussed. The purpose of Chapter 3 is to illustrate how sequencing and pacing have played a dominant role in the selection and adjustment of SOE reform strategies in China.

Over the course of China's SOE reform, the government's policy priority has experienced a gradual shift. At an early stage of China's transition, the government had adopted various strategies for SOE reform which did not involve ownership restructuring. Reform programmes under such strategies mainly emphasized the expansion of enterprise autonomy, the building of managerial incentives, and the introduction of competition from the non-state sector to the state sector. At a later stage of the transition, particularly in the mid-1990s, the government began to experiment with new strategies that started to address ownership reform of SOEs, mainly through partial or full privatization. In other words, wider-scale privatization had not become an attractive policy option until recently.

China's WTO membership acquired in 2001 has brought about an external lever for the government to push forward SOE reform, which is now characterized by the acceleration of decentralized privatization and the emphasis of corporate governance primacy. In the meantime, as a complementary element of institution-building to the ongoing corporate governance reform in China's enterprise sector, financial reform in the banking and securities sectors has also gained momentum at a time when the five-year grace period for China to fully open its domestic financial market under its WTO commitments ended in December 2006.

Major findings in Chapter 3 can be summarized as follows.

First, alternative reform strategies adopted at an early stage of China's transition, which did not involve ownership restructuring, had not worked particularly well to bring about efficiency gains to China's SOEs. Some of these strategies, such as the managerial performance contract system, had an initial positive impact on firm performance, but did not maintain such positive results due to inherent ownership and control problems in the SOE sector that can only be effectively mitigated through ownership reform.

Second, the corporatization and shareholding experiments since early 1990s started to address the ownership problem of SOEs, and have yielded some preliminary results. Existing evidence indicates that of two widely used measures for firm performance in privatization literature as well as competition policy literature — the so-called "ownership effect" and "competition effect" — the ownership effect on Chinese SOEs is significant and may well dominate the competition effect on SOE performance at later stages of the transition.

Third, privatization in China has proceeded in a gradual and decentralized manner, whereby regional competition and central-local arrangements under China's fiscal federalism have largely shaped the pattern of privatization of small SOEs and TVEs at local levels. While privatization has become a favorable policy option at a later stage of the transition, the government still insists on continuing state ownership, primarily due to its concern about retaining control over strategic sectors and preserving fundamental bases for its political regime.

Fourth, privatization and corporate governance reform in the enterprise sector, despite preliminary positive results, have encountered serious challenges in an underdeveloped legal and institutional environment. The primary challenge is the lagging reform of the state assets management system during the process of expanded privatization at local levels. As a result, asset stripping and self-dealing have become evident in many privatization transactions, and have raised concerns and criticism from both the central government and the general public. Another challenge is the lagging financial reform in the banking and securities sectors, which until recently (particularly before 2004) had not proceeded as promptly as it should have to complement the enterprise reform. Accordingly, future reform strategies should take into account these two challenges, and emphasize the importance of both sequencing and complementarity of reform initiatives in related sectors of the national economy.

Chapter 3 consists of four sections. Sections 3.1 to 3.3 recount the three stages of China's SOE reform since the late 1970s. These three sections examine various alternative strategies and review important debates over the direction and methods of reform, such as the debate over whether to privatize, when and how to privatize, and whether "more growth" or "more regulation" should be a policy priority in the reform of the stockmarket. These debates have enriched the understanding of the Chinese public of the dynamics of economic transition, and at times also inspired the central government's new thinking on workable reform strategies as the country's institutional environment evolves. Section 3.4 summarizes the implications of the history of China's gradualist enterprise reform for future reform directions.

3.1 The First Stage of SOE Reform: Autonomy, Incentives, and Competition (1978–1992)

China has had a well known "SOE problem" for a long time, which is manifested by the systemic inefficiency of the state sector. Chinese SOEs, after nearly three decades of reform, have not experienced significant improvement in financial performance.[1] The SOE problem not only imposes a major tax on the national economy, but also poses financial risks to the banking sector as the "big-four" state banks have accumulated a mounting pool of non-performing loans (NPLs) to technically insolvent SOEs. In addition, because SOEs consume large quantities of social and financial resources and use them inefficiently, other parts of the economy, in particular the vibrant private sector, are hindered by capital starvation and a non-level playing field due to preferential government treatment of SOEs. This is characterized by economists as the "spill-over" effect of the SOE problem to the banking and private sectors.[2]

SOE reform has always been a priority on the government's policy agenda since the beginning of China's economic reform, but the government only moved to address the ownership issue at a later stage. The first stage of China's SOE reform was identified with increasing the operational autonomy granted to enterprise managers, largely by allowing them greater authority over the allocation of profits. In addition, partial profit retention also replaced the previous practice of remitting all enterprise incomes to the state.[3]

---

1.   Major financial indicators of China's SOE performance are profitability, incidence of loss-making, fiscal subsidies, liability-to-asset ratios (leverage), and unfunded pension liabilities. See Nicholas Lardy, *China's Unfinished Economic Revolution* (Washington, DC: The Brookings Institution Press, 1998), pp. 33–47.

2.   Harry G. Broadman, "The Business(es) of the Chinese State," 24:7 *World Economy* 851 (2001), pp. 859–860.

3.   Lardy, *supra* note 1, p. 22.

The major cause for China's "SOE problem," as the discussion in Section 3.3 also points out, is the inherently inefficient ownership structure and the resulting corporate governance deficiencies. The separation of the cash flow rights, which belong to the impersonalized "state," and the control rights split between managers and government officials supervising the firm's operation, has rendered efficient production very difficult.[4]

3.1.1 Changing the method of SOE financing

Since 1985, the means of SOE financing has changed from direct capital allocation by the Ministry of Finance to state bank loans. The soft budget constraints under the old financing system, however, still remained. After the implementation of this reform, what followed were two new problems: (a) the "insolvency problem" of SOEs due to their high leverage, and (b) the resulting "NPL (non-performing loans) problem" of the "big four" state banks caused by the heavy indebtedness of SOEs and their failure to repay bank loans. Because banks are also politicized as are SOEs and the heads of the "big four" are essentially not professional bankers but bureaucrats, China's SOE problem could not be mitigated by the reform of financing methods alone.

3.1.2 Autonomy expansion and building incentives for profits

Beginning in 1979, the central government started to grant operational rights and authority to SOE managers. In the meantime, the government also changed the system of profit remittance from the transfer of all profits to the government to tax payments at fixed rates. These measures had led to wage increases for both managers and workers and at first increased their incentives to maximize value. This was known in China as the "responsibility contract system" (*chengbao jingying zerenzhi*), which spelled out terms under which SOE managers were permitted to retain profits after submitting to the state a negotiated amount of remittance. The managers could then use the retained profits to either increase workers' wages or bonuses, or reward themselves with higher salaries. This system was similar to managerial performance contracts used in other counties to create incentives to perform.

However, the positive effect of the "responsibility contract system" was short-lived, since managers and workers only took the upside of profit increases and

---

4. Maxim Boycko, Andrei Shleifer & Robert Vishny, *Privatizing Russia* (Cambridge: MIT Press, 1995), p. 30.

the downside was still borne by the state. As a result, proper incentives were still hard to establish. Despite the original enthusiasm on the part of the central government, the "responsibility contract system" was not successful in solving China's SOE problem.

3.1.3 Dismantling barriers to competition in the state sector: the "dual-track" system and the "parallel economies"

The following discussion will provide answers to two questions: (a) how markets and the non-state sector have evolved in China; and (b) how China's economy has grown so substantially "out of the plan" that it can be characterized as "a market economy with a mixed ownership base."[5]

As a defining characteristic, China's gradualist economic reforms have adopted a "dual-track" system, in which the non-state sector has gradually developed alongside the state sector. In other words, there had been two "parallel economies" in the course of China's transition. China began its reforms by permitting entry of non-state firms and state firms to sell outside the plan, while the old planning system was not immediately abolished but only vanished gradually.[6] Markets then spread and gradually revealed inadequate institutional arrangements, thus pushing forward the process of "marketization" and institutional changes.[7] The primary reasons for adopting the "dual-track" system were the lack of clear objectives or a guiding blueprint at the outset of reforms, as well as weak administrative capabilities China then had.[8] Contrary to the early prediction of some economists that an economy with such mixed structure as China's was unviable, the "dual-track" system has worked out its own pattern of economic growth, or has "muddled through" under institutional constraints.

During the first decade of China's economic reforms, some economists had come to conclude that China's "neither this nor that" economy was an unstable condition — economically and ethically, and would eventually be dominated by

---

5. Stanley Lubman, *Bird in a Cage: Legal Reform in China After Mao* (Palo Alto, CA: Stanford University Press, 1999), p. 105.
6. Under the "dual-track" system, goods produced by SOEs were sold at planned prices, while above-quota production was sold at higher prices, some set by the market and other set by the state. As a result of further decontrol of prices, by 1997 more than 95 percent of industrial output was being sold at market prices. See Lubman, *ibid.*, p. 103. As China has continuously progressed in its market-oriented reform, it can be said that in today's China, prices are basically all determined by the market.
7. Dwight Perkins, "Completing China's Move to the Market," in Ross Garnaut & Yiping Huang (eds.), *Growth Without Miracles: Readings on the Chinese Economy in the Era of Reform* (New York: Oxford University Press, 2001), p. 38.
8. John McMillan & Barry Naughton, "How to Reform a Planned Economy: Lessons from China," in Garnaut & Huang, *ibid.*, p. 470.

a single system — either market or plan. In their words, the unstable nature of China's mixed economy was vividly described as "half-plan, half-market; neither-plan, nor market; pretend-socialism, pretend-capitalism; with ill-defined borders between legality and illegality; socialist moral codes and principles of market efficiency; neither this nor that; in short a condition of 'market socialism,' or 'socialism with Chinese characteristics'."[9]

Despite the mixed nature of the Chinese economy in early years of reform, the non-state sector emerged alongside the state sector, and had quickly started to show its stronger competitiveness than SOEs. The non-state sector in China is primarily made up of the collectively-owned TVEs, private enterprises and foreign-invested enterprises. These firms have been the driving forces for China's export expansion and economic growth. The competition they have brought to the state sector has been intense, putting pressures on SOEs to reform and improve performance. However, the competition brought by the non-state sector only addressed the SOE problem to some degree because the intensity of competition was not strong enough to achieve a level playing field. In reality the non-state sector has still encountered a number of barriers and policy discrimination in favor of SOEs, such as limited access to state bank loans, technological disadvantage due to insufficient input in research and development (R&D), and regulatory impediments imposed by the government.

3.2   The Second Stage of SOE Reform: Restructuring, Corporatization, and Ownership Diversification (1993–1997)

The year 1993 marked a turning point of China's SOE reform. The government in that year introduced the shareholding experiment and corporatization program aimed at transforming traditional SOEs into a new form of enterprise — shareholding companies. There are three types of shareholding companies under the Company Law, which was first promulgated in 1993, with subsequent amendments made in 1999 and 2005: limited-liability companies, joint-stock companies and wholly state-owned companies. Western-type corporate governance mechanisms were introduced, including boards of directors, supervisory boards and general shareholder meetings. Moreover, two stock exchanges in Shanghai and Shenzhen were also set up in the early 1990s for the purpose of raising funds for the now transformed but cash-strapped SOEs.

---

9.   Geoff Raby, "The 'Neither This Nor That' Economy," in Garnaut & Huang, *supra* note 7, p. 19.

3.2.1 The Chinese characteristic of corporate governance reform

Corporate governance reform in China concerns primarily SOEs, especially after their transformation to shareholding companies under the corporatization program. Strictly speaking, corporatization in China does not amount to privatization. The main purpose of corporatization is not to sell off state assets to private investors, whereby the state can then withdraw from enterprises. Rather, the essence of corporatization is to adopt a new form of enterprise (the shareholding company) to replace the old form of traditional SOEs under the central planning system, whereby the state can manage its assets in a new capacity of shareholder.[10]

3.2.2 From traditional SOEs to shareholding companies

It is necessary to describe the "traditional SOEs" in China. The traditional SOEs in China were enterprises run by government-appointed managers, who were under the supervision of multiple government agencies with multiple, sometimes conflicting, objectives. Managers of traditional SOEs were not entrepreneurs, but agents of government ministries responsible for managing state assets in particular industries or sectors. These managers had a mixed identity of both "party cadres" and "bureaucrats," because they usually had to be Communist Party officials themselves to run state enterprises. They were not evaluated on the basis of performance, and their most important job was to guarantee that the quota requirements set by the central plans were met. Managerial strategic decisions, such as what to make, at what prices to sell products and how much revenue to retain, were not their concern. All such matters were taken care of by governmental bureaucracies.

Under the corporatization program, most traditional Chinese SOEs have been transformed to shareholding companies and have installed new organizational structures similar to those of Western public corporations, such as boards of directors, general shareholder meetings, and supervisory boards. However, the establishment of these "modern" corporate governance organs does not change the nature of these enterprises as SOEs, because the state usually maintains a full or controlling ownership in those shareholding companies considered of strategic importance to the Chinese government. In this sense, shareholding companies are only a new form of SOE in China, as compared to the traditional form.

---

10. For an illustrative account of major differences between traditional SOEs and enterprises that have been incorporated under the Company Law while still state-owned or under state control, see Donald C. Clarke, "Corporate Governance in China: An Overview," 14 *China Economic Review* 494 (2003), pp. 495–497.

3.2.3   **Corporatization and privatization: Two separate, but sometimes combined, steps**

Although corporatization is not privatization, the two concepts are interlinked in China's transition context. In particular, in a dynamic sense, corporate governance reform in China has been a process combining both corporatization and privatization. For one thing, when the traditional SOEs were transformed to shareholding companies, except for those still maintaining full state ownership, new enterprises had usually undergone some level of restructuring to diversify their ownership base. Such restructuring typically involves the participation of private and foreign capital, and the prominence of such non-state capital in these new shareholding companies varies greatly. In general, small SOEs have undergone much deeper restructuring and ownership diversification, in the sense that many of them have been genuinely divested. Large SOEs, particularly those largest ones under the supervision of the central government, have not been open to full privatization and still remain in state control. Nevertheless, privatization has been an integral element in the process of corporatization, especially for small SOEs.

Accordingly, the "Chinese characteristic" of corporate governance reform can then be understood as a combination of corporatization and privatization. However, this description does not highlight a unique feature of privatization in China, which is also not fully addressed by the existing privatization literature. Most importantly, "privatization" of Chinese SOEs is markedly different from privatization in Russia and other post-communist transition economies.[11] This is so not only because China has not adopted the mass and rapid privatization strategy, which is a matter of speed and volume, but also because China has insisted on maintaining state ownership and control in "privatized" SOEs in strategic sectors, especially the large ones, which is a matter of degree and intensity. This type of privatization is not seen anywhere in other transition economies. In this sense, "privatization" in China, as has been practiced so far, is not mainly about reducing the state's control over strategic sectors, but about making that control more effective. Indeed, after private capital began to participate in the ownership restructuring of SOEs, the state has in many cases been able to retain the same level of control as in the past, but with less capital investment.[12]

---

11.   See William Megginson & Jeffry Netter, "From State to Market: A Survey of Empirical Studies on Privatization," 39:2 *Journal of Economic Literature* 321 (2001).

12.   "We are the Champions," in "Behind the Mask: A Survey of Business in China," *The Economist*, March 18, 2004, p. 14.

3.3 The Third Stage of SOE Reform: Decentralized Privatization and the Need for Complementary Financial Reform (1997 to Present)

The third stage of SOE reform, starting from the 15th Communist Party Congress of 1997 and still in progress, is characterized by the accelerated and expanded shareholding reform and decentralized privatization (*minyinghua*) at local levels, after the government decided that it will gradually withdraw from the competitive elements of the national economy and only concentrate on the "strategic" sectors. The participation of private and foreign investors in the ownership restructuring of SOEs has been encouraged by the government, and developing a "mixed economy" with a multiple ownership base was announced as the purported destination of China's shareholding reform. China's WTO accession in 2001 has provided an external lever to deepen and strengthen the structural reforms of the state enterprises and financial institutions, in the face of enhanced competition from overseas.

Significantly, in April 2003, a new government agency, the State-owned Assets Supervision and Administration Commission (SASAC), was established to push forward state assets management reform. The SASAC is in charge of overseeing state assets and is entrusted with the exercise of ownership rights in SOEs on behalf of the state. With a relatively short period of regulatory experience, the SASAC has already encountered serious challenges in responding to a latest round of the privatization debate spurred by the public outcry over widespread irregularities during the process of privatization, in particular with regard to insider privatization to managers, i.e., the Chinese-style management buyouts (MBOs). Despite the heated controversy over MBOs, which culminated in the summer of 2004, the government seems resolved to continue to pursue ownership reform of SOEs. In the meantime, the government has also voiced its concerns with asset stripping and other forms of expropriation by enterprise insiders and local officials through collusion.

As complementary measures to SOE reform, shareholding and corporate governance reforms at state banks and a new trend of tightening regulation in the stockmarket to afford investors stronger protection have also been implemented in recent years. Therefore, it seems that the logic of sequencing and pacing of China's enterprise and corporate governance reforms has been under dynamic adjustment, in the sense that the pace of structural reforms and institution-building has been accelerating over the past few years while coordination and synchronization have increasingly been incorporated into the implementation of these related reforms.

The following discussion focuses on some important debates over the directions and methods of privatization. Through these debates, a broader picture can be drawn of how reform strategies have evolved.

3.3.1 **The privatization debate: Whether or not to privatize?**

For the Chinese government and public, a central question that has been under debate in the course of SOE reform is whether there is a genuine need for privatization in addressing the persistent problem of SOE inefficiency.

The debate on "ownership effects *versus* competition effects"

For researchers of privatization, the debate on "ownership effects *versus* competition effects" is a familiar theme. This debate has been centered on the respective role of ownership reform (particularly privatization) and competition in enhancing the efficiency of SOEs. While a number of studies on competitive market economies have generally offered privatization-positive observations, evidence from transition economies is more equivocal and in some cases negative, indicating that privatization may not always work in addressing operational inefficiencies of SOEs. The reasons why transition economies have presented mixed results of privatization are many, and will be discussed closely in Chapter 7 where Russian privatization is examined.

To obtain a balanced understanding of whether privatization works for developing countries like China, it is important to look beyond transition economies. For example, a comprehensive review paper on the empirical results of privatization in less developed countries visits the topic of "ownership effects *versus* competition effects" and reaches the following conclusion:

> Empirical evidence on the economic performance of SOEs generally yields negative results and suggests that SOEs are a major tax on the economies of developing countries reflected in the large operating subsidies required to sustain them. These inefficiencies seem in part attributable to ownership effects and partly to lack of competition effects.[13]

It is worth noting that in addition to financial subsidies, whether through fiscal advancement or policy bank lending, there are other social and economic resources consumed in large quantity and generally inefficiently by SOEs, such as government technological support and cheap (or free) land use. In China, SOEs arguably receive all but one of the common forms of government preferential treatment offered to favored firms, the sole exception being tax breaks. Chinese SOEs had generally paid considerably higher taxes than private and foreign enterprises had. This had been the case throughout China's transition to a market economy over the last three decades or so, and was best reflected in the discriminatory income tax rate imposed on China's SOEs, which

---

13. Andrew Smith & Michael Trebilcock, "State-Owned Enterprises in Less Developed Countries: Privatization and Alternative Reform Strategies," 12 *European Journal of Law and Economics* 217 (2001), p. 217.

was set at 33 percent, almost doubled the 17 percent borne by foreign-invested firms until a new Enterprise Income Tax Law was enacted in 2007 to set out a uniform tax rate of 25 percent for all types of enterprises operating in China.[14] The tax factor may mitigate the negative results of SOE performance to some extent. However, since the state pays high costs via subsidies in exchange for the tax revenues collected from SOEs, often exceeding what it receives in return, the tax factor does not significantly affect the level of systemic inefficiency in China's state sector, as measured by a variety of financial indicators, such as profitability and return on assets.

Why is state ownership inefficient?

Around the world, state ownership is widely viewed, and has been repeatedly demonstrated, as inefficient.[15] Briefly put, this is because both profit motives and political motives of government officials have the potential to distort policy objectives significantly.[16] The political targets that state enterprises are charged with are not compatible with economic targets and are often in sharp conflict with profit maximization.

Moreover, there is a problem of "SOE externalities." This term refers to the high cost to the general economy created by the over-consumption of social resources, such as fiscal subsidies and state bank loans, as well as extractions of firm value by managers, workers and government officials. Those extractions include asset stripping by managers, shirking by workers, predatory taxes, fees and bribes levied by government officials, and non-pecuniary benefits for workers and their relatives in the form of housing and social services.[17]

Not only does the government often lack adequate means to pursue given ends, the so-called "meta-agency" problem in government firms or programs also frequently causes the government to fail to choose correct ends.[18] In other words, government agents may not seek to maximize the welfare of their principals (i.e., the public), but more likely prefer to maximize their own welfare. This problem will have a greater impact after a particular activity has been allocated to the public sector, because such an allocation creates new interest groups.[19]

---

14. The unequal tax burdens among different types of enterprise will be phased out soon. In March 2007, The Chinese government enacted a new Enterprise Income Tax Law, under which a unified tax rate of 25 percent will be imposed on both domestic and foreign-invested enterprises in January 2008. Meanwhile, a preferential income tax rate of 20 percent will apply to small and low-profit enterprises to support their development.
15. See, for example, Boycko, Shleifer & Vishny, *supra* note 4; Smith & Trebilcock, *supra* note 13.
16. Michael Trebilcock & Edward Iacobucci, "Public Values in an Era of Privatization: Privatization and Accountability," 116 *Harvard Law Review* 1422 (2003), p. 1441.
17. Gary Jefferson, "China's State Enterprises: Public Goods, Externalities, and Coase," 88:2 *The American Economic Review* 428 (1998), p. 428.
18. Trebilcock & Iacobucci, *supra* note 16, p. 1443.
19. *Ibid.*

Can alternative strategies solve China's "SOE problem"?

According to some researchers, empirical evidence on the effect of privatization of SOEs in both developed and developing countries suggests that privatization is often likely to lead to major improvement in economic performance. However, where privatization is not politically feasible, SOE reform alternatives such as management contracts, performance contracts and greater exposure to competition may, in some contexts, enhance SOE performance, although typically they are second-best policy options to privatization when both economic and political preconditions for privatization are not ready.[20] China has given credence to the above observations: it has tried alternative strategies to privatization over the course of SOE reform, but in general did not see much success in terms of achieving stable and sustainable performance improvement measured by financial indicators, such as profitability and return on assets.[21]

3.3.2 When and how to privatize?: A matter of sequencing and pacing

Another persistent theme of debate in the context of China's SOE reform relates to the timing, speed and method of privatization. While many economists agree that privatization would be a better policy choice after repeated failures of alternative strategies which did not directly address the ownership issue, their opinions often differ on when and how to privatize. Meanwhile, the Chinese government has also been reluctant to embark on rushed privatization upon seeing the privatization discontents in Russia. It is also unwilling to relinquish control in strategic sectors, particularly in large SOEs operating in security-related industries (such as armaments), natural monopolies and natural resources (such as power generation and distribution, oil, petrochemicals and telecommunications), sectors providing infrastructure and important public goods and services (such as highway transportation and civil aviation), as well as pillar and high-tech industries. Therefore, the debate over when and how to privatize has significantly shaped the current policy framework for SOE reform in China.

Continuing state ownership during the process of shareholding experiment and privatization

In rhetoric, a massive privatization program was announced in China in 1997, under the slogan "grasp the large, release the small" (*zhuada fangxiao*), which

---

20.   Smith & Trebilcock, *supra* note 13, p. 217.
21.   See, for example, Broadman, *supra* note 2; Lardy, *supra* note 1.

is roughly interpreted as privatizing all but the largest SOEs, numbering 155 as of July 2007.[22] In practice, however, ownership restrictions on the actual implementation of privatization, such as the requirement that publicly listed former SOEs must keep a controlling state shareholding which, until very recently, had been non-tradable in the stockmarket, have resulted in a very unusual feature of privatization in China. This feature is that "privatized" SOEs have not become genuine "private" enterprises, but enterprises with mixed ownership dominated by the state.

Therefore, corporate governance reform in China needs to deal with the issue of continuing state ownership. The impact of this characteristic of privatization in China is particularly acute if seen through the lens of the mainstream post-communist transition framework adopted in other countries, in which the Communist Party no longer functions as an economic agent. Given that China is the only transition economy still ruled by the Communist Party, it is reasonably easy to see why state ownership is still protected: without state ownership, the Party would lose its most effective tool to control national economic resources, which is among the fundamental pillars of its regime. This can be better understood in the context of the "party-state" bureaucratic and political styles in China.[23]

In this sense, state ownership in China carries other functions than organizing industrial production or realizing distributional objectives, as is commonly the case in other economies — including developed market economies — that also have SOEs. These other functions are largely non-economic and often charged with political motivations, such as the above-mentioned Party grasp of political ruling capital. State ownership is also used to realize China's desire to produce globally competitive "national champions" through vigorous domestic and overseas expansions, so that big Chinese SOEs, often in state-orchestrated industrial grouping, can have a strong international presence to show the rest of the world the advantages of "socialism with Chinese

---

22. Source: SASAC, online < http://www.sasac.gov.cn/zyqy/tbts/200707200192.htm >.
23. It is not uncommon to find the term "party-state" in China research, which entails a vague idea that the Communist Party apparatus is absorbed by, and intertwined with, the governmental establishments in China. This notion, which was appropriate in early contexts, does not tell much about the evolving nature of the party-state relationship in today's China, where the legitimacy of communist rule has been under redefinition. For example, in addition to being a political ruling machinery of the Communist Party, the Chinese state is "becoming more as a machinery for pluralist interest-mediation," which can be illustrated by the recent emphasis on rural development and the admission of private entrepreneurs to the Party. See Masahiko Aoki, "The Dual Aspects of the Institutional Transformation of the Chinese Economy," China Institute for Reform and Development (CIRD) (2002), online < http://www.chinareform.org/cgi-bin/ResearchPaper/ResearchPaper_main.asp?Ggwk_ID=36&Ggwk_Type >.

characteristics" (*zhongguo tese de shehui zhuyi*), which, if successful, would yield more ideological than economic returns.[24]

Finally, there is another important reason why state ownership is difficult to withdraw from the Chinese economy. In China, it is SOEs, rather than the government itself, that have served as the country's social safety net.[25] The heavy policy burdens assumed by state firms, such as maintaining urban employment and providing various welfare entitlements and benefits to state employees, are a direct reflection of this particular welfare function of state ownership. The welfare benefits that have been traditionally provided by SOEs to their employees ranged from child education and medical care to housing and recreation.

In order to reconcile continuing state ownership with the market orientation of economic reform at the ideological level, the Chinese government coined a new notion that "mixed ownership under the shareholding system is the primary form of realizing public ownership, especially state ownership."[26] By looking forward, maintaining the state as the controlling shareholder of partially-privatized SOEs may only be a transitional arrangement as required by the logic of sequencing. From a long-run perspective, the maintenance of state control in these firms cannot achieve the purported goal of improved performance and very likely will lead to the waste of both state and private capital inputted in these firms. As the country's institutional environment develops and both political and government reforms proceed, the further relinquishment of state control in partially privatized SOEs will become feasible.

The gradualist and decentralized nature of privatization in China

In the vast volumes of economic literature on privatization and enterprise reform in China, it is widely noted that privatization has proceeded in a gradualist and decentralized manner in this country. The following text offers explanations as to why this has been the case.

The rationales for a gradualist approach to privatization in China

The gradualist approach characterized by experimentalism and proper sequencing and pacing has been praised as accounting for China's success in

---

24. Whether political or ideological objectives can *in some cases* be compatible with economic efficiency is not a settled question. With respect to transition economies that had been advised to pursue mass privatization in the 1990s, some economists comment that although the specific design of the programs was largely dictated by politics, politically feasibly programs can still be made attractive from an economic standpoint in terms of maximizing value, fostering free and efficient markets, and promoting corporate governance. See, Maxim Boycko, Andrei Shleifer & Robert W. Vishny, "Voucher Privatization," 35 *Journal of Financial Economics* 249 (1993).

25. Megginson & Netter, *supra* note 11, p. 1137.

26. Jiang Zeming, "Report at the 15th Communist Party Congress (zai zhongguo gongchandang di shiwu ci quanguo daibiao dahui shang de baogao)," September 1997.

achieving high rates of GDP growth over the last decade. Many economists in the West have endorsed this reform strategy in comparing Russia and China, including Nobel Prize winners in economics Kenneth Arrow and Joseph Stiglitz, who visited China and exchanged ideas on economic reform with Chinese government officials. As Stiglitz reports, both he and Arrow emphasized to the Chinese government the positive effects of experimentalism and the merits of proper sequencing and pacing:

> The contrast between China's strategy and that of Russia could not be clearer, and it began from the very first moves along the path to transition. China's reforms began in agriculture, with the movement from the commune (collective) system of production in agriculture to the "individual responsibility" system — effectively, *partial* privatization. It was not complete privatization: individuals could not buy and sell land freely; but the gains in output showed how much could be gained from even partial and limited reforms... The evidence was so compelling that the central government did not have to *force* this change; it was willingly accepted. But the Chinese leadership recognized that they could not rest on their laurels, and the reform had to extend to the entire economy.
>
> ... [H]e [Arrow] and I each stressed the importance of competition, of creating the institutional infrastructure for a market economy. **Privatization was secondary...**[27]

To the same effect he remarks elsewhere that China shows "...that an economy might achieve more effective growth by focusing first on competition, **leaving privatization until later.**"[28]

Clearly, Stiglitz does not rule out the privatization option for China, but cautions against imprudent timing, speed and method of privatization in the transition process. In his opinion, premature and rushed privatization is a flawed policy product of political imperative and economic imprudence, and could be a major cause for substantial economic losses when the sequence of reform is ignored or wrongly devised.[29] As discussion in Chapter 7 indicates, Russia has provided a negative example of "rushed" privatization. China should learn this lesson. Indeed, while counter-factually it is difficult to speculate what would have happened if China adopted the same approach of mass and rapid privatization when markets had not expanded and critical institutions, such as an effective

---

27. Joseph E. Stiglitz, *Globalization and Its Discontents* (New York: W. W. Norton & Company, 2002), p. 182 [italics in original; emphasis added].
28. Joseph Stiglitz, "Knowledge for Development: Economic Science, Economic Policy, and Economic Advice," paper presented at the *Annual World Bank Conference on Development Economics*, Washington, DC, April 20–21,1998, p. 2 [emphasis added].
29. Stiglitz, *supra* note 27.

financial system, were weak or missing, the undeniable fact that it has achieved remarkable economic growth without massive privatization at the early stage of reform testifies to the merits of sequencing and pacing.

The determinants of the decentralized feature of privatization in China: Fiscal federalism and regional competition

There are two major determinants of China's decentralized privatization.

The first factor is the arrangements under the so-called "fiscal federalism" between the central and local governments. It should be pointed out that although China is not a constitutionally professed federalist state, it shows notable features of federalism in the fiscal arrangements between the central and local governments.

In China, the relationship between the central and local governments resonates with the typical structure under the "market-preserving federalism" model developed by political scientists and economists in recent years.[30] Although not optimal, the Chinese-style "fiscal federalism" is generally conducive to promoting market-oriented reform and economic prosperity at the local levels. The issue of incentive compatibility has been well addressed in China's fiscal contracting system as well as in its fiscal and tax reforms since 1994.

The fiscal contracting system is an arrangement between the central and local governments dealing with revenue sharing under fixed terms, which provides local governments with strong financial incentives to pursue market-oriented reform. For example, faced with hard budget constraints, local governments have actively encouraged the development of non-state enterprises and greater reform in local SOEs, typically through partial or full privatization to generate more revenues.[31] As a result, the fiscal incentives of local governments to reform enterprises have largely shaped the decentralized feature of privatization in China.[32] In addition, local governments have also played a very important role in corporate governance of local enterprises. For example, in local government-controlled enterprises (usually the collectively-owned township and village enterprises or TVEs), managers have been given partial or total residual shares by the local governments to pursue firm efficiency.[33]

---

30. See, for example, Rui J. P. de Figueiredo, Jr. & Barry R. Weingast, "Pathologies of Federalism, Russian Style: Political Institutions and Economic Transition," working paper (2002), available at < http://faculty.haas.berkeley.edu/rui/mpfrussia.pdf >; Olivier Blanchard & Andrei Shleifer, "Federalism with and without Political Centralization: China versus Russia," 48 IMF Staff Papers 171 (2001); Hehui Jin, Yingyi Qian & Barry R. Weingast, "Regional Decentralization and Fiscal Incentives: Federalism, Chinese Style," Working Paper, Center for Research on Economic Development and Policy Reform at Stanford University (2001), pp. 36–37.

31. Jin, Qian & Weingast, *ibid.*, pp. 36–37.

32. Michael Burawoy, "The State and Economic Involution: Russia through a China Lens," 24:6 *World Development* 1105 (1996).

33. Shaomin Li, Shuhe Li & Weiying Zhang, "The Road to Capitalism: Competition and Institutional Change in China," 28 *Journal of Comparative Economics* 269 (2000).

The second important factor in shaping the decentralized feature of privatization in China is enhanced inter-regional competition in product markets during the process of market expansion and economic liberalization in the areas of trade and investment.[34] In order to compete with firms from other regions with lower costs of production, a local firm (as well as the local government overseeing it) has strong incentives to improve performance. The best way of achieving such improvement is through ownership reform, whereby private entrepreneurs receive partial or full residual rights from the government. Not only local small SOEs, but also TVEs have experienced widespread privatization since the mid-1990s in this manner. China's accession to the WTO has added more strength to inter-regional competition and accordingly provided an external lever to push forward China's decentralized privatization.

3.3.3   The latest round of the privatization debate: The culmination of the controversy over privatization (*minyinghua*) and MBOs

Over the course of China's decentralized privatization, largely due to the underdevelopment of complementary institutions, such as a strong stockmarket and an effective system of state assets management, there have occurred a number of incidents of rampant asset stripping. This has generated controversy among the Chinese public over the means, and most recently the very direction, of privatization. The spill-over or pull-back effect of such controversy has the potential to undermine the legitimacy of privatization as it has been so far practiced, thereby risking the reversal of SOE reform, despite having accelerated since 1997 towards decentralized privatization of small and medium-sized SOEs at local levels.

This controversy reached its culmination in the summer of 2004, when an economist at the Chinese University of Hong Kong, Larry H. P. Lang, launched a fierce attack on several well-known Chinese entrepreneurs, accusing them of stealing state assets during the process of China's SOE reform. In particular, he dismissed the legitimacy of insider privatization (Chinese-style MBOs) as a method of acquiring controlling stakes in SOEs.[35] This has sparked a heated

---

34.   Shaomin Li, Shuhe Li & Weiying Zhang, "Cross-Regional Competition and Privatization in China," 9:1 *Economic Policy in Transitional Economies* 75 (1998), p. 84.

35.   Lang Xianping, "Questioning the Method of Ownership Reform at TCL (zhiyi TCL chanquan gaige fang an)," *Sohu Caijing,* June 17, 2004, online < http://business.sohu. com/2004/06/17/35/article220573551.shtml >; Lang Xianping, "The Transformation of Haier: A Complete Analysis of A Long and Complicated Process of MBO (Haier bianxing ji: manchang quxian MBO quanjiexi)," *Sohu Caijing,* August 2, 2004, online < http://finance.sina.com.cn/t/20040802/1417919523.shtml >; Lang Xianping, "Cautions over The Collusive Expropriation of State Assets by Private and State Enterprises (Lang Xianping: jingti minqi huotong guoqi hefa tunbing guoyou zichan)," *Phoenix TV,* August 26, 2004, online < http://www.phoenixtv.com/home/finance/ fortune/200408/26/317941.html >.

debate over privatization that has lasted to date and engaged not only scholars, but also the general public. A thorough discussion of this debate is provided in Chapter 4.

Despite the controversy and debate surrounding privatization, the government seems resolved to continue to pursue ownership reform at small and medium SOEs, while voicing in the meantime its concerns with asset stripping and other forms of expropriation by enterprise insiders and local officials through collusion. In the wake of the MBO controversy, the SASAC, the national watchdog of state assets, was quick to release a policy report on the principles, achievements and problems of SOE reform that had proceeded thus far.[36] This report largely reassured the public that the direction of ownership reform will be maintained, and that the state will not change its determination to withdraw from competitive sectors of the economy and to support private firms to take over these sectors. Specifically, the SASAC expressed its opinion that MBOs are only suitable for privatizing small SOEs on a case-by-case basis, and that such transactions must be subject to a set of restrictions and be conducted in a fair, transparent, and competitive manner. This means that outside and foreign investors should be able to bid against managers for the assets on sale in an open market.[37]

This latest round of debate has a significant impact on the current understanding of privatization strategies among China's policy circles, which impact was demonstrated in a review by the central government of local enforcement of privatization. This review was conducted by officials from the SASAC and the Ministry of Finance in September 2004. Such prompt response from the government to the privatization debate indicates that the government has taken notice of the irregularities in the process of decentralized privatization, and that it is poised to initiate new measures, mostly through the SASAC's rule-making, to curb asset stripping and to ensure that privatization is implemented with higher transparency to the public and more scrutiny from the central government.

3.3.4   The complementarity between corporate governance reform in the enterprise sector and reforms in the banking and securities sectors

As has been heavily documented, privatization in transition economies is only the first step to efficient ownership.[38] For China, corporate governance reform

---

36. SASAC, "Insisting on the Direction of SOE Reform and Orderly Pushing Forward SOE Reform with Regulation (jianchi guoqi gaige fangxiang, guifan tuijin guoqi gaizhi)," *People's Daily*, September 29, 2004, online < http://news.xinhuanet.com/ fortune/2004-09/29/content_2036001.htm >.

37. SASAC, *ibid.*

38. See, for example, Bernard Black, Reinier Kraakman & Anna Tarassova, "Russian

accompanied by reforms in the banking sector and securities markets has become a new strategy on the government's reform agenda as the country enters the next stage of transition to a full market economy, especially in light of China's accession to the WTO.

According to a number of researchers studying transition economies and emerging markets, corporate governance reform in these countries is closely associated with the development of capital markets as privatization has occupied the centre of these countries' reform agenda in recent years.[39] The economic logic behind this link is that privatization is not likely to succeed unless capital markets are able to facilitate the restructuring of privatized firms, whereby efficient ownership structures can be established.[40] China is no exception to this observation. Aside from financing and investment functions, China's stockmarket is entrusted with an additional task to facilitate the ownership reform of SOEs by offering a place to trade property rights. However, in practice this task is by no means properly executed, or executable, given the political logic of China's stockmarket that works against the economic rationales described above.[41] Chapter 5 will elaborate on this issue.

3.3.5 Major debates about China's stockmarket

A defining feature of China's stockmarket at the current stage of economic development is that it is generally inefficient in allocating capital, where unscrupulous issuers are obsessed with a practice of *quanqian* ("free lunch" style, predatory fund-raising), and engaged in a race for value destruction at the expense of huge wealth losses for investors. For an overwhelming majority of companies listed on China's two stock exchanges in Shanghai and Shenzhen, numbering 1,477 as of June 2007,[42] the only purpose of going public is to raise money as a "free lunch" without caring about improving corporate governance

---

Privatization and Corporate Governance: What Went Wong?", 52 *Stanford Law Review* 1780 (2000); Boycko, Shleifer & Vishny, *supra* note 24; John J. Coffee Jr., "Privatization and Corporate Governance: The Lessons from Securities Market Failure," 25 *Journal of Corporate Law* 1 (1999).

39. See, for example, Simon Johnson, "Coase and the Reform of Securities Markets," Federal Reserve Bank of Boston Conference Series [Proceedings], 187 (2000); Edward Glaeser, Simon Johnson & Andrei Shleifer, "Coase versus Coasians," 116 *Quarterly Journal of Economics* 853 (2001).

40. Johnson, *ibid*; Glaeser, Johnson & Shleifer, *ibid*.

41. See Stephen Green, *China's Stockmarket: A Guide to Its Progress, Players and Prospects* (London: Profile Books, 2003), pp. 4–6.

42. Source: CSRC, online < http://211.154.210.238/cn/tongjiku/report/200706/ c/8070101M200706_1.htm >.

quality or rewarding investors with adequate returns. Major debates about China's inefficient stockmarket are introduced below.

The debate about the most fundamental problem of China's stockmarket

With respect to the most fundamental problem of China's stockmarket, or the root cause of the endemic practice of *quanqian*, there has been a constant debate over what is more damaging to the market: the poor quality of listed companies, or the fragmentation of the stockmarket manifested by the non-tradability of state shares.[43] In answering this question, China's scholars and securities regulators share a common understanding that both these problems are equally serious and need to be addressed in tandem.

Given the problems with China's nascent stockmarket, what is particularly puzzling is that with both a weak legal system and largely inadequate regulation in terms of enforcement effectiveness, China's stockmarket still attracts many domestic investors who in general do not pay much attention to the quality of corporate governance of the companies they put their money in. This mysterious investment pattern demands explanations.

In addition to the scarce alternative channels to make capital investment for the Chinese public, which means the only other place to put personal savings in is the "big four" state banks which offer very low interest rates, another more important reason for investing in the stockmarket without considering the quality of listed companies is that Chinese investors widely hold an expectation that the government will bail out the market if it faces a collapse out of the concern for social stability.

This explanation seems to have found its resonance in the work of the 2004 Nobel Prize winners in economics, Edward Prescott and Finn Kydland, although the thrust of their theory is more vigorously tested by macro-economic booms and busts.[44] According to the two Laureates, the credibility of government to sticking to its economic policies is important to the success of these policies. If the government is perceived as not credible because it has a history of repudiations of promises, its policies will be ignored and the public will generate opposite expectations. In other words, if the government cannot fulfill its promises made *ex ante*, it will lose credibility and the public will act in opposite ways in anticipation of government compensation *ex post* if they suffer losses.

---

43. Wang Chenbo, "Liu Hongru, the First Chairman of China Securities Regulatory Commission: Government Abidance by Promises Is a Precondition for Stockmarket Development (zhengjianhui shouren zhuxi Liu Hongru: zhengfu jiannuo gushi caineng xianghao)," *China Newsweek* (*Xinwen Zhoukan*), October 19, 2004, online < http://www.chinanews.com.cn/news/2004/2004-10-19/26/496237.shtml >.

44. The 2004 Nobel Prize in economics honored these two economists for their contribution to the reshaping of macroeconomic thought and policy. See "Cycles and Commitment," *The Economist*, October 14, 2004, p. 74.

This conundrum is summarized by the two economists as the "time consistency problem."[45]

The "time consistency problem" is precisely the major cause for the abnormal investment pattern in China's stockmarket. Investors, believing that the government will not risk social unrest by letting the market collapse, bet on an *ex post* bail-out should there be a meltdown, and accordingly recklessly engage in rampant speculative trading activities. It seems that the "time consistency problem" is fully recognized by the government itself, as reflected in the comments on reviving investor confidence by a top regulator of China's securities markets, who considers government's abidance by its promises a "precondition" for stockmarket development in China.[46] Therefore, while investor education is by no means of secondary importance to the development of China's stockmarket, it is perhaps more critical that the government should commit itself to stringent regulation and fulfill its promise not to bail out the market or rescue the market participants, be they state-controlled listed companies, state-owned financial intermediaries or individual investors, in the event of a collapse or meltdown in the market.

The debate about "development versus regulation": A matter of sequencing

On the issue of which of the following dimensions assumes a higher policy priority — promoting the development of the stockmarket or strengthening the regulatory regime, the Chinese government seems to favor a pragmatic stance of "discovering and solving problems over the course of market development."[47] This position has a clear "development" tilt, despite the rhetorical clarification by the government that it is unnecessary, as well as unreasonable, to regard these two dimensions as reflecting opposite or contradictory values.

There is a good example to illustrate the vigor of the philosophy of "more development, lesser regulation." Laura Cha, the former vice chairwoman of the China Securities Regulatory Commission or the CSRC (China's SEC) who was hired by the Chinese government in 2001 from Hong Kong for her reputation as an "iron-handed regulator," left her post in October 2004 following criticisms from the market participants (surprisingly, many being small investors) about her unbending stance on tough regulation. Some say that her departure was a verdict that stringent regulation may not be suitable to the Chinese stockmarket at its early development stage. Chapter 5 will shed more light on the issues raised here regarding the direction of China's stockmarket reform.

---

45. *Ibid.*
46. Wang, *supra* note 43.
47. Wang, *supra* note 43.

3.4 **Summary**

The history of China's enterprise reform over the past three decades or so has provided some useful lessons for contemplating future reform strategies. The following discussion seeks to summarize these lessons and consider the directions of China's corporate governance reform and related financial reforms at a later stage of the transition. Arguably, there are five lessons that developing and transition economies could learn form China's experience.

First, alternative reform strategies adopted at an early stage of China's transition, which did not involve ownership restructuring, did not work well to bring about efficiency gains to China's SOEs. In general, previous reform strategies all failed to effectively solve the "SOE problem." Some of these strategies, such as the managerial performance contract system, had an initial positive impact on firm performance, but did not maintain such positive results due to inherent ownership and control problems in the state sector that can only be effectively mitigated through ownership reform.

Second, the corporatization and shareholding experiments started to address the ownership problem of SOEs, and have yielded some preliminary results. Existing evidence indicates that the "ownership effects" on Chinese SOEs are significant and may well dominate the "competition effects" on SOE performance at later stages of the transition. Although with some notable problems, such as limited participation of private and foreign capital in the ownership restructuring of large SOEs, particularly those in strategic sectors, the corporatization and shareholding experiments have overall proved effective with small and medium SOEs at local levels.

Third, privatization in China has proceeded in a gradual and decentralized manner, whereby regional competition and arrangements under China's fiscal federalism have largely shaped the pattern of privatization of small SOEs and TVEs at local levels. Unlike Russia, China did not pursue a radical approach toward privatization. Instead, it has adopted a gradualist and experimental approach that emphasizes the merits of local innovative pilot schemes. Local initiatives are often useful for the discovery of a better road to the market through experiments at lower costs. Moreover, the gradualist nature of China's privatization approach has also been illustrated by the fact that while privatization has become a favorable policy option at a later stage of the transition, the government still insists on continuing state ownership, primarily due to its concern about retaining control over strategic sectors and preserving fundamental bases for its regime.

Fourth, compared to a radical approach toward privatization, China's gradualist strategy has proved a better approach toward the market. There has been a huge debate among students of transition economics over the question of the optimal pace and sequence of economic reforms in transition economies.[48]

---

48. Lardy, *supra* note 1, p. 2.

Russia had implemented its privatization programs in a "big-bang" manner in anticipation of economic prosperity, but experienced significant stagnation and decline through the following decade and has only seen signs of growth over the past several years due to high oil and metal commodities prices in the international market. China's enterprise and corporate governance reforms have followed a gradualist path that takes into account proper sequencing and pacing and allows for the implementation of alternative strategies at different stages of economic development.

The gradualist strategy is largely a sensible approach, for two reasons. On the one hand, a developing country cannot build well-functioning institutions overnight under economic, political, social and human resource constraints, because these institutions take time to develop. On the other hand, when old systems are no longer suitable, it is important to avoid an institutional vacuum which has a potentially destructive impact on the whole society. Therefore, some transitional solutions, even if not the best in a more developed institutional environment, can still play a positive role in promoting economic growth. More importantly, today's imperfect solutions can provide a starting basis to accumulate resources for future reforms, thus serving as "stepping stones" to the ultimate destination of a market economy. Therefore, the merits of sequencing and pacing in the dynamics of transition should be appreciated.

Fifth, China's gradualist approach toward privatization and corporate governance reform in the enterprise sector, although with preliminary positive results, has also encountered serious challenges in an underdeveloped legal and institutional environment. The primary challenge has been the lagging reform of state assets management system, particularly in relation to expanded privatization at local levels since the late-1990s. As a result, asset stripping and self-dealing have become evident in many privatization transactions, and have raised concerns and criticism from both the central government and the public. The second challenge is the lagging financial reform in the banking and securities sectors, which until recently had not proceeded as promptly as it should have to complement the enterprise reform. Accordingly, future reform strategies should take into account these two challenges, and emphasize the importance of both sequencing and complementarity.

It is important to point out that "sequencing" is not a static concept that does not allow for self-adaptation and self-adjustments when constraints on reform have been relaxed or removed at later stages of economic development. For example, there are potential high costs associated with delaying the structural reforms of SOEs and the financial system when China is rapidly integrating with the global economy. In order to generate synergies and complementarity, the reforms of the SOE sector, banking sector and the stockmarket need to proceed simultaneously and in a syncronized manner.[49]

---

49. Lardy, *supra* note 1, pp. 3–5 and p. 221.

4

Corporate Governance Practices of Major Types of Chinese Enterprises and Institutional Constraints on Corporate Governance Improvements during Transition

Chapter 4 examines the design and implementation of corporate governance mechanisms at Chinese enterprises and assesses their effects on both firm performance and the growth prospects of Chinese economy. Under investigation are four types of Chinese enterprises: state-owned enterprises or SOEs, listed companies, township and village enterprises or TVEs, and private enterprises. Major issues to be discussed in Chapter 4 are reform strategies adopted by the Chinese government for difference types of enterprises, as well as typical corporate governance problems arising from reforms and their causes. In addition, Chapter 4 also investigates the current legal and institutional environments for China's corporate governance reform and the constraints they impose on corporate governance improvements.

The major findings of Chapter 4 are reflected in the following four aspects.

First, due to legal and institutional constraints at the current stage of China's economic development, whereby market basics are not firmly established, the role of the government is still under transformation and investor rights are not adequately protected, the quality of corporate governance practices of Chinese enterprises in general is not satisfactory and requires further reform or enhanced implementation of existing reform schemes.

Second, privatization in China had not become a favored policy option until 1997, when the central government decided that the state should withdraw from competitive sectors of the economy and only concentrate on strategic sectors. In terms of implementation, privatization in China has proceeded in a decentralized and experimental manner, whereby local governments have been the driving force in seeking workable reform strategies for local SOEs and TVEs under existing federalist and government structures. Corporatization and shareholding reform have been the primary methods of corporate governance reform in the SOE sector aimed at transforming traditional SOEs into shareholding companies with diversified ownership structures. Currently, while privatization has been extended to a much broader scale at the local levels, large SOEs, especially state monopolies under central government's control, have not experienced much privatization, or have only been partially privatized. What is more, the reform of SOEs in China, in particular since 2000, has been primarily identified not with mass privatization, but with "gradual participation of private capital in the ownership restructuring of SOEs" (*jianjinshi minyinghua*).

Third, although at an early stage of reform some transitional corporate governance mechanisms had played a positive role in bringing about efficiency gains, such as local government ownership and control of TVEs that served as the second-best solution to the agency problem, these transitional mechanisms are no longer efficient at later stages of reform. As China's transition proceeds, these "stepping stones" toward a full market economy need to be replaced by more market-oriented institutions. One such example is the widespread privatization of TVEs since the mid-1990s.

Fourth, under a "dual track" system at the early stage of reform, which encouraged competition between the state and non-state sectors without addressing ownership reform of SOEs, China's indigenous private enterprises were permitted to grow alongside the state sector, but were also subject to various forms of policy discrimination, particularly with regard to financing and eligibility for industry entry. After three decades of development, Chinese private enterprises have become the primary contributor to the country's economic growth and employment expansion, but the policy discrimination against them has only started to be addressed seriously by the government. Moreover, although the private sector, now consisting of both "born private" firms and privatized former SOEs and TVEs, is widely expected to dominate China's economy in the future as the most competitive sector, it has also encountered serious challenges of corporate governance reform. These challenges are primarily associated with the overall transformation of traditional business patterns in China's private sector, such as the "lock-up" pattern of family business lines, lax internal controls, "founder's dictatorship," and the practice of "private entrepreneurs paying for a government identity card." These old patterns of doing business are unlikely to sustain global competition and need to be reformed and replaced by modern corporate governance mechanisms, particularly with respect to effective internal checks and monitoring of the owner-manager.

Based on the above observations, Chapter 4 argues that careful sequencing and pacing should be regarded as the central feature of corporate governance reform in China, which requires realistic and workable schemes that accommodate available economic and political resources and existing legal and institutional environments. Because of the huge size of China's economy and diverse local conditions and levels of development, local experiments with innovative pilot schemes should be encouraged in the process of corporate governance reform, which has been a major characteristic of China's gradualist approach toward transition. These local experiments are not only useful for the accumulation of collective knowledge of transition across the country, but can also facilitate the discovery of effective reform strategies suitable for a broader scope of application through trial-and-error at lower costs.

Chapter 4 is divided into seven sections. Section 4.1 draws a broad picture of the current landscape of China's enterprise sectors by introducing relevant statistics and data on major types of Chinese firms. Based on the statistics, Section 4.1 also assesses the respective importance of different types of enterprises to China's economy, as well as their prospects for contributing to the country's future growth and enhancement of global competitiveness.

Section 4.2 reviews corporate governance reform of China's SOEs, including large SOEs controlled by the central government ("central SOEs") and small and medium enterprises controlled by local governments ("local SOEs"). The focus of examination in Section 4.2 is the progress of shareholding reform and decentralized privatization over the past decade or so, and in particular after 1997 when the central government decided that the state should withdraw from competitive sectors of the economy and only concentrate on strategic industries. A strategy of "grasp the large, release the small" (*zhuada fangxiao*) was announced in 1997 by the central government as the guiding principle for SOE reform. After various experiments at the local levels, this strategy has been interpreted as privatizing all but the largest SOEs, primarily the largest "central SOEs," numbering 155 as of July 2007. Accordingly, Section 4.2 closely examines the core elements, implementation and effects of the "*zhuada fangxiao*" strategy.

A key subject of investigation in Section 4.2 is the role of the State-owned Assets Supervision and Administration Commission or SASAC in corporate governance reform of SOEs. The SASAC was established in April 2003 and has been overseeing state assets in the SOE sector as the *sole* representative of the state owner through extensive rule-making and monitoring activities. The term "sole" is particularly important, because it marks a notable difference between the newly established practice and the old practice of supervising SOEs. Under the new design of state assets management system, the SASAC is solely responsible for exercising the ownership rights in SOEs and ensuring the maintenance and increase of the value of state assets. By contrast, before the SASAC was established, multiple government agencies with different (and at times conflicting) objectives had split the state ownership rights in the SOE sector, yet none had been made ultimately responsible for firms' performance.

Section 4.2 also discusses policy issues associated with decentralized privatization, primarily in relation to the reform of local SOEs. Local experiments with innovative schemes of privatization are presented as an example of a gradualist and experimental approach to SOE reform, even though some of these pilot schemes were not always workable. Controversies over management buyouts (MBOs) as a method of privatization and the local practice of "business people wearing 'red hats'" are also examined, which indicate the challenges and difficulties of SOE reform and, to a broader extent, of building market fundamentals in China under legal and institutional constraints.

Section 4.3 offers a brief assessment of corporate governance of Chinese listed companies in both domestic and overseas capital markets. The domestic capital markets are the Shanghai Stock Exchange and Shenzhen Stock Exchange. The primary overseas capital markets for Chinese listings are those in Hong Kong, New York, London and Singapore. To illustrate the important issue of the interaction between capital markets and corporate governance of Chinese listed companies, case studies of corporate governance controversies in both domestic and overseas capital markets are presented.

Section 4.4 and Section 4.5 address corporate governance issues at Chinese TVEs and private enterprises, respectively. Specifically, Section 4.4 reviews the rise and possible fall of TVEs, with an emphasis on the function of local government ownership and control as a transitional corporate governance institution in addressing the agency problem. In examining China's private enterprises, the primary finding of Section 4.5 is that although these firms have outperformed SOEs over the past three decades and gradually become more competitive to meet the challenge of globalization, their corporate governance structures have displayed some worrying signs of inefficiency. Examples include the "lock-up" pattern of family business and the phenomenon of "founder's dictatorship," which need to be addressed in future reforms. Section 4.5 also points out that although the removal of "red hats" from private enterprises originally registered as pseudo-TVEs was a significant improvement on their corporate governance structures, the problem of lax internal controls has increasingly become a significant impediment to the future growth of these firms.

In light of the empirical review of corporate governance practices in major types of Chinese firms presented in the preceding sections, Section 4.6 then raises important questions that have emerged from China's corporate governance reform, and attempts to explain these questions under the analytical framework of a gradualist reform strategy. The concluding Section 4.7 follows by describing the positive and negative lessons of corporate governance reform in major types of Chinese enterprises.

4.1 The Enterprise Landscape in China

By reviewing the landscape of Chinese enterprises, Section 4.1 points out that among China's major enterprise sectors, the relative importance of SOEs to the national economy has been in decline, while the private sector has become the main contributor to China's GDP growth. It is also suggested that future competitive Chinese enterprises on both domestic and international markets will be found not in the SOE sector, but in the private sector. While SOEs have been the primary concern of China's corporate governance reform and whether they can be transformed into competitive firms will have a huge impact on China's growth prospects, private enterprises have demonstrated tremendous potential to contribute significantly to China's transition to a market economy and international competitiveness in an age of economic globalization. The following discussion is aimed at providing relevant statistics and data on major types of Chinese enterprises, which indicate their respective importance to China's economy. For the reason identified in Chapter 1 (i.e., the still limited influence of foreign-invested enterprises or FIEs on China's corporate governance regime), FIEs are not covered by Chapter 4.[1]

4.1.1 State-owned enterprises (SOEs), including large SOEs controlled by the central government ("central SOEs") and SMEs controlled by local governments ("local SOEs")

According to recent statistics, as of December 2003, there were about 150,000 SOEs in China, of which more than 147,000 were small and medium enterprises under local government control (i.e., "local SOEs").[2] The largest SOEs under central government control with the State-owned Assets Supervision and Administration Commission or SASAC as their custodian (i.e., "central SOEs") numbered 155 as of July 2007.[3] These firms have been described as "white elephants" by some western observers because of their sheer size.[4] Under a gradualist strategy, the central SOEs and local SOEs are treated differently

---

1. For an excellent comprehensive overview of FIEs in China, see Yasheng Huang, *Selling China: Foreign Direct Investment during the Reform Era* (New York: Cambridge University Press, 2003).
2. SASAC, "Insisting on the Direction of SOE Reform and Orderly Pushing Forward SOE Reform with Regulation (jianchi guoqi gaige fangxiang, guifan tuijin guoqi gaizhi)," *People's Daily*, September 29, 2004, online < http://news.xinhuanet.com/fortune/2004-09/29/content_2036001.htm >.
3. Duan Xiaoyan, "The SASAC Admonishing SOE Bosses," *21st Century Business Herald* (*21 Shiji Jingji Baodao*), December 15, 2004.
4. "The Other China: Parts That The Bulldozers Have Not Yet Reached," *The Economist*, January 8, 2004, pp. 59–61.

with regard to ownership reform. On the one hand, the central SOEs are the subject of the "grasp the large" (*zhuada*) scheme whereby the state owner retains control of these firms. On the other hand, the local SOEs are the major concern under the "release the small" (*fangxiao*) scheme aimed at introducing foreign and private capital into the ownership structures of these firms, which usually involves deeper ownership diversification or fuller privatization.

Even after three decades of reform, China still has the world's largest number of SOEs in an era marked by global waves of privatization. This is a sharp dissonance with the prevailing theme of the day. With such a huge size, China's SOE sector has continuously underperformed its non-state counterparts, especially the vibrant private enterprises which now account for nearly two thirds of China's annual GDP output according to independent estimates.[5] Despite the decline of their importance to the growth of the national economy, SOEs are still a huge burden on the government and the success or failure of their reform will have a significant impact on China's overall growth prospects.

4.1.2 Listed companies

As of June 2007, there were 1477 listed companies on China's two stock exchanges in Shanghai and Shenzhen.[6] The state owns two-thirds of equity in all listed companies, which, for the purpose of retaining control, had been non-tradable until very recently.

Partially privatized SOEs, many of which lose money and are badly governed, dominate China's stockmarket. On the other hand, most profitable private firms have been denied public listings in China. For example, Standard & Poor's, a credit-rating agency, counted only 35 "private" listed companies in China in 2003 out of a total number of 1300 listed companies, and pointed out that a good number of these so-called "private" listed companies were in fact controlled by local governments and even the military.[7]

---

5.   Official estimates by the Chinese government, which are more conservative and viewed by many as "unreliable," generally put this number at 50 percent. See Xu Xiaonian, "From 'the Withdrawal of the State and the Expansion of the Private Sector' to 'the Withdrawal of Government Officials and the Expansion of the Private Sector' (cong 'guotuiminjin' dao 'guantuiminjin')," *Caijing*, February 5, 2007, online < http:www.caijing.com.cn/home/opinion/other/2007-02-15/16190.shtml >.

6.   Source: China Securities Regulatory Commission (CSRC), online < http://www.csrc.gov.cn/en/statinfo/index1_en.jsp?path=ROOT>EN>Statistical % 20Information>Listed >.

7.   "Casino Capital," in "The Weakest Link: A Survey of Asian Finance," *The Economist*, February 6, 2003, pp. 10–12.

4.1.3 Township and village enterprises (TVEs)

Having prospered in early years of China's economic reform, Chinese TVEs have been in decline since the mid-1990s and undergone widespread privatization. However, recent statistics show that they are still relevant to employment generation and income increases for China's rural population. For example, TVEs are estimated to have employed a total number of 138 million rural workers over the periods of 1978–2004.[8] Even though in decline, they were projected to still have employed 3 million workers in 2004 alone.[9] TVEs are also an important source of income increases for China's rural residents. For instance, in 2003, TVEs contributed 35 percent to the annual total income of China's rural population.[10]

4.1.4 Private enterprises

In January 2005, there were about 3 million private enterprises with an employment size of more than 8 people and more than 23.5 million private businesses with an employment size of less than 8 people. Until June 2004, these firms in combination had employed a total number of 90 million workers.[11] According to the statistics released by All-China Federation of Industry and Commerce (ACFIC), the Chinese private sector now accounts for roughly one half of the country's annual GDP output and 70 percent of the aggregate employment.[12] If measured by employment expansion, the private enterprises stand out even more remarkably. Since 1992, they have added 5 to 6 million new employment posts per year. In 2004, they provided 90 percent of all newly created employment posts in China.[13] The above statistics strongly support a prediction that is widely shared by Chinese economists: in the future landscape of competition among Chinese enterprises, the dominant players with the most vigorous competitiveness are not likely to be found in the SOE sector but in the non-state sector, in particular the private enterprises.

---

8. Zhao Yongping, "TVEs Absorbed 1.4 Million Rural Workers in the First Half of 2004 and Are an Important Source of Rural Income Increases (shangbannian xina 140 wan laodongli, xiangqi cheng nongmin zengshou zhongyao laiyuan)," *People's Daily*, September 28, 2004, online < http://www.chinanews.com.cn/news/2004/2004-09-28/2 6/488937.shtml >.

9. *Ibid.*

10. *Ibid.*

11. Wang Zi, "The Non-State Sector in Chinese Economy Is Now Given Proper Evaluation and Treatment (feigong jingji 'zhengshen')," *21st Century Business Herald* (*21 Shiji Jingji Baoda*), January 24, 2005, online < http://www.nanfangdaily.com.cn/jj/20050124/ zh/200501240001.asp >.

12. *Ibid.*

13. *Ibid.*

4.2 **Corporate Governance of SOEs**

Corporate governance reform of China's SOEs as a policy priority has been underway since the shareholding reform was expanded nationwide in the mid-1990s. The shareholding reform, starting from local pilot programs of corporatization, has transformed traditional SOEs into a new form of firm — shareholding companies. As reported in Chapter 3, as an alternative approach to SOE reform after previous schemes had all failed, the shareholding experiment marked the first attempt by the government to tackle ownership reform in the SOE sector. The shareholding reform has been aimed at diversifying the ownership structure of SOEs and transforming them into shareholding companies with Western-style corporate governance structures.

Corporate governance reform of Chinese SOEs has generated some encouraging results as the shareholding experiment and privatization have extended to a wide application across the country. There are some reports showing that, through corporate governance reform, especially privatization, SOEs have improved their performance. For example, according to a recent empirical study of China's privatization, during 1990–97 newly privatized SOEs had shown "significant improvements in real output, real assets, and sales efficiency" in addition to "significant declines in leverage" and "significant improvements in profitability" compared to fully state-owned firms.[14] Another study reports that China's shareholding reform has had huge impacts on levels of both firm efficiency and social equality.[15] On the one hand, for SOEs and collectively-owned enterprises such as TVEs, their conversion to joint stock companies "contributes to overall increases in both current productivity and innovation" and paves a way for the emergence of "a domestic managerial and entrepreneurial class." On the other hand, the greater concentration of shareholding reform in wealthier coastal areas is also likely to contribute to regional inequality in China.[16]

Although the corporate governance reform of Chinese SOEs has produced some positive results, the remaining problems and challenges must not be underestimated. Section 4.2 reviews several important aspects of corporate governance at Chinese SOEs to demonstrate this point.

---

14. Zuobao Wei *et al.*, "The Financial and Operating Performance of China's Newly Privatized Firms," 32:2 *Financial Management* 107 (2003), p. 107.
15. Gary H. Jefferson *et al.*, "The Impact of Shareholding Reform on Chinese Enterprises, 1995–2001," William Davidson Institute Working Paper No. 542 (2003).
16. *Ibid.*

4.2.1 **The politics of privatization: The political economy constraints on privatization in China**

The politics of privatization is chiefly a reflection of the current political economy constraints on China's economic reform and transition to the market. Broadly speaking, privatization in China has taken, and had to take, a gradualist approach in terms of both speed/scope and method.

The speed/scope of privatization concerns issues such as when to privatize and which types of SOEs should be privatized. The method of privatization primarily centers on the following issues: (a) how to transfer state assets to private hands (e.g., through IPOs, MBOs, open market auctions, or government-coordinated mergers and acquisitions); (b) how to solve the problems of labor reallocation and debt payment to workers, such as salary arrears, unpaid welfare benefits and pensions; and (c) how to reach an agreement with bank creditors with respect to usually huge amounts of un-recovered loans to the firm.

These issues are all practical challenges and always a headache for local governments which supervise state firms during the process of privatization, primarily because the necessary legal rules and regulations governing the management and transfer of state assets have been in short supply at the central level. As a consequence, the experiments with privatization at the local levels have been subject to a variety of diverse practices and to a considerable level of uncertainty surrounding the legitimacy of already executed deals.

In China's decentralized privatization, local governments have been engaged in a "game" with the central government. To the central and local governments, the problems and challenges arising from privatization as mentioned above raise different political as well as social and economic implications.

From the point of view of the central government, privatization should be conducted in a "stable and cautious" manner, given various legal and institutional constraints on ownership reform of SOEs. The most cited constraints include the explicit debts (e.g., salary arrears and unpaid welfare benefits) and implicit debts (e.g., a huge deficit in the current national pension account) owed to workers, the fairness between coastal and interior areas with different levels of industrial growth, potential social instability caused by massive lay-offs, the lack of necessary laws and regulations to ensure transparency of state assets transfers, weak monitoring by the central government of asset stripping at local levels, and an inadequate social security system.

The local governments, however, are generally driven by different incentives in the process of privatization. It has been repeatedly reported that local governments, especially those with larger bases of state-owned industries, have a strong "impulse" for embarking on rapid ownership reform. Two reasons are behind this "local impulse." First, local governments are eager to get rid of the huge fiscal and social burdens of running SOEs as quickly as possible and to improve local economic performance, which is closely linked to the promotion prospects of local officials. Second, because the SASAC is now in charge of SOE reform and is poised to introduce vigorous regulation and monitoring over the implementation of assets transfers at local levels, some local officials are afraid of losing the last opportunity to "catch fish in turbid water" or "enjoy the last free supper" when rules and disciplines were not fully in place, which usually involves irregular transactions.[17] Some local governments, such as Nanjing municipality of Jiangsu province, even set up a timetable to speed up privatization and impose "execution targets" on local SOEs, forcing them to conduct expedient ownership transfers.[18]

Seen from the central-local power play or a dynamic "game" between different levels of the Chinese government, the conclusion is that the politics of privatization has a huge impact on China's gradualist approach to privatization and corporate governance reform.

4.2.2 Privatization and corporate governance reform of local SOEs: "release the small" (*fangxiao*)

For China's state-owned small and medium enterprises or SMEs, which are usually controlled by local governments, corporate governance reform has been gradually taking place and achieved some meaningful results. Through ownership restructuring guided by the policy of "grasp the large, release the small," the majority of China's state-owned SMEs have been privatized by insiders, including former managers and employees. As a result, insider shareholding, particularly the controlling shareholding by managers, has become the dominant ownership structure of these firms. This type of insider privatization was largely an accommodation to the strategic consideration of the Chinese government to "buy consent" from managers and employees, in order for reforms to take place.[19]

---

17. Liu Xuemei, "The SASAC in Swift Action: A Sudden Break on Local SOE Reforms at the End of 2003 (guoziwei fengbao: difang guoqi gaizhi niandi jishache)," *21st Century Business Herald* (*21 Shiji Jingji Baodao*), December 24, 2003, online < http://www. nanfangdaily.com.cn/jj/20031225/cj/200312240799.asp >.

18. Lou Yi & Li Qing, "The Mystery of Hunan's Sale of State Shares," *Caijing*, September 20, 2003; Wang Chenbo, Chen Xiao & Pan Songtao, "The Window-Dressing Role of Property Rights Trading Centre: Jiangsu Province Reviewing Expedient Reform of State Assets (chanquan jiaoyi zhongxin cheng baishe, Jiangsu zicha ganchaoshi guozi gaige)," *China Newsweek* (*Xinwen Zhoukan*), October 25, 2004, online < http://finance.sina. com.cn/roll/20041025/13501106279.shtml >; Li Jing & Wang Shengke, "A Thorough Review of the Transfer of State Assets Worth RMB200 billion: Jiangsu Province Under Central Government Scrutiny (2000 yi guozi zhuanrang dachoucha, zhongyang lianhe diaochazu nanxia jiangsu)," *21st Century Business Herald* (*21 Shiji Jingji Baoda*) October 9, 2004, online < http://finance.sina.com.cn/g/20041009/17211067501.shtml >.

19. Zhang Chunlin, "The Ownership Reform of Small SOEs," *Caijing*, February 5, 2002.

While this kind of ownership structure (i.e., managerial controlling shareholding) may have advantages over the old firms, the problems associated with insider control and lack of transparency and competition from outside bidders in transferring state assets have also caused corporate governance failures, such as poor management and asset stripping. Some Chinese economists have proposed a solution to these problems: introducing outside investors either through direct transfer of managerial shareholding to new owners, or by issuing new shares to outsiders to replace the controlling shareholders. In either case, fairness, transparency and competition from outside bidders should be guaranteed in searching for the optimal owner.[20]

It is also important to note that in the process of privatizing local SOEs, some pilot reform schemes have been designed by local governments to experiment with workable strategies that accommodate distinct local conditions and levels of economic development. There had been some successful examples in the 1990s. For example, the experience of three localities, including Zhucheng county of Shandong province, Shunde county of Guangdong province and Yibin county of Sichuan province, has received positive remarks from Chinese economists.

In a widely noted empirical study of the three examples, it is reported that in Zhucheng county of Shandong province, its initially controversial but ultimately successful privatization experiment began in September 1992.[21] The county eventually transformed 37 of the 50 SOEs controlled by the local government into non-state enterprises.[22] The researchers note:

> Of the 37 transformed former SOEs, 32 became stock cooperatives collectively owned by their managers and employees, three larger firms were incorporated into limited liability companies under the *Company Law*, one firm was merged with a Beijing-based non-state enterprise, and one firm went bankrupt, which was rare at the time when bankruptcy was still an unfamiliar notion to China's SOEs. The remaining 13 SOEs not included in the privatization experiment were all in public utility and transportation sectors, which the county regarded as appropriate for continuing government control in order to serve its duty to provide public services to the local community. Moreover, the county also privatized 235 of its 238 urban collectives.[23]

The reported results of privatization in Zhucheng county were impressive. Before the reform, many of the local SOEs were losing money. After the reform, all transformed enterprises started making profits. According to the researchers,

---

20. *Ibid.*
21. Yuanzheng Cao, Yingyi Qian & Barry R. Weingast, "From Federalism, Chinese Style, to Privatization, Chinese Style," 7:1 *Economics of Transition* 103 (1999), pp. 127–129.
22. *Ibid.*
23. *Ibid.*

"the total profits made by the reformed firms, the average rate of return on capital in local enterprises, the average annual growth rate of local government revenue, and the average annual incomes of employees of local enterprises all increased significantly in the first three years after privatization."[24]

The second example, Shunde county of Guangdong province, was well known across China in the late 1980s for its successful TVE sector. As China's transition proceeded in the 1990s, TVEs started to show signs of decreased competitiveness and some localities, including, notably, Shunde county, began to privatize TVEs. In 1993, the county launched its reform of both local SOEs and TVEs by changing their ownership structures and introducing ownership diversification.[25] For example:

> The local government changed the ownership structures of 743 former SOEs and collectively-owned enterprises (including TVEs and urban collectives), accounting for 69 percent of the total in Shunde county. Of these 743 enterprises, 249 were sold to the public, 331 were transformed into stock cooperatives owned by their managers and employees, 21 changed their controlling owners (i.e., the local county or township government) to minority shareholders, and 142 in public utility, transportation, real estate and foreign trade sectors remained solely owned or controlled by the country or township government.[26]

As privatization has expanded to a much broader application nationwide after 1997, when the central government gave its endorsement to the "grasp the large, release the small" policy, Shunde country has experienced much deeper and accelerated privatization. It is currently one of the best performing local economies in China, with local private enterprises now contributing nearly 60 percent to the county's annual GDP output and 57.2 percent to the annual tax revenues of the local government.[27] More recently, the projected annual GDP growth rate of Shunde county for 2005 was estimated to reach 20 percent.[28]

The third example, Yibin county of Sichuan province, started ownership reform of local SOEs and collective enterprises (including TVEs and urban collectives) in 1992 through privatization, which was a pioneering experiment at the time.[29] As recounted in the study mentioned above:

---

24. *Ibid.*
25. *Ibid.*
26. *Ibid.*
27. "Private Sector Now Accounts for 59.7 Percent of Shunde's Aggregate GDP Output (minying jingji yi zhan Shunde GDP zongliang de 59.7%)," *South Daily* (*Nanfang Ribao*), November 2, 2004, online < http://www.southcn.com/news/dishi/foshan/ttxw/200411020421.htm >.
28. Ma Zhenhua, Wang Maolang, Ma Hongsheng & Zhang Tao, "The Projected GDP Growth Rate of Shunde County for 2005 Has Been Increased to 20 Percent (Shunde GDP zengzhang tiaogao 20%)," *Pearl River Times* (*Zhujiang Shibao*), April 11, 2005, online < http://county.aweb.com.cn/2005/4/11/8144648.htm >.
29. Cao, Qian & Weingast, *supra* note 21.

By 1995, of the total 110 local SOEs and collective enterprises, 86 had been transformed into private enterprises. What distinguished the Yibin model of privatization was its adoption of a method of non-cash mortgage sales, whereby buyers, usually former managers and employees of the transformed enterprises, paid 30 percent of the book value of the firm assets and paid off the balances in installments over the following three years. Before the full value of the sold assets was paid off, buyers in general had paid an annual fee to the state as rents for using state assets. The results of privatization in Yibin county were positive in the immediate three years. For example, between 1993 and 1995, the profits and taxes contributed by the reformed enterprises to the local economy had increased seven times, while workers' average incomes increased by 30 percent per year.[30]

While the examples of Zhucheng, Shunde and Yibin were generally positive, there have also been local experiments that were not always workable, at least at a particular stage of reform when the necessary political and institutional conditions were not yet receptive to such pilot schemes. For instance, in September 2003, the provincial government of Hunan pooled together all the state shares in its listed companies and put these shares on sale as a wholesale package at the annual China High-Tec Fair held in Shenzhen, with the expectation to sell off these shares to private investors (including foreign investors). However, this move was very controversial and raised criticism from both the public and central government as "too radical," as the central government had yet to clarify its position and policy on the non-tradable state shares in listed companies. In the end, the Hunan provincial government had to withdraw its privatization plan under external pressures, particularly from the SASAC.[31]

4.2.3 The controversies over MBOs

Compared to how it is generally understood in the capital markets of mature market economies, the term "MBO" (management buyout) has a different meaning in the Chinese context. In China, MBO is a new concept to the business community and only started to emerge several years ago during the process of privatizing SOEs. In the first place, the target firms of many MBO deals were not public companies, as is usually the case in Western capital markets, but state-owned, non-listed firms. Managers of these firms usually

---

30. *Ibid.*
31. Hu Yifan & Lou Yi, "Some Puzzles Surrounding the Transfer of State Assets Still Waiting for Clear Answers (guozi zhuanrang xuannian daijie)," *Caijing*, November 20, 2003, online < http://www.caijing.com.cn/econout/other/2003-11-20/3342.shtml >.

became their new owners by acquiring controlling stakes or full ownership via off-market negotiations with local governments. Because there have been some irregularities associated with this method of privatization, such as asset stripping, extraction of state resources, self-dealing, corruption and violation of workers' rights, public scrutiny and criticism have intensified over the past several years, which eventually amounted to a storm of attacks on MBOs.

In particular, controversies over a few high-profile Chinese enterprises which had been transformed from old SOEs, through which process capable managers successfully turned loss-making SOEs into profitable private firms through explicit or implicit MBOs, have raised the issue of the legitimacy of this particular method of privatization, given the lack of necessary legal rules that govern MBO transactions. The MBO controversy reached its culmination in the summer of 2004 when an economist of the Chinese University of Hong Kong, Larry H. P. Lang, publicly questioned the legitimacy of the controlling stakes acquired by several well-known Chinese entrepreneurs in their firms, including Zhang Ruimin, the CEO of Haier, a white goods maker, Li Dongsheng, the CEO of TCL, a TV and phone maker, and Gu Chujun, the CEO of Greencool, an electronics manufacturer. Mr. Lang accused these managers of accumulating personal wealth through stripping state assets during the process of China's SOE reform.[32] He dismissed the legitimacy of Chinese-style MBOs as an acceptable method of acquiring controlling stakes in SOEs, because in his view this is no much different from the much criticized Russian style of privatization, whereby some large SOEs were sold at ridiculously low prices to insiders.

Lang's open criticism of MBOs, which first appeared in a popular Chinese financial internet forum, *Sohu*, and later began to be aired in a Shanghai-based TV program, *Larry Lang Live*, has resulted in a wave of debate over privatization among Chinese public, media and academic circles. This debate is still commanding the height of public attention today. Almost every well-known Chinese economist has joined this debate, either concurring with Lang or challenging his position by criticizing him for "reaching a general conclusion based on limited case studies" or "relying on questionable data."[33] Hundreds

---

32. Lang Xianping, "Questioning the Method of Ownership Reform at TCL (zhiyi TCL chanquan gaige fang an," *Sohu Caijing*, June 17, 2004, online < http://business.sohu. com/2004/06/17/35/article220573551.shtml >; Lang Xianping, "The Transformation of Haier: A Complete Analysis of A Long and Complicated Process of MBO (Haier bianxing ji: manchang quxian MBO quanjiexi)," *Sohu Caijing*, August 2, 2004, online < http://finance.sina.com.cn/t/20040802/1417919523.shtml >; Lang Xianping, "Cautions about The Collusive Expropriation of State Assets by Private and State Enterprises (Lang Xianping: jingti minqi huotong guoqi hefa tunbing guoyou zichan)," *Phoenix TV*, August 26, 2004, online < http://www.phoenixtv.com/home/finance/ fortune/200408/26/317941.html >.

33. See, for example, Liu Jipeng, "Leftism and Rightism both Harmful in Ownership Reform (chanquan geming ji yao 'fanzuo' ye yao 'fangyou')," *Sohu Caijing*, October 19, 2004, online < http://business.sohu.com/20041019/n222560185.shtml >; Qin Hui,

of commentaries and newspaper reports have been pouring into the public domain, mostly on the internet. Gu Chujun, the CEO of Greencool and one of the entrepreneurs criticized by Lang, even brought a libel lawsuit against him, which was much publicized by the media and added in more dramatic flavor to this episode.

Greencool expanded operations through acquiring controlling stakes in declining state enterprises. Gu was attacked by Lang for "stealing state assets" through a series of "illegitimate acquisitions" of rival SOEs in the electronics industry.[34] The libel case was famously known to the Chinese public as the "Lang-Gu dispute." The latest state of the "Lang-Gu dispute" highlighted the spectacular trial of Gu in November 2006 in a local court in Foshan of Guangdong province, on charges of economic crime centered on financial fraud, allegedly taking place in the process of his acquisitions of former ailing state enterprises.[35]

It is important to examine why Lang's attacks on MBOs have obtained widespread support from the Chinese public. At a time when the Chinese public has increasingly become critical of widened social inequality and of an enlarging wealth gap during the country's economic reform, Lang has become a "cult hero" by criticizing the managers of China's best-known enterprises. Lang had

---

"The Battle between Leftists and Rightists, the Danger in the Institutions, and the Fair Reform of SOEs (zuoyou zhizheng tizhi zhixian yu guoyou qiye gongzheng fenjia)," *Sohu Caijing*, October 11, 2004, online < http://business.sohu.com/20041011/n222424113.shtml >; Qiu Feng, "Seeking the Legitimacy of Ownership Reform of SOEs (xunzhao chanquan zhidu gaige de zhengdangxing)," *China Newsweek* (*Xinwen Zhoukan*), October 4, 2004, online < http://www.chinanewsweek.com.cn/2004-10-10/1/4425.html >; Chen Zhiwu, "Preserving SOEs or Returning the Assets to the People? (yao guoying haishi yao 'huanchanyumin'?)," *Securities Market Weekly* (*Zhengquan Shichang Zhoukan*), September 25, 2004, online < http://blog.icxo.com/read.jsp?aid=4980&uid=863 >; Zhou Qiren, "Why My Response to Lang Xianping? (wo weishenme yao huiying Lang Xianping?)," *Business Watch* (*Jingji Guancha Bao*), September 11, 2004, online < http://finance.sina.com.cn/jingjixueren/20040911/16341016995.shtml >; Zhang Weiying, "Zhang Weiying's Response to Lang Xianping: Those with Contributions to Our Society Deserve Good Treatment (Zhang Weiying huiying Lang Xianping: shandai wei shehui zuochu gongxian de ren)," *Business Watch* (*Jingji Guancha Bao*), August 30, 2004, online < http://economy.enorth.com.cn/system/2004/08/30/000853872.shtml >; Yang Ruifa & Yao Jian, "Zhang Wenkui: the Direction of Ownership Reform of SOEs Cannot be Dismissed (guoyan zhongxin Zhang Wenkui: guoqi chanquan gaige fangxiang burong fouding)," *21st Century Business Herald* (*21 Shiji Jingji Baodao*), August 21, 2004, online < http://www1.people.com.cn/GB/jingji/1037/2735027.html >.

34. Li Ranzhou, "The Lang-Gu Case Is A Focus of Public Attention: Lang Took the Challenge with High Profile (Lang-Gu zhisu zaidu chengwei gejie guanzhu jiaodian, Lang Xianping gaodiao yingsu)," *The Oriental Outlook Weekly* (*Liaowang Dongfang Zhoukan*), October 21, 2004, onine < http://www.yn.xinhuanet.com/focus/2004-10/21/content_3075517_5.htm >.

35   Su Dandan, "Gu Chujun on Trial (Gu Chujun shoushen)," *Caijing*, November 13, 2006, online < http://www.caijing.com.cn/ruleoflaw/other/2006-11-13/13283.shtml >.

used his newly launched but widely popular TV show in Shanghai, *Larry Lang Live*, as a platform to continue his attacks on the managers who were able to buy state assets at alledgely cheap prices through MBOs.[36] Widely speculated to be partly prompted by recent public debate over privatization led by Lang, in December 2004, the SASAC prohibited MBOs of large SOEs and set stringent conditions for MBOs of smaller SOEs.[37]

Interestingly, according to his interview with the *Financial Times*, Lang's claims about the private wealth obtained by the managers of SOEs were based on a list of China's richest business leaders, published in January 2005 by Euromoney China, a financial and business journal.[38] According to Euromoney China, five of 50 enterprise managers on its list acquired their shares through MBOs. For example, Ma Mingzhe started off in 1988 with no shares as general manager of Ping'An Insurance, a formerly state-owned insurance company. However, he has gained effective control of the firm, now listed overseas with a total capitalization of USD 4.5 billion, through an "employee shareholders association (ESA)." Such ESAs have been used as an incentive mechanism through issuing shares to managers of SOEs. However, in some cases these ESAs have been deployed by the managers as a tool of implicit MBOs to dilute state holdings.[39] These firms include previously mentioned Haier and TCL, as well as Lenovo, a PC maker that acquired IBM's PC business in December 2004 and is currently the world's third largest PC maker by annual revenue and product output.

Supporters of these firms' managers argue that they have earned their success through hard work and innovation in business strategies and therefore deserve decent reward, including a controlling stake in their firms. These supporters pointed out that all three firms — Haier, TCL, and Lenovo — have prospered at home and also started to launch ambitious overseas operations, largely at the initiative of their top managers. However, in the view of Mr. Lang, the process of MBOs in China, including those transactions involving Haier, TCL and Lenovo, is inherently flawed, because it is usually the managers themselves who decide on what prices should be paid for the state assets they acquire.[40]

As already pointed out, the government quickly took notice of the MBO controversy. In December 2004, the SASAC made it clear that it is not permitted to privatize large SOEs through MBOs.[41] While acknowledging that MBOs to some extent do improve the vitality of enterprises, the SASAC expressed deep

36. Geoff Dyer & Richard McGregor, "China's Answer to Larry King," *Financial Time*, February 1, 2005, p. 13.
37. *Ibid.*
38. *Ibid.*
39. *Ibid.*
40. *Ibid.*
41. "Reform: State CEOs Salaries Linked to Profit," *Asia Times Online*, December 17, 2004, online < http://www.atimes.com/atimes/China/FL17Ad04.html >.

concerns over implementation irregularities, such as self-dealing and insider expropriation in some of the MBO transactions completed so far. In its recent review of the implementation of SOE reform at local levels, the SASAC found that in most MBO transactions, asset stripping and stealing by managers through unfair or non-transparent procedures of valuation, pricing and transfer were widespread, usually in conspiracy with local officials who oversaw the privatized firms and accepted bribes to give the deals a green light. In addition, there had been cases where managers tried to transfer risks to the buy-out targets and state banks by using state shares and assets as loan guarantees to finance their MBO deals. The SASAC also pointed out that some MBO transactions also harmed the rights of investors and employees.[42]

In summary, an overall assessment of the policy consequences of the recent MBO controversy is two-fold. On the one hand, the Chinese government has not shifted from the general direction of ownership reform of SOEs, nor has it dismissed privatization as a favorable policy option. On the other hand, the government has also cautioned against irregular or illegal implementation of privatization at local levels which had resulted in asset stripping and self-dealing and had harmed the rights of employees. Out of this caution, the government banned MBOs as a method of privatization with regard to large SOEs. While MBOs are permitted in the case of small SOEs, their implementation is now closely monitored by the central government, specifically by the SASAC.[43] Since its establishment in 2003, the SASAC has been working diligently to draft rules to govern proper methods and procedures of state assets transfer, and the pace of its rule-making has accelerated in the wake of recent debate over the "Lang-Gu dispute."

It seems that the policy signal at the present time is generally opposed to those managers with an MBO ambition. The position of the SASAC on MBOs could however be a double-edged sword, because while its ban on MBOs of large SOEs and tightened monitoring of MBOs of small SOEs may well put irregular practices to a halt, its toughened position could also block or deter potentially efficiency-enhancing privatization transactions.

Some economists in favor of MBOs argue that MBOs are an effective way to realize the intrinsic value of entrepreneurs, and are also a much-needed cure for the pathology of "the world's cheapest entrepreneurs but most expensive entrepreneurial system" in China.[44] On the one hand, Chinese entrepreneurs in SOEs are "cheap," because their compensation packages are generally very shabby and cannot yield adequate incentives, which often

---

42. "Monitoring State Assets: The SASAC Is Facing A Supervision Deficiency," *China Newsweek* (*Xinwen Zhoukan*), October 18, 2004.

43. SASAC, *supra* note 2.

44. Xu Peihua, "Seeking the Road to the Realization of the Value of Chinese Entrepreneurs (xunzhao zhongguo qiyejia jiazhi shixian zhilu)," *Caijing*, November 20, 2002, online < http://www.caijing.com.cn/cjzl/ds1/2002-11-20/9346.shtml >.

leads to underperformance or mismanagement. On the other hand, China's entrepreneurial system is "expensive," exactly because the lack of incentives and the resulting poor performance usually cause huge losses and waste. The issue of managerial compensation will be revisited shortly when new reform strategies designed by the SASAC for the largest SOEs ("central SOEs") are examined below.

4.2.4 Reforming the state assets management system

As mentioned previously, in 1997, the central government decided that the state should withdraw from the competitive sectors of the national economy and only concentrate on strategic industries. A strategy of "grasp the large, release the small" (*zhuada fangxiao*) was announced as the guiding principle for SOE reform, which, after various experiments at local levels, has been interpreted as privatizing all but the largest SOEs controlled by the central government or the "central SOEs," numbering 155 as of July 2007. The following discussion mainly concerns the *zhuada* part of the policy and with a specific emphasis on the role of the SASAC.

State assets management system in transformation: from "centralized ownership and decentralized control" to "decentralized ownership and control"

The SASAC was established in April 2003 as the sole representative of the central government to oversee state assets nationwide. It reports directly to the State Council (the cabinet) and its officials and staff are appointed by the State Council. The SASAC also has established its local branches at both municipal and provincial levels, but the progress has varied with different localities. The mandate of the SASAC is to represent the state owner in China's largest SOEs under central government's control (the "central SOEs"), with a primary responsibility of maintaining and increasing the value of state assets in these firms. In the past, local SOEs, which are largely small and medium enterprises, had been controlled by local governments which did not officially have the ownership rights. By comparison, under the new state assets management system the local governments are granted ownership rights to local SOEs.

Under the old system, the central government was nominally the sole owner of SOEs at all levels, including those it did not directly supervise. Local governments, although with direct control of SOEs in their jurisdictions, did not formally enjoy the status of "owner" and were obliged to obtain central government's approvals of significant transactions or ownership reform involving local SOEs. This is described as a system of "centralized ownership and decentralized control." The old system was replaced by a new system of "streamlined decentralized ownership and control" in June 2003, when local governments were granted the *de facto* ownership rights to local SOEs. This means that local governments now enjoy the status of owners of the state assets under their control, and have the rights to transfer or auction off these assets as well as make personnel decisions in local SOEs, without first having to obtain central government's approvals.[45]

Accordingly, the key feature of the current reform of state assets management system in China can be categorized as a transformation from "centralized ownership" of all SOEs by the central government and "decentralized control" by local governments of local SOEs, to "streamlined decentralized ownership and control" of local SOEs by the local governments. Moreover, this policy shift also means that the old practice of multiple government agencies splitting the ownership rights to SOEs, i.e., "five dragons fighting the flood" (*wulong zhishui*) as vividly summarized by Chinese economists, has been replaced by a new system, whereby the SASAC is the sole representative of the state owner with a consolidated range of ownership rights.[46]

The phenomenon of "five dragons fighting the flood" had been the primary cause of the agency problem of Chinese SOEs. On the one hand, multiple government agencies with different, and sometimes conflicting, objectives were each responsible for assets management, personnel decisions (such as appointments and removals of managers) and routine business operations (such as investment and R&D strategies). On the other hand, none of these agencies assumed the ultimate responsibility for firms' performance.[47] As the SASAC now bears sole responsibility for assets management, personnel decisions and business operations of SOEs, many Chinese economists and policy makers believe that agency costs will be significantly reduced.

Regulating state assets transfer and improving transparency of transactions

On February 1, 2004, the SASAC and the Ministry of Finance jointly issued rules that require all transactions involving state assets transfer be executed in the open market, i.e., the trading centers for property rights. Currently, China has three trading centers for state assets transfer, located in Shanghai, Tianjin and Beijing. In addition, the information of state assets transfer, such as the identity of the buyers and the prices paid, must be disclosed to the public.[48]

---

45. Shi Dong, Zhao Xiaojian & Hu Yifan, "A Close Look at the SASAC – Part One: State Assets Management System in Gradual Clarification after the 16th Party Congress (xijie guoziwei 1: shiliuda hou guozi guanli jiagou jianci qingxi)," *Caijing*, February 24, 2003.
46. "The Path Taken by the Pioneers (xianxingzhe zhilu)," *Caijing*, November 20, 2002. "Dragon" is a powerful symbol in ancient Chinese legends with expertise in curbing flood.
47. Shi Dong & Zhao Xiaojian, "The Direction of State Assets Worth RMB10 trillion (shiwanyi guozi zouxiang)," *Caijing*, November 20, 2002.
48. Jean-Marc Deschandol, "Breaking New Ground in State-owned Assets Transfers," *China Law & Practice*, March 1, 2004, p. 1; Jia Quanxin, "SASAC: 'Sunshine Transactions' Required for State Assets Transfer (guoziwei: qiye guoyou chanquan de zhuanrang yao

4.2.5 Strengthening the central SOEs: the quest for "national champions"

As of July 2007, there were 155 large SOEs owned and directly controlled by the central government with the SASAC as their supervisor.[49] These firms are commonly known to the Chinese public as the "central SOEs" and are described by some Western observers as "the state-owned white elephants."[50] These central SOEs are generally in strategic sectors and industries, such as oil, telecommunications, civil aviation, highway, steel and power. The SASAC has taken actions to implement a strategy of "grasping the large" (*zhuada*) aimed at building global competitiveness of the central SOEs and producing 30 to 50 "national champions" through industrial grouping by 2010.[51] The following discussion introduces major schemes adopted by the SASAC to implement the "grasping the large" (*zhuada*) strategy.

Encouraging industrial rationalization to achieve operational integration and capacity expansion

Mergers and acquisitions involving Chinese SOEs include both domestic transactions between themselves and overseas transactions with foreign enterprises. Domestically, the SASAC has ordered a series of restructuring and grouping among central SOEs operating in key industries such as telecommunications, civil aviation and shipping. As a result, as of July 2007 the number of central SOEs was reduced to 155, down from 196 when the SASAC was first established in April 2003.

Recently, there have also been some significant overseas M&A negotiations and deals, including two notable examples. The first example is the acquisition negotiations in 2005 between China Minmetals and Canada's Noranda in the mining industry, which eventually had not produced substantial results despite active initiatives by China Minmetals to reach a deal. The primary reason was that the Canadian enterprise, also state-owned, had been under both political pressure and public criticism for negotiating an acquisition deal with a state monopoly from a regime with a "poor human rights record." The second example is the transfer of IBM's personal computer unit to China's computer maker Lenovo in December 2004, which hugely surprised U.S. capital markets.[52]

---

shixian 'yangguang jiaoyi')," *China News*, September 29, 2004, online < http://www.chinanews.com.cn/news/2004year/2004-09-30/26/489835.shtml >.

49. Source: SASAC, online < http://www.sasac.gov.cn/zyqy/tbts/200707200192.htm >.
50. *The Economist, supra* note 4.
51. Mary Boyd, "The State Sector," Q3 China Economic Quarterly (2003). Also see Zhao Huanxin, "China names key industries for absolute state control," *China Daily*, December 19, 2006, p. 1, online < http://www.chinadaily.com.cn/china/2006-12/19/content_762056.htm >.
52. Jayanthi Iyengar, "China's Misstep in Canada," *Asia Times Online*, November 23, 2004, online < http://www.atimes.com/atimes/China/FK23Ad07.html >; "M&A's New Giant: IBM Deals Shows How Normal China Has Become," *Financial Times*, December 9, 2004.

However, the Lenovo-IBM deal had also been under close scrutiny by the U.S. government on grounds of "national security." These complexities imply that the level of difficulty in overseas expansion for Chinese SOEs might well exceed their original expectation. The sheer challenges facing Chinese SOEs with an ambition for overseas expansion were highlighted in the aborted takeover attempt by China's biggest oil producer CNOOC at America's Unocal in 2005, whereby a hostile U.S. congress successfully blocked the deal on "national security" grounds.[53]

The industrial policy of building "national champions" in the state sector has drawn criticism from some Western observers, who consider that this policy is likely to create future problems. They warn the Chinese government that there have been failed examples in China of state-mandated industrial rationalization and grouping through forced mergers, which did not succeed in integrating managements or reducing surplus capacity because "the commanding heights beloved by government planners can turn into costly economic sink holes."[54] Seen from reality, this caution has some merits in it. A big problem of using M&As as a means to integrate and restructure China's state monopolies is that some transactions are not market-driven, but orchestrated by the government through "coordinative efforts" of the SASAC, which usually involves administrative intervention in business decision-making.[55] This problem indicates that at the current stage of China's transition, the line between the role of the government and that of the market is still not clear cut. As a result, corporate governance reform of Chinese SOEs, especially the central SOEs, is subject to strong non-market influences.

Introducing competition to state monopolies in strategic sectors

Recently, private enterprises have been permitted to enter previously forbidden sectors where state monopolies dominate, such as oil, automobile, steel, electricity, transportation and banking industries. The purpose of relaxing entry restrictions on private enterprises is to bring competition to monopoly SOEs and improve their performance. However, where the private enterprises are involved, abrupt policy changes and the government's arbitrary repudiation of contracts have sometimes proved serious impediments to the enhancement of competition in monopoly sectors. As a result, private enterprises have suffered losses, in some cases significant losses, as demonstrated in the much publicized incident of "government seizures of private oil wells," erupted recently in Shaanxi province.

---

53. See "The Myth of China Inc," *The Economist*, September 3, 2005, p. 63.
54. See Guy de Jonquieres, "China's industrial policy should think small," *Financial Times*, September 7, 2006, p. 17.
55. Hu Yifan & Zhu Xiaochao, "Restructuring the Central SOEs: Searching for Market-Driven Solutions (yangqi chongzu: tanlu shichanghua)," *Caijing*, September 20, 2004, online < http://www.caijing.com.cn/econout/other/2004-09-20/3222.shtml >.

As one of the most egregious examples of violating private property rights by the government, in the spring of 2003, the local government of the northwest Shaanxi province ordered the seizure of about 5,500 private oil wells in over 15 counties as part of an environmental cleanup and overhaul of the industry. These oil wells had been explored by private investors since 1994, when the Shaanxi government started to encourage private investment in local oil industry to both increase efficiency and enhance competition.[56] Outraged by the government's arbitrary change of policy, investors, largely private entrepreneurs from China's heartlands, started their preparations in November 2004 for bringing collective lawsuits against both the provincial, municipal and county governments involved, over the forced seizures without due process and proper compensation. These investors claimed that the closed wells were worth nearly RMB 7 billion yuan (USD 845 million).[57] This case has been marked by both lawyers and academics as "the flagship case of protecting private property rights" in China after the Constitution was amended in March 2004 to declare that "legally obtained private property is inviolable."

Consolidating "core business lines" (zhuye) and decoupling ancillary operations (fuye)

China's central SOEs are required by the SASAC to gradually split from their core business lines ancillary operations and social burdens, such as schools, hospitals and employees' housing services.[58] The split had been completed with 49 central SOEs and some 800 large-sized local SOEs by December 2004.[59] Although the effect of removing social burdens and ancillary operations remains to be seen, it is widely believed that such measures will have a positive impact on firm efficiency.

"Going out": overseas investment and expansion

At the SASAC's encouragement, the "going out" strategy for enhancing global competitiveness of China's state monopolies may be implemented through the following channels: (a) expanding industrial operations abroad, such as reaching M&A deals with foreign partners, (b) making overseas investments in

---

56. Zhu Yuchen, "The Flagship Case of Protecting Private Property Rights (baohu sichan diyi an)," *China Newsweek (Xinwen Zhoukan)*, November 1, 2004.

57. Antoaneta Bezlova, "China Seizes Private Oil Wells, Mirrors Russia," *Asia Times Online*, November 2, 2004, online < http://www.atimes.com/atimes/China/FK02Ad03.html >.

58. Xinhua News Agency, "China Axes Redundant Operations of SOEs," *China Daily*, April 30, 2004, online < http://www.chinadaily.com.cn/english/doc/2004-04/30/content_327745.htm >.

59. Wang Shengke, "49 Central SOEs Have Consolidated Core Business Lines, Li Rongrong Kicks Off the Start of The Restructuring of Central SOEs (49 hu yangqi zhuye qiaoding, Li Rongrong kaiqi zhongyang qiye chongzu damu)," *21st Century Business Herald (21 Shiji Jingji Baodao)*, December 1, 2004, online < http://finance.sina.com.cn/g/20041201/08151192837.shtml >.

"strategic" industries, such as mining, oil and power, and (c) seeking overseas listings of large SOEs.[60]

Of the major channels of "going out," overseas listings have become a primary method to facilitate industrial restructuring and corporate governance reform of China's state monopolies. For example, several state-owned airliners, such as Air China, Hainan Airlines, Shenzhen Airlines and Xiamen Airlines, have gone public on overseas stock exchanges in Hong Kong or London to both raise funds and change ownership structures. Apart from the fact that they can raise money on the overseas markets, an important change for these airlines is that they all become public companies.[61] The government hopes that by going public overseas, these firms can have much better incentives to perform and make profits. However, although overseas listings to a considerable extent indeed provide stricter regulatory oversight, tougher market disciplines and higher corporate governance standards, overseas-listed Chinese SOEs have nevertheless experienced some dramatic corporate failures due to lapses in internal control systems. These corporate governance failures have dampened the confidence of international investors. Chapter 5 will provide a close analysis of some significant cases.

4.2.6 Corporate governance reform of the central SOEs

Experimenting with a board system

Since June 2004, the board of directors has been introduced as a new form of supervising central SOEs by the SASAC. The purpose of this new practice is to change the old pattern of monitoring SOEs by the state owner, whereby direct intervention by the government had dictated the appointment of management. Under the new board system, members of the board of directors are appointed by the SASAC.[62]

However, there remains a major problem with the implementation of the board system: the Communist Party still retains direct control over firms' operations through taking part in decision-making on "significant matters," such as firms' growth strategy, investment projects, fund-raising plans, as well as

---

60. James Mackintosh, Richard McGregor & Francesco Guerrera, "Chinese Companies Acquire a Taste for Western Targets," *Financial Times*, October 19, 2004, p. 20; Arthur Kroeber, "Chinese Invasion Has Yet to Happen," Q4 *China Economic Quarterly* (2004).

61. "Air China Debuts on HK and London Markets," *Asia Times Online*, December 18, 2004, online < http://www.atimes.com/atimes/China/FL18Ad03.html >.

62. Wang Chenbo, "Central SOEs: Saying Goodbye to the Board of One-Person (yangqi: gaobie yigeren de dongshihui)," *China Newsweek* (*Xinwen Zhoukan*), June 28, 2004, online < http://www.chinanewsweek.com.cn/2004-07-04/1/3815.html >.

appointments to the management team.[63] Certainly, the board system cannot function well under this constraint. However, this problem is beyond the scope of corporate governance issues and extends to the area of political reform, which is not far advanced in China today.

Hiring managers on the open market and building managerial incentives

To help SOEs improve their performance, the central government has decided to hire senior executives on the open market, including the overseas market. This is a significant improvement on the traditional system of internal appointments.[64] The open-market recruitment exercise started in 2003 under the oversight of the SASAC, aiming at attracting talented top managers as well as qualified chief accountants and chief legal counsels. By the end of 2005, the SASAC had hired 50 senior executives in central SOEs who stood out in open market competition. The target number for 2006 was set at 26.[65] The SASAC has expressed the idea that such market-driven recruitment practice, though currently at an experimental stage and with a limited scope of application, will gradually extend to more firms and to more posts as the reform of central SOEs proceeds.[66] It is expected however that the obvious incompatibility between the orientation of open-market hiring and the current policy emphasis on the Party's control over top cadres in central SOEs (which naturally results in political appointments to top managerial posts) will need to be reconciled in the future, which is a real challenge for the SASAC.[67]

Meanwhile, managerial compensation systems are also under reform. In December 2004, the SASAC for the first time signed a performance contract with the CEOs of 30 central SOEs, linking their salaries and bonuses to the profitability of their firms.[68] According to the SASAC, other more advanced schemes of incentive compensation, such as stock options, will be under consideration when the necessary conditions, including a well-functioning stockmarket, are in place.

As the first step to experiment with equity incentive schemes in central SOEs, in September 2006 the SASAC and the Ministry of Finance jointly issued

---

63. Li Yizhong, "Li Yizhong, Vice Director of the SASAC on the Role of the Party in the Decision Making at Central SOEs (Li Yizhong qiangdiao zhongyang qiye yao jian dangwei canyu juece de lingdao tizhi)," *China News*, June 24, 2004, online < http://www.chinanews.com.cn/news/2004year/2004-06-24/26/451885.shtml >.
64. Hu Yifan, "We Want You: State-owned Companies Pay for Talented Managers," *Caijing*, October 5, 2003.
65. Sun Bing, "What Kind of Top Managers at Central SOEs Does SASAC Want? (guoziwei xuyao shenmeyang de yangqi gaoguan)," *China Economic Weekly* (*Zhongguo Jingji Zhoukan*), July 10, 2006, online < http://paper.people.com.cn/zgjjzk/html/2006-07/10/content_7350484.htm >.
66. *Ibid.*
67. *Ibid.*
68. Asia Pulse/XIC, "Reform: State CEOs Salaries Linked to Profit," *Asia Times Online*, December 17, 2004, online < http://www.atimes.com/atimes/China/FL17Ad04.html >.

a circular on the trial measures for implementing equity incentive schemes in state-controlled companies that are listed domestically. This document was intended to both set out benchmark criteria for the introduction of equity incentive schemes to state-controlled listed companies and put a brake on some schemes that had been proposed, without proper guidance and supervision from the central government, by a group of companies in the process of recent share structure reform aimed at making non-tradable shares tradable.[69]

According to this circular, the prerequisite for a company to adopt equity incentive schemes is to have a sound corporate governance structure in place. External directors, including independent directors, must hold more than half of the directorships on the board. The remuneration committee must be chaired by an independent director and the majority of the committee must be made up of external and independent directors. Other major requirements include sound financial performance and good assets quality. It can be seen that the SASAC sets out stringent benchmarks for the equity incentive schemes to take place, as reflected in both the preconditions for their introduction and specific execution details with regard to lock-up periods and pricing.[70] This shows the extreme caution on the part of the SASAC in experimenting with such new compensation mechanisms in China's SOEs — understandably, a politically sensitive issue where asset stripping can occur under the guise of market-driven reform — when both the corporate governance reform and stockmarket reform are reaching a critical turning point.

Apart from reforming the recruitment and compensation systems, the new round of incentive-building at central SOEs is also carried out through the establishment of a new performance evaluation system introduced by the SASAC in October 2006. Under this system, there are five levels of performance, ranking from A to E (A being the highest level). Significant technological innovation is weighted heavily in assessing positive performance, while negative indicators include significant loss of assets, significant failures involving operational safety and product quality, as well as accounting irregularities and large amounts of overdue debt.[71] Predictably, the new performance evaluation system will put considerable pressures on managers to improve the performance of their firms, which is directly linked to their personal compensation and promotion prospects.

---

69. Zhang Yuzhe, "SASAC Forges 'Golden Handcuffs' (guoziwei dingzhi 'jinshoukao')," *Caijing*, June 12, 2006, online < http://caijing.hexun.com/text.aspx?sl=2328&id=1682235 >.
70. *Ibid.*
71. Zhang Xinyue, "Evaluating Performance of Central SOEs at Five Levels (wu dangci huafen yangqi jixiao pingjia)," *China Business News* (*Diyi Caijing Ribao*), October 30, 2006, online < http://dycj.ynet.com/article.jsp?oid=16910496 >.

Strengthening risk control and internal monitoring

Risk control and internal monitoring have been traditionally lax in many SOEs. In order to strengthen internal control and risk management systems in central SOEs, the SASAC has asked these firms to establish necessary corporate governance organs and mechanisms for monitoring purposes, such as a chief accountant and a chief legal counsel.[72] Besides, managers are now responsible for significant operational losses caused by irresponsible investment decisions and asset stripping. In serious cases where the state suffers huge losses, the responsible managers are now subject to legal liabilities.[73] It was reported that the SASAC has been pondering over the idea of releasing regulations on the liability to be imposed on top managers at central SOEs who cause significant losses of state assets and who make missteps in investment decisions due to violations of law.[74]

Adopting a new dividend policy

In December 2006, the SASAC suggested that state-controlled companies start to pay dividends to the state. Although the SASAC, as the representative of the state owner, would at first only take a small amount in dividends and the money would be reinvested in restructuring the state sector and strengthening research and development, this was a remarkable change of policy toward managing SOE profits on the part of the central government.[75] This move shows that the state started to assert its right to dividends as the owner of central SOEs, marking a welcome step toward better corporate governance practices in the state sector.

4.2.7   Abolishing the local practice of "business people wearing 'red hats'" (*hongding shangren*)

"Business people wearing 'red hats'" (*hongding shangren*)

The term "business people wearing 'red hats'" refers to those communist party officials who hold managerial posts in local SOEs or private enterprises.

72. Duan Xiaoyan, "The SASAC Admonishing Bosses of Central SOEs (guoziwei xunzheng)," *21st Century Business Herald* (*21 Shiji Jingji Baodao*), December 15, 2004, online < http://www.nanfangdaily.com.cn/jj/20041216/zh/200412150005.asp >.
73. Fan Lixiang, "Guarding Central SOEs: the SASAC is Armed with Legal Tools," *21st Century Business Herald* (*21 Shiji Jingji Baodao*), October 18, 2004.
74. Zhang Yuzhe, "SASAC Is Considering the Introduction of Accountability of Top Managers at Central SOEs (guoziwei zhiding yangqi lingdaoren wenzezhi)," *Caijing*, July 20, 2006, online < http://caijing.hexun.com/text.aspx?lm=2550&id=1742104 >.
75. "Chinese Dividends Payouts from State Companies Are Just the Beginning," *Financial Times*, December 7, 2006, p. 22.

Economists in China have expressed deep concerns about this phenomenon. They have pointed out that such practice entails a potential danger of driving China into a trap of the so-called "crony capitalism," which is a "bad model of market economy," as has been observed across East Asia.[76] The central government seems to have received the warning from some Chinese economists that China may likely fall into this undesirable track, if administrative power is aligned with "socially advantaged or privileged classes" to jointly expropriate public resources at the expense of social equality. In the association between public power and private interests, the "socially advantaged or privileged classes" primarily refer to China's emerging private entrepreneurs, who have gotten rich ahead of the majority of the country's general population, especially their countrymen in rural areas.

The central government taking on "business people wearing 'red hats'"

By nature, the widespread local practice of "business people wearing 'red hats' " is a manifestation of public power entering the market for private gains. This is a serious distortion of market principles and also a hotbed for breeding corruption. The central government has become increasingly concerned about this local irregularity and decided to act upon it. Recently, the Party's Central Committee issued a memo to address this problem. According to this memo, as of May 2004, Chinese Communist Party cadres as well as government officials were no longer permitted to work in SOEs as managers.[77]

However, the implementation of the central government's memo has largely lagged. This is because local governments have discovered some "merits" in having officials sit on the management teams of local SOEs, such as their role in helping these firms obtain loans from local branches of state banks, as well as communicating with different government regulatory agencies on behalf of these firms. In the view of local governments, the transaction costs of local firms could be reduced if "business people wearing 'red hats' " can effectively deal with regulatory red-tape, thus saving firms considerable time and resources that they can put into productive business operations.

This "transaction costs" argument has found echoes in some localities where local governments are benign to business. With regard to implementing measures to abolish the practice of "business people wearing 'red hats'," these localities have become sophisticated in playing a "game" with the central government: they take little action in reality, but submit positive reports on

---

76. Hu Shuli, "Choose A 'Good Market Economy' (xuanze 'haode shichangjingji')," *Caijing*, October 20, 2003, online < http://www.caijing.com.cn/home/editorial/2005-05-08/2606.shtml >.

77 Peter Morris, "Chinese Cadres Must Give Up Corporate Posts," *Asia Times Online*, March 26, 2004, online < http://www.atimes.com/atimes/China/FC26Ad05.html >.

paper to the central government. This attitude of local governments has impeded the effective implementation of the 2004 memo.[78]

Therefore, the dynamics of the relationship between China's central and local governments needs to be understood in assessing the prospects of China's market-oriented reform. It is important to note that seen from some local market-distorting practices, a danger of the country falling into the trap of a "crony market economy" should not be underestimated. If not brought under control, this emerging danger may well contribute to future problems at later stages of China's transition.

4.3 Corporate Governance of Listed Companies

Section 4.3 introduces a brief assessment of corporate governance of China's listed companies. In-depth analyses and case studies are presented in Chapter 5, which deals with the important issue of the interaction between capital markets and corporate governance of Chinese listed companies.

4.3.1 State dominance in the stockmarket and "the dictatorship of a single largest shareholder"

With regard to Chinese listed companies, a majority of them are either state-owned or state-controlled. Corporate governance improvement of these firms is closely associated with the development of the stockmarket. Because the state owns two-thirds of equity in all listed companies, which, for the purpose of retaining control, had been non-tradable until a share structure reform started to take place in April 2005, the state shareholder or the state-owned legal-person shareholder as the controlling shareholder faces no market discipline. As a result, expropriation of minority shareholders is widespread. This phenomenon is described by investors as "the dictatorship of the single largest shareholder" (*yigu duda*), which has its root in the non-tradability of state shares (*guoyougu*) and legal-person shares (*farengu*). The artificial split of shares into three categories — individual shares, state shares and legal-person shares — has not only resulted in the fragmentation of the stockmarket, but also led to corporate governance failures in listed companies.

Although the *Company Law* spells out basic governance structures for all shareholding companies, it incorporates special provisions to accommodate

---

78. Fan Lixiang, "Public Power Flirting with the Market: the Crisis of the 'Government-Business' Model in Yixing City (quanli bonong shichang: yixing 'guanshang moshi' weiji)," *21st Century Business Herald* (*21 Shiji Jingji Baodao*), December 18, 2004, online < http://www.nanfangdaily.com.cn/jj/20041209/zj/200412080014.asp >.

continuing state ownership. However, the Chinese-style shareholding system cannot reconcile the dual goals of maximizing shareholder value and maintaining state ownership. This is because wealth maximization and other social and political aims that the state imposes on firms, such as maintaining urban employment, are incompatible with the interests of shareholding companies. As a result, this incompatibility has caused conflicts of interest between the state shareholder and minority shareholders.[79] This is an important cause of corporate governance failures in state-owned listed companies.

4.3.2 A "vicious circle"

In terms of the implementation of corporate governance mechanisms spelled out in the *Company Law* and in various enactments by China Securities Regulatory Commission (the CSRC), many listed companies did not strictly follow the letters of such requirements. For example, in reality, even though the legal and regulatory requirements on paper have been satisfied and basic corporate governance organs have been established, such as the general meeting of shareholders, the board of directors, independent directors and the supervisory board, these institutions do not function effectively. More than often, managers (the "insiders") and controlling shareholders disrespect the rights of small investors by extracting corporate funds, stealing corporate assets and resources and engaging in rampant related-party transactions.

Moreover, China's stockmarket is not well-regulated in underdeveloped legal and institutional environments. The state frequently intervenes in market activities, and securities regulators, primarily the CSRC, frequently submit their independence to political will. As a result, fraudulent behavior and violations of investor rights have become widespread. In other words, ineffective regulation of China's stockmarket and the geneally poor quality of corporate governance of listed companies are mutually reinforcing, thus constituting a "vicious circle."

4.4 Corporate Governance of Township and Village Enterprises (TVEs)

China's TVE sector had prospered in the 1970s and 1980s in the country's coastal areas. This sector had been an important driver for China's economic growth and trade expansion until its decline since the mid-1990s when many TVEs started to adopt privatization schemes. The following discussion will show how the TVE sector developed under a set of innovative corporate governance

---

79. See Donald C. Clarke, "Corporate Governance in China: An Overview," 14 *China Economic Review* 494 (2003); Donald Clarke, "Corporatization, not Privatization," 7:3 *China Economic Quarterly* 27 (2003).

arrangements, which were transitional at early stages of China's reform. The prospects of the TVE sector at a new stage of China's economic transition will also be examined.

4.4.1 The puzzle of China's growth in defiance of conventional property rights theory

For many curious Western observers, there remains a major mystery in the pattern of China's economic growth, which is lucidly summarized in the following commentary:

> China's economy has grown rapidly despite the absence of any systematic attempt to clarify "property rights."...Chinese economic success defies conventional theory, which requires that "to function anywhere near its potential, an economic system must have property rights that are much better defined and enforced than is true of China's mixed economic system today."...However, not only have the ambiguities and uncertainties in clarifying property rights done "surprisingly little" harm to Chinese reform, but they may have a longevity that will surprise Western observers.[80]

Competing interpretations of such a puzzling anomaly have proliferated in recent years, but all share a common ground: in China, it is often the social and cultural forces, such as social networking (*guanxi*), personal bonds (*ganqing*), reciprocity, sense of shame (*mianzi*), as well as invocation of the state administrative apparatus, that had functioned to allocate and enforce property rights in practice, while formal legal institutions had been largely avoided.[81]

Here, *guanxi* is a key notion in understanding Chinese business culture. Though inconsistent with the idea of "rule of law," *guanxi* seems to work well in many circumstances involving reciprocity and long-term business ties. As a social norm, *guanxi* has penetrated into the Chinese society at almost every level. It usually does not lead to "disorderly" social behaviors, as some western commentators have speculated and criticized when disappointed with unsuccessful business ventures in China.[82] On the contrary, *guanxi* by and large works effectively within Chinese business society, including overseas ethnic Chinese people, to facilitate business transactions exactly because it embodies certain commonly recognized rules of behavior among local communities that

---

80. Stanley Lubman, *Bird in a Cage: Legal Reform in China After Mao* (Palo Alto, CA: Stanford University Press, 1999), p. 117.

81. *Ibid.*

82. "A Disorderly Heaven," in "Behind the Mask: A Survey of Business in China," *The Economist*, March 18, 2004, pp. 10–13.

function as "tacit knowledge" and informal agreements to guide or restrain individual actions. This interpretation of *guanxi* bears equal implications for Chinese TVEs as well as private enterprises in their running of businesses, as later discussions will reveal.

However, it should also be noted that the personalized pattern of transactions built upon *guanxi* cannot sustain the challenge from globalization at the new stage of China's transition to the market, especially after its accession to the WTO which marked China's commitment to abiding by international business principles and commercial rules of the market. As will be pointed out, in order to survive and grow in an evolving business environment that is destined for competitive markets, corporate governance reform of Chinese TVEs as well as of private enterprises need to tackle the issue of their dependence on *guanxi*, although this process may take long. Hopefully, Chinese enterprises will one day no longer have to invest heavily in *guanxi* with their financial and human resources, and will be able to use these resources for their value-creating business operations.

4.4.2 **The rise of TVEs**

TVEs were a major driving force of China's economic growth and export expansion during the early stage of transition. They showed robust performance during the 1970s and 1980s as compared to SOEs, but started to decline since the mid-1990s and have been subject to widespread privatization.

According to many China experts, there are two primary reasons for the success of TVEs by the mid-1990s. First, reforms in the 1970s and 1980s created competition in product markets and incentives for profit of local government officials and TVE managers, because they can share economic benefits generated from running TVEs efficiently at local levels without remitting the profits to the central government, which their SOE counterparts had to remit. Second, policy discrimination against, and societal suspicion of, private enterprises had suppressed these firms' growth, primarily due to ideological constraints at the early stage of reform.[83]

In particular, banks were very reluctant to lend to private businesses in support of their operation and expansion, and local governments were not at all helpful in providing technological assistance and facilitating the allocation of funds and factors of production, such as land use. Therefore, TVEs enjoyed a relatively comfortable playing field for better performance, as local governments, as well as local branches of state banks in their jurisdictions and hence susceptible to local government influence, were generally supportive

---

83. See, for example, Brett H. McDonnell, "Lessons from the Rise and (Possible) Fall of Chinese Township-Village Enterprises," 45 *William and Mary Law Review* 953 (2004).

of these firms in terms of favorable policies of credit, land use, technological assistance and property rights protection.

4.4.3 Ownership control and incentive structures of TVEs

Transitional but efficient corporate governance mechanisms adopted by China's TVEs can partly explain the country's growth by the mid-1990s. Government ownership and control identified with the corporate governance structure of Chinese TVEs was a second-best solution to the agency problem at the early stage of reform when private enterprises did not enjoy a favorable institutional environment and their growth was suppressed by various forms of discrimination.

The TVE sector had showed the most significant progress by the mid-1990s when local governments, by taking control of TVEs, had facilitated financing, provided technical assistance, helped with allocating funds, accumulating assets and accessing factors of production such as land use. Government ownership also yielded more secure property rights and helped contain corruption through granting ownership rights to government officials, thus reducing the agency costs and enhancing entrepreneurial incentives. Although the relative advantage of China's TVEs in productive efficiency has been in decline in recent years as China enters a new stage of reform, and some authors have started to discuss their "possible fall," the function of those transitional corporate governance mechanisms in the middle of China's transition should not be underestimated.

The major strengths of the corporate governance mechanisms of Chinese TVEs as a transitional institution (or to some an "institutional innovation") include the following four aspects:

(a) The hard budget constraints and the possibility of bankruptcy faced by TVEs;

(b) The ability of local officials to find solutions to the "delegation problem," whereby local officials appointed by higher bureaucrats may have conflicting incentives to seek higher profits, as opposed to pursuing revenue and employment generation at the expense of higher profits;

(c) The profit sharing arrangements between managers, local governments and community members that largely aligned competing interests; and

(d) More secure property rights under local government protection as compared to private enterprises.[84]

Given their robust performance by the mid-1990s as a result of relatively efficient corporate governance structures that effectively solved problems of

---

84. See Barry Naughton, "Chinese Institutional Innovation and Privatization from Below," 84:2 The American Economic Review 266 (1994), p. 270; Andrew G. Walder, "Local Governments as Industrial Firms: An Organizational Analysis of China's Transitional Economy," 102:2 *American Journal of Sociology* 263 (1995); McDonnell, *ibid.*

delegation and incentive design as compared to their SOE counterparts, Chinese TVEs were regarded by many economists as an alternative to privatization during the early stage of reform.[85]

4.4.4 A "helping hand" interpretation of TVEs success

In China, the economic roles of central government and local governments in transition are different. Local governments have generally played a more active role in promoting non-state enterprises as well as reforming SOEs. As discussed in Chapter 3, the decentralized feature of privatization in China is primarily a result of the fiscal incentives of local governments to improve firm performance. If local governments were not faced with hard budget constraints and revenue inducements, they would not have had a strong fiscal motivation to take supportive measures. The central government is certainly the dominant force in designing and promoting reform agendas, but the implementation and enforcement of particular reform schemes are carried out by the local governments. The success of China's TVEs is a good example to show that the economic role of the Chinese government in transition has been largely a "helping hand," as opposed to a "grabbing hand."[86] As already pointed out, how this works can be explained by the corporate governance function of local governments in TVEs, which is exercised through their ownership and control in these firms. For example, government ownership is shown to serve as a second-best commitment mechanism, through which the government agency will restrain itself from rent seeking activity and even offer the manager support and favor, such as tax breaks and subsidies.[87]

Certainly, local governments are not always destined to be supportive of or benevolent to businesses. They need to be induced to do so. The motivation and incentive for preferring a role of a "helping hand" to that of a "grabbing hand"

---

85. See, for example, Naughton, *ibid.*, p. 270; Walder, *ibid.*
86. The terms "grabbing hand" and "helping hand" as different models of government in transition were first coined in Timothy Frye & Andrei Shleifer, "The Invisible Hand and the Grabbing Hand," 87:2 *The American Economic Review* 354 (1997), pp. 354–355. According to the authors, under the "helping hand" model, bureaucrats, though subjected to limited and organized corruption, are intimately involved in promoting private economic activity, while law plays a limited role. Under the "grabbing hand" model, government is not just as interventionist, but much less organized and more corrupt, than in the "helping hand" model, while predatory regulations are usually adopted to extract rents from private businesses. Russia was regarded by the authors as a typical example of the "grabbing hand" model, while Poland was considered in conformity with the "helping hand" model.
87. Jiahua Che, "From the Grabbing Hand to the Helping Hand: A Rent Seeking Model of China's Township-Village Enterprises," United Nations University Discussion Paper No. 2002/13 (2002), p 1.

reflect local governments' fiscal interest in helping firms improve performance so that they can collect more revenues. An important consideration for the local governments in this calculation is that predatory taxation is inferior to supportive policy combined with a well designed revenue sharing scheme. Clearly, the local governments are most likely to adopt such a business-friendly position when they can be sure that the central government does not take away too big a piece of the pie. Therefore, whether the local governments are willing to serve as a "helping hand" depends on how arrangements under China's fiscal federalism can reconcile the interests at both central and local levels, especially with regard to the sharing of fiscal revenues. This factor of central-local relationship has also featured significantly in China's financial reform, as Chapters 5 and 6 demonstrate.

4.4.5 **The decline of TVEs**

The rapid privatization of China's TVEs has been underway since the mid-1990s, while private enterprises have flourished and prospered in China. Government control in corporate governance of TVEs as a second-best solution played a positive role in addressing the agency problem at the first stage of China's enterprise reform (1978–1994) when conventional market supporting institutions, such as the rule of law and property rights protection, were not well established. However, at the second stage of China's enterprise reform starting from 1994, the costs of government control in corporate governance have increased because of the changing institutional environment that has become more conducive to the emergence of private ownership. At this point, the "exit" of government control from corporate governance of TVEs seemed a better choice.[88]

While some transitional corporate governance mechanisms in China had proved to be efficient and had generated positive development outcomes, this is not to deny that these mechanisms may become inefficient when China's transition enters a new stage, where the demand for new institutions in conformity with a full market economy must be met. As a result, the once thriving Chinese TVEs have undergone rapid privatization since the mid-1990s, whereby managers and employees have become partial or full owners as many of these firms have been transformed into joint stock cooperatives or sold off to private hands.

As a policy response, the central government has shown remarkable tolerance toward the conversion of TVEs into shareholding cooperatives and

---

88. Yingyi Qian, "Government Control in Corporate Governance as a Transitional Institution: Lessons from China," University of Maryland Department of Economics Working Paper (2000), pp. 28–30.

the removal of "red hats" by pseudo-TVEs.[89] In other words, privatization has become a widespread practice and a practical way out for the declining Chinese TVEs since the mid-1990s, and the government is in favor of this option, although without explicit endorsement.

4.4.6 A possible revival?

On the subject of the prospects of Chinese TVEs, it can be safely predicted that in the immediate future, they will be less important and their advantages over private enterprises will fade. However, they are not likely to disappear from the layout of the national economy, but rather may preserve a distinctive presence in the Chinese economic landscape. Some recent numbers can illustrate the relevance of TVEs to China's economy today.

According to government statistics, TVEs are estimated to have employed a total number of 138 million rural workers over the periods of 1978-2004. Even though in decline, they were projected to still have employed 3 million workers in 2004 alone. TVEs are also an importance source of income increases for Chinese rural residents. For instance, in 2003, TVEs contributed 35 percent to the annual total incomes of China's rural population.[90]

A cautious conclusion, therefore, is that under the industrial policy of "giving priority to employment expansion," China's TVEs still have a role to play in the national economy. This is primarily due to their contribution to income increases of China's rural population, which understandably has a significant impact on the much emphasized "social stability" in an age of rapid economic transformation and a resulting wealth gap between China's urban dwellers and their less fortunate rural countrymen. Seen from the current structure of the Chinese economy, a permanent "fall" of Chinese TVEs, as some western observers might have in mind, is not likely in the immediate future. However, a "revival" is only possible if Chinese TVEs can upgrade their technologies, modes of production and management style, and can move quickly from traditional strongholds of sectoral growth, such as the manufacturing of toys, clothing and shoes, to services sectors with higher added-value. However, since private enterprises may have considerable advantages in achieving these same goals more efficiently and more quickly, given their better designed ownership and incentive structures, Chinese TVEs may well become even more marginal in years ahead.

---

89. Jeffrey D. Sachs & Wing Thye Woo, "Understanding China's Economic Performance," NBER Working Paper 5935 (1997), p. 43. The issue of "red hats" is discussed in Section 4.5 where corporate governance of Chinese private enterprises is reviewed.
90. Zhao, *supra* note 8.

4.5   Corporate Governance of Private Enterprises

Section 4.5 examines corporate governance practices of China's private enterprises and the fundamental implications of their reform for building a strong private sector in the Chinese economy. Section 4.5 also analyses the current legal and institutional environments in which China's private sector operates and the constraints they impose on corporate governance improvement.

4.5.1   Property rights in the private sector: the removal of "red hats"

An intriguing example of ambiguous property rights in China is the so-called "red hat" phenomenon. The "red hat" is a metaphor referring to a popular practice among Chinese private entrepreneurs in early years of reform, whereby private businesses were registered as rural collective enterprises or TVEs, with the consent of local governments (i.e., putting a "red hat" on the firm as a cover). The purpose of doing so was twofold. On the one hand, the entrepreneurs could avoid breaking the ideological taboo on overtly promoting private business and become qualified for business facilitations controlled by local governments, such as bank loans and technological support. On the other hand, by offering a "red hat," local governments could share a considerable portion of profits. A major drawback is that controversies over whether the "red hat" should amount to an "ownership investment" by the local governments have frequently arisen. Matters have improved as more and more private enterprises have removed the "red hats" in recent years, especially after the Constitution was amended in 1999 to upgrade the non-state sector from "beneficial" and "necessary" supplement to the public sector to "important component" of the national economy.

The 2004 constitutional amendment that finally declared private property "inviolable" is a vivid illustration of China's gradualist transition path with regard to property rights. It took over 15 years and four rounds of constitutional amendments to eventually establish full constitutional recognition and protection of private property in China. The Constitution was amended the first time in 1988 to affirm the legal status of the private sector, stating that it "complements the socialist economy"; the second was in 1993 when the Constitution declared China will practice a market economy instead of a planned economy; then in 1999 the Constitution was amended again to upgrade the private sector from a "complementary" status to "an important component" of the country's market economy; finally, the 2004 amendment started to provide full recognition and protection to private property rights.[91] More recently, a new

---

91. "Constitution to be Amended a Fourth Time," *China Daily*, March 3, 2004, online < http://www.chinadaily.com.cn/english/doc/2004-03/content_311108.htm >.

Property Law was also enacted in March 2007 to give equal protection to public, collective and private property rights.

4.5.2 An improved business environment for the private sector

While the private sector has been elevated to a prominent status now that China's Constitution declares "lawful" private property rights inviolable and under the protection of law, in reality it still faces a number of barriers that impede its growth. As evidenced by descriminatory policies favoring SOEs, China's private sector does not enjoy a level playing field. Capital starvation resulting from limited access to state bank loans, technological disadvantage due to insufficient R&D input, as well as regulatory impediments in the routine conducting of business are major constraints on the further development of China's private sector.

For example, according to an early survey of start-up bureaucracy in 75 developing countries by Harvard University in 2000, China was ranked 51st overall for delay and 43rd for cost.[92] The situation for doing business in China has improved over the past several years in terms of a more benign regulatory environment.[93] More recent findings in a survey by the World Bank on global business environment showed a further remarkable improvement made by China, ranking it No.4 of the top 10 reformers during the period from January 2005 to April 2006.[94] China's reforms had resulted in speedier business entry, increased investor protections and reduced red tape in trading across borders, as well as the establishment of a credit information registry for consumer loans.[95] Meanwhile, the World Bank report also pointed out that despite this encouraging sign of advancement, China's overall ranking on the ease of doing business in 2007 — 93rd of 175 economies surveyed — was still considered falling within the lower half of all economies surveyed.[96]

It is important to note that China's accession to the WTO in 2001 has stimulated domestic government and administrative reforms. To submit itself to the requirements under the WTO agreement indicates that the government is willing to reduce administrative intervention and to adapt core government functions to a market economy. According to recent announcements by the

---

92. See Joe Studwell, *The China Dream: The Elusive Quest for the Greatest Untapped Market on Earth* (London: Profile Books, 2002).
93. World Bank & IFC, *Doing Business in 2004: Understanding Regulation* (co-published by the World Bank and Oxford University Press, 2004).
94. World Bank & IFC, *Doing Business 2007: How to Reform* (Washington: co-published by the World Bank and Oxford University Press, 2006), p. 3.
95 *Ibid.*
96 *Ibid.*, p. 6.

government, China will further enhance deregulation through streamlining regulations and simplifying administrative procedures. In fact, the deregulation reform has already produced some positive results. For example, some 4,000 permits and authorizations previously issued by the government had been reduced to 789 by the end of 2003.[97] Moreover, in August 2003, China enacted a new *Law on Administrative Licensing* after heated debate among scholars and policy makers. The purpose of the new law is to limit and standardize the government's power with regard to granting licenses to citizens, particularly those applying for starting a private business.[98] Although China has been undertaking a new round of government and administrative reforms aimed at reducing regulatory barriers and enhancing the business environment, it will take time for the reform initiatives to have real effects on the economy. The effectiveness of reforms will depend crucially on the actual enforcement and implementation capacities of the government.

4.5.3   Capitalists now "welcome to the Party"

In today's China, a significant number of private entrepreneurs are communist party members, and a significant number of government officials hold corporate posts in SOEs. According to a recently published survey by China Academy of Social Sciences (CASS), in 2003, 30 percent of 2 million private entrepreneurs in China were communist party members; another 11 percent expressed an interest in joining the Party.[99]

The mutual penetration of the Party and businesses has not resulted in "state capture," but signals a certain level of "the mutual penetration between the party and business," which the government only partly endorses. What the government supports, and even actively promotes, is a "one-way" interaction between the Party and businesses: private entrepreneurs are welcome to join the Party, but party officials must resign from their corporate posts.[100]

To a large extent, this is a very encouraging position for the government to take. On the one hand, the withdrawal of party officials from corporate posts would help insulate businesses from government intervention. On the other hand, the decision to admit "capitalists" carries a message that the Party is now willing to share some of its political power and responsibility with wider segments

---

97. Chi Fulin, "China's Reform Focuses on Streamlining Government," 14:1-3 *Transition* 10 (2003).
98. Shi Dong, "Another Effort to Limit the Administrative Power," *Caijing*, September 5, 2003.
99. "An Investigation Report of Private Enterprises in China (zhongguo siying qiye diaocha baogao)," *Caijing*, February 20, 2003.
100. Peter Morris, "Chinese Cadres Must Give Up Corporate Posts," *Asia Times Online*, March 26, 2004, online < http://www.atimes.com/atimes/China/FC26Ad05.html >.

of Chinese society.[101] The decision to admit private entrepreneurs to the Party was announced by then China's president Jiang Zemin in 2001, which sparked an immediate round of controversies within China. This change of heart by the Party has been well received, however, by some western observers who think that it signaled the Party's increasing desire to strengthen both the private sector and the party links to the burgeoning private business elite.[102] Seen from some recent improvements in the government's support for the private sector, there is much truth to this assessment.

4.5.4 The government's new pledge to promote the private sector

A positive sign is that the government has recently taken a decisive move in addressing the development of the non-state sector. It was announced in a government work report released in March 2004 that the Chinese government would "promptly eliminate or revise regulations and policies" that restrict the development of the non-state sector and "implement measures that relax market access." In addition, the non-state sector is "encouraged to participate in the reform of SOEs" and assured to "receive the same treatment as other enterprises in investment, financing, taxation, land use and foreign trade."[103] How long it will take to put these promises into action and make them generate genuine effects remains to be seen, but at least the signal is encouraging.

4.5.5 The "original sin" and its redemption

It is often described as the "original sin" (*yuanzui*) of some private entrepreneurs that they had conducted irregular transactions when participating in the ownership reform of SOEs and made personal fortunes through questionable channels in China's underdeveloped legal and institutional environments. The primary causes of this "original sin" include the ambiguities of property rights, the lack of fair rules and transparent procedures to govern the transfer of state assets to private hands, personal greed to steal and extract state assets, and corruption among government officials supervising local SOEs. For example, some dishonest private entrepreneurs had bought state assets at ridiculously low prices in conspiracy with local government officials who took bribes. In other cases the buyers were themselves insiders (usually managers) of the old firms

---

101. Gregory C. Chow, *China's Economic Transformation* (Blackwell, 2002), p. 82.
102. Mary E. Gallagher, "Reform and Openness: Why China's Economic Reforms Have Delayed Democracy," 54 *World Politics* 338 (2002), p. 353.
103. "Premier: China to Boost Non-Public Sector Economy," *People's Daily*, March 5, 2004, online < http://english.peopledaily.com.cn/200403/05/print20040305_136611.html >.

who grossly undervalued the state assets. Those practices have to a large extent mirrored the Russian experience of mass and rapid privatization in the 1990s.

Accordingly, these private entrepreneurs may well have acquired state assets illegally, and, in the view of some Chinese commentators, have to pay "redemption" to clean their property rights at a later stage when rules and procedures have been put in place and transactions have become more transparent and in more conformity with market basics. The methods of "redemption" have been under discussion primarily among China's academic circles, since it is understandable that private entrepreneurs have largely avoided taking part in this discourse. How to redeem the "original sin," however, is still subject to an ongoing debate in China, and some economists have proposed such methods as BOT (build-operate-transfer) and levying inheritance taxes.[104]

4.5.6 Doing business in the private sector

Contract enforcement

According to a new study on the role of institutions in economic development,[105] recent research on contract enforcement during China's economic transition reveals more aspects of the interaction between local governments and private businesses. Most notably, Huang Shaoqin finds that local government officials have often acted as liaisons between private contracting parties in assuring contract enforcement, especially when one contracting party is from outside the local jurisdiction.[106] Because local government officials have at their disposal both formal administrative powers (which usually dictate the allocation of local economic and social resources) and favorable access to local networks of *guanxi*, they have a huge advantage in linking the formal and informal elements of local business environment, both of which are required for effective enforcement of contracts.[107] According to Huang, Chinese private entrepreneurs have established an innovative method of enforcing contracts for impersonal transactions when they conduct business with partners from other localities: find in the host jurisdiction a local government official as their "agent for contract enforcement."[108] Sometimes this requires assistance from a third party who acts

---

104. Gu Ming, "Lang Xianping in Quest for a Way Out for Those with the 'Original Sin' (Lang Xianping tanqiu minying qiye 'yuanzui' chulu)," *Nan Feng Chuang Magazine*, August 6, 2003, online < http://business.sohu.com/33/02/article211880233.shtml >.
105. Michael Trebilcock & Jing Leng, "The Role of Formal Contract Law and Enforcement in Economic Development," 92 *Virginia Law Review* 1517 (2006), pp. 1559–1560.
106. Huang Shaoqin, A Study of Contract Enforcement Mechanisms in China during Transition (zhongguo zhuangui shiqi hetong zhixing jizhi yanjiu), 3 *Journal of Legal & Economic Studies (Hong Fan Ping Lun)* 184 (2006), p. 192.
107. *Ibid.*, pp. 188–189.
108. *Ibid.*, p. 192.

as the broker between the local official and the outside entrepreneur. In most cases, personal investment by the outside entrepreneur through contributions of in-kind consumption to local officials (instead of outright bribes) is a prerequisite to the establishment of a stable relationship.[109] As a result, the local government official, now acting as the "agent" on behalf of the outside contracting party, exercises influence or pressure on local contracting parties in their fulfillment of contractual commitments.[110] Huang concludes that, although this informal mechanism for contract enforcement has been beneficial for promoting cross-region commerce and expanding local markets at early stages of China's transition,[111] in the long term, it will lead to the worsening of multiple deficiencies in China's social, political, economic and legal institutions, eventually making the country fall into the trap of "crony capitalism."[112]

Financing: the credit constraint and the demand for an active "curb market"

It is commonly known to Chinese private enterprises that credits from state banks are very difficult to obtain. The "big four" state banks heavily discriminate against private enterprises in allocating loans. As a general rule, state banks are more likely to lend to private enterprises with the lobbying of local governments hoping to give a hand to their local private sector. However, this latter case is not always a common practice among China's different localities.

As a result of the difficulty in receiving capital from the state banks, Chinese private enterprises have incurred higher operating costs by resorting to more expensive trade credits.[113] Worse still, capital starvation not only induces private enterprises to hide profits and thus embark on tax evasions in order to save enough for business expansions, it also distorts the banking system when money irregularly flows out of the banks to underground credit markets for higher returns, where private enterprises, not able to obtain money through normal channels, are willing to pay generous rates of interest. This poses a huge challenge to the stability of China's banking system because it could accumulate serious financial risks.

Therefore, credit discrimination against the private enterprises has negative impacts on both corporate governance of these firms, which are best exemplified by their tax evasion activities and distorted borrowing practices in the underground markets, and the stability of China's banking system. The chain effects of the collapse of underground curb markets could be enormous, and enormously dangerous for the health of the national financial system, as recently shown in the widely discussed Wu Ying case. The summer of 2007 was

---

109. *Ibid.*
110. *Ibid.*
111. *Ibid.*, pp. 198–204.
112. *Ibid.*
113. Loren Brandt & Hongbin Li, "Bank Discrimination in Transition Economies: Ideology, Information, or Incentives?", 31 *Journal of Comparative Economics* 387 (2003), p. 387.

unsettling for those closely involved in the case, where Chinese police were investigating the sudden rise to riches of a young Chinese woman who turned a foot massage parlor into a multibillion-yuan conglomerate in just 10 years.[114] Wu Ying, the centre figure in the unfolding saga that could lead to the biggest collapse of informal financing networks in China's reform era, was a 26-year-old business woman in the well known manufacturing base, Yiwu city of the coastal Zhejiang province, which operates the country's largest curb market due to its prominent private sector which is the most buoyant of China's localities. She was reported to have accumulated personal wealth worth RMB3.8 billion through vigorous business expansions financed by the curb market, and was detained on suspicion that she illegally acquired funds for her business empire, the Bense Group. Wu Ying was charged with two accounts of "economic crime" — "illegal solicitation of public funds" and contract fraud.[115] If found guilty, she could face up to 10 years in prison. The case has shed light on the huge sums of money in the "underground" credit market that are flowing independent of regulated financial institutions. In Zhejiang, this pattern of informal financing is particularly rife where huge loans are made among family, friends and social connections for speculative investments.

Joint ventures with foreign partners and the pitfalls

Chinese private enterprises have shown their increased participation in both domestic and international competition not only through going public for a share listing, but also by forming joint ventures with foreign partners who hope to tap the enormous Chinese consumer market. However, for some foreign investors, doing business with Chinese partners can be an uneasy experience as the gap in managerial styles and other aspects of business operation still persists and the pitfalls in the current practice of joint ventures may lead to serious conflicts. This is most vividly demonstrated in the Danone-Wahaha dispute which first erupted in the summer of 2007 and had reached an intensified level of hostility on both sides where nationalist sentiments were at one time deployed by the Chinese partner in an alleged attempt to enlist government support in a commercial dispute.

Zong Qinghou, one of China's most prominent entrepreneurs, founded a popsicle company in Zhejiang province and turned it into one of China's biggest beverage makers, Wahaha. In 1996, the French food conglomerate Group Danone SA started a joint venture with Wahaha. After 11 years of the joint venture, Wahaha and Danone started to fight over the use of the Chinese

---

114. "Chinese Police Detain Millionaire Wu Ying," *Guardian*, February 12, 2007.
115. "Wu Ying, the 'beauty tycoon' in Zhejiang, has been charged with two accounts of crime involving 1 billion yuan (Zhejiang meinü fuhao Wu Ying beisu liang zuiming shean da shiyi)," *21st Century Business Herald* (*21 Shiji Jingji Baodao*), July 13, 2007.

company's brand name, Wahaha, which had been valued at millions of dollars. As one news report put it:

> ...The antagonism between Zong and Danone seems as much about culture as about modern business. It surfaced after the Wahaha side, which is partly government owned but run more like a private company, rebuffed a proposal by Danone to buy out some of the Chinese company's assets. Zong, his powder-blue shirt monogrammed with the characters "Wahaha," accuses Danone of attempting a hostile takeover and of failing to contribute much to the joint venture's success.[116]

> ... Danone contends that it paid US$100 million to Wahaha for "exclusive and irrevocable" use of the brand name. It accuses the Chinese side of undermining the joint venture by selling Wahaha products in competing, non-joint venture companies. Zong resigned as chairman of the joint venture after Danone filed a lawsuit in Los Angeles seeking more than $100 million for the alleged illegal sales. It also filed for arbitration in Stockholm to help resolve the dispute... Zong contends that the government never approved Danone's request that their joint venture have exclusive use of the Wahaha brand name... "They don't understand the Chinese market," Zong says. "Culture is a very big problem. There is a very big gap between East and West."[117]

Encouragingly, after an initial appeal to the nationalist sentiments for solving the dispute (allegedly in an attempt to seek government support), Wahaha had turned to take moves to respond to Danone's effort in seeking legal solutions to their dispute. Most notably, Wahaha filed a commercial arbitration application with the Hangzhou Arbitration Commission in Zhejiang province, and also brought lawsuits in two of China's local courts against senior executives in the joint venture dispatched by Danone for breach of non-compete duties.[118] These moves showed that the Chinese company was trying to discipline itself with market basics and to subject itself to formal legal and institutional arrangements for dispute resolution.

The management gap

Some observers have noticed that compared to their counterparts in the SOE sector, managers of Chinese private enterprises are "overly entrepreneurial"

---

116. Elaine Kurtenbach, "Wahaha-Danone Feud Highlights Pitfalls," *Associate Press*, June 27, 2007.
117. *Ibid.*
118. "The Danone-Wahaha Joint Venture Dispute Is Gradually Entering into Legal Channels ('Danone-Wahaha' hezi zhengduan jianru falü guidao)," *Caijing*, July 12, 2007.

and are used to "taking bold risks without the constraints of a functional legal system or independent capital markets."[119] These managers are reported to be just as "undesirable" as their counterparts in SOEs when foreign companies from developed market economies come to China and consider recruiting local managerial talents.[120] Currently, there is an observed urgent need for the private sector to train qualified professional managers, not least for the purpose of addressing the pressing issue of successful succession of family firms whereby the second generation entrepreneurs are faced with the challenge of carrying on with the business built by the founders, which in many cases does not prove to be smooth and may have the negative prospect of reducing firm value. Given the current management gap, it is indicative that the potential value of the market for managerial education in China, through programmes such as MBA or EMBA, is estimated to amount to RMB10 billion in Zhejiang province alone.[121]

"Paying for a government identity card"

Another worrying sign in China's private sector is that there has been a "bureaucracy-business complex," whereby government officials are closely associated with private entrepreneurs in daily operations of private firms. In terms of the bureaucracy-business complex, the same can be said of Chinese government officials and party cadres keeping posts in SOEs where "business people wearing 'red hats'" are widely found. What makes this link between bureaucracy and business different in the case of Chinese private enterprises is that the direction of influence is the reverse. Here, the private entrepreneurs usually voluntarily pay higher taxes to local governments, especially those in a desperate need of fiscal incomes to run local affairs, in exchange for a post in local government agencies.

Typically, the government posts obtained by private entrepreneurs are not "strategically important" and also lack significant licensing power, and accordingly carry less rent-seeking opportunities. Rather, these posts largely function as an "identity card," which implies government connections and social resources.[122] Needless to say, although the government posts assumed by

---

119. Jack Perkowski, "Mind China's Management Gap," 168 *Far Eastern Economic Review* 38 (May 2005).
120. *Ibid.* See also Wang Jianmao, "China's Thirst for Middle Managers," 169 *Far Eastern Economic Review* 44 (Jul/Aug 2006).
121. Zong Xinjian, "The impulse to upgrade business management in Zhejiang's private sector opens a training market worth RMB 10 billion (Zhejiang minqi shengji chongdong baokai baiyi yuan peixun shichang 'dangao')," *China Business News* (*Diyi Caijing Ribao*), November 2, 2006, online < http://gov.finance.sina.com.cn/zsyz/2006-11-02/92414.html >.
122. Sun Zhan, "The Government and Market in A County of Prosperous Private Enterprises (yige minqi daxian de guanchang yu shichang)," *China Newsweek* (*Xinwen Zhoukan*),

private entrepreneurs may not have much of the licensing power that is likely to invite corruption, in a number of circumstances the "identity cards" do help private business people access other implicit benefits, such as promoting their business profiles when dealing with foreign partners or businesses from outside, as well as facilitating negotiations with other government agencies in conducting transactions where the local governments are among the parties or have a stake.

It is clear that this bureaucracy-business complex has a negative impact on the building of market basics and a healthy commercial environment in China's localities. It does not guarantee a level playing field among private entrepreneurs and only favors those with a close link with the bureaucracy. This practice, which has unfortunately started to spread to a wider range of China's local communities over the past few years as private enterprises have grown stronger, should be curbed effectively before it evolves into a new variety of "cronyism, Chinese style."

4.5.7 Chinese private enterprises in expansion: going public and going overseas

Although with very limited success, Chinese private enterprises have started to raise capital in the country's nascent stockmarket by applying for an IPO. However, since China's stockmarket is inefficient in allocating capital at the present stage of development, where unscrupulous issuers are obsessed with "*quanqian*" (predatory money-raising) and engaged in a race for value destruction at the expense of the huge wealth loss to investors, the "adverse selection" problem has become increasingly serious. The high possibility of the mis-pricing of firm value, in addition to policy discrimination against private enterprises in share issuing under the priority of reforming the ownership structures of SOEs through capital markets, have propelled some well-performing and genuinely competitive Chinese private enterprises to seek overseas listings. Hong Kong is the favorite destination for these firms.

However, although the much higher quality of securities regulation and a much healthier market environment in overseas capital markets do serve as effective disciplines for good behavior, some inherent weaknesses in the corporate governance practices adopted by Chinese private enterprises during the overall transition of the private sector, such as "founder's dictatorship" and lax internal controls, have led to corporate governance failures on both domestic and overseas markets.

March 1, 2004, online < http://www.chinanewsweek.com.cn/2004-03-05/1/3136.html >; Tang Jianguang, "Why 'Wealthy People Assuming Public Offices'? ('furen congzheng' weishenme?)," *China Newsweek* (*Xinwen Zhoukan*), March 1, 2004, online < http://www. chinanewsweek.com.cn/2004-03-05/1/3135.html >.

4.5.8 The need for upgrading corporate governance: the "Wenzhou model" and its possible decline

Recently, there has been much discussion of the prospects of the "Wenzhou model" of private sector development in China, in light of some discouraging signs of its vitality at a new stage of China's transition to the market. The "Wenzhou model" was once a prize model of market-driven local growth, in which the private sector was allowed to release its productivity and competitiveness, while subject to few policy and regulatory constraints by the local government during the early years of China's reform. The local government was very supportive and served as a strong "helping hand" in aiding the growth of private enterprises in terms of allocating factors of production, removing local red-tape and facilitating the cooperation between local businesses and external as well as foreign partners. In other words, the workings of the market were relatively undistorted and the private sector was left relatively autonomous to pursue business opportunities. As a result, Wenzhou municipality had been the strongest performer in the province of Zhejiang, an affluent coastal province in China.

However, things took a dramatic turn in 2002 when Wenzhou municipality, the long leading performer in the province throughout the 1990s, suddenly found itself in seventh place on the list of "Rankings of Municipal GDP Growth Rates in Zhejiang Province in 2002." The case was even worse in July and August of 2003, when the proud Wenzhou municipality learned that it had to settle with the lowest rank in the monthly provincial GDP report.[123]

Did this signal a sign of "decline" or more precisely, the "crossroads" of the "Wenzhou model," a local innovation of economic growth path that once not only gained nationwide admiration, but also attracted some level of international attention from Western observers eager to decipher the "China Exceptionalism"?

Perhaps the answer should be drawn from a perspective of political economy. There are several major reasons for the recent under-performance of Wenzhou's private enterprises, some with corporate governance implications and some resulting from the political economy constraints on the growth of China's private sector as a whole.

The crisis of the "lock-up" pattern of family business in the "Wenzhou model"

The "lock-up" pattern of family business in Wenzhou refers to the widely observed phenomenon in which the young generation of firm owners continue to follow their parents' footsteps in almost every aspect of operations. They have

---

123. Zhong Weizhi, Liu Mingjuan & Shi Chunhua, "GDP Ranking A Dramatic Fall to the 7th in Zhejiang Province: Death Bell Ringing for the Wenzhou Model?", *Economy Watch* (*Jingji Guancha Bao*), April 17, 2004.

inherited from the first generation (i.e., the founding generation) of private entrepreneurs the same business practices, including the same industries in which the firms operate, the same client bases, the same business culture, the same "local knowledge" of business norms and rules, the same educational background, and the same sales network.

This "lock-up" pattern has restrained the ability of the younger generation of private entrepreneurs to expand to more promising markets with better growth potential, and to gain new business opportunities in other sectors or industries. Certainly, the "lock-up" pattern of family business is not consistent with the much needed creativity, flexibility and risk-taking spirit for Chinese private sector in an age of global economic integration. According to some Chinese economists, this is the primary reason behind Wenzhou's recent decline.

An unfavorable macro-economic environment and the central government's intervention with local economic activities

The current macro-economic policy of the central government is not necessarily in line with local interests, especially for those localities in the prosperous coastal areas that have hugely benefited from the "open door" policy friendly to foreign direct investment (FDI) and export expansion. In 2004, the central government, wary of signs of an overheating economy, decided to put a hold on local engines of investment expansions and ordered by administrative fiats that local branches of the "big four" state banks stop allocating credits to a few overheating sectors, such as the steel industry. Because many private enterprises, particularly those from Wenzhou, had been heavily investing in these industries with an expectation to profit from China's gigantic need for raw materials and energy goods, this sudden withdrawal of capital suport amounted to a lethal blow.

The result was not surprising: private enterprises, including those from Wenzhou, suffered huge losses from the government intervention with local business activities in an arbitrary and dramatic manner. This example indicates that the government, still not tightly constrained by market fundamentals, is an impediment to effective corporate governance as detrimental as are the lapses in firms' internal control system. While lax internal controls cannot discipline reckless investment activities of dictatorial CEOs, arbitrary government intervention in private businesses is equally bad for even the most prudent CEOs to make sound financing and investment decisions.

The mutual penetration of public power and private businesses and a prevailing "personalized pattern" of business transactions

A "personalized pattern" of business transactions is based on an invisible but seamless web of *guanxi*, which affords unequal protection of property rights in favor of local businesses but at the expense of non-local businesses. This has resulted in a reduction of external investment and a wave of capital flight from Wenzhou over the past several years. This factor of an unfavorable investment environment for outsiders had significantly contributed to Wenzhou's GDP decline and a local scarcity of capital needed for the expansion and growth of its private sector.[124]

4.5.9 Summary

The primary finding of Section 4.5 is that although Chinese private enterprises have outperformed their state-owned counterparts over the past three decades and gradually become more competitive to meet the challenge of globalization, their corporate governance structures have displayed some worrying signs of inefficiency. Main examples of such corporate governance deficiencies include the "lock-up" pattern of family business and the phenomenon of "founder's dictatorship." Section 4.5 also points out that although the removal of "red hats" from many Chinese private enterprises was a significant improvement on their corporate governance structures, the problem of lax internal controls has increasingly become a serious impediment to the future growth of these private firms. In addition, the prevailing bureaucracy-business complex, in which many Chinese private enterprises have stranded themselves, is frequently manifested in the practice of private entrepreneurs "paying for a government identity card." This practice has a pervasive negative impact on the building of market basics and a healthy commercial environment in China's localities, and should be curbed effectively before it evolves into a new variety of "cronyism, Chinese style."

In light of the identified problems, future reform strategies for improving the corporate governance regime for Chinese private enterprises should emphasize the importance of complementary and supporting reforms in related areas, including government and administrative reforms aimed at further dismantling the various links between private businesses and public offices, in order to firmly establish market basics and conducive legal and institutional environments in which Chinese private enterprises operate.

4.6 Important Questions Arising from Corporate Governance Reform in China

Based on the examination of corporate governance practices at major types of Chinese enterprises, it can be seen that there are some important questions

---

124. *Ibid.*

arising from enterprise and corporate governance reforms in China under legal and institutional constraints at the current stage of transition. From different angles and to various degrees, those questions signal the rationale as well as the dynamics of a gradualist approach to corporate governance reform.

4.6.1 How to redeem the "original sin" of private entrepreneurs?

It is often described as the "original sin" of some private entrepreneurs that they had conducted irregular transactions when participating in the ownership reform of SOEs and made personal fortunes through questionable channels in China's underdeveloped legal and institutional environments. The primary causes of this "original sin" include the ambiguities of property rights, the lack of fair rules and transparent procedures to govern the transfer of state assets to private hands, personal greed to steal and extract state assets, and corruption among government officials supervising local SOEs. For example, some dishonest private entrepreneurs had bought state assets at ridiculously low prices in conspiracy with local government officials who took bribes. In other cases the buyers were themselves insiders (usually managers) of the old firms who grossly undervalued the state assets. Those practices have to a large extent mirrored the Russian experience of mass and rapid privatization in the 1990s.

Accordingly, these private entrepreneurs may well have acquired state assets illegally, and, in the view of some Chinese commentators, have to pay "redemption" to clean their property rights at a later stage when rules and procedures have been put in place and transactions have become more transparent and in more conformity with market basics. The methods of "redemption" have been under discussion primarily among China's academic circles, since it is understandable that private entrepreneurs have largely avoided taking part in this discourse. How to redeem the "original sin," however, is still subject to an ongoing debate in China, and some economists have proposed such methods as BOT (build-operate-transfer) and levying inheritance taxes.[125]

4.6.2 Has the performance of China's SOEs improved over the last three decades of reform, especially after the shareholding reform since the early 1990s?

To the question of whether the performance of China's SOEs has improved over the last three decades of reform, especially after the shareholding reform since the early 1990s, there are three different answers.

---

125. Gu, *supra* note 104.

The first answer is that if measured by profit increases, the performance of transformed SOEs, especially listed SOEs, has not improved. Where firms have shown signs of performance improvement, it might well be because managers of SOEs have strong incentives to misreport performance by overstating profits or understating costs. Typical incentives and practices with regard to misreporting take two forms. The first type is the window-dressing of financial performance by listed companies to cheat investors and regulators in order to remain in the stockmarket where they can continue to raise money. The second type is the reporting of false performance improvement of local SOEs by officials at lower levels to higher-ranking officials in order to preserve positions or receive promotions.

The second answer is that some large SOEs do make profits at comfortable rates, but the sources of their profits are the monopoly positions they hold in strategic industries or sectors under government protection, such as the electricity, telecommunications and oil industries. Because these firms do not face intensive competition from private firms, their profits cannot reflect the real situation of productivity efficiency, managerial effectiveness, and the quality of corporate governance.

The third answer is that although some SOEs have recorded accounting profits, these profits are usually obtained at huge costs of capital input and government subsidies that outweigh the gains of reported profits. These costs are recorded as unpaid debts in the books of these firms and non-performing loans or NPLs in the books of state banks.

It seems that these three answers all have some validity, and in combination they speak to the fact that Chinese SOEs, despite three decades of reform, are still not up to the task of meeting the challenge of competing with both domestic private enterprises and overseas players.

4.6.3   How has the interaction between central and local governments affected China's corporate governance reform?

The relationship between the central government and local governments has significantly influenced the pattern of corporate governance reform in China, particularly in relation to Chinese SOEs and TVEs. The rise of TVEs was largely a result of experimental reform strategies driven by the local governments, and the decentralized feature of privatization of both SOEs and TVEs to a large extent was shaped by the arrangements under China's fiscal federalism.

Specifically, at the new stage of China's transition when mass privatization of small and medium SMEs seems a favorable policy option, the dynamics of China's central-local relationship needs to be understood in predicting the prospects of China's market-oriented reform. On the one hand, the central government has been very cautious in extending the implementation of privatization of

SOEs to a wider scope. Its primary consideration is that potential social unrest may be prompted by increased unemployment rates and controversies over the distribution of rights and benefits among various social groups where "fairness" matters. On the other hand, local governments and managers of SOEs have been proactive in privatizing middle and small-sized SOEs. The primary reason is that for local governments and enterprise managers, there are considerable local and private benefits generated from privatization, in many cases at the expense of the state. Specifically, when legal and institutional environments are underdeveloped, insider dealing, asset stripping and corruption are often involved in local implementation of privatization schemes.

4.6.4 On the road of transition from the state to the market, is China heading towards a "good market economy" or a "bad (crony) market economy"?

From what has been discussed regarding such market-distorting practices as "business people wearing 'red hats'," "business people paying for a government identity card," and the dubious "bureaucracy-business complex" in China's localities, it is not surprising that the question arises as to whether China is heading towards a "good market economy" where the state stays out of the business of the market, or a "bad (crony) market economy" as has been observed with some East Asian countries. Seen from the identified local market-distorting practices, the danger of China falling into the trap of a "crony market economy" is emerging. If not under control, this danger may well contribute to future problems at later stages of China's transition. Accordingly, future corporate governance reform should proceed in combination with reforms in other related areas, including, among others, government and administrative reforms.

4.6.5 What are the implications of the Party's role during China's transition for corporate governance reform?

The Communist Party in China is not only a political organization; it also plays a role of an economic agent in many circumstances. China's market-oriented reform over the years may have reduced the Party's tight control on ideology to a large extent, but has not excluded the Party's influence from state businesses, which is still significant in the running of SOEs. Earlier discussion demonstrates that the Party's control of personnel decisions at large SOEs is not likely to loosen even after a series of corporate governance reform schemes have been introduced to make these firms more look like modern enterprises. Chinese SOEs cannot fully capture the benefits of corporate governance reform under continuing political intervention with business. It remains to be seen how the Party's role will evolve at the new stage of transition, which of course is not a pure economic matter but largely depends on further political liberalization in China.

4.6.6   How long will it take to accomplish necessary legal and institutional reforms?

The necessity of emphasizing sequencing and pacing of reform is determined by the reality of the general underdevelopment of legal and market-supporting institutions in transition economies at the early stage of reform, as well as by the reality that it will take a long time to establish well-functioning legal and institutional environments in an economy in transition given the constraints of government resources and human capital. For example, the establishment of rule of law, the education of qualified investors, and the emergence and development of a managerial market that prices professional corporate managers properly are difficult tasks and will need continuing input of time and energy from all levels of society, not to mention the potentially huge amount of financial and human resources needed. Therefore, a full transition to a market economy is predicted to entail a long process of legal and institutional reform.

4.7   Summary

The experience of corporate governance reform in major types of Chinese enterprises has provided a unique perspective on the dynamics of transition under legal and institutional constraints. In general, the empirical review presented in Chapter 4 offers strong support to ownership reform aimed at expanding private ownership in the competitive sectors of the Chinese economy. However, corporate governance reform has also encountered a number of challenges, especially those attributable to legal and institutional constraints. As a result, corporate governance reform in China has proceeded in a gradual, experimental, and at times decentralized manner. Some general conclusions can be drawn, as stated below.

First, the "politics" of economic reform and the underdevelopment of legal and institutional environments are the major determinants of a gradualist approach to corporate governance reform in China.

Second, there has been a considerable distance between "design on the paper" and "implementation on the ground" of corporate governance reform in China. On the one hand, the deficiency or ineffectiveness in local enforcement of certain centrally mandated reform policies not only reflects the interaction between the central and local governments whereby interests often diverge, but also indicates practical constraints on the country's political resources and institutional capacities needed to push forward reforms during the transition. On the other hand, local experiments with innovative pilot schemes, aimed at discovering a better road to the market that suits distinctive local conditions, have also been an important source of new understanding of institutional development at the central level.

Third, corporate governance reform, in particular ownership restructuring through privatization of local SOEs, has produced positive results in terms of efficiency improvements, but has also contributed to inequality between different social groups and regions. Therefore, the balance of "efficiency" and "equality" needs to be addressed to reduce social resistance and discontent that could hamper China's successful transition to the market.

Fourth, transitional institutions can serve as second-best solutions to build efficient corporate governance structures at the early stage of reform, but need to be adjusted to meet new challenges when reform has proceeded to the next stages and the institutional environment evolves.

Fifth, in reforming China's enterprise sector, it is crucial to avoid the danger of falling into a "bad (crony) market economy." Some worrying signs of the state intervening with the workings of the market during the process of corporate governance reform in both SOE and private sectors, such as using public power for private gains, must be addressed seriously if China is to build a truly competitive enterprise sector and complete a successful transition to the market.

In summary, the overall conclusion of Chapter 4 is that careful sequencing and pacing should be regarded as the central feature of corporate governance reform in China, which requires realistic and workable schemes that accommodate available economic and political resources and existing legal and institutional environments. Regarding future direction of corporate governance reform, as a major characteristic of China's gradualist approach toward transition, local experiments with innovative pilot schemes should continue to be encouraged, especially with regard to privatization strategies. These local experiments are not only useful for the accumulation of collective knowledge of transition across the nation, but can also facilitate the discovery of effective reform strategies suitable for a broader scope of application through trial-and-error at lower costs.

5

The Interaction between Capital Markets and Corporate Governance of Chinese Listed Companies

There is an important qualification of the subject of study in Chapter 5: the term "capital markets" used here primarily refers to the stockmarket in China and overseas. This is primarily because equity financing is the dominant method for Chinese listed companies to raise capital, compared to the small proportion of debt financing in their capital structures.

China's stockmarket was established in the early 1990s when two stock exchanges in Shanghai and Shenzhen officially came into being. The stockmarket in China's transition economy is a nascent financial institution with a short history and operates on a totally different basis compared to mature capital markets in the West. To many western observers, China's stockmarket serves as a good example of the contradiction of the country's "socialist market economy," in which private enterprises and markets now play important roles in promoting growth, while political reform has not progressed at a comparable pace to introduce a more transparent and democratic political system.[1]

The reflection of the fundamental and unresolved contradiction between China's economic and political aspirations in the capital markets is that the state, as the owner of SOEs, hopes to attract foreign and private capital to strengthen the financial base of these firms, but does not wish to cede control over the "commanding heights" of the economy by adopting full privatization.

---

1. See Stephen Green, *China's Stockmarket: A Guide to Its Progress, Players and Prospects* (London: Profile Books, 2003), p. 3.

The "commanding heights" of Chinese economy, such as the strategic industries of telecommunications, banking, transportations and energy, are still controlled by the government where state monopolies dominate. This ambivalence remains at the heart of the government's failure, at least so far, to create a properly functioning stockmarket in China.

As a result, China's stockmarket is largely ruled by political logic rather than by economic rationales, and remains inefficient after almost two decades of operation.[2] According to some harsh critics, China's stockmarket is "little more than funny-money casinos built on foundations of sand and populated by manipulators."[3] One of China's most respected economists, Wu Jinglian, even considers the corruption-ridden stockmarket "worse than casinos in foreign countries," because the latter still operate on the basis of rules.[4] Doubts about possible exaggerations aside, these critical statements indeed reveal much of the truth about China's stockmarket at its early stage of development.

The political logic of China's stockmarket is the root cause of the poor quality of listed companies, which are dominated by partially privatized SOEs with their minority stakes issued to the public and which have rewarded investors with shabby returns. Despite the government's insistence that listed companies with good corporate governance are the fundamental basis of a well-functioning stockmarket and therefore should be given paramount emphasis by both regulators and market participants, the overall performance of China's listed companies on corporate governance has created many disappointments. As a result, the interaction between China's stockmarket and corporate governance of listed companies seems to have formed a "vicious circle," as the poor-quality listed companies and the fraud-filled stockmarket are mutually reinforcing.

In light of this unfavorable assessment of the interaction between China's stockmarket and corporate governance of listed companies, Chapter 5 argues that removing the political logic from China's stockmarket and replacing it with market basics is the ultimate solution to building good corporate governance of listed companies and attracting foreign and private capital. More importantly, reforming China's stockmarket is a critical condition for the country to sustain steady economic growth and complete a successful transition to a full market economy.

---

2.   *Ibid.*, p. 4.

3.   Gary LaMoshi, "China's Stock Market Binge," book review of Carl E. Walter & Fraser J.T. Howie, *Privatizing China: The Stock Market and Their Role in Corporate Reform* (Singapore: Wiley (Asia), 2003), *Asia Times Online*, August 30, 2003, online < http://www.atimes. com/atimes/China/EH30Ad02.html >.

4.   Wu Jinglian, "China's Stockmarket Worse than Foreign Casinos (zhongguo gushi buru duchang)," interview with China Central Television (CCTV) in the "Conversation" ("Duihua") program, January 13, 2001.

While urgent, the reform of China's stockmarket is a difficult task, given the existing political, legal and institutional constraints which suggest that it would be unrealistic to find a quick fix to the existing compounding problems. Therefore, a more workable strategy for the government is to push forward necessary structural reforms of the stockmarket on the basis of what is already in place, and seek improvements on the existing market structure and practices. In this context, compared to a rapid and complete overhaul of the existing market structure or "starting anew," which would involve a wide range of parties and likely entail extraordinarily high costs with uncertain prospects for success, a strategy of sequencing and pacing, which focuses on improving — instead of destroying — the existing market structure, seems to be a more practical approach.

In terms of its key proposal, this strategy of sequencing and pacing advocates a two-fold solution to China's stockmarket reform. On the one hand, necessary market regulation, such as rules on disclosure and related-party transactions, must be strengthened to become truly effective, i.e., not only "admonishing" but also "deterring" to wrongdoers. On the other hand, the stockmarket should be encouraged to grow and expand without excessive government intervention and over-regulation, especially in relation to regulators' efforts to import "advanced" institutions from mature capital markets that not yet have a working foundation in China. One such example is the mandatory requirement for listed companies to have a fixed number of independent directors. In the process of stockmarket reform, the most important constituencies of investor protection — the investors themselves — also need to develop a strong awareness of rational and value-based investment and to form a powerful interest group to assert their own rights.

China's accession to the WTO in December 2001 and its commitments to the opening up of the financial industry have generated external pressure and stimulus for the reform of the stockmarket. Among other things, the WTO factor can help propel the Chinese government to take decisive actions to clean up the stockmarket before competitive overseas market players, such as highly sophisticated international investment banks and fund management companies, have obtained wider access to China's financial market. It is widely predicted that foreign competitors would force a number of weak domestic financial institutions to exit the market if unreformed, of which the most vulnerable are the approximately 130 securities companies currently facing an industry-wide insolvency crisis.

Accordingly, Chapter 5 suggests that alongside China's ongoing banking and SOE reforms, one priority on the government's policy agenda at the new stage of transition should be making the stockmarket a better regulated and safer place to invest as a beneficial component of the national economy. As Chapter 5 indicates, stockmarket reform not only is critical to the establishment and strengthening of investor confidence, but also matters greatly for the health of the entire financial system and, in particular, for the sound operation of the banking sector.

Chapter 5 further points out that given the complementarity between structural reforms of SOEs, state banks and the stockmarket, a much improved stockmarket will bring about significant benefits to both China's banking system and SOE sector. At a time when China is experiencing remarkable GDP growth, a properly functioning stockmarket could relieve the "big four" state banks of overwhelming financing burdens, currently accounting for four fifth of the sources of funds for China's annual new investment. Similarly, the success of China's SOE reform also partly depends on the progress of stockmarket reform.

There are two important reasons for the complementarity between the SOE reform and stockmarket reform. The primary reason is that the privatization of SOEs needs a well functioning stockmarket as an effective channel to reshape their ownership structures, thus facilitating their transformation into modern enterprises. Another reason is that China's national social security fund will need a safe place to invest and make adequate returns to fund the country's pressing pension liabilities.

Chapter 5 is organized into five sections. Section 5.1 reviews some basic aspects of China's stockmarket, including the following: (a) a snapshot of the stockmarket, such as its size, major players, capital and regulatory structures, fundamental problems and relevance to the national economy, (b) the political logic beneath the inner workings of the stockmarket and the resulting consequences, and (c) the operational quality of the stockmarket under its political logic. Section 5.2 examines relevant aspects of corporate governance of China's domestically listed companies, such as their capital structure, ownership structure, financial performance and typical forms and causes of poor corporate governance. Section 5.3 examines the role of overseas capital markets in China's transition, with an emphasis on the risks associated with investing in Chinese companies that are largely attributable to corporate governance deficiencies. Section 5.4 reviews the process of important legal and regulatory reforms of China's stockmarket and related corporate governance reforms of listed companies since 2000, in the context of both accelerated transition to markets and greater financial liberalization under China's WTO commitments. Drawing on the assessment of the effects of reforms that have been implemented, Section 5.4 also discusses an appropriate strategy for future reforms that is centered on sequencing. Section 5.5 concludes by pointing out the peculiar pattern of interaction between China's stockmarket and corporate governance of listed companies which has formed a "vicious circle," and by reiterating the urgency of fundamental reforms of the stockmarket, of which solving the split share structure is a critical and challenging reform. Section 5.5 also proposes the appropriate sequencing of future reform measures in the short run, medium term and longer term that are aimed at addressing the "vicious circle" problem and providing support to the reforms of SOEs and banks .

5.1 An Overview of Important Aspects of China's Stockmarket

Section 5.1 reviews three important aspects of China's stockmarket: (a) a snapshot of its basic structure, fundamental problems and relevance to China's economy, (b) its political logic and the resulting consequences, and (c) its operational quality. This overview provides some critical facts about China's stockmarket during the transition and their implications for the country's economic development, thus providing the context for later discussions of solutions to the identified structural problems and future reform directions.

5.1.1 A snapshot of China's stockmarket

From a very low level, the development of China's stockmarket has been rapid. Until 1990 China had no securities markets at all, and until 1993 no Chinese company was listed abroad. Today, the Shanghai Stock Exchange and its smaller counterpart in Shenzhen had about 1,477 listings as of June 2007 and a combined market capitalization of around RMB 4420.79 billion (approximately USD 566 billion), second in Asia only to Japan.[5] Officially, as of June 2007, some 75 million individuals — more than the population of Britain or France — had invested in the stockmarket, where 130-odd securities companies and 50 investment fund companies are the major market intermediaries and components of China's nascent institutional investor base.[6] The primary regulator of the stockmarket is China Securities Regulatory Commission (CSRC), which was established in 1992.

China's stockmarket has been undergoing cautious or "prudent" liberalization, compared to other vibrant sectors of the economy that have been more receptive to globalization, such as trade and foreign investment. Indeed, according to former chief negotiator for China's WTO accession, Long Yongtu, one reason behind China's acceptance of unfavorable conditions attached to its standing in anti-dumping disputes with the U.S. was to maintain protection in its securities industry for a longer period of time. By accepting the condition that China should be regarded as a "non-market economy" when dumping margins are calculated, China received a concession from the U.S. that its securities industry would not be liberalized as quickly as would the insurance and banking industries.[7]

---

5. Source: CSRC, online < http://211.154.210.238/cn/tongjiku/report/200706/ c/8070101M200706_1.htm >.
6. CSRC, *ibid.* Also see "Casino Capital," in "The Weakest Link: A Survey of Asian Finance," *The Economist*, February 6, 2003, pp. 10–12.
7. Zhang Fan, "Interview with Long Yongtu on the Early Years of China's WTO Negotiations (rushi tanpan hua dangxian)," *Caijing*, November 29, 2004, online < http://www.caijing. com.cn/coverstory/2004-11-29/2353.shtml >.

Over the past few years, under China's WTO commitments, rules which had previously operated to prohibit foreign ownership of securities companies and investment fund companies have been relaxed. Approved foreign investors have been gradually allowed into the domestic markets under a Qualified Foreign Institutional Investor (QFII) scheme, which draws on the example of Taiwan's earlier financial liberalization. The government has hoped that the opening up of China's capital markets will mark its integration with the global financial system. Meanwhile, Hong Kong has become a more important financial centre by helping to raise foreign capital for the transformation of SOEs in mainland China, and increasingly also for the development of China's growing private sector. Chinese companies now make up 42 percent of Hong Kong's stock market capitalization, compared to only 7 percent in 1995.[8] As of April 30, 2006, 344 mainland enterprises had gone for Hong Kong for public listings; the top 10 IPOs in Hong Kong had all been made by mainland enterprises.

Despite the impressiveness of the rapid development of China's stockmarket, it has many serious problems. The most fundamental problem that has for years lingered and raised investor concern is the fragmentation of share structure resulting from the split of tradable and non-tradable shares. In the early years of the development of China's stockmarket, the government sold overpriced minority stakes in mostly badly run SOEs, confident that retail investors, who were mostly urban households, with few alternatives for capital investment and enamored of China's growth prospects, would buy these shares regardless. With the state able to intervene in the market as both regulator and controlling shareholder and through government owned or controlled brokerage firms, stock prices soared, multiplying earnings by 60 times in the summer of 2001.[9]

However, plagued by the deep-rooted structural problem of non-tradable shares and investors' persistent concerns about steps that the government may take to their detriment, such as abruptly pouring large chunks of state shares into the market to dilute their holdings, the market started to decline in June 2001 in the wake of the government's plan to relinquish a portion of residual state shares to the public. This plan was short-lived due to strong negative market reactions. The decline had continued to 2005 in the face of the uncertainty of a new attempt by the government to sell state shares. Both the Shanghai Composite Index and Shenzhen Composite Index reached their five-year lows in February 2005. Remarkably, however, the stockmarket recovered rapidly since the government started to experiment with a share structure reform in April 2005 to make non-tradable shares tradable. The Shanghai Composite Index reached 5,000 points in August 2007, an all-time high (in some analysts' view showing the making of a "bubble"), in sharp contrast to the declining markets

---

8.   "Casino Capital," *supra* note 6.
9.   "A Marginalized Market," *The Economist*, February 24, 2005.

in the U.S. and the rest of Asia in the wake of the sub-prime mortgage crisis that had spread globally.[10]

Measured by both market capitalization and the percentage of capital markets financing in aggregate investment, the size of China's stockmarket is not impressive by international comparison. For example, as of December 2003, the total capitalization of China's stockmarket was RMB 4,245.8 billion yuan (around USD 500 billion), which was equivalent to 36.38 percent of the country's 2003 GDP. However, the market capitalization of the tradable shares was only RMB 1,317.9 billion yuan and equivalent to only 11.29 percent of the 2003 GDP.[11] While in terms of gross size China's stockmarket dominates those of transition economies in Russia and East Europe, when measured as a proportion of GDP, China's stockmarket does not fare well. For example, compared with 34 percent in Hungary and 25 percent in the Czech Republic, China's stock market capitalization only accounted for less than 12 percent of GDP in 2003.[12] Meanwhile, China's stockmarket only financed less than 2 percent of total investment in China for the year 2003, which was negligible compared to the dominant role of banks in funding the country's investment projects.[13]

Finally, the composition of Chinese investors is also in notable contrast with the prevailing pattern of institution-driven equity investment in most overseas capital markets. In China, institutional investors account for only a very small fraction of the total number of the A-share investors. For instance, as of December 2003, there were 68.35 million A-share trading accounts at Chinese banks, of which 68.02 million were registered by individual investors and only 330,000 were held by institutional investors, representing 99.52 percent and 0.48 percent of the total, respectively.[14] In other words, China's stockmarket is largely retail-oriented and lacks a strong base of institutional investors.

5.1.2 The political logic of China's stockmarket

According to the original design of the government, China's stockmarket should be, and in fact has been, primarily a tool to take over part of the financing of SOEs from the state banks burdened by huge amounts of non-performing loans. Clearly, when the government first advanced the idea of creating a stockmarket, concepts such as protection of investor rights, equal access to

---

10. Geoff Dyer, "Bullish China Breaks through 5,000 Barrier," *Financial Times*, August 24, 2007.
11. Source: CSRC, "An Introduction to China's Securities and Futures Markets: 2004 Edition," April 2004. This document can be accessed at the CSRC website < http://www. csrc.gov.cn >.
12. Green, *supra* note 1, pp. 34–35.
13. "Casino Capital," *supra* note 6.
14. Source: CSRC, *supra* note 11.

the capital markets of different types of enterprises and effective financial intermediaries which provide information authenticity and market liquidity did not feature at all in the blueprint. This should not be surprising, given the still limited understanding of markets by the government at the time, and one would reasonably expect that as China's reforms advance the situation will improve.

However, the irregular start, marked by the mandated role of the stockmarket as a cash cow for the SOEs (bluntly embodied in a policy statement that the stockmarket should "save SOEs from financial difficulties," or "*wei guoqi jiekun*"), has not to date re-directed itself to a regular course. For example, after more than 15 years of operation, China's stockmarket not only failed to reward investors with adequate rates of return on capital, which have been lower than the actual interest rates of fixed-term bank deposits over the same time periods, but also saw little achievement in improving the books of listed SOEs despite a stunning pool of money injected into them by China's investors, standing at RMB 890 billion (USD 107.36 billion) over the years of 1998-2004 alone.[15] Much of the money raised by the listed companies has been wasted, or in many cases stolen. The root cause of the vanishing capital is poor corporate governance of most listed companies, whereby managers, commonly known as "insiders," are not subject to effective monitoring and often direct capital to inefficient use or simply steal it. The controlling shareholders of many listed companies have gained a reputation for extracting corporate funds and expropriating minority shareholders. The root cause of the poor corporate governance of China's listed companies, in turn, is the distorted stockmarket, driven by its political logic.[16]

There are a few notable examples of the political logic of China's stockmarket. First, the government has used editorials in the state run newspaper *People's Daily* and three major securities newspapers to influence the trading of shares in the stockmarket, such as encouraging investors to trade when the market sentiment was low, and discouraging investors to trade when the market seemed "excessively speculative." Second, the government has plenty of room for indirect influence and direct interference in market transactions through the dominance of state ownership in almost every type of major market player, including the listed companies, securities brokerage companies, institutional investors such as securities investment funds and insurance funds, accounting firms, credit-rating and assets appraisal agencies, and lastly, the stock exchanges.[17] Third, in addition to helping finance SOEs as mandated by the government, the CSRC started to assume another seemingly unsuitable responsibility since 1999: to help achieve China's GDP growth targets and stabilize the society by propping up the

---

15. Jiao Qian, "High Costs Yet Low Returns: 40 Percent of Chinese Investors Want to Quit," *Beijing Yule Xinbao* (January 25, 2005), online: < http://www.chinanews.com.cn/news/20 05/2005-01-25/26/532685.shtml >.
16. Green, *supra* note 1, p. 4.
17. *Ibid.*

stock indexes. It was believed by some decision makers in the government that by maintaining high stock indexes, the aggregate demand would be stimulated and therefore the GDP growth would be sustained. This line of reasoning was criticized as questionable.[18]

The political logic of China's stockmarket was embedded at the very outset of its establishment, and has served to implement the government's industrial policy of supporting SOEs. It is commonly understood that in transition economies, the functions of the stock markets are not limited to providing financing to enterprises, but also include helping with the privatization of SOEs by facilitating the transfer of their ownership rights to private hands. However, China's stockmarket seems to largely disregard its "investing" function and pays only limited attention to its "privatizing" function, but heavily leans toward the "financing" function, which has in practice been translated into a notorious game of *quanqian* ("free lunch" style, predatory money-raising). The natural results of this single-dimensional function of China's stockmarket, as discussed below, are frequent infringements of investor rights, widespread fraud and manipulation of share prices, and poor corporate governance of listed companies.

An important extension of this unfavorable assessment of China's stockmarket relates to the country's pre-communist industrial history.[19] Perhaps not accidentally, in imperial China in late 19th and early 20th century, there was a similar pattern of stockmarket operation which emphasized only its financing function. After China lost the Sino-Japanese war in 1895, in order to promote private industrial businesses as a means to rebuild China's national strength, some reformers in the imperial government enacted a new Corporation Law in 1904, which was modeled after contemporary English and Japanese law and designed to codify modern corporate governance practices and attract investment from public shareholders.[20] However, partly because these reformers saw capital markets only as sources of funds, but overlooked their use as mechanisms for improving corporate governance, such as disciplining errant corporate insiders, the 1904 Corporation Law was remarkably ineffective.[21] Other potential factors that likely contributed to this failure of legal transplantation included an asserted "cultural

---

18. Zhang Weiying, "Some Problems in China's Stockmarket," *Caijing* (April 2000). Also see "An Overview of Shang Fulin's First Year as CRSC Chief: Reshaping the Regulatory System of the Stockmarket (Shang Fulin jiuren zhengjianhui zhuxi yinian huigu)," *China News*, January 12, 2004, online < http://www.chinanews.com.cn/n/2004-01-12/26/390584.html >.

19. For an interesting investigation of the reasons behind the emerging prominence of historical studies in contemporary law and economics scholarship, see Ron Harris, "The Uses of History in Law and Economics" (2003) 4:2 *Theoretical Inquiries in Law* 659.

20. Randall K. Morck & Lloyd Steier, "The Global History of Corporate Governance: An Introduction," NBER Working Paper, No. 11062 (2005), pp. 6–7.

21. *Ibid.*

inertia" that prevented real change because China's long culture of family businesses paying for the patronage of imperial bureaucrats proved too deeply ingrained, and the lack of an independent and trustworthy judiciary in China's traditional legal system to implement the law effectively.[22]

Seen from these peculiarities of corporate legal reform in imperial China, it is reasonable to suggest that path dependence may explain to some extent why corporate governance reform in China's transition economy has encountered similar problems as in the pre-communist periods. For example, the incompetence of the judiciary is still a serious barrier to effective corporate governance reform in China today, which makes punishing and deterring wrongdoers in the stockmarket difficult.

Given the historical lesson learned from the imperial China, corporate governance reform in China's transition economy should avoid the missteps of the past. The reform today should extend the functions of the stockmarket from the single dimension of financing cash-starving SOES to other critical aspects, such as facilitating privatization of SOEs that is efficiency-enhancing, as well as improving corporate governance practices of listed companies. This change cannot be realized unless the political logic beneath the inner workings of China's stockmarket is removed. Understandably, this will require complementary reforms to take place in China's SOE sector that would extend privatization on an even wider scale than is permitted under the current "grasping the large, releasing the small" (*zhuada fangxiao*) strategy. From a long-term perspective on China's economic transition, the government will eventually come to a point where it needs to not only "release the small," but also "release the large," including state monopolies in strategic industries, which means to adopt a comprehensive privatization strategy covering the entire SOE sector. For this to happen, complementary reforms in China's political and government systems are necessary. Predictably, these are more challenging tasks than China's economic transition.

5.1.3   Main consequences of the political logic of China's stockmarket

There are several negative consequences of the political logic of China's stockmarket, which have formed the basis of its deep-rooted structural problems.

State dominance among major market players

State dominance among major stockmarket players, including listed companies, brokerage firms, investment fund management firms, accounting firms, assets appraisal firms and the stock exchanges, allows the government a number of mechanisms to indirectly influence and directly interfere in the market.

---

22. *Ibid.*, p. 7.

First of all, SOEs make up the majority of China's listed companies. Under the government policy of using the stockmarket to "save SOEs from financial difficulties," or *"wei guoqi jiekun,"* SOEs have been heavily favored by the regulators in receiving the green light to launch IPOs on the Shanghai and Shenzhen stock exchanges. These firms often received IPO approvals through window-dressing financial books and "packaging" (*baozhuang*) less rotten assets with the assistance of local governments. By contrast, most profitable private firms have hitherto been denied access to the stockmarket. For example, Standard & Poor's, a credit-rating agency, counted only 35 "private" listed companies in China as of 2003 out of a total number of 1300 listed companies, and pointed out that a good number of these so-called "private" listed companies were in fact controlled by local governments and even the military.[23] Because of the significant political and regulatory barriers to the listing of private companies, some well performing private companies have sought overseas listings.[24]

Another result of this discriminatory listing policy is that most of the investment in the dynamic non-SOE sector that is propelling China's industrial growth in the new century is self-financed, or dependent on foreign capital. As economist and China observer Deepak Lal remarks, with few of the non-state enterprises being allowed to issue shares, trade on China's domestic stock exchanges is mainly in SOEs, whose "non-transparent accounting practices and perceived lack of viability deter retail investors from holding much of their savings in these firms for the purpose of long-term and value-based investment."[25] Hence the thinness and volatility of China's domestic stock exchanges, where "even a little news from the opaque SOEs can trigger big price movements."[26] The issue of volatile stock price movements is also related to the discussion below about China's "government policy-driven" stockmarket that has been identified with the politicization of economic activities.

In addition to the dominance of SOEs among listed companies, state ownership or control of other major players has also caused serious problems of moral hazard and insolvency, most critically for China's approximately 130 brokerage firms that are supposed to be one of the pillars to provide market liquidity in the institutional structure of the stockmarket. The brokerage industry in China is a loss-making and scandal-prone sector that has been plagued by malpractice for years, primarily due to its lack of incentives to operate on a market basis due to state ownership and control. The most notorious and widespread types of malpractice by China's brokerage firms include misappropriation of clients' funds (i.e., clients' "margin deposits"),

---

23. "Casino Capital," *supra* note 6.
24. Green, *supra* note 1.
25. Deepak Lal, "How Foreign Reserves Could Make China yet Stronger," *Financial Times*, December 29, 2004, p. 11.
26. *Ibid.*

insider trading, guaranteeing returns to investors (which could in some cases reach double-digit rates regardless of market movements), and falsifying financial statements to cover losses and retain qualifications for business.[27]

As of January 2005, the accumulated debts in the entire brokerage sector were estimated by some financial analysts at a staggering amount of RMB 200 billion yuan (roughly USD 24 billion).[28] This threatened an imminent meltdown of China's stockmarket as the share prices on both stock exchanges in Shanghai and Shenzhen hit their five-year lows. How to deal with the insolvency crisis of China's brokerage firms is a serious concern for China's securities regulators in designing proper reform strategies, and will presumably be a high priority on the government's reform agenda at the next stage.

Government intervention in the stockmarket

As a prevailing "local distinction" in China's stockmarket, Chinese investors hold an enduring belief that share prices are dictated by political signals, not by the laws of supply and demand.

Because China's two stock exchanges are dominated by mostly poorly-run SOEs, the government has developed a habit of influencing stock prices by controlling the flow of information. The periodic release of "good news" (*lihao*) to the public has been part of the drive to keep stock prices buoyant, although with diminished effect over past several years. The government's practice has been to "talk up poor-quality SOEs while preventing information on their true financial health from making its way into the media."[29] For example, during the period of 1991–2001, the 25 highest and lowest records of the Shanghai Composite Index had been all correlated with policy announcements and information releases by the government.[30]

Indeed, policies filtering out the "bad news" (*likong*) were partly responsible for a spectacular boom in China's two stock exchanges between January 2000 to June 2001 before the stockmarket started its decline which had lasted to 2005. At that time, the "bad news" released was that the government tried to relinquish its remaining holdings by selling off the non-tradable state shares through a "full flotation" (*quanliutong*) plan.

The history of the emergence, strengthening and entrenchment of the belief of Chinese investors in the role of government intervention in stockmarket

---

27. Geoff Dyer, "Brokerages Face Audit as China Starts Clean-up," *Financial Times*, January 22, 2005, p. 4.

28. Li Zhenhua, "Is Government Taking Over 'the Best Solution' to those 'Problem Brokerage Firms'?", *21st Century Business Herald* (*21 Shiji Jingji Baodao*) January 4, 2005, online < http://nanfangdaily.com.cn/jj/20050103/jr/200501040026.asp >.

29. Chen-Ee Lee, "Dish the Dirt: China's Markets Need the Info," *Asian Wall Street Journal*, August 17, 2000, p. 6.

30. Cheng Siwei, "Walk Out of the Vicious Circle of the 'Government Policy-Driven Stockmarket (zouchu 'zhengceshi' guaiquan)," *Caijing*, October 10, 2004.

operation has its roots in the early 1990s when China's stock exchanges were first established. First of all, it should be pointed out that the active involvement, and indeed the driving influence, of the Chinese government in the stockmarket — primarily with regard to IPO qualifications and pricing in the primary market and share price movements in the secondary market — had its origins at the very beginning of capital market development in the country when economic reforms initially started. The establishment of a stockmarket, then a completely alien notion to most Chinese citizens accustomed to years of central planning, was not an "autonomous institutional innovation by the market," but a direct result of government actions and administrative fiats.[31]

In other words, China's stockmarket was originally not a product of market mechanisms, but a government creation at a time when there was virtually no visible presence of private equity investment, financial intermediaries and firms with public shareholdings. Therefore, government actions were a necessary determinant of the establishment of China's stockmarket. Even though from the start it was a "irregular," or "state-dominated," or "government policy-driven" market, it was still better than "no market at all," because an imperfect market may well serve as a "transitional institution" and could still improve at later stages when China's economic transition had progressed.

However, the problem is that the "transitional period" turned out to have been protracted, and necessary reforms that would have improved the imperfect market have been largely delayed. After nearly two decades of operation, China's stockmarket is still dictated by the political logic, which has increasingly proved detrimental to the effective and efficient workings of the market. The policy-driven share prices, which reflect the immediate effect of government intervention, now usually taking the form of bail-outs (*jiushi*) every time the Shanghai Composite Index is headed downwards, have politicized economic activities and distorted investment culture in the stockmarket.

The fragmentation of the stockmarket: the problem of non-tradable shares

The political logic of China's stockmarket has also led to the fragmentation of shares, low market liquidity and poor corporate governance of listed companies. Under closer scrutiny of the causal relationship among these three identified structural problems, the fragmentation of shares, specifically the A-shares, is in turn the major cause of the other two problems.

Basically, there are three categories of shares issued by China's A-share listed companies, each with different rights, benefits and prices: state shares, legal-person shares, and public shares. The A-shares are shares issued by listed companies on China's stock exchanges in Shanghai and Shenzhen, which are

---

31. Zhang Weiying, *The Theory of the Firm and China's Enterprise Reform* (Beijing: Peking University Press, 1999), pp. 383–385.

denominated in Chinese currency *yuan* (RMB) and until November 2002 had been restricted to domestic investors. Since November 2002, foreign institutional investors that have obtained the joint approval by the CSRC, the central bank and the State Administration of Foreign Exchange (SAFE) can also trade A-shares with an allotted quota of funds. This is called the "qualified foreign institutional investors" (QFII) scheme, which is borrowed from Taiwan's experience during the earlier years of its capital market development when the conditions for full financial liberalization were not mature.

As of December 2003, a total of 642.8 billion shares were outstanding, of which 226.8 billion were tradable and represented 35.38 percent, or about one-third, of the total shares.[32] The non-tradable shares, accounting for almost two-thirds of the outstanding shares, primarily consist of state shares and legal-person shares.[33] The legal-person shares are usually held by state-owned or controlled enterprises. Therefore, it can be said that the structure of China's stockmarket is dominated by the state. Such a split share structure had put the public investors in a worse position than the actual controllers of the listed companies in making corporate policies and disposing of the companies' profits and assets.[34] The structural fragmentation of the stockmarket has seriously distorted valuations of tradable shares. For example, in 2004 the average A-share traded at an expensive 25 times earnings on China's domestic stock exchanges, even when precisely the same asset, if listed in Hong Kong or New York, was priced at half that price/earnings ratio.[35]

As the non-tradable shares have increasingly become a serious structural problem in the stockmarket, making them tradable and abolishing the current split share structure is an urgent task that could not afford extended delay. However, this task can only be achieved if a reform strategy can be designed to both satisfy the government, which hopes to use proceeds from selling state shares to fund its pension liabilities, and meet investors' demand that they be compensated for the dilution of their holdings. As to how to "compensate" the public investors, proposals include offering them discounts on the state shares being sold, or attaching rights warrants to the shares investors already hold that will allow them to buy state shares proportionately at lower prices to avoid the dilution of their holdings. It seems that a consensus on pricing had been reached between the Chinese government and investors as the CSRC finally started to seriously address the fragmentation problem in April 2005 by introducing a share structure reform aimed at making non-tradable shares

---

32. Source: CSRC, *supra* note 11.
33. Other less dominant components of the non-tradable shares are employee shares, transferred rights issues, shares placed to investment funds and strategic investors, etc. See *ibid.*
34. Asia Pulse/XIC, "Shanghai Stock Market Hits Six-Year Low," *Asia Times Online*, February 2, 2005, online < http://www.atimes.com/atimes/China/GB02Ad08.html >.
35. "A Marginalized Market," *supra* note 9.

tradable. Under this reform, the minority shareholders holding tradable shares are paid a "consideration," in the form of cash or warrants, by controlling shareholders for the latter to obtain convertibility of their non-tradable shares.

A pathological investment environment

The political logic of China's stockmarket has also resulted in a pathological investment environment characterized by widespread fraud, manipulation of share prices by large investors or the so-called *zhuangjia* (manipulators), and speculative short-term share transactions other than merit-based investments by small investors, who usually do not care about the corporate governance of the firms they invest in.[36] As discussed before, the political logic is the root cause of pervasive fraud in China's stockmarket. The government, especially at local levels, is directly responsible for, and in some cases even has an active part in, the cheating. A typical example is that a company in the northeast province of Heilongjiang, *Daqing Lianyi*, went public on false accounts fabricated jointly by the local government and the Commerce and Industry Administration, an agency whose very job was to ensure that all business activities comply with rules and regulations.[37]

Even if regulators have punished some of the most outrageous manipulators in the stockmarket, insider trading is still rampant. This is primarily because the punishment has not been severe enough to effectively deter wrongdoing. Fines, even in huge amounts, are still deemed by the unscrupulous as a price worth paying in return for much lucrative gains from share price manipulation. Simply put, the potential benefits far outweigh the possible costs (when the fraud is discovered) of committing wrongdoing, hence the weak deterrent effect of punishment. According to the estimate of China's stock exchange executives, the real number of investors may only be around half the official number, which was at approximately 70 million in 2004, because many investors have used multiple accounts for questionable or illegal share transactions.[38]

Before the adoption of the delisting system in February 2001 and the first actual delisting of a listed company, the Shanghai-based Narcissus Electronic Appliance (Narcissus) on April 23, 2001, Chinese investors would buy the shares of companies which were threatened with delisting in the knowledge they would inevitably be bailed out by local governments. Regional authorities also used numerous deceptive tools to ensure that favored local companies did not continue to record losses, including injecting assets into the enterprises and showering them with preferential policies. However, the ending of the old listing system in 2001, which allocated quotas to provinces to take local companies

---

36. Green, *supra* note 1, p. 154.
37. Yong Yan Li, "China's Equity Markets: Buyer Beware," *Asia Times Online*, May 9, 2003, online < http://www.atimes.com/atimes/China/EE09Ad01.html >.
38. "Casino Capital," *supra* note 6.

public, has removed companies such as Narcissus of their value for regional governments as fund-raising vehicles. Local investors once considered clever for pouring money into loss-making companies in anticipation of their recovery were instead mocked in the local media for buying shares in Narcissus.[39]

Poor quality of corporate governance and the "adverse selection" problem

While non-profitable and debt-ridden SOEs are given strong preference for public listings on the domestic stock exchanges, better performing private enterprises are largely excluded from seeking an IPO on mainland exchanges and have been increasingly propelled to overseas capital markets. In addition, with respect to companies that have been listed domestically, their share prices often do not reflect true levels of financial performance and operational efficiency in a pathological and speculative investment environment. It is not unusual that shares of some poorly-run listed companies may be hotly pursued by investors, not because they have good performance prospects, but because they are decorated by some market manipulators with such glamorous concepts, as "restructuring" and "mergers and acquisitions (M&As) prospects" that usually entail profit opportunities through capital gains. On the contrary, for some better performing companies, the real "blue chips," which are a minority group in the stockmarket, their shares may be traded at lower prices than should be the case, because of the large size of their capital base and their lack of "restructuring" prospects that would fuel the imagination of speculative traders for abnormal and quick gains.[40]

Indeed, the adverse selection problem is so severe in the domestic stockmarket that some well-performing issuers would rather go to overseas capital markets for listings, even though their shares are usually sold at a considerable discount, as compared to comparable foreign counterparts listed in the same market.

The CSRC's conflicting roles, lack of independence, and resulting ineffective regulation

Under the political logic of the stockmarket, the principal regulator, the CSRC, has been entrusted with conflicting responsibilities. First, in theory it should assume the primary responsibility to supervise and monitor the stockmarket through promoting good behavior and truthful disclosure and punishing wrongdoers. However, the function of "supervision and regulation" has largely been compromised by a more compelling function: to facilitate the raising of capital for SOEs to help mitigate their financial distress. These two functions are inherently incompatible. Because SOEs are generally unprofitable and poorly

---

39. Richard McGregor, "First Chinese Company to be Delisted Today," *Financial Times*, April 24, 2001, p. 11.

40. Huang Huimin, "Delisting: Another Driving Force for Stockmarket Development," 4 *Listed Companies* (ShangShi GongSi) (2001).

managed, the preservation of their financing opportunities translates to *de facto* weak regulation and disregard for investor protection. Otherwise, these firms would have long ago been excluded from the stockmarket. In addition, since 1999, a curious position has been adopted by some policy makers in the central government that maintaining high share indexes would be beneficial and stimulative to the achievement of high GDP growth targets because a booming stockmarket with more capital inflows would contribute to high aggregate demand in the economy. Accordingly, the CSRC started to assume a new function: to prop up the stock indexes. However, when the indexes did reach their highs, any possibility that they could fall engendered investors' dismay and outcry. Thus the primacy of "social stability" always prevailed to prevent the indexes from declining, which has created a perverse pattern of interaction between the state, the market, the regulators, and the investors.

Obviously, these competing functions have deprived the CSRC of regulatory vigor and effectiveness. On the one hand, the controlling shareholders of most listed companies are usually local governments or entities controlled by them. On the other hand, as a quasi-governmental agency, the CSRC lacks independence and is ultimately subject to government will. Therefore, it is usually difficult for the CSRC to effectively rectify the misdeeds by listed companies and their government controlling shareholders. More than often, providing investors with adequate protection through vigorous regulation is an empty promise, especially when the interests of the state and that of the investors are not aligned.[41] Partly due to this significant drawback on the independence of the CSRC, the presumed function of the stockmarket in facilitating privatization of SOEs in China's transition economy, as is generally expected of its counterparts in other transition economies, has been at best limited.[42]

5.1.4 The operational quality of China's stockmarket

An overall assessment of the operational quality of China's stockmarket is that, except for channeling funds to poorly-run SOEs under its political logic, which has eventually led to the drying up of investment resources in the society, it has not been very successful in realizing all other important functions that it is supposed to perform. These functions include the following: (a) allocating capital to deserving firms, (b) protecting investor rights through punishing wrongdoers, (c) promoting good corporate governance and disciplining firms

---

41. Chen Xiao, "Judicial Enforcement Intervenes into the Stockmarket, but Effective Regulation Is Still a Long Way Off (sifa jieru gushi, youxiao jianguan luyao)," *China Newsweek*, January 12, 2004, online < http://www.chinanewsweek.com. cn/2004-01-14/1/2935.html >.
42. Han Zhiguo, "China's Stockmarket on the Verge of Demise," *Securities Market Weekly*, January 15, 2005.

with market basics, (d) building market credit mechanisms and a value-based investment culture, and (e) offering adequate returns on capital to investors that reflect the risks they bear.

From June 2001 to early 2005, the share prices on China's stockmarket had been moving in the opposite direction to the strong growth trend of the country's economy. It is telling that the world's greatest economic success story had produced Asia's, and the world's, worst share performance in 2004. The Shanghai Composite Index, which covers yuan-denominated A-shares and hard currency denominated B-shares, fell 14 percent in 2004 and experienced a free-fall to a six-year low on February 1, 2005. At the same time, the Shenzhen Composite Index hit its lowest level since 1997.[43] The root cause of receding investment confidence was the very low (or negative) return for investors in the stockmarket. For years, many listed companies have regarded the stock exchanges as places for *quanqian* and do not care about investor rights. Instead, they rarely pay dividends and often provide false information. The market remains dysfunctional as the mechanism for protecting investors' rights has yet to be fully established and enforced.[44]

5.2 Corporate Governance and Performance of Listed Companies in Domestic Market

Section 5.2 examines important aspects of corporate governance and performance of China's domestically listed companies, including their capital and ownership structures, financial performance and typical forms of corporate governance deficiencies.

Before proceeding to more substantive topics, it is necessary to explain the relationship between the stockmarket and listed companies. On the one hand, in the words of China's principal securities regulator, the CSRC, the quality of listed companies, which is chiefly reflected by their corporate governance practices, is "the fundamental building block of the stockmarket." On the other hand, a better regulated stockmarket would help encourage good corporate behavior. As the strategy for China's SOE reform has shifted from granting autonomy, building managerial incentives and promoting competition, to reforming the ownership structure of SOEs through partial or full privatization, stockmarket seemed a necessary institution to promote the ownership reform of SOEs. However, because there is no true market for corporate control in China due to the underdevelopment of a property rights regime, the role of the stockmarket in disciplining listed companies and their management and promoting good corporate governance is not strong at this stage of reform. In

---

43. "Shanghai Stock Market Hits Six-year Low," *supra* note 34.
44. Asia Pulse/XIC, "China Moves to Cage its Rampaging Bears," *Asia Times Online*, January 20, 2005, online < http://atimes01.atimes.com/atimes/China/GA20Ad02.html >.

addition, at a time when legal and regulatory reforms for the stockmarket are still progressing and their results have so far been limited, advanced corporate governance mechanisms, such as an independent director system and equity incentive schemes for rewarding management, may not work as effectively as in a better developed market.

5.2.1 The capital structure of Chinese listed companies

Overwhelmingly, Chinese listed companies prefer equity financing over debt financing. Issuing shares to raise capital has been an enduring favorable option for these firms, as compared to corporate bonds. The key feature of the capital structure of most listed companies in China, therefore, is low leverage. For example, in 2001, the average leverage rate for Chinese listed companies was 44.8 percent, compared to 62.4 percent for the national average, 52.1 percent for the group of shareholding companies (listed companies included), and 65.8 percent for the group of collectively-owned enterprises.[45]

The fundamental reason for the low leverage rate of China's listed companies is the underdevelopment of the capital markets where investors have very few alternatives for capital investment. Specifically, the corporate bond market has long been depressed under the government policy to control credit flows, because state banks had not been genuine commercial lenders (which situation started to change after a new round of banking reform was initiated in 2003, featuring shareholding reform and overseas listings of state-owned banks) and interest rates are not the primary monetary tool to adjust currency flows. With inadequate liberalization of the financial system, in particular the banking sector, an active corporate bond market has not developed in China. An encouraging sign of improvement is that the Chinese government has been considering the promotion of a corporate bond market. In August 2007, the CSRC enacted formal rules governing the issuance of corporate bonds, which greatly reduce the previously stringent requirements for listed companies to sell bonds for trade on the two stock exchanges.[46]

In addition, because China's stockmarket is inefficient and deviates from standard rules of capital costs, many firms feel that they do not have to worry about either the costs or the risks of issuing equity capital. One example is that the price/earnings ratio in the primary market is set artificially high (as high as 60 times) as a result of administration-driven share issuing and pricing systems that do not reflect the true market value of assets. This means firms can raise equity capital at a very low cost, and that they provide investors with virtually

---

45. Gu Weiping, "Why Do Chinese Listed Companies Prefer Equity Financing to Debt Financing?", *Listed Companies* (*Shangshi Gongsi*) (2001).

46. Jamil Anderlini, "China Move Starts Corporate Bond Surge," *Financial Times*, August 15, 2007.

no meaningful returns on assets. Given the fact that most of China's listed companies do not pay dividends at all, the costs of raising equity capital for these companies are even lower than the average level.[47]

From the perspective of investors, why on earth would they want to buy these shares if returns are so low? The answer is that most investors view stock buying as a speculation tool for gains from short-term share trades in the secondary market, not as a long-term, value-based investment vehicle. Therefore, they buy into these shares regardless of their long-term return prospects.[48]

In further examining why investors would buy these shares and why there could be short-term gains for (at least some) investors, there are two factors that explain to a large extent the irrational investment pattern. First, in the early years of stockmarket development, some economists, who were then seen by investors as representatives of the government's "think tanks" or policy advisors, had assured investors that "60 to 80 times price/earnings are absolutely normal" and that "the government will definitely not allow the stockmarket to decline," which had misled small investors into buying shares at high prices, in the hope of making lucrative returns at a later time.[49] The second factor is that although on average public investors as a whole will lose in buying inflated shares issued by poorly-run listed companies, there had existed a well known "fool's game" ("*bosha*") in the Chinese stockmarket. Many investors believed that as long as there was a "fool" willing to buy shares from the previous holders, everybody can make gains in share trades until the last "fool" could not find anyone else to buy the shares from him/her, thus bearing all losses as the unlucky end chain of the "fool's game."

However, as the problems of the stockmarket become increasingly evident, many investors could not realize their hope of exiting the market by selling shares at high prices to a "fool," because more and more investors have become aware of this game. Instead, they have remained "locked" in the market, desperate to find a buyer of the shares they hold. As a result, investing in the stockmarket has become "one of the most risky businesses" in China, and there have been reported cases where retail investors, many of them pensioners, took radical actions such as protesting on the streets upon losing all their savings in the stockmarket.

5.2.2 The ownership structure of Chinese listed companies

The prevailing ownership structure of China's listed companies is the so-called "sole controlling shareholder dictatorship" (*yigu duda*), whereby the state,

---

47. Gu, *supra* note 45.
48. Gu, *supra* note 45.
49. "Forcing China's Stockmarket Down to the Bottom: Tails of Robbing Wealth in China's Stockmarket," *Business Watch*, December 12, 2003.

or a state-controlled entity, is the sole largest shareholder with a controlling stake. Of Chinese shareholding companies, many have been transformed from traditional SOEs. These firms have to various degrees experienced the diversification of ownership structure by introducing private or foreign capital. However, in most cases such ownership restructuring process primarily involved inviting customers, suppliers and other related enterprises to participate in the diversification, thus creating an ownership structure with *de facto* control by the sole largest shareholder.[50] For example, in 2001 there were 890 listed companies, or 79.2 percent of the total, that had a single shareholder holding at least 50 percent of their outstanding shares. The state, or a state-controlled legal person, is usually the largest shareholder of Chinese listed companies.[51]

This peculiar ownership structure has caused a widely observed problem of insider control among Chinese listed companies, as the state shareholder usually lacks effective mechanisms to exercise its ownership rights. This is also the most fundamental source of various corporate governance failures or misbehavior. The most typical forms of corporate governance failure in the Chinese stockmarket include the following: (a) the extraction of corporate funds and resources and expropriation of minority shareholders by controlling shareholders, (b) expropriation and stealing by managers of corporate funds and resources, (c) the preference of listed companies for issuing new shares that dilutes the interests of minority shareholders, and (d) manipulating shareholder meetings by the controlling shareholders to pass new issuing plans against the will of minority shareholders.[52] Later discussions will feature some notable cases where serious corporate governance deficiencies in the above aspects were exposed.

5.2.3   The financial performance of Chinese listed companies

Performance on major financial indicators

An abnormal phenomenon in China's stockmarket is that the performance of many listed companies is even worse than before listing. In a recent study on the empirical results of the relationship between an IPO and the operational performance of Chinese listed companies, it is found that in measuring firms' growth, profitability and stability after IPO, the only industries in which China's listed companies displayed signs of strong performance were public utilities,

---

50. Liu Zhaohui, "The Stockmarket Needs a Double Adjustment of both Corporate Governance and Industrial Structure of Listed Companies," 7 *Listed Companies* (*Shangshi Gongsi*) (2003).
51. Wen Zhao, "Is 'Sole Controlling Shareholder' the Culprit for Corporate Governance Failures?: Part V of a Report on Corporate Governance Structure," *China Business Times,* August 27, 2001.
52. Liu, *supra* note 50.

transportation and finance, which are all in the "sunrise sectors" during China's transition where SOEs still hold a monopoly status.[53] As to the changes in the financial indicators of listed companies following the IPO, the evidence shows that with the exception of earnings related indicators, such as EPS (earnings per share) and ROE (returns on equity), there are no significant changes.[54] Moreover, the financial indicators tend to fall rapidly on a year-on-year basis. These findings indicate that the IPO is of little help to companies' operational performance, and in some cases may actually worsen it.[55]

Measured against the performance of those overseas-listed Chinese companies, the A-share companies as a group display a much lower level of financial performance. For example, for the year 2003, the average P/E (price/earnings) ratio for the A-share companies was 29.5 percent, against 14 percent for overseas-listed Chinese companies; the average ROE ratio for the A-share companies was 7.3 percent, compared to 13.5 percent for their overseas counterparts.[56] In particular, almost a half of the A-share companies recorded ROE ratio lower than 5 percent, despite the fact that 2003 was a fast growing year for China's economy, which means that many of these poorly-performing firms should have been excluded from the stockmarket.[57]

Why relatively poor performance?

As the above discussion indicates, for many listed companies in China, going public did not improve their corporate governance and financial performance, and for some their performance and financial condition became even worse after listing.[58] There are three major reasons suggested for the disappointing results of financial performance of Chinese listed companies.

The first reason for the declining performance of China's listed companies is that in order to be qualified for an IPO and secure an equity listing, Chinese companies often submit inflated figures in their financial statements that they are required to provide as part of the listing documents.[59] In other words, firms cooked their books to pass the review of IPO applications and their subsequent performance decline is only an inevitable reflection of the previously disguised fact. It is not uncommon that after these firms have raised money from the

---

53. Chen Chien-Hsun & Shih Hui-Tzu, "Initial Public Offering and Corporate Governance in China's Transitional Economy," NBER Working Paper, No. 9574 (2003).

54. Chen & Shih, *ibid.*

55. Chen & Shih, *ibid.*

56. Chen Changhua, "Before the Bad Companies Go, the Good Companies Will Not Come (huaide buqŭ, haode bulai)," *Caijing*, November 29, 2004.

57. Chen, *ibid.*

58. Erika Leung, Lily Liu, Lu Shen, Kevin Taback & Leo Wang (with advice from Stewart C. Myers), "Financial Reform and Corporate Governance in China," MIT Sloan School of Management, 50th Anniversary Proceedings (2002).

59. Chen & Shih, *supra* note 53.

public, they suddenly become truthful and disclose a stunning loss. A critical commentary on China's stockmarket thus reported:

> ...[T]here is no telling the extent to which the listed companies resort to cheating (in order to get listed). But the dozens of cases that have been made public are alarming in their sheer contempt for laws. From financial reports to accounting books, and from bank statements to related transaction contracts, everything can be falsified. From management to auditors, and from law firms to securities brokers, everybody can be a paid co-conspirator. Non-existent sales are recorded, imaginary profits are announced, while in reality the companies are insolvent even before they get listed.[60]

The second reason is incomplete privatization. According to some empirical estimates, exposure to capital markets through public equity offerings has been scarcely more effective in imposing disciplines on Chinese managers than under the old management system of SOEs. Many so-called privatization schemes so far have simply parceled out dominant shareholdings to different arms of government, leaving only minority stakes for private investors.[61] Although ministries' direct interference in day-to-day management has been curbed, companies still face pressure to fulfill sometimes conflicting social and industrial policy priorities, which helps explain why studies have repeatedly found that many Chinese companies perform worse after privatization than before.[62]

The third reason is the commonly observed poor corporate governance of Chinese listed companies that usually leads to performance failure. Specifically, the endemic phenomenon of pervasive corporate litigation usually leads to huge financial losses and heavy debt burdens of China's listed companies. Such litigation often results from disputes over the extraction of corporate funds by the controlling shareholders and irregular guarantees by the listed companies for bank loans to related entities.

In most cases, the defendant is a listed company that experienced financial losses in failed business transactions or because of extractions by managers and controlling shareholders. The plaintiff usually includes the following categories: (a) the defendant's creditors, such as banks that made unrecovered loans to a related-party of the defendant with the defendant as the loan guarantor, (b) minority shareholders of the defendant who demanded that the corporate funds extracted by the controlling shareholders be returned or compensated by the defendant, and (c) public investors who entrusted funds with the financial services arm of the defendant for guaranteed returns that were promised, yet not realized, by the defendant, many of whom were not only defaulted on the

---

60. Yong Yan Li, *supra* note 37.
61. Guy de Jonquieres, "Investors are Drawn to China in Spite of the Risks," *Financial Times*, February 1, 2005, p. 19.
62. *Ibid.*

promised returns, but also lost their original funds.[63] The average loss arising from the costs of such litigation for the A-share companies reached more than RMB 15 million yuan (around USD 1.81 million) in 2003.[64] Clearly, the litigation burden has eroded the profit margins and increased the debt burdens of many listed companies.

5.2.4 The quality of corporate governance of Chinese listed companies

As pointed out above, poor corporate governance is an important contributor to the performance failure of listed companies in China. Even some of the better-regarded listed companies indulge in various forms of market abuses, such as lending money raised on the stockmarket to the parent company rather than investing it as promised in their IPO prospectuses, or speculating in the stockmarket on their own accounts. Almost all companies that were allowed to list are the beneficiaries of government favoritism. As *The Economist* magazine sharply criticizes, "their profitability is usually abysmal, their levels of disclosure poor, and — with the state holding roughly two-thirds of the shares of companies listed in Shanghai and Shenzhen — their treatment of minority shareholders appalling."[65] Meanwhile, it should be pointed out that state-controlled companies and private companies both bear their own share of the blame, and both contribute to the problem of corporate governance pathology in China's stockmarket, as the cases reported below reveal. Therefore, listing more private companies would not be sufficient to improve the general quality of corporate governance. As the later discussion of corporate governance failures of China's private enterprises listed overseas suggests, these firms face similar problems of insider control, in the form of "the founder's dictatorship."

Among China's listed companies, typical forms of corporate governance pathology include the following five categories: (a) related-party transactions, (b) insider control and the resulting misappropriation of corporate funds and resources by managers, (c) fraudulent listing applications and disclosure, (d) the extraction of corporate funds and expropriation of minority shareholders by controlling shareholders (usually the state and legal-person shareholders), and (e) weak internal controls and risk management.

From the following cases of high profile corporate governance failures that have raised serious concerns to investors, it can be seen that the listed companies in China need an effective cleanup across the board, as both private and state-

---

63. Li Zhongdong & Li Hongwei, "The Fatal Litigation Trouble for Chinese Listed Companies (shangshi gongsi zhiming susong)," *Securities Market Weekly* (*Zhengquan Shichang Zhoukan*), October 25, 2004, online < http://news.hexun.com/detail.aspx?id=879820 >.

64. Li & Li, *ibid.*

65. "Casino Capital," *supra* note 6.

controlled companies, including those previously regarded as "better governed" firms, have recorded egregious misbehavior. It should also be noted that some of China's "new rich" — an emerging class of wealthy private entrepreneurs — turned out to be big corporate thieves and, in some cases, criminals engaged in economic crimes. This phenomenon has been described as China's new epidemic of "questionable tycoons" (*wenti fuhao*) or "tycoons with the original sin" (*yuanzui fuhao*).

The Xi'an Diamond fraudulent listing and embezzlement case

One such "questionable tycoon" as described above was the former chairman of Xi'an Diamond, a listed private enterprise that fabricated financial papers to obtain a fraudulent listing. In January 2005, the People's Congress of Xi'an city approved "compelling measures" against the fugitive chairman of Xi'an Diamond, Xu Zonglin. Xu was accused of taking nearly RMB 500 million yuan in public funds between 1996 and 2004, before absconding with the stolen money overseas. Prosecutors approved his arrest in December 2004, but Xu has still remained at large.[66]

The Xinjiang Hops embezzlement case

Another recent embezzlement case involved Aikelamu Aishayoufu, the chairman of Xinjiang Hops, a Shanghai-listed company, who has been missing since November 2003. In a recent *Asiamoney* list, Mr. Aishayoufu, an ethnic Uighur from western China, was listed as one of China's richest businessmen in 2003, ranked 22nd in the country according to the value of his shares in Xinjiang Hops.[67] *Asiamoney* calculated that Mr. Aishayoufu's personal wealth was USD 351 million, based on his shareholding declared in Xinjiang Hops' annual report. Compared to his stunning personal wealth, Mr. Aishayoufu did not leave his company in a good financial condition, however. In a statement to the Shanghai Stock Exchange following his disappearance, the company's board disclosed loan liabilities of RMB 987 million (USD 119 million), doubled the company' net assets, as well as receivables of RMB 265 million.[68] What is more, Xinjiang Hops had a further RMB 140 million in overdue loans and RMB 800 million in already disclosed loans guarantees. After the disappearance of Mr. Aishayoufu, the board announced that it "only became aware that the former chairman had absconded" when it received a request to contact him on October 30, 2003 from the Shanghai Stock Exchange.[69]

---

66. "Measures to Track Down Fugitive Xi'an Diamond Chief," *South China Morning Post*, January 29, 2005, p. 6.
67. Richard McGregor, "Head of Xinjiang Hops Goes Missing," *Financial Times*, November 5, 2003, p. 16.
68. *Ibid.*
69. *Ibid.*

The Changhong-Apex dispute

While the cases reported above basically involved fraud and embezzlement, which are commonly seen in China's stockmarket, the recent Changhong-Apex dispute reflected a new, but potentially critical, source of corporate governance failure: the disregard for risks in overseas expansion at a time when China's enterprises are seeking to increase their participation in the global economy.

In December 2004, China's biggest television maker and exporter, Shanghai-listed Sichuan Changhong Electric Appliances, admitted that it was in serious financial difficulty, largely because of its reliance on Apex Digital, its U.S. distributor. Changhong was likely to recover only USD 150 million of the USD 467.5 million in debts that were allegedly owed by Apex. As a result, Changhong, hitherto a much praised "favorite son" to Chinese leadership for its remarkable success in transforming itself from a small local SOE to the country's biggest TV maker, was facing significant losses in 2005. It later declared to its shareholders that it was making provisions to incur losses of USD 310 million, implying that the shareholders will not receive any dividends for at least ten years to come.[70] Apex's co-founder, David Ji, a U.S. citizen, was detained by Chinese authorities over suspicions of financial wrongdoing.[71]

Many analysts believe the sour relationship between Changhong and Apex reflected a strategic decision by Changhong to focus on sales growth in the U.S. while neglecting its profit margins in recent years.[72] In other words, Changhong sacrificed profit for market share. According to expert estimates, Apex was selling Changhong products at such low prices that after taking into account various costs, Changhong's profit margins on its exports to the U.S. had been close to zero, compared with an industry export profit margin of 2 to 5 percent.[73] This pattern of overseas expansion not only entailed great risk of profit losses, but had also forced Changhong's domestic competitors into a vicious circle of price competition, which was hurting the overall competitiveness of China's TV industry. The two companies' unusual business relationship, whereby Apex acted as an agent but not the owner of Changhong's goods and took a 10 percent commission from sales, encouraged Changhong to continue sending orders despite slow demand in the U.S. market.[74]

This case reminds Chinese enterprises with an ambition to expand overseas that business prudence and risk control are crucially needed when tapping global markets, and the typical problem of insider control, whereby

70. Justine Lau & Andrew Yeh, "Picture Suddenly Goes Fuzzy for One of China's Favorite Sons," *Financial Times*, January 4, 2005, p. 15.
71. Chris Buckley, "Leading Chinese TV Exporter Has Huge Loss," *New York Times*, December 28, 2004.
72. Lau & Yeh, *supra* note 70.
73. Lau & Yeh, *supra* note 70.
74. Chris Buckley, "For Entrepreneur, Business Trip Ends in a Chinese Jail," *New York Times*, January 18, 2005, p. C6.

top managers make important business decisions without broad consultation, could lead to spectacular losses. As a local government controlled company (the government of Mianyang city where Changhong's headquarters are located holds a 53 percent stake in its listing entity), Changhong demonstrated precisely this danger: its former CEO, Ni Runfeng, who stepped down before the Apex affair was exposed to the greater public, made decisions to continue to cooperate with Apex, despite warnings from other managers when criticism of Apex's credibility was being spread among the industry and media circles by some firms with unhappy experience with the U.S. distributor in the past.[75] Indeed, the reckless business adventure of Changhong with its U.S. distributor was so bereft of reasonable care that the contract detailing the rights and responsibilities of each party was only one-page long, and Changhong even did not set up a representative office in the U.S., a remarkable oversight for such a large exporter with a significant market share for imported TV sets in the U.S..[76]

The D'Long debacle

Since July 2004, Tang Wanxin, the former president of D'Long, had been under investigation by Chinese authorities for alleged financial crimes involving the firm's spectacular collapse in the summer of 2004. Tang Wanxin was indicted in December 2005 in a local court in Wuhan city of Hubei province for "illegally accepting deposits and manipulating stock prices," facing a maximum of 15 years in prison.[77] D'Long was a flagship Chinese private enterprise with a wide range of operations, which also had an international presence by acquiring Western brands. In the shadow of the D'Long debacle, the Chinese government had been preparing the biggest debt-restructuring plan in China's financial system since the collapse of Guangdong International Trust & Investment Corporation in 1998.[78] It is indicative to examine the reasons for the D'Long debacle, which reveal some serious challenges faced by China's private enterprises, many of which are experiencing a transformation of business strategies from local operations and usually a narrow scope of business lines to vigorous expansion.

Before its collapse, D'Long had pursued its business on two fronts. On the one hand, D'Long "invested heavily to acquire hundreds of companies in a range of industries, including tomato jam, cement, auto parts, electric tools,

---

75. Yang Ruifa & Wang Yunfan, "(Ji Longfen: the Collapsing Point of the 'Domino' ('gupai' Ji Longfen)," *21st Century Business Herald* (*21 Shiji Jingji Baodao*), December 27, 2004, online < http://www.nanfangdaily.com.cn/jj/20041227/zh/200412270003.asp >.
76. Lou Yi *et al.*, "Sichuan Changhong's US$472 million Dispute with Apex," *Caijing*, January 10, 2005, online < http://www.caijing.com.cn/english/2005/05-1-10/05-1-10-4.htm >.
77. Ling Huawei & Zhou Fan, "Finale in Sight for Delong Saga," *Caijing*, January 9, 2006, online < http://caijing.hexun.com/english/detail.aspx?issue=150&sl=2482&id=148815 2 >.
78. Mark O'Neil, "D'Long Officials under House Arrest," *South China Morning Post*, August 24, 2004, p. 2.

heavy trucks, seeds and mining."[79] On the other hand, D'Long took control of dozens of financial service firms, including brokerage firms, trust companies and financial leasing companies.[80] These two fronts were closely interrelated: because of its pursuit of an aggressive expansion strategy that was capital-intensive, D'Long had to invest large amounts of capital into the restructuring of the companies it had acquired or merged with. The primary solution to D'Long's continuing expansion was to borrow money, and the need for funds eventually prompted D'Long to take direct control of financial institutions. In 2002, after it obtained control of several trust and securities companies, D'Long started to extend its business scope to the banking industry.[81]

The result was remarkable: over a short period of time, D'Long had acquired shares, including controlling stakes, of six or seven city commercial banks and had made appointments to the boards or management teams of these banks.[82] According to an investigation report by China's banking regulators in their probe into the firm's irregular financial transactions, D'Long had borrowed from these banks a total of RMB 20–30 billion yuan (USD 2.4–3.6 billion). Many of these loans were guaranteed by connected companies or pledged with stocks.[83] Adding in other funds obtained by D'Long from other financial institutions, D'Long was estimated to have ultimately controlled RMB 40–50 billion yuan (USD 4.8–6.0 billion) of funds in China's financial system.[84] According to *Caijing*, the most vigorous investigative financial magazine in China:

> A report by one of the "big four" state banks revealed that although D'Long ostensibly had "reasonable projects" for all its bank loans, it actually had used many of its loans to buy shares in acquisition transactions to pursue its expansion strategy. Most of the loans were not lent on adequate collateral, and many of them were guaranteed by third-parties — usually the most risky type of loans for banks.[85]

The China Banking Regulatory Commission (CBRC), the country's primary banking regulator, started to be alerted to the fact that D'Long and several other companies (mostly private enterprises) had excessively high leverage ratios, which increased the possibility of generating huge amounts of bad loans in the banking sector. After the CBRC sent risk alerts to local banking regulators, D'Long was doomed, because "its fragile financing chains could not sustain an

---

79. Ling Huawei, "D'Long Bubble Bursts," *Caijing English Newsletter*, April 22, 2004, online < http://www.caijing.com.cn/english/2004/040420/delong.htm >.
80. *Ibid.*
81. *Ibid.*
82. *Ibid.*
83. *Ibid.*
84. *Ibid.*
85. *Ibid.*

overall tightening of credit in the banking industry."[86] The result was the chain collapse of the share prices of the "D'Long Fraction," which quickly caused the spectacular failure of the financial conglomerate.

5.2.5 The limited effect of advanced corporate governance mechanisms from overseas

From the cases reported above, it can be seen that both China's private enterprises and partially privatized SOEs listed on domestic stock exchanges have widespread corporate governance problems. Would, then, introducing advanced mechanisms of checks and monitoring to combat these corporate governance deficiencies work — such as the installation of an independent director system? While it is necessary to seriously consider such measures, in the short run the effect of such effort is not always positive. This is mainly because the advanced corporate governance mechanisms lack necessary operational conditions in China's current institutional environment, where many basic market mechanisms are either still at their early stage of development or simply absent. Recent incidents surrounding several "dismissed independent directors," as discussed below, offer a typical example of where the distance between the intended goals and actual consequences of corporate governance reform can be much larger than one might expect.

In the summer of 2004, independent directors of at least three listed companies in China were forced off their boards after challenging management decisions, including requesting an audit of one company's accounts. The board of a listed company, Leshan Power Electric, held a special meeting in August 2004 to sanction the resignation of a director who had hired an auditor from outside the province to investigate charges that the company had not disclosed loan guarantees to other enterprises. Two other companies — Xinjiang Tunhe Investment, part of a private financial conglomerate, the failed D'Long group, and Inner Mongolia Yili Industrial, a dairy company — also both lost their independent directors around the same time in controversial circumstances.[87] Although many analysts commented that it was wrong for companies to remove independent directors because they were trying to disclose possible misbehavior, in the business reality of many Chinese listed companies, independent directors are largely considered "guests" or "vases" only for decorating purposes, which makes it doubtful whether they can play any material part in the operation of the company.[88] In particular, as a large proportion of the independent directors

---

86. *Ibid.*
87. Richard, McGregor, "Director Loses Seat for Hiring Auditor," *Financial Times*, August 18, 2004, p. 26.
88. *Ibid.*

in China, now more than 1400 in total, consists of people from academic circles, including universities and research institutions, their expertise in commercial matters and the time and energy they are able to spend on corporate affairs are also doubtful.

It is worth noting that compared to China's situation, recent empirical studies have provided preliminary evidence indicating a better record of independent directors in listed public companies in South Korea. It has been found that Korean firms with 50 percent outside directors have 0.13 higher Tobin's *q* (roughly 40 percent higher share price), after controlling for other components of an overall corporate governance index. Moreover, this effect is found to be likely causal, which suggests the first evidence consistent with the proposition that greater board independence causally predicts higher share prices in emerging markets.[89] The difference in the effect of independent directors on share performance between China and South Korea may be partly attributable to the better regulated capital markets in South Korea, as well as the different composition and incentive structure of independent directors in Korean listed companies.

5.3   Overseas Listings and Corporate Governance of Chinese Companies

Since the listing in 1993 on the Stock Exchange of Hong Kong of the first mainland company, Tsingtao Brewery, Chinese companies have gone overseas to raise capital. Major overseas capital markets for Chinese listings are the Stock Exchange of Hong Kong (including both its main board and GEM board), the New York Stock Exchange, NASDAQ, the London Stock Exchange and the Singapore Stock Exchange.[90] The major components of China's overseas listed companies are large SOEs with better performance, usually in such strategic sectors as energy, telecommunications, transportation, civil aviation, and finance. Meanwhile, since the 2001 IPO in Hong Kong of Zhejiang Glass, private enterprises have also increased their interest in seeking overseas listings, partly because of the restrictions on domestic listings these firms face.

The reasons for China's companies to list in overseas capital markets are largely related to positive considerations, including the following: (a) reaching a much wider base of international investors guided by value-based

---

89.   Bernard S. Black, Hasung Jang & Woochan Kim, "Does Corporate Governance Predict Firms' Market Values? Evidence from Korea," University of Texas Law School Law and Economics Working Paper, No. 26 (2004).

90.   Lu Wenying, "A Study of the Relationship between Cross-Border Listing and Corporate Governance," in Zhu Congjiu (ed.), *Shanghai Stock Exchange Research: the 1ˢᵗ Issue of 2004* (*Shang Zheng Yan Jiu*) (Shanghai: Fudan University Press, 2004).

investment ideas, (b) accessing deeper and more liquid capital markets where not only more funds are available but the regulatory quality is much higher, (c) improving information disclosure and accounting practices, (d) facilitating the ownership reform of large SOEs, (e) promoting enterprise image and reputation internationally, and (f) expanding participation in the global economy.

While headway has been made in terms of improved corporate governance under stricter regulation and market discipline, Chinese companies listed overseas have shown some critical weaknesses in internal controls and other forms of corporate governance deficiencies closely associated with the country's incomplete transition to a market economy, thus creating potential investment risks for investors.

5.3.1 The likely fading attraction of the NYSE to Chinese firms in the wake of SOX

Before the coming into force of the Sarbanes-Oxley Act (SOX) in 2002, the New York Stock Exchange (NYSE) had been an attractive destination for many potential Chinese issuers. After all, a listing on the world's most dynamic and liquid capital market would naturally carry a significant reputational premium for firms ambitious to acquire global recognition and expansion.

However, tightened regulation under the SOX has given some of China's big companies second thoughts about seeking a NYSE listing. Passed in the wake of the Enron and WorldCom scandals, this law calls for auditors to approve a company's procedures for preventing fraud and ensuring that its accounts are correct. It also requires managers to certify the effectiveness and adequacy of internal controls in year-end filings. For foreign companies registered with the Securities and Exchange Commission (SEC), compliance with the internal-controls rule started with the financial year ending on or after July 15, 2005.[91] Given the increased costs of compliance, two of China's "big four" state banks, the Bank of China (BoC) and China Construction Bank (CCB), which were planning billion-dollar international offerings in 2005, publicly expressed reservations about listing on the NYSE. Also, as a result of the negative impact of the SOX on the listing plans of potential Chinese issuers, the London Stock Exchange eventually replaced the NYSE as one of the listing destinations for Air China, the country's largest civil aviation carrier, which launched a dual-listing in December 2004 in London and Hong Kong.[92]

Although according to the former chairman of the NYSE, William Donaldson, non-American firms may be granted more time to comply with the internal-controls clause under the SOX and the rules on delisting from

---

91. "Foreign Listings in New York: Big Apple Blues," *The Economist,* January 27, 2005, p. 73.
92. *Ibid.*

American exchanges may also be relaxed, Chinese companies would still find these concessions inadequate, given their generally higher difficulty in improving corporate governance as compared to their European counterparts.[93] Faced with the serious threat of class action for corporate governance failures in American capital markets, Chinese issuers on the NYSE have already found life uneasy. For example, China Life, China's largest life insurer, had been under a formal investigation by the SEC since December 2004 and had a class-action suit pending, having failed to disclose accounting irregularities of RMB 5.4 billion (USD 652 million) at its state-owned parent company, which were uncovered by China's National Audit Office after China Life's dual-listing on the NYSE and the Stock Exchange of Hong Kong in December 2003.

5.3.2 Hong Kong's stockmarket as the primary channel of raising foreign capital for mainland Chinese companies

Many of China's biggest companies are listed in Hong Kong and are generally well received by overseas investors. At the height of the investment fever over China's growth story, overseas investors raced to buy every new issue, leading to exponential over-subscription of IPO shares.

The history of mainland listings in Hong Kong shows a steady and rapid increase in market presence of Chinese issuers, measured by both the number of IPOs and total capitalization. The listings of so-called "red-chips" in Hong Kong started in the 1980s, followed in 1993 by the first H-share listing, made by Tsingtao Brewery. By the end of 1994, 15 H-share companies had gone for public in Hong Kong, accompanied by the release of the *Mandatory Provisions for Companies Listed Overseas* by the Chinese government. Since 2000, mainland enterprises also started to be listed on the GEM board. By the end of April 2006, 344 mainland issuers had been listed on the Stock Exchange of Hong Kong, accounting for 30 percent of total lists and with a combined capitalization of HKD 4,043 billion, which amounted to 42 percent of the market total. By the end of August 2007, the top 10 IPOs in Hong Kong had all been made by mainland issuers, including the world's largest IPO — the IPO of the Industrial and Commercial Bank of China or ICBC, China's largest state-owned commercial bank, in October 2006.

In terms of the attractiveness of its capital markets for Chinese companies, Hong Kong has three important comparative advantages: (a) a language advantage, as Hong Kong is the only overseas capital market that uses both English and Chinese as working languages; (b) a transportation advantage due to Hong Kong's location adjacent to the mainland; and (c) a human capital advantage, as most financial analysts with an expertise in the mainland companies are located in Hong Kong.

---

93. *Ibid.*

As already mentioned above, there are two types of Chinese companies listed in Hong Kong: H-share companies and red-chip companies. H-share companies refer to companies incorporated in the PRC and approved by the CSRC for a listing in Hong Kong. The par value of the shares of these enterprises is denominated in RMB, and the shares are subscribed for and traded in Hong Kong dollars or other currencies.[94] Red-chip companies have the following characteristics: (a) if the companies have at least 30 percent shareholding held in aggregate by mainland China entities, and/or indirectly through companies controlled by them, with the mainland China entities being the single largest shareholders in aggregate terms, or (b) if the shareholding of the company held in aggregate directly and/or indirectly by mainland China entities is below 30 percent but is 20 percent or above and there is a strong influential presence, on a judgmental basis, of mainland China-linked individuals on the company's board of directors.[95]

H-share companies are usually state-controlled entities, and many of them are state monopolies in strategic industries such as oil, telecommunications, steel, aviation, highway transportation, banking and insurance, even though competition is eroding their franchise.[96] By contrast, the red-chip companies are largely controlled by private enterprises which registered parts of their businesses overseas (e.g., in the Virgin Islands) as listing vehicles to circumvent domestic regulatory approval requirements for overseas public listings, which apply to all H-share companies.

5.3.3   Dual listings of mainland companies and cross-border regulatory cooperation

Some Chinese enterprises have gone for public listings in both domestic and overseas markets. The majority of these firms have a dual listing in the Shanghai Stock Exchange and the Stock Exchange of Hong Kong. Notably, Hong Kong-traded H-shares are generally priced 50 to 90 percent lower than their Shanghai or Shenzhen A-share counterparts, even though each of these different shares represents the same assets in the same company.[97] This has been described by some financial analysts as a system of "one country, two valuations." Indeed, ever since the first overseas listing of Chinese companies in 1993, shares of mainland companies have traded at a sharp discount on international markets compared with the home market.

---

94. Securities and Futures Commission of Hong Kong, online < http://www.sfc.hk/sfc/doc/ TC/research/stat/b01.doc >.
95. *Ibid.*
96. "Capital Markets Are Good for You, But In Asia They will Take Time to Build," in "The Weakest Link: A Survey of Asian Finance" *The Economist*, February 6, 2003, pp. 14–16.
97. LaMoshi, *supra* note 3.

Currently, the valuation gap, which had shrunk from 90 percent in 2001 to about 40 percent in 2005, is poised to fall further with the advent of simultaneous listings of mainland companies on both mainland and Hong Kong's stock exchanges.[98] The first simultaneous "A&H" dual listing was made by ICBC in October 2006, where the valuation gap was reduced to minimal and could be seen as negligible. The CSRC, burdened with an overvalued domestic A-share market, is widely expected to push for pricing parity on future simultaneous listings.[99] Although the different valuations of the A-shares and H-shares may move closer in the future if the reform of China's stockmarket achieves meaningful results and greater liberalization brings stricter market discipline to domestic market players, for the USD 3.5 billion of foreign funds currently qualified to invest in China's A-share market under the QFII scheme, A-shares remain unattractive.[100]

As mainland enterprises have rapidly increased their presence in Hong Kong's capital markets, cross-border regulatory cooperation has become a critical issue for regulators on the mainland and in Hong Kong. The current framework for regulatory cooperation is built upon the Memorandum of Regulatory Cooperation and the Memorandum of Regulatory Cooperation Concerning Futures between the Securities and Futures Commission (SFC) in Hong Kong and the CSRC on the mainland, which were exchanged in March 2007. Under these arrangements, the SFC may request assistance from the CSRC in obtaining information in the mainland for SFC investigations, as well as exercise its investigatory powers to help the CSRC in its investigations that have a Hong Kong element.[101] Remaining challenges in cross-border regulatory cooperation primarily lie in further strengthening the effectiveness of enforcement and increasing the consistency of regulations and rules between Hong Kong and the mainland.

5.3.4 Risks associated with investing in Chinese companies

International private equity investment entities, such as large funds and investment banks, have made comfortable returns in Hong Kong-listed Chinese companies over recent years. However, this does not negate the fact that there are also risks, which could potentially be significant, associated with investing in overseas-listed mainland companies, including both state-controlled companies and private enterprises.[102]

---

98. "Chinese dual listings," *Financial Times,* January 12, 2005, p. 1. **[Is article title correct?]**
99. *Ibid.*
100. *Ibid.*
101. Securities and Futures Commission of Hong Kong, "Cross Border Enforcement Enhanced," April 2, 2007, online < http://www.sfc.hk/sfcPressRelease/EN/sfcOpenDoc Servlet?docno=07PR52 >.
102. "Capital Markets Are Good for You," *supra* note 96.

Although China's growth has been remarkable, investing in this boom economy remains a risky proposition. For instance, some international investors who had hoped to make money by buying shares in overseas-listed mainland companies have instead suffered large losses as a consequence of corporate governance failures.[103] There are three major types of risk associated with investing in China's overseas-listed companies.

The first type of risk: state intervention in firms' daily operation

The first type of risk comes from the still firm habit of the government to view SOEs, especially large ones, as quasi-government agencies rather than independent profit-making commercial entities. Accordingly, top members of SOE management are often treated as government officials in their promotion or transfer, as suggested in the recent incidents of sending the CEO of a listed oil company to a government post in Hainan province and more controversially, rotating top managers of the listed telecommunications companies among one another.

The changes of senior management in the telecommunications industry included moving China United's chairman and chief executive, Wang Jianzhou, into the top spot at the country's largest wireless operator, China Mobile. The government also shifted China Mobile's chairman, Wang Xiaochu, into the equivalent position at fixed-line operator China Telecom, while China United was assigned a new chairman, Chang Xiaobing, then a vice president of China Telecom. All three companies have publicly listed units that trade in Hong Kong and New York. In fact, the Chinese telecommunications industry had undergone personnel rotations before this reshuffling, and according to the telecommunications regulators, these shifts reportedly "have not directly resulted in noticeable, significant operational strategy or policy changes." Indeed, telecommunications regulators at the Ministry of Information Industry and executives of phone companies sometimes have even swapped jobs.[104]

This reshuffling of senior managers of China's telecommunications companies was one of the latest moves by the government to restructure the industry, which restructuring did not go through any board approval procedures at all. Such pattern of personnel decisions at large and strategic Chinese SOEs partly revealed that administrative orders often trump commercial calculations in the running of China's state monopolies. Indeed, if managers believe that their next positions will be at the head of their direct competitors, why bother trying to build a competitive company in the first place?[105] Moreover, by simply

---

103. "The Quest for Fair and Open Markets," *South China Morning Post,* July 24, 2003, p. 10.
104. Rebecca Buckman, "China Plans Job Shifts for Telecom Executives; Changes to Come Ahead of Mobile-License Awards and China Netcom's IPO," *Asian Wall Street Journal,* November 2, 2004, A.1.
105. Murc Dickie & Richard McGregor, "Chinese Business at Risk from Monopoly Mindset," *Financial Times,* December 7, 2004, p. 34.

moving telecommunications executives into different positions at competitors, the government might have missed an opportunity to bring in professional managers from the outside. In the view of some overseas investors, the management shifts showed that a company's leaders are "ultimately accountable not to investors, but to the Party." That might not be a positive message for foreign investors trying to judge the companies based on their growth prospects and profitability.[106] Needless to say, this enduring mindset of government intervention has made good corporate governance difficult to maintain, or to be established in the first place.

The second type of risk: related-party transactions at large SOEs

The second type of risk is the high likelihood of related-party transactions created by the peculiar pattern of restructuring China's large SOEs before their domestic as well as overseas listings. Over the past decade, China has been restructuring its massive SOEs and selling pieces of them to international investors, raising billions of dollars. The most common method, which has so far been applied to telecommunications companies, power producers and oil companies, is to hive off the best businesses of an inefficient state giant and then package them into a new company with stronger management to set up a listing entity, and finally sell shares of the new firm to the public. This pattern of restructuring has unavoidably led to a number of incidents of related-party transactions that could result in unsecured business dealings and risks for investors. The recent deposit controversy surrounding Hong Kong-listed China Oilfield was just a latest example of how conflicts can arise over how the listed companies conduct business with their parent companies and related parties.

To better understand the pervasiveness of related-party transactions among Chinese companies, it is useful to review the recent deposit controversy surrounding China Oilfield mentioned above. In 2004, a fight over a request from China Oilfield, the Hong Kong-listed Chinese oil services company, to deposit up to 40 percent of its 2003 revenue, about USD 148 million, with a finance company owned by its parent illustrated how China's approach to accessing global capital markets can generate corporate governance concerns among investors. Corporate governance advocates and some investors asserted that it is poor corporate governance to put so much of the firm's cash into a company controlled by its main shareholder. Because its deposits would not be secured, China Oilfield would have no recourse if the finance company were to make bad investments.

The request from China Oilfield was viewed by the firm itself— and indeed many other large Chinese companies listed overseas — as "business as usual," which indicated the widespread nature of such practice among

---

106. Buckman, *supra* note 104.

Chinese companies. For instance, in 2001, Hong Kong regulators uncovered that Guangdong Kelon Electrical Holdings, a Chinese refrigerator and air-conditioner maker, had failed to disclose a RMB 1.26 billion yuan (USD 52.2 million) loan to its parent. The company later received a warning from its auditors. Another example was that when China Oilfield went public in 2002, Hong Kong regulators permitted it to deposit up to 10 percent of its previous year's revenue at CNOOC Finance Ltd., which was controlled by its parent company. Again, in April 2004, a sister company of China Oilfield, Hong Kong-listed CNOOC Ltd., won shareholder approval to deposit as much as RMB 6.8 billion yuan, which was equal to 17 percent of its 2003 revenues, at the group's finance company.[107]

Although similar deposit or loan plans had gained shareholder approvals, investors of China Oilfield regarded this type of practice as a veiled way for the parent company to effectively borrow from its listed subsidiary on an unsecured basis. According to a prominent shareholder rights activist in Hong Kong, David Webb, it was simply "bad behavior" to finance the parent company with the listed company's funds.[108] Eventually, the deposit proposal was voted down by shareholders of China Oilfield.

The third type of risk: moral hazard of international investors

Finally, the third type of risk is the dangerous belief held by investors in government bail-outs of troubled state firms, which is very likely to cause moral hazard and distort rational judgments about firms' financial health and operational efficiency. It has become increasingly clear that with a favored position within China's economy which has only started to diminish recently, China's large SOEs, usually state monopolies in strategic sectors, have been considered compelling and relatively low-risk investments by many investors. These investors often justify putting money into state-controlled entities with questionable records of governance by pointing to the likelihood that the state would bail them out. However, this belief, or indeed moral hazard on the part of investors, started to founder in 1998, when the local government controlled Guangdong International Trust & Investment Corporation defaulted on USD 4.7 billion in debt and investors were left with huge losses.[109]

Thus, it is clear that investing in China's state-controlled companies entails potentially significant risks. Global investors are supposed to be aware of the risks, because Chinese companies are allocated risk-weightings by brokerages and fund managers to reflect their relative regulatory and political risks. The weightings build in a discount from the returns that might be expected from

---

107. Kate Linebaugh, "China Oilfield Fight Highlights Questions about Governance," *Asian Wall Street Journal*, November 2, 2004, M.1.

108. *Ibid.*

109. *Ibid.*

a stock in a similar industry in a developed country. For China, the discount is about 13–14 percent. However, even aware of the risks, many investors buy shares of these companies regardless.[110] Obviously, there is a pressing need to educate investors in international capital markets about the old principle of "buyer beware" when investing in China's companies.

5.3.5 The enormity of the CAO scandal: "China's Barings"

In December 2004, in a shock that was soon to reveal the biggest corporate scandal in Singapore's financial markets, China Aviation Oil (Singapore), a locally listed subsidiary of the monopoly oil giant, China Aviation Oil Holding Corporation (CAOHC), stunned investors by disclosing massive trading losses, worth USD 500 million, in oil future transactions. CAO filed for bankruptcy protection with a local court in Singapore. Its biggest creditors, including Japan's Sumitomo Mitsui Banking, the SK Energy of South Korea, South Africa's Standard Bank, Australia's Macquarie Bank, SG Asia, Barclays Capital, Goldman Sachs and Fortis, had all been negotiating with CAO for a restructuring plan. Some of them sued the firm for unrecovered loans.[111] Moreover, a group of local investors launched a class action against CAO and its parent, CAOHC, for failing to disclose the losses when CAOHC sold a 15 percent stake in CAO to the public in late October 2004, allegedly to fund a bail-out of its troubled subsidiary, which was widely considered a violation of rules banning insider trading. This spectacular collapse was infamously billed as "China's Barings."[112]

In this case, three things have become clear: (a) due to insider control, CAO had inadequate internal controls over its derivatives trading, since deals were supposed to be suspended if any of the company's 10 traders assumed a loss of more than USD 500,000; (b) the company, as well as its parent, failed in their obligation to make timely disclosure when beset by financial disaster, and (c) domestic regulators, including the CSRC and the SASAC, failed to monitor the company's risky financial transactions overseas.[113]

The "monopoly mindset" as a major contributor to the CAO debacle

Trading scandals are not unique to China: Britain's Barings and Japan's Sumitomo have demonstrated the potential dangers of derivatives trading to

---

110. Dickie & McGregor, *supra* note 105.
111. John Burton, "CAO Seeks $500m Debt Write-offs," *Financial Times*, January 5, 2005.
112. In 1995, Nick Leeson, a British "rogue trader," triggered the collapse of Barings Bank, a respected British bank with a history of more than 100 years, as a result of massive losses of USD 1.2 billion from failed speculation on foreign exchange transactions in Singapore's financial markets.
113. "China's Champions: Markets Have Been Too Eager for 'Red-Chip' Companies," *Financial Times*, December 3, 2004, p. 22.

corporations from any country.[114] However, few analysts doubt that CAO's woes are an important reminder of the particular problems that plague many Chinese companies listed abroad, and an indication that these problems stem in part from structural issues as much as individual failures of corporate governance. While Chinese companies that have gone overseas for listings are generally considered the best performers of the state sector, their performance often depends on the lack of liberalization and competition in the industries they operate in rather than entrepreneurial spirit or managerial skill. For the SOEs that are highly profitable, an important source of their profits is the near "risk-free" monopoly rents in home markets.[115]

While the monopoly mindset has led the Chinese government to treat state-controlled companies as quasi-government agencies, as pointed out earlier, the debacle at CAO shows that for companies with a monopoly mindset, the pressure to generate profits embodies great dangers. In this particular case, because CAO had a monopoly in market distribution of jet oil for China's domestic civil carriers, the thirst for profits, combined with the fact that the company had been seeking growth in aggressive overseas investments and oil and derivatives trading, paved the road to perdition.

According to many domestic commentators, this thirst for profits was likely driven, at least partly, by the profit-linked compensation package of CAO's CEO, Chen Jiulin, who bore the primary responsibility for the firm's reckless gambling in the oil futures market. While some may think that in most cases profit-linked managerial compensation will deter foolish speculative investments, the CAO was an exception. As a layman in future market transactions, without consulting either the board or his supervisors at the parent company, Chen turned out to have made all critical trade decisions by himself alone that eventually led the firm to collapse. It is hard to imagine that a big Western company listed on a mature capital market would hire a non-professional CEO to run its daily business. In a sense, Chen's ignorance of financial basics and the high risks associated with speculative trades in oil futures market was unparalleled: even after CAO filed for bankruptcy protection, Chen, himself also under an investigation by the local financial regulators, still claimed that if he could have another USD 500 million, he can "make a turnaround and recover all the losses incurred." This was bitterly swallowed by commentators in the domestic financial industry as "beyond madness."[116] What inspired particular cynicism was that before its dramatic fall, CAO was once praised as one of "the best governed companies" and one of "the most transparent listed companies" in Singapore,

---

114. Dickie & McGregor, *supra* note 105.
115. Dickie & McGregor, *supra* note 105.
116. Gao Yu, "Why There Was No One to Stop CAO from Going Crazy? (weishenme meiyou ren zuzhi Zhonghangyou fafeng?)," 24 *Business Watch* (*Shangwu Zhoukan*) (2004).

and Chen Jiulin was ranked among the "new economic leaders in Asia" by the World Economic Forum in 2003.[117]

Was CAO an isolated exception?

Some financial analysts are less discouraged by the potential risks in investing in China's companies demonstrated in the CAO scandal. In their opinion, CAO's collapse was purely the result of a breakdown in internal controls caused by pressure to increase profits, and is therefore similar to western corporate scandals such as Enron and WorldCom in the U.S. and Parmalat in Italy, in which executive greed and disregard for shareholder rights led powerful managers to pursue a reckless course that sent their firms into spectacular collapses. More skeptical observers, however, believe that the transformation of China's partially privatized SOEs is plagued by structural problems, typical of a country in transition from a command economy to a market economy.[118] In the wake of the CAO scandal, one should carefully assess the impact it may have on international investors' perceptions of Chinese firms in general. The question for investors impressed by China's growth story is whether CAO was an aberration caused by one or more "rogue traders," or the first of many disasters waiting to happen as the country proceeds further on its transition to a market economy and hidden structural problems caused by incomplete privatization and industrial liberalization start to emerge and ultimately explode.[119]

The likely answer does not seem encouraging. In fact, in many respects CAO was not an isolated exception, but a typical example of a Chinese state enterprise to which the government had granted a monopolistic market status: CAOHC, its state-owned parent, had a near-total monopoly in domestic supply of aviation fuel, and had made CAO its sole supplier of imports. That monopoly prompted investors to buy into CAO's 2001 IPO, which was Singapore's biggest that year. Supported by the parent, which retained a 75 percent controlling stake, CAO's mission was clear: use foreign capital to increase profits and expand operations, while keeping a strategic industry under state control.[120]

This is a familiar model of industrial restructuring of China's "strategic sectors," which has enabled the Chinese government to restructure and inject market discipline into sectors that used to be huge economic burdens, such as oil, telecommunications and power, without ceding ultimate control. The resulting mix of entrepreneurial energy and state ownership has made the listed entities of China's state giants attractive for foreign investors as they hold a belief in government bail-outs in times of difficulty.

---

117. John Burton, Mure Dickie, Francesco Guerrera & Joe Leahy, "A Collapse that Waves a 'Big Red Flag' about Business with Beijing," *Financial Times*, January 21, 2005, p. 15.
118. *Ibid.*
119. *Ibid.*
120. *Ibid.*

Regulating overseas businesses of Chinese SOEs is a particular challenge

Finally, from the perspective of Chinese regulators, the dramatic losses at CAO made clear the importance of regulating state enterprises' overseas businesses. For example, according to the State-owned Assets Supervision and Administration Commission or SASAC, which until January 2005 had been slow and weak in responding to the debacle, it would step up efforts to establish an effective supervision system to avoid another CAO scandal. While this pledge to improve offshore regulation marked the SASAC's most substantive public response to the CAO scandal, it gave no details of the regulatory system it planned to develop. Therefore, domestic critics who saw the SASAC's reaction to the scandal as representative of its failure to improve corporate governance of state companies, were not convinced by this pledge.[121] Indeed, with weak governance and corruption endemic among state ventures and government offices even at home, regulating managers stationed overseas presents a particular challenge.[122]

5.3.6 China's private enterprises listed overseas are not immune from corporate governance controversies

While state-controlled companies may carry potentially significant investment risks, their private counterparts have not done better and had recorded a series of corporate governance controversies between 2002 and 2005, which had dealt a blow to the confidence of international investors who had been previously chasing with enthusiasm the so-called "p-chips" on the Stock Exchange of Hong Kong .

Recent corporate governance controversies surrounding China's private enterprises listed overseas

The following cases are notable examples of corporate governance controversies involving Chinese private enterprises listed in Hong Kong over the past several years. These cases have drawn wide attention in Hong Kong's financial media and raised concerns to investors about the quality of corporate governance of the supposedly well-run Chinese private enterprises with an overseas public listing.

The trial of Skyworth executives

In December 2004, Skyworth, a Hong Kong-listed private enterprise and China's fourth-largest TV manufacturer by volume, insisted that business was continuing

---

121. Mure Dickie, "Beijing Promises Better Offshore Rules," *Financial Times,* January 27, 2005, p. 9.
122. *Ibid.*

as usual even as authorities in the territory, most notably the Independent Commission Against Corruption (ICAC), formally charged the company's chairman, Wong Wang-sang, and his brother Wong Pui-sing, an executive director, for allegedly misappropriating HKD 48 million (USD 6 million) in company funds. The two Mr. Wongs, who were among 15 people arrested in relation to the case, were jointly charged with conspiracy to steal.[123] The arrests were a humiliating fall from grace for a company favored by foreign fund managers and once again highlighted the risks facing investors in Hong Kong-listed mainland Chinese companies, of which the difficulty of the regulators to reach the management based in the mainland is a serious one.

In the Skyworth case, Mr. Wong Wang-sang founded the company about 15 years ago and was its largest shareholder with a 40 percent stake when the scandal erupted. The "founder's dictatorship" and disregard for investor rights have been the major reasons for corporate governance failures at China's private enterprise, and this case was merely exemplary. Another of those arrested in the Skyworth case was a former accountant who allegedly took bribes and falsified Skyworth's accounts for its Hong Kong listing in 2000.[124] In July 2006, a court in Hong Kong found the two Mr. Wongs guilty of stealing from the Skyworth and its sister companies USD 70 million in cash and stock options in conspiracy with their mother, and subsequently sentenced both to jail for six years, respectively.[125]

The investigation surrounding Skyworth was not the first incident involving potential criminal manipulation of the listing process by mainland private enterprises. Back in July 2003, the ICAC charged five people, including an accountant, with alleged conspiracy to defraud connected to the listing of Gold Wo International.[126] In addition, among Chinese companies listed in Hong Kong, companies ranging from the Hong Kong branch of Bank of China, where three senior managers were charged with embezzlement of corporate funds, to Shanghai Land, a land developer controlled by a local tycoon, Zhou Zhengyi, who has been in jail in the mainland for corporate crimes, have been at the centre of similar probes over alleged corporate governance failures in recent years.

The incidents of "auditor walk-out" at China Rare Earth

In April-May 2003, the consecutive walk-out of two auditors in five weeks highlighted the accounting controversy at China Rare Earth Holdings. KPMG quit as its auditor, 36 days after the resignation of Ernst & Young due to

---

123. Alexandra Harney & Justine Lau, "Skyworth Officials Charged with Theft of Funds," *Financial Times*, December 2, 2004, p. 26.
124. *Ibid.*
125. Toh Han Shih, "Skyworth pair found guilty of $70m theft," *South China Morning Post*, July 8, 2006.
126. Harney & Lau, *supra* note 123.

disagreement on proper accounting measures with the firm. Unfortunately, China Rare Earth's quarrels with its auditors were not a rare phenomenon in mainland China and hilighted just how difficult the relationship can be between auditors and Chinese firms steeped in a tradition of non-transparency.[127]

The jail of Euro-Asia founder

Another notable case of corporate governance controversy involved Euro-Asia Agricultural Holdings, an orchid-grower listed on the Stock Exchange of Hong Kong . In December 2002, Hong Kong police launched an investigation into the company, after documents were seized from its offices by the Commercial Crime Bureau in Hong Kong.[128] Euro-Asia had been probed by mainland regulators for allegedly overstating its revenues by 20 times in the previous four years, and was under investigation by both mainland and Hong Kong securities regulators.[129] The founder of Euro-Asia, Yang Bin, was reputedly China's second-richest man in 2002 and has since July 2003 been serving an 18-year jail sentence for illegal real estate deals at his Holland Village development in Shenyang city of Liaoning province. After the company's mainland assets were stripped by the Chinese government, the regulators and investors in Hong Kong were left with little or no recourse to the firm's business interests in the face of uncertainty.[130]

Accounting irregularities at Chaoda

Moreover, another Chinese private enterprise listed in Hong Kong, Chaoda Modern Agriculture (Holdings), tried to convince the local market of its good practice by announcing in October 2002 that it was ready to report quarterly to improve transparency and restore confidence in private mainland firms, after its auditors refused to sign off on its financial results. Chaoda's move was an attempt to distance itself from the scandal-ridden Euro-Asia. The difficulty for Chaoda was that it looked very similar to Euro-Asia: privately owned, in the agriculture business and with abnormally high profit margins and startling growth rates in revenues and profits. The suspected inflation of profit margins and growth rates by Chaoda had raised deep investors' concern over its accounting practices.[131]

As new and continuing scandals started to affect a wider scale of Hong Kong-listed mainland private enterprises, the need for better corporate governance seemed to extend across the board, rather than involving just a few isolated cases. The investigations into financial dealings of Shanghai Land and Shanghai Merchants, together with the doubt auditors had cast over the accounts of Guangdong Kelon and China Rare Earth, were prominent examples

---

127. Eric Ng, "Auditors Walk China Tightrope," *South China Morning Post,* May 6, 2003, p. 18.
128. Clifford Lo & Raymond Ma, "Police launch probe into Euro-Asia," *South China Morning Post,* October 30, 2002, p. 2.
129. *Ibid.*
130. "The Quest for Fair and Open Markets," *supra* note 103.
131. Lo & Ma, *supra* note 128.

in 2003 alone.[132] In particular, the practices that flourished at Shanghai Land and Euro-Asia, which followed a pattern of making real estate investment funded by bank loans and then diverting funds or funneling proceeds into even more leveraged businesses, could only have persisted as long as they were implemented in a corporate environment where oversight was lax and checks and balances were poor, as has been generally the case with corporate governance of most mainland companies.[133]

Reasons for increased corporate governance controversies at Chinese private enterprises

Three main reasons explain why incidents of corporate governance controversies have increased among China's private enterprises listed overseas in recent years.

The first reason is that China's private entrepreneurs have built their businesses in China's transition economy where a well defined property rights system has not been established, which has resulted in uncertainty surrounding the legitimacy of the personal wealth and business interests of some private entrepreneurs. In cases where the government decided that a private business was illegitimate and its profits were illicit, the risk of government seizures of personal and corporate property, which usually triggers a business collapse, could be very serious. The jail terms for both Yang Bin of Euro-Asia and Zhou Zhengyi of Shanghai Land, are two notable examples.

The second reason is that China's private entrepreneurs are faced with a challenge of transforming the pattern of their business practices from a "primitive" stage of wealth accumulation, whereby hard work and prudent savings had been the primary source of success and expansion, to a new stage of more advanced market practices whereby knowledge of modern business operation, commercial ethics and risk management are critical to sustained corporate growth. Given that most of the first generation of China's private entrepreneurs only had limited education and business training and their understanding of modern accounting and reporting rules in mature capital markets is inadequate, the likelihood of violation and misbehavior in corporate governance practices is significant after they enter international capital markets.

The third reason is that the pattern of "founder's dictatorship" has been common in corporate governance structures of many Chinese private enterprises, which makes effective internal controls impossible. This was the primary cause for the massive stealing of corporate funds by Wong Wang-sang of Skyworth. While in China's domestic capital markets this pattern of running private businesses is more tolerable when transition is still in progress, in more advanced overseas capital markets it may be subject to stricter scrutiny and if not mitigated may well become an important source of corporate governance failures.

---

132. "The Quest for Fair and Open Markets," *supra* note 103.
133. *Ibid.*

5.4 Legal and Regulatory Reforms to Improve China's Stockmarket and Corporate Governance of Listed Companies

Section 5.4 reviews important legal and regulatory reforms over recent years to improve China's stockmarket and corporate governance of listed companies. In this process, the CSRC has played a central role in designing and implementing reform initiatives, usually in coordination with regulatory efforts of other financial regulators, such as the China Banking Regulatory Commission, the China Insurance Regulatory Commission, the Ministry of Finance and the State Administration of Foreign Exchange.

The CSRC was established in 1992. However, significant moves to improve the effectiveness of securities regulation and capacity-building at the CSRC to enhance regulatory oversight did not happen until 2000. Since being placed in charge of the centralized supervision of China's stockmarket in 1998, the CSRC has taken a number of measures to improve corporate governance of listed companies and to crack down on bad behavior and fraud in the stockmarket.[134]

Meanwhile, until recently the role of the courts in punishing securities fraud and protecting investor rights had been largely absent in the institutional structure of China's securities regulation. Until January 2002, the courts did not accept lawsuits brought by investors for damages suffered from securities fraud and market manipulation. This situation began to change after the Supreme People's Court (SPC) issued its first judicial interpretation in this regard to assert court jurisdiction over cases involving false disclosure. Later, the SPC again released its second interpretation on private securities litigation, detailing the rules on damage calculation and the scope of compensation, which was an improvement on the first interpretation. After the release of these two important pieces of judicial interpretation, investors have increasingly brought private securities litigation to the courts. A landmark case was adjudicated in August 2004, whereby the Harbin Intermediate People's Court rendered judgment in favor of shareholders against a listed company, Daqing Lianyi, and its underwriter, Shenyin Wanguo Securities Company, for damages resulting from a false statement. This was the first private securities litigation judgment after full trial. In this case, 109 plaintiffs sued the firm and its underwriter for damages worth RMB 3.04 million, with 98 of them being awarded a total of RMB 1.87 million.[135]

Moreover, the central government had not paid adequate attention to stockmarket reform until very recently, compared with its emphasis on the urgency of China's banking reform and its tremendous input of resources into the restructuring of the "big four" state-owned commercial banks. This

---

134 Leung *et al.*, *supra* note 58, pp. 18-19.
135 Zhu Yin, "The Court Renders Judgment in the Daqing Lianyi Case: Investors Won the Fist Case of Collective Securities Litigation (Daqing Lianyi an xuanpan, shouli touzizhe gongtong susong an shengli)," *Xinhua News*, August 25, 2004, online < http://news. xinhuanet.com/stock/2004-08/25/content_1878929.htm >.

imbalance of government input only started to be mitigated after the release of a nine-point policy guideline by the State Council on February 1, 2004 to address the urgency of the development and opening up of the capital markets. This policy statement was entitled *The Nine-Point Guideline on Promoting Reform, Opening up and Steady Development of China's Capital Markets,* or the so-called *guojiutiao,* and has since become a roadmap document at a new stage of China's capital markets reform in the wake of the broader financial liberalization in 2006 under China's WTO commitments.

5.4.1 Important legal and regulatory reforms

Broadly, there are six specific areas of legal and regulatory reforms that are aimed at improving the quality of both stockmarket operation and corporate governance of listed companies.

Improving information disclosure and accounting standards

The CSRC has gradually tightened information disclosure requirements in an effort to make listed companies more transparent and to protect minority shareholder rights. In 1998, new disclosure rules and accounting standards were introduced by the CSRC to improve the transparency and financial reporting of listed companies. In addition, since 2001, listed companies have also been required to provide quarterly financial statements.

In November 2004, China's two stock exchanges published rules aimed at improving corporate disclosure, including a tight definition of related-party transactions and a requirement aimed at giving investors more information about company officers.[136] In December 2004, the CSRC again tightened reporting rules for listed companies, requiring, among other things, more information on relationships between major shareholders. The revised rules on information disclosure for annual reports started to apply to the full-year 2004 annual reports. The revised rules also seek to make shareholder ties clearer. For example, companies must disclose the party that is actually in control of the firm, which may not always be the same as the largest shareholder. In addition to previous requirements to publish the top 10 shareholders and the top 10 shareholders of tradable shares, the revised rules require companies to detail relationships that might exist among these shareholders. The revised rules also strengthen requirements on disclosure for related-party transactions, loan guarantees extended by the company and major accounting changes.[137]

---

136. Kate Linebaugh, "Holders Reject Revenue Plan by China Oilfield," *Asian Wall Street Journal,* December 1, 2004, M.1.
137. "Chinese Regulator Tightens Reporting Rules for Listed Firms," *Asian Wall Street Journal,* December 21, 2004, M.2.

Reforming share issuing mechanisms

Until 2001, the share issuing process had been governed by a quota system, which was first introduced when China's stockmarket was established in the early 1990s, to limit the number of companies to be listed and the amount of shares to be issued. Under the quota system, local governments were responsible for the primary review of the qualifications of local firms for IPOs before they submitted their decisions to the CSRC for final approval. The central feature of the quota system was that it was driven by administrative direction. For example, the number of listings that a province could have each year was determined by the central government, while the IPO prices were jointly decided by regulators and brokerage firms.[138] In 1999, the Public Offering Review Committee (PORC) under the CSRC was established as the responsible agency for the final approval of IPOs.[139]

In 2001, a registration system replaced the quota system governing the share issuing process. The registration system was aimed at liberalizing the processes of IPO pricing and the review of listing qualifications previously controlled by regulators and administrative agencies, by introducing a more market-oriented screening system whereby the role of the CSRC was expected to be less substantive in judging firms' listing qualifications. However, in practice the reviewing body, the PORC, has still played a substantial part in the IPO review process, making the purported goal of reducing administrative intervention largely unrealized.

Since February 2004, a sponsorship system has been put in place to introduce more market forces into the share issuing process, whereby a "sponsor," usually a brokerage firm, was to be responsible for supervising an IPO applicant for one year before making a listing recommendation to the CSRC. The sponsor must undertake certain responsibilities after it submits recommendation documents to the CSRC. Despite the intended goal of introducing more market forces into the listing review process, administrative intervention has not been removed, especially after new rules were released to limit the number of IPO applicants that each sponsor can supervise each year to eight, thus artificially controlling the size and capital flows of each year's new listings.

One of the main questions now is how the PORC and the sponsor system can co-exist. On the future direction of reform, some brokerage firms have suggested that the PORC must be reformed together with the sponsor system, to ensure that the sponsor system would succeed in its intended task of making the IPO review more transparent and market-driven. A more radical suggestion

---

138. Duan Haihong, "Ten Years of the Reform and Development of Stock Issuing System in China," 5 *Listed Companies* (*Shangshi Gongsi*) (2001).
139. Yu Ning, "Reform of Stock Issuing Mechanism," *Caijing English Newsletter*, December 3, 2003, online < http://www.caijing.com.cn/english/2003/1120/1120ReformStock.htm >.

is that since the sponsors eventually bear some responsibilities for issuers recommended by them, the right to approve IPO applications should also be decentralized and ultimately left to the exchanges.[140]

The latest move to reform the share issuing system was the introduction of a new IPO pricing method in 2005. The CSRC had temporarily suspended IPOs since August 30, 2004 to draft new rules on IPOs, which took effect on January 1, 2005, and which were expected to increase transparency and ensure fairness in the pricing of initial public offerings. Under the old IPO system, IPO prices were approved by the CSRC and already set by the time a prospectus was issued. Prices were often set artificially low in order to ensure a large jump on the opening day of trading, which would then be followed by a gradual fall to below the listing level. The result was that many retail investors applied for shares in the IPO and quickly sold their holdings in order to make short-term profits, thus fueling the market with a more speculative sentiment.[141] To change this situation, the new rules were aimed at bringing markets-driven pricing to IPOs.

Under the new rules, a two-step pricing process is implemented after an issuance plan receives regulatory approval. The first step is to seek initial pricing levels from at least 20 approved institutional investors, depending on the size of the IPO.[142] The second and final pricing of the IPO takes place via bids during the IPO's subscription period. In an effort to keep pricing reasonable and prevent any price manipulation, depending on the size of the IPO, approved institutional investors participating in an IPO price discovery and subscription are limited to between 20 percent to 50 percent of the placement. The rules also set a minimum three-month lock-up period for approved institutional investors receiving placement of shares from an IPO.[143]

The delisting system

On February 22, 2001, the CSRC issued a circular to clarify rules on suspending and terminating the listing status of a loss-making company. Under these rules, a company which had recorded three years of consecutive losses can apply to the relevant stock exchange for a "grace period" to restructure its business.[144] Following these rules, a Shanghai electronics company, Narcissus Electric Appliances, was delisted on April 24, 2001, in a landmark event for China's stock

---

140. *Ibid.*
141. Geoff Dyer, "Huadian Debut a Blow to China Listings Reform," *Financial Times*, February 4, 2005, p. 17.
142. Six types of institutional investors are allowed to participate in price discovery for IPOs: approved fund-management companies, brokerage firms, investment trusts, finance companies, insurance institutions and Qualified Foreign Institutional Investors (QFII).
143. J.R. Wu, "China to Change Rules for the Pricing of IPOs," *Asian Wall Street Journal*, December 13, 2004, M.2.
144. Richard McGregor, "First Chinese Company to be Delisted Today," *Financial Times*, April 24, 2001, p. 11.

exchanges, which had never lost a listing in their 11-year trading history as of that date.[145]

However, in practice it is still difficult to delist companies because both local governments and investors are unwilling to see this happen. While for the local governments, delisting a local firm would mean losing a low-cost fund-raising tool, for the investors it could result in huge losses if the companies in which they invest were to be excluded from the market.

Strengthening the protection of shareholder rights

In January 2001, drawing on the OECD Corporate Governance Principles, a *Code of Corporate Governance for Listed Companies* was jointly released by the CSRC and the State Economic and Trade Commission to ensure better corporate governance practices of listed companies. In December 2001, the CSRC released the *Guideline for the Establishment of an Independent Director System*, aimed at the reform of the board of directors of listed companies through the adoption of an independent directors system. Under this guideline, all listed companies were required to have at least two independent directors by June 30, 2002. This number must be increased to one-third of all board seats by June 30, 2003.

Since late 2004, a new round of rule-making has been underway at the CSRC to emphasize the protection of shareholder rights in the stockmarket. Most importantly, the CSRC announced sweeping regulations on December 7, 2004 that gave minority investors their strongest voice to date in corporate affairs, essentially subordinating the role of big government owners to proposing major transactions, not approving them. Under these new regulations, decisions on whether to proceed with large corporate investment projects and new fund-raising plans would depend on the majority vote of public shareholders attending annual meetings. The regulations were aimed at constraining the voting power of the government, the biggest shareholder of listed companies in China and affording small shareholders more protection against expropriation by controlling shareholders.[146] In addition, under these new rules, if profitable companies do not pay dividends, they have to explain such decisions in detail and explain how the profits will be used instead. Where a listed company fails to pay dividends for three consecutive years, it shall not be eligible for issuing new shares or convertible bonds. These requirements were expected to have a huge impact on the previous practice of many listed companies that for years have paid meager or no dividends to investors.

Apart from the proactive role of the CSRC in enacting rules to strengthen investor rights, allowing the courts to play a role in the enforcement of securities

---

145. *Ibid.*
146. James T. Areddy, "China's Smaller Investors Get Bigger Voice in Company Affairs," *Asian Wall Street Journal*, December 9, 2004, M.1.

regulation is also an important aspect of enhancing shareholder protection. In China, courts had for years refused to hear securities-related lawsuits, denying investors legal remedies for damages suffered from fraudulent securities dealings. As discussed earlier, this situation began to change in January 2002, when the Supreme People's Court issued a notice allowing such suits to be filed. This long delay in providing judicial protection to investors should not be viewed as a surprise, however, given the fact that a *Securities Law* was not promulgated until 1998, eight years after the stock exchanges were established.[147]

Meanwhile, by revising the *Company Law* and *Securities Law*, the government has begun to allow the courts to rule on private suits brought by investors compared to the previous practice where only the CSRC had been empowered to punish fraudulent behavior. The CSRC is likely to increasingly resort to the courts to prosecute wrongdoers instead of its previous practice of only invoking its own administrative sanctions.[148]

In 2005, progress was made in terms of legal reform in strengthening shareholder protection. Revisions to the *Company Law* were approved in March 2005 by the National People's Congress, China's highest legislative body, although the actual effect of legal reform remains to be seen, as implementation is much more difficult than writing nice rules into law. The revised *Company Law* includes new rules on shareholder protection and securities litigation. First, while the old law only vaguely spelled out the principle of shareholder rights protection without elaborating on enforceable procedural rules and clarifying punishment of violations, the new law, aside from reiterating the primacy of shareholder rights, mandates the representation of independent directors on the boards of listed companies and introduces the mechanisms of cumulative voting and derivative actions. In the meantime, the mandatory quorum for provisional shareholder meetings has been reduced from 25 percent to 10 percent of outstanding shareholding. The drawback is that the new law does not yet introduce a class action system, to the disappointment of some enthusiastic advocates of shareholder rights. This omission was probably deliberate, given lagging judicial reform in relation to corporate litigation, as judges are not yet ready for a likely influx of lawsuits brought to them that could be spurred by the introduction of class actions.[149]

So far it is still unclear whether a "self-enforcing" model of company law which places great faith in *ex post* corporate governance mechanisms, such as establishing judicial standards of fiduciary duty or piercing of the corporate veil, will be made genuinely effective in China's still weak legal and institutional

---

147. Yong Yan Li, *supra* note 32.
148. Green, *supra* note 1.
149. "Revising the Company Law: Re-allocating Rights Is Only a Starting Point," *Southern Daily* (*Nanfang Ribao*), March 2, 2005, online < http://www.nanfangdaily.com.cn/southnews/ spqy/200503020483.asp >.

environments. Indeed, Russia's experience in this aspect did not offer encouraging results: at the advice of Western legal scholars, a "self-enforcing" corporate law was enacted in the mid-1990s to offer investors better protection in privatized Russian firms, but only to be lamented later for lacking effectiveness in putting *ex post* mechanisms, such as shareholder litigation, into meaningful practice as there were no complementary institutions to curb managers' insider dealing.[150]

Developing an institutional investor base

China's major financial regulators, including the CSRC, China Banking Regulatory Commission and China Insurance Regulatory Commission, have been very proactive in promoting the establishment of an institutional investor base in China, and a series of supportive measures have been adopted in recent years.

To help China's insolvent brokerage firms, in November 2004 major financial regulators jointly announced that they would allow brokerages to use securities as collateral to obtain bank loans as a means to fund the ailing industry. In addition, fund managers also received a reduction of the stamp duty from 0.2 percent to 0.1 percent in January 2005. The government has also agreed to permit some commercial banks to set up fund management companies, a move designed to introduce more institutional investment to the equity markets. Moreover, securities companies are now allowed to issue bonds; investment funds have their mutual fund products approved much faster and easier than previously; insurance and pension funds have obtained wider access to stock investment, providing a fresh source of funds.

Since 2005, another round of supportive initiatives has been taken by the regulators to promote the performance of the stockmarket. On February 21st, 2005, the CSRC and the Ministry of Finance announced the establishment of an investor protection fund, which was estimated to be worth up to USD 6 billion, to compensate investors for the bankruptcy or incompetence of local brokerage firms. In addition, regulators launched a pilot program allowing commercial banks to set up mutual fund arms. In 2005, selected insurers also received the green light to invest up to USD 7 billion in shares.[151]

While the government has been very supportive of the development of an institutional investor base in China, many of its newly introduced stimuli will not bring about an active institutional investor base, without adopting fundamental solutions to the insolvency crisis of the brokerage industry. One fundamental solution to the insolvency crisis of China's brokerage industry is to introduce

---

150. See Bernard Black & Reinier Kraakman, "A Self-Enforcing Model of Corporate Law," 109 *Harvard Law Review* 1911 (1996).
151. "A Marginalized Market," *supra* note 9.

ownership reform and market-based sectoral integration, which would not only reduce state dominance and the resulting moral hazard and poor management, but would also optimize the capacity of the brokerage industry and increase its competitiveness. In this process, participation of international investment banks through establishing joint ventures with domestic brokerages would be a beneficial factor.

While the financial regulators have increased their policy support for domestic institutional investors, the continued exclusion of foreign investors has limited the amount of capital that flows into the Chinese securities markets. While foreign investors can invest in Chinese companies listed overseas, generally without restrictions, on the Chinese domestic exchanges there are two kinds of stocks available for foreign investors: (a) hard currency-denominated B-shares that are sold to foreigners — and since February 2001 also to domestic investors — but are mostly worthless,[152] and (b) yuan-denominated A-shares that are only open to domestic investors and a group of foreign investors who fall under the Qualified Foreign Institutional Investor or QFII scheme.[153] Under the QFII scheme, large institutional investors such as UBS, Citigroup and Bill Gates' charity foundation are allotted a quota by the government to invest in the A-shares and bonds. As of December 2004, 27 overseas institutions had been granted quotas worth a total of about USD 3 billion, and another 10 were pending approvals.[154]

In a move to further liberalize China's financial system, recently the government gave its approval to the "qualified domestic institutional investors" (QDIIs) to invest in overseas capital markets. The QDII scheme is expected to provide China's major institutional investors, including insurance funds, securities investment funds and the national social security fund, with an opportunity to gain investment experience in more advanced international capital markets, thus helping to cultivate a rational investment culture and strengthen the base of China's capital markets.

Reforming the split share structure

The government had in the past made attempts to reform the split structure of the stockmarket, identified with a large portion of non-tradable shares, but to little avail, because the interests of the government and public investors were so divergent on this issue that they could not reach consensus and agree on a

---

152. For some investors in the B-share market, a main reason for buying the "worthless shares" at all is their speculation that the now separate A-share and B-share markets will eventually converge, and when this finally happens they will make huge gains by selling these shares at much higher prices.

153. Jamil Anderlini, "The Stock Market a Casino for Communists," *Asia Times Online*, October 9, 2004, online < http://www.atimes.com/atimes/China/FJ09Ad05.html >.

154. *Ibid.*

mutually acceptable plan. The key obstacle to implementing a "full flotation" scheme was the controversy over pricing — while the government wanted to sell non-tradable shares at the market value at which the tradable shares traded, the investors, concerned about the prospect that their current holdings would be diluted when flows of state shares poured into the market, expected huge discounts.

It is also necessary to point out that before the establishment of the SASAC in 2004 and the subsequent reform of state assets management system it has been undertaking, which has granted local governments ownership rights to local SOEs, oppositions to the idea of "full flotation" (*quanliutong*) had also come from local governments. The reason is simple: during China's SOE reform in the pre-SASAC periods, the central government had only granted local governments the right to manage daily operations of local SOEs, with the ownership rights still held by the central government, which means that under such circumstances the local governments would not receive any financial gains from selling state shares. For some localities, both the financing of their fiscal expenditures and tax revenues largely come from local SOEs. Therefore, adopting the "full flotation" scheme in pre-SASAC periods meant virtually taking away an important source of income from the local governments.

Since the summer of 2001, the government has attempted to make the non-tradable shares tradable. For the state shares, the favored option was to sell a portion of them to investors in the secondary market and use the proceeds to balance the account of China's social security fund, which has been in poor financial condition because of a huge deficit in unfunded pension liabilities. For the legal-person shares, the favored option was to put them up at auctions in an already existing, though informal, "C-share" market where negotiated transfers of legal-person shares had been underway for some time. In fact, although the non-tradable shares had not been openly sold to investors in the secondary market at discount, over-the-counter (OTC) transfers to private and foreign buyers had flourished over recent years, usually with rather opaque procedures whereby both the transfer prices and the identity of buyers were not disclosed to the public, thus leading to irregular MBO transactions which grossly benefit management. In June 2001, a plan called "reducing the state shareholding in the listed companies" was implemented to sell a portion of outstanding state shares to investors, but was aborted a year later due to strong negative market reactions as investors' discontent with "state exploitation" mounted.

The latest move in reforming the split share structure was a pilot "full flotation" scheme that was adopted with a limited number of listed companies which had a smaller size of state shareholding. In February 2005, shares in Shanghai Automotive, a carmaker, Handan, Wudan and Angang (all steelmakers), and Yangzi and Qilu (in petrochemicals) rose on the expectation that they would be first to be fully privatised. However, for this pilot scheme to go ahead, the prerequisite conditions required favorable market conditions and restored investor confidence. These, understandably, entailed some difficult tasks in the short run.

To address the problem of unfavorable market condition at that time, the government had taken some moves. For example, in order to revive the then declining market which discouraged good quality issuers from listing on the domestic exchanges, the government was trying to persuade some well performing firms to "stay home" and thus gradually dilute the market share of poorly governed companies. For example, in March 2005, the Bank of Communications (BoCom), China's fifth largest lender, was reportedly planning to split its IPO between Hong Kong and Shanghai after the government approached it with the suggestion of "staying home." [155]

5.4.2   Assessing the effects of reforms

The limited results of reforms

If the quality of legal and regulatory reforms was measured by the volume of newly enacted regulations, China would be a good role model. In recent years, its financial regulators have released rules and regulations to promote market disciplines and good corporate governance almost weekly. In term of enforcement and implementation, however, there is still a large gap between intended goals and actual consequences. Despite the vigor and intensity of rule making, meaningful results of reform measures have been limited, as spectacular corporate governance failures in both domestic and overseas capital markets have been reported with serious negative repercussions for investor confidence.

Although China's regulators recognize that systematic corporate misconduct undermines economic development and could deter the foreign capital on which it depends, to effectively address such a fundamental problem takes much more regulatory input and political determination. In this respect, the government has been remarkably cautious, as solutions to the problem of the split share structure had been delayed until recently and market forces have not been introduced into the share issuing system as adequately as they should be.

Progress in reforming China's stockmarket and corporate governance of listed companies has undoubtedly been made, albeit from a very low level. The outlines of a clearer regulatory and legal framework are emerging, corporate boards are being established and some companies have begun to take corporate governance seriously in the face of a delisting threat. Therefore, some corporate governance experts argue that judged by the opaque cronyism and weak corporate accountability prevalent in much of Asia, China does not look quite

---

155. "A Marginalized Market," *supra* note 9.

so bad. Yet even optimists expect that the curbing of rampant abuses will take a decade or more, and that the path ahead is paved with obstacles, such as the still very limited role of the courts in protecting shareholder rights and the efforts of some entrenched interests in the stockmarket to delay urgently needed reforms.[156]

Indeed, there is much more challenging work to be done, primarily with regard to making the non-tradable shares tradable and replacing the political logic of the stockmarket with an economic agenda. One worrying sign is that under a weak market condition, even presumably stimulating measures would not bring about expected benefits. For example, all of the reforms in 2004 to implement the *Nine-Point Guideline* (*guojiutiao*) were supposed to be positive news that should have made the stockmarket turn around. However, apart from short-lived rebounds, the market gave a cold reaction to the stimuli and relentlessly headed downwards. As of February 2005, the market still had not recovered from its five-year low share price performance.[157]

Why limited results?

There are three main reasons for the limited results of reform. The first reason is the lack of determination on the part of the government to address some fundamental problems of the stockmarket in a timely fashion. Although the government has been making efforts to strengthen stockmarket reform under both internal and external pressures, especially after China's accession to the WTO which required much greater liberalization of China's domestic financial markets from 2006, it had missed some opportunities to tackle the fundamental structural problem of the split share structure in a timely fashion.

In the meantime, one important reason why corporate governance reform of listed companies has had limited effects is that the government has insisted on retaining state ownership and control of partially privatized SOEs. This has made modern corporate governance mechanisms difficult to work, because, among other things, the conflicts of interest between the state controlling shareholder and minority shareholders are hard to mitigate. Besides, even though advanced corporate governance mechanisms, such as the independent director system, are written into legal and regulatory documents, implementation and enforcement are usually ineffective.

The second reason is related to the pursuit of divergent interests by different government agencies in the process of reform, which has prevented some reform measures, which would require collaboration between different government agencies, from being implemented effectively. For example, in the process of designing the QDII scheme, while the State Administration of Foreign Exchange has been an active promoter, out of concerns about pressure on

---

156. de Jonquieres, *supra* note 61.
157. Asia Pulse/XIC, *supra* note 44.

yuan reevaluation, the QDII scheme had been delayed because of fears by the CSRC that allowing Chinese institutions to invest in overseas stocks will remove even more liquidity from the home market and further depress share prices. Another example is found in the differing opinions among the central bank, the Minsitry of Finance, and the CSRC about a workable solution to the insolvency crisis of the brokerage firms, because this issue raised a controversy over which government agency should be paying for the bail-out.[158]

The third reason is the problematic sequencing of certain reform initiatives. For example, although some decision makers believed that introducing the new IPO pricing method was an essential step to establishing a market-driven share issuing system, its immediate effect was contrary to their expectation. One reason was that some institutional investors conspired to deliberately offer low prices in the price-bidding process, thus causing a perverse impact on price movements in the secondary market. As a result, the old pattern of share price volatility has not been mitigated after the new IPO pricing method was introduced.

According to many financial analysts, until the current administrative control over share issuing process is dismantled, merely introducing a new pricing method may not only be ineffective, but could even worsen the current situation.[159] When some important decisions relating to IPOs are still determined by the government, such as how many firms should launch IPOs each year, at what time they should launch IPOs, and how much money these firms should raise from the stockmarket, it is impossible that market-driven mechanisms and institutions could work properly in China. Accordingly, in terms of proper sequencing of reform, removing administrative control of the share issuing system and reducing excessive government intervention in the daily workings of the stockmarket should be more fundamental and urgent tasks than providing piecemeal stimuli.

5.4.3   Regulatory corruption at the CSRC

In the context of developing a strategy for future reform, it is necessary to review the important issue of regulatory corruption at the CSRC, which is primarily a result of its excessive intervention in the market — such as its role in the IPO review process — and the delay in reducing it. This has cost the

---

158. Mo Fei, "The Stockmarket Slumped to 1200 Points at the Anniversary of the 'Nine-Point Guideline' (shengshi fanrong xia de 1200 dian: 'guojiutiao' zhounian ji)," *21ˢᵗ Century Business Herald* (*21 Shiji Jingji Baodao*), January 31, 2005, online < http://www.nanfangdaily.com.cn/jj/20050131/cj/200501310035.asp >.

159. Guo Ba & Wang Chenbo, "Why the Newly Adopted IPO Pricing Method Not Only Unable to Bail Out the Market, But Also Making the Market Down Further? (xingu xunjia: jiushi yuanhe you wushi)," 216 *China Newsweek*, February 7, 2005, online < http://www.chinanewsweek.com.cn/2005-02-23/1/5238.html >.

CSRC investor confidence it has actively sought, and diminished the credibility of regulatory oversight. According to an index of financial corruption in 2003 in China compiled by two Chinese economists, the securities industry was assigned a staggering figure of 7.26 on a 1 to 10 scale (the higher the number, the more severe the corruption) and was described as "the most severe" among China's financial sectors.[160] The recent "Wang Xiaoshi case" was only the latest manifestation of regulatory corruption at the CSRC.

Wang Xiaoshi, a deputy division director in the CSRC's Department of Public Offering, was arrested in November 2004 on corruption charges, including taking bribes from a businessman to facilitate the IPO application review of a favored company. This case had led to a more comprehensive probe into stockmarket listing approvals.[161] Financial analysts pointed out that the arrest of Wang showed that there were still problems with the approval procedures for public offerings and new share issues, despite the CSRC's efforts to promote regulatory transparency and accountability. In 2003, the CSRC changed its procedures for IPO review by posting on its website the names of listing applicants and the names of the members appointed to the listing committee (i.e., the Public Offering Review Committee, or PORC), who are responsible for reviewing and approving the IPO applications. Until then, the names of the applicants and PORC members had remained secret, which led to allegations that many listing candidates paid huge bribes to find out whether they were short-listed or to get the names of PORC members appointed to review a particular case. Despite the 2003 reform, financial analysts believed that it was still an open secret that listing candidates and investment banks gave massive payments to public relations firms to lobby the PORC members.[162]

Based on the above assessments, proper sequencing seems to be a more critical determinant of the progress and effect of China's stockmarket reform than writing good rules that are in practice not well implemented. Specifically, removing the political logic and the resulting excessive intervention by the regulators in the workings of the market, as well as timely resolution to the problem of non-tradable shares, should be priority tasks on the reform agenda at the next stage.

5.4.4. **The prospects of future reforms**

At the next stage, the reform of China's stockmarket must put more emphasis on a strategy and approach centered on proper sequencing. Specifically, it is

---

160. Xie Ping & Lu Lei, "A Study on Financial Corruption (jinrong fubai qiujie)," *Caijing*, January 10, 2005, online < http://www.caijing.com.cn/coverstory/2005-01-10/2019.shtml >.

161. "Securities Official Held for Allegedly Taking Bribes," *South China Morning Post*, November 17, 2004, p. 6.

162. *Ibid.*

necessary to draw on the experience of securities markets building in other transition and developing economies under legal and institutional constraints. The following discussion attempts to introduce some important lessons from international experience as to what institutions are needed for a strong securities market and how to build these institutions.

The core institutions for a strong securities market: "necessary" *versus* "nice to have"

Scholars have studied the experience of transition economies in building functioning securities markets after privatization. They have come to realize that various corporate governance failures during and after privatization have much to do with the lack of institutions that control self-dealing and asset stripping. One of these missing institutions is strong securities markets that can discipline corporate behavior and afford investors effective protection. Therefore, establishing the legal and institutional preconditions for strong securities markets is regarded as critical to achieving a successful transition. Among the core institutions suggested by scholars, the most needed are those that address information asymmetry and self-dealing.[163]

For example, Bernard Black has suggested the following core institutions that control information asymmetry and self-dealing: (a) effective regulators, prosecutors and courts, (b) financial disclosure and procedural protection for investors, (c) reputational intermediaries, such as sophisticated accounting firms, investment banks, securities lawyers and stock exchanges, (d) company and insider liability, including criminal liability, (e) legal and regulatory rules that control insider trading, (f) rules ensuring market transparency and banning manipulation of trading prices, and (g) cultural and informational institutions that can uncover and criticize misleading disclosure or fraudulent transactions, such as an active financial press and securities analysis profession.[164]

Notably, Black makes a clear distinction between core institutions that are "necessary" and those that are "merely nice to have," particularly for countries at their early stage of capital markets development with limited institutional resources, such as transition economies.[165] While choosing not to offer a definitive and universal calcification because of the complex interrelationships among institutions (i.e., complements in some respects and substitutes in others), he suggests that a practical approach would be to evaluate the importance of each institution, both on its own and as part of an overall economic system. For instance, while a ban on insider trading is considered a

---

163. Bernard Black, "The Core Institutions that Support Strong Securities Markets," 55 *Bus. Law.* 1565 (2000); Bernard S. Black, "The Legal and Institutional Preconditions for Strong Securities Markets," 48 *UCLA L. Rev.* 781 (2001).
164. Black 2001, *ibid.*, pp. 789–814.
165. Black 2001, *ibid.*, p. 803.

core institution, it is not absolutely critical. By comparison, because legal and regulatory enforcement is critical, honest courts and regulators, without which a strong securities market cannot exist, are critical.[166]

The issue of sequencing

As to which steps a developing country should take first — reforming the legal system or building supporting market institutions — to strengthen its securities markets, a practical answer is that this is a futile question because a central characteristic of these institutions is that they interrelate and develop together and reinforce each other.[167] However, for transition economies, there does exist an issue of "sequence," whereby caution is needed with respect to legal reform and transplantation: corporate governance reform in these economies should be much more basic and less "advanced." In other words, transition economies need "honest judges and regulators, good disclosure rules, and the beginnings of a culture of honesty," before it makes sense to worry about independent directors.[168] This emphasis on sequencing is particularly relevant for the ongoing corporate governance reforms in China, where calls for adding independent directors to corporate boards are very strong at present. Given the current underdevelopment of both institutional environment and human capital in China, the applicability of this relatively "advanced" practice may need reconsideration.

Based on the current progress of legal and regulatory reforms, a primary assessment of the prospects of China's stockmarket is that deeper and more fundamental reforms must accelerate as China's economic transition enters a critical new stage, whereby not only is the SOE reform expanded to a far broader scale of privatization, but much greater financial liberalization under China's WTO commitments is also imminent. In terms of the sequencing of stockmarket reform, an urgent task in the immediate term is to mitigate and eventually solve the deep-rooted structural problem of share fragmentation that had severely dampened investor confidence. If this particular task was further delayed, the "marginalization" of China's stockmarket in the country's economic structure could very likely become a reality.[169] In the meantime, significantly reducing the state ownership and control of Chinese listed companies through further or full privatization to change their ownership structure is a key determinant of real improvements of corporate governance.

According to Stephen Green, the author of a recent book on China's stockmarket,[170] the best scenario for solving the problem of non-tradable shares would probably be if the government could just carry on privatizing these

---

166. Black 2001, *ibid.*
167. Black 2000, *supra* note 163, pp. 1606–1607.
168. *Ibid.*, p. 1607.
169. "A Marginalized Market," *supra* note 9.
170. Green, *supra* note 1.

companies in a slow and steady way. According to him, afte ten years, when these companies are private and better run, selling the non-tradable shares in the open market would be much easier.[171] However, although ideally this forward looking and less radical approach would avoid a shock that would follow a sudden introduction of all non-tradable shares to the stockmarket, the immediate situation is that China needs a healthy capital market right now in the wake of accelerated SOE and financial reforms. One critical reason for this urgency is the government's plan to clean up the NPL-laden banking sector which centers on listing three of the "big four" state-owned commercial banks, the Industrial and Commercial Bank of China (ICBC), Bank of China (BoC) and China Construction Bank (CCB), on domestic and overseas stock exchanges. Therefore, the problem of the non-tradable state and legal-person shares must be dealt with as an urgent priority if there was to be enough capital available in the future when investor confidence can sustain to fund such large and important listings.[172]

5.5 **Summary**

Chapter 5 offers a comprehensive review of the interaction between capital markets, both domestic and overseas, and corporate governance of China's listed companies during transition. Many issues discussed in Chapter 5 are interrelated and if understood in isolation would generate misperception of mutually dependent or highly associated reforms. The primary finding of Chapter 5 is that while there exists a dynamic interaction between the reform of the institutional structure of China's stockmarket and the reform of corporate governance practices of the listed companies, legal and institutional reforms aimed at improving both have so far only produced limited results, which partly explains the failure of the stockmarket to serve as an efficient resource allocator in China's economic structure and the poor quality of corporate governance of most listed companies plaguing the stockmarket.

Over the past two decades or so, China's biggest achievement in developing its capital markets is that under a gradualism strategy, China's stockmarket has gradually obtained a legitimate status as a necessary economic institution for the country to build a market economy, having been subject to controversies during the early years of reform when the ideological debate over "socialism *versus* capitalism" was not solved and private ownership was a marginal factor in the economic landscape. However, this legitimacy has come at a high price — the fragmentation of the market, which has brought a huge negative impact on its operational quality. The artificial creation of a split share structure, marked

---

171. Anderlini, *supra* note 153.
172. *Ibid.*

by the division of tradable and non-tradable shares, was a compromise with the initial institutional environment where safeguarding state ownership was a major imperative. In order to come into being under such condition, the stockmarket had to install the split share structure to show that it indeed had the function of "preserving state ownership and preventing the eroding of state assets," and was thus compatible with a "socialist market economy." The split share structure has been the fundamental cause of major problems in the stockmarket, including corporate governance failures of listed companies caused by the "sole controlling shareholder dictatorship."

Looking forward, initiating deeper and more fundamental reform to solve this structural problem is both necessary and urgent, as China's transition to a market economy enters a new stage. At this stage, China faces increased internal and external pressures to accelerate structural reforms of its SOEs and financial sectors. These reforms are interrelated and need to proceed simultaneously to generate synergies. The following discussion attempts to provide some thoughts about the strategy and prospects of future reforms.

5.5.1   Overseas listing ("piggy-backing") is not a full substitute for good legal, financial and corporate governance institutions at home

Since the early 1990s, China's companies have increasingly gone overseas to raise capital. Of the overseas capital markets, Hong Kong has played a critical role in providing a channel of fund-raising to finance Chinese enterprises, including large state-controlled entities and local firms transformed from formerly government or collectively-owned enterprises, thus facilitating their ownership restructuring. Especially for those private enterprises hoping to remove their "red hats," Hong Kong's capital markets provide them with a platform to implement full privatization schemes. According to some economists, this institutional function of Hong Kong in helping with China's transition stems partly from the British colonial legacy of the rule of law and the territory's rich human and regulatory resources in managing financial transactions. Another important reason for the preference of China's companies for Hong Kong's capital markets is the slowness of legal and institutional reforms in China to protect and finance private businesses, which has propelled these firms to access both capital and good institutions in Hong Kong.[173] From a positive perspective, the Chinese government has been supportive of this "going out" trend, which enabled some entrepreneurs to escape an unfavorable system and insufficient capital in the home market.

---

173. Yasheng Huang, "China's Big Hope Is Not Hong Kong," *Financial Times*, January 14, 2005, p. 13.

Therefore, borrowing good legal and financial institutions in overseas capital markets through firms' "piggy-backing" has been an important factor in explaining China's economic success in the past. However, while during the early stage of reform this strategy worked reasonably well, it cannot become a full substitute for building good legal, financial, and corporate governance institutions at home when China's transition has gradually moved to a more advanced stage and its participation in the world economy has become increasingly active. As China has gradually become an important contributor to the growth of the world economy over recent years and the presence of Chinese companies in the world market has expanded, the underdevelopment of its domestic institutions may generate a negative "spill-over" effect across borders. For example, while "exporting democracy" seems to have become a Western political agenda these days, China is likely to be seen as entering into an infamous business of "exporting corruption" through serious corporate governance failures of its firms listed overseas. The CAO debacle was just a warning.

Accordingly, instead of continuing reliance on borrowing good institutions from abroad, it is now time for China to build good legal, financial and corporate governance institutions at home. This will not only help China's own transition, but will also reduce the possibility of negative impacts of poorly governed Chinese companies on overseas markets.

5.5.2 The necessity and urgency of fundamental structural reform of the stockmarket in the wake of accelerated reforms of SOEs and the banking sector

At the new stage of reform, China's SOE sector has been experiencing a process of expanded privatization under the "grasping the large, releasing the small" strategy. In the meantime, the banking sector has also started sweeping structural reforms to transform the "big four" state banks into modern commercial lenders. In order to facilitate these reforms, or make them much easier, the stockmarket needs to accelerate its own structural reform, both to provide a functioning platform for the implementation of ownership restructuring of SOEs, and to relieve the banks of heavy financing burdens. Moreover, since domestic listings are part of the banking reform strategy, a well functioning stockmarket is necessary.

5.5.3 Proper sequencing is required for the reforms of the stockmarket and corporate governance of listed companies

How to design proper sequencing is a critical concern in the process of reforming China's stockmarket and corporate governance of listed companies.

Generally speaking, there are competing priorities on the reform agenda of the government, all of which seem necessary. These priorities include the following:

(a) solving the insolvency crisis of the brokerage industry and optimizing its operational capacity through sectoral restructuring;

(b) increasing regulatory oversight to discover and punish fraud and violations committed by corporate insiders, controlling shareholders and managers of financial intermediaries;

(c) reforming the share issuing system to introduce more market forces, fairness, and transparency;

(d) combating regulatory corruption at major securities regulators, especially at the CSRC;

(e) developing an institutional investor base with a rational and value-based investment culture;

(f) providing investors with stronger protection both by giving shareholders a stronger voice in corporate decision-making process and by instituting a securities litigation system;

(g) abolishing the split share structure to generate higher market liquidity and mitigate corporate governance failures caused by the "sole controlling shareholder dictatorship"; and

(h) further liberalizing the capital markets and allowing greater participation of international players.

This long list of priorities indicates not only that there are indeed many important issues to be addressed in the process of financial development for a country that has only experienced stockmarket for less than two decades from a very low starting point, but it also implies that future reforms will be extremely challenging and much more difficult than at the early stage, primarily because accumulated problems and institutional inefficiencies have all emerged at the new stage and may reinforce each other. Although these identified tasks all need to be addressed at some point, as both the economic and political resources of the government are limited, selecting the most urgent tasks with which to proceed first is necessary.

There are two basic assessments of what should be done first. First, at the current stage of transition, building basic-level institutions should precede introducing more advanced institutions, as indicated in the discussion of the role of independent directors in the corporate governance of listed companies. In that case, delisting and punishing errant corporate insiders, including the imposition of criminal liability, may be more effective than counting on independent directors to deter wrongdoing. Second, because the political logic of the stockmarket is the source of its various deviations from expected functions, most importantly allocating capital efficiently and disciplining firms through good corporate governance practices, replacing the political logic with an economic rationale should be the guiding principle in designing the sequencing of reform.

5.5.4 **The proposed sequencing of future reforms**

Based on the above assessments, a reasonable order of reform measures at the next stage can be contemplated.

The essential first step is to remove the split share structure and make nontradable shares tradable. The difficulty is to design a selling plan that could be accepted by both the government and the public investors. Some Chinese economists have suggested that the government should compensate investors for their losses, because minority shareholders bought their shares at artificially inflated prices under government-driven share issuing and pricing systems which implicitly mandated a fixed high P/E ratio. While this proposition is not without reason, the government should be cautious in "compensating" investors as it could generate moral hazard. If the government chooses to compensate public investors, it should point out that the compensation is the "last supper," and that the government will not assume any future compensation responsibilities if investors incur losses again.

In the meantime, another urgent task is reducing government intervention in the day-to-day workings of the stockmarket and making the CSRC independent of the government and free from conflicting responsibilities. This will essentially strengthen the regulatory capacity of the CSRC and make it easier for the CSRC to punish violations, thereby creating a favorable external environment for corporate governance reform of listed companies.

The second step is to solve the debt crisis of the brokerage industry and to restructure it on a market-basis through ownership reform and sectoral integration, which would avoid a systemic crisis of the stockmarket as the brokerage firms are the most important financial intermediaries and also a component of the institutional investor base in China's stockmarket.

The next step is to deepen legal and regulatory reforms aimed at improving information disclosure and corporate transparency. Meanwhile, implementing newly enacted rules on the protection of shareholder rights, such as those spelled out in the recently revised *Company Law* with regard to shareholder voting rights and derivative actions, is also critical to improving corporate governance at the next stage. Accordingly, the role of courts in hearing securities-related cases should be enhanced.

The fourth step is to expand privatization to a wider scale to change the overwhelming shareholding structure of the listed companies, identified with the "sole controlling shareholder dictatorship." More efficient ownership structure with less concentrated shareholdings will redress the problems of "insider control" and expropriation of corporate funds and resources by both managers and controlling shareholders.

After the preceding reform measures have achieved meaningful results, further liberalization of the stockmarket should follow. Although opening up the stockmarket to international players is important and necessary, it must proceed with great caution and prudence. On the one hand, greater financial liberalization in the stockmarket will introduce higher standards of corporate governance and market ethics; the experience and expertise of international fund managers and investment bankers will be beneficial for the knowledge and skill upgrading of domestic financial institutions. On the other hand, because structural reforms in the SOE, banking, and securities sectors are complementary, at a time when the general level of liberalization and marketization in the entire financial system is still advancing gradually, rushed liberalization of the stockmarket could cause a systemic crisis. Specifically, because both interest rate and currency rate systems in China have been lagging in market-oriented reform, a sudden flux of capital flow into the stockmarket could be disruptive as it is possible that international capital with an appetite for betting on the re-evaluation of yuan will always have the incentive to make speculative transactions, as the 1997-98 Asian financial crisis revealed. As the pressure for fully liberalizing China's capital markets and banking sector under its WTO commitments intensifies, preparing domestic financial institutions for greater competition from overseas and accelerating financial reforms to bring more market forces into the banking and securities sectors must be pushed forward promptly by the government without protracted delay.

6

Corporate Governance Reform of China's Banking System

Chapter 6 examines corporate governance reform of China's state-owned commercial banks (the "big four") in the context of globalization and China's transition to a market economy.[1] Specifically, the critical issues of NPL (non-performing loan) disposal and the preparations of the "big four" for overseas listings are under close investigation.

As a special type of SOE (i.e., state-owned financial enterprise), the reform of the "big four" is by nature aimed at solving the same problem as China's SOE reform has targeted: state ownership and its costs. There exists strong complementarity between China's SOE and banking reforms, primarily because the "big four" are the principal lenders to SOEs while SOEs are the main contributor to the NPL problem in the banking sector. Accordingly, the success or failure of the "big four" in the wake of a new round of reforms in China's banking sector since late 2003, including foreign exchange reserve injections, shareholding restructuring and corporate governance reform, will ultimately affect the results of China's SOE reform. In addition, China's banking reform also has a significant impact on the country's buoyant private enterprises. Despite their remarkable performance over the last three decades, China's private enterprises have not yet gained equal access to state bank credit as their state counterparts, thus suffering from widespread capital starvation that has hindered their development.

---

1. As pointed out earlier, the "big four" banks are Industrial and Commercial Bank of China (ICBC), China Construction Bank (CCB), Bank of China (BoC) and Agricultural Bank of China (ABC).

The importance of China's banking reform for the country's growth prospects in the era of globalization and transition cannot be understated. Specifically, if China's banks cannot eventually operate on a commercial basis and become independent of government intervention in their lending decisions, even a successfully implemented privatization scheme will not bring global competitiveness to Chinese enterprises. Examples of politically-directed loans to private firms as beneficiaries of government favoritism abound when one looks to Japan, South Korea and Latin America where bank crises resulting from government intervention have not been an uncommon phenomenon. In this regard, ownership reform alone is not a sufficient condition for China to transform its SOEs into modern enterprises that can perform and compete in the global economy. Replacing the soft budget constraints on SOEs with hard budget constraints is also necessary, and this cannot be achieved without a successful transformation of the "big four" from state-dictated credit allocators to modern commercial lenders.

Given these broad implications, Chapter 6 argues that as China is increasingly integrating itself with the global economy, its banking reform must proceed swiftly and decisively to address some of the most difficult and politically challenging tasks, such as considerably reducing state ownership and introducing foreign and private capital in the banking sector. As China's SOEs are currently implementing an accelerated privatization scheme on a much wider scale under the "grasping the large, releasing the small" (*zhuada fangxiao*) policy, and the stockmarket has also come to a turning point of reform by tackling the problem of a split share structure, corporate governance reform of the banking system carries great weight for the health and stability of China's overall economic structure. In terms of effective reform strategies, shareholding restructuring and overseas listings would provide China's state banks with improved governance mechanisms and incentive structures, as well as international management skills and much stricter commercial discipline.

Although only a start, the reform measures that have recently been implemented in China's banking sector, as Chapter 6 reviews, are positive signs of the government's determination to fix the country's vunerable financial system. This encouraging trend must be sustained. It has also become clear that any progress in China's banking reform will have profound implications for the privatization of SOEs as well as the stabilization and development of the stockmarket. As has been pointed out by concerned observers, funds irregularly diverted from the banks to the stockmarket for lucrative returns are likely to pose a systemic risk for China's entire financial sector. Therefore, the structural reforms of the banks, SOEs and the stockmarket should proceed simultaneously to gain synergies and complementary support from one another. Failing that, it will be impossible for China to successfully complete its transition to a market economy.

6.1 The NPL Problem and the Urgency of China's Banking Reform

China's "big four" state banks have dominated the country's credit allocation system. Having been under control by the state to channel funds to SOEs for years, they were unable to price loans and allocate capital efficiently. As a result, they were stranded in a minefield of bad loans before a new round of banking reform initiated in 2003. Given the government's plan to sell off minority stakes in the "big four" to international investors through their overseas listings, the task of fixing the NPL problem is formidable: according to an estimate by UBS, to bring these banks into a "saleable" condition, the minimum amount of government NPL carve-out could reach RMB 2.4 trillion, or 21 percent of GDP.[2]

6.1.1 The severity of the NPL problem

Compared to the small capitalization of China's stockmarket, the banking system collects an overwhelming portion of China's domestic savings, which is equivalent to nearly 40 percent of GDP. At present, nearly 90 percent of household savings are held in deposits with state-owned banks, partly because of the lack of alternatives.[3] Unfortunately, the banks misallocate these funds on an even grander scale than China's stockmarket, whose dysfunction and inefficiency in disciplining listed companies and rewarding good corporate governance are widely recognized by both domestic and international investors.

The "big four" in combination account for the lion's share of the NPLs in the entire banking sector, which at some point reached as high as USD 400 billion. The poor operational quality of the "big four" and their discrimination against private enterprises are widely known. For example, the "big four" direct 80 percent of their lending to generally unprofitable SOEs. The purpose is to prevent unemployment and the loss of welfare benefits to former and current SOE employees. By comparison, the vibrant private sector, which has been the main driving force of China's economy and created around 40 million new jobs during the period of 1998-2003 alone, is largely left to seek self-financing. In order to achieve growth and expansion, most of China's private enterprises rely on retained earnings, foreign capital, or informal sources of expensive credit.[4]

---

2. Jonathan Anderson, "How to Fix China's Banking System?" *Caijing English Newsletter*, November 5, 2003, online < http://www.caijing.com.cn/english/2003/1105/1105how%20to%20fix.htm >.

3. Deepak Lal, "How Foreign Reserves Could Make China yet Stronger," *Financial Times*, December 29, 2004, p. 11.

4. "Casino Capital," in "The Weakest Link: A Survey of Asian Finance," *The Economist*, February 6, 2003, pp. 10-12.

6.1.2 **The causes of NPLs**

According to empirical studies by Chinese economists and working reports of China's central bank, the causes of NPL creation are multiple and not all of them are attributable to the state's intervention. In general, both "the ownership effect" and "the size effect" have an impact on NPL generation at the "big four." The "ownership effect" usually leads to state intervention in banks' lending decisions and for that matter the accumulation of policy loans. The "size effect," on the other hand, implies that the "big four" are indeed too big[5] to manage their business efficiently when the command chains are multiple under their five-layer organizational structure, whereby it is difficult for orders from the headquarters to reach the ground level of local branches and be implemented precisely. Understandably, the agency problem caused by information asymmetry between the state owner and bank managers is particularly severe at the "big four," which makes measuring performance difficult.[6]

The governor of the central bank, Zhou Xiaochuan, once provided some reliable statistics on the causes of China's NPLs. According to his work report released in May 2004, the causes of NPLs can be roughly divided into the following five categories:[7]

(a) direct administrative orders and intervention at various levels of Chinese government, primarily the local governments, were responsible for 30 percent of NPLs;

(b) another 30 percent was caused by banks' routine lending practice of supporting SOEs;

(c) local legal and administrative environments explained a portion of 10 percent;

(d) another 10 percent was a result of the adjustment of China's industrial structure organized by the central government during the country's transition, and

(e) the remaining 20 percent can be attributed to banks' own mismanagement and business losses.

Interestingly, in another study a senior Chinese banking regulator revealed that "poor local credit environments" were the primary variable of NPLs,

---

5. Take the example of ICBC, China's largest lender: in 2003, it reported around 100 million depositors and 24,000 branches, plus USD 638 billion in assets, or 19 percent of the Chinese banking system total. See "China's Biggest Lender Is Ripe For December Recapitalization," *Asian Wall Street Journal*, December 23, 2004, M.1.

6. Ye Weiqiang, "Professor Yi Gang on the Breakthrough in the Thoughts about China's Banking Reform Strategy (yinhang gaige, silu poti: Yi Gang jiaoshou zhuanjia jianjie)," *Caijing*, November 20, 2002.

7. Zhou Yang, "The 'Cult' of Banks' Shareholding Reform (yinhang gugai mixin)," 70 *The Economics Monthly (Jingji Yuekan)*, October 2004, online < http://www.jingji.com.cn/show.aspx?id=681 >.

which accounted for almost 70 percent of NPL creation, while government ownership and mismanagement of bank officials can only explain the remaining 30 percent.[8] This in turn raises the question of what has caused the poor local credit environments, and the answer relates to the role of local governments in promoting regional economies under existing performance evaluation system for government officials. The chief problem lies in the central government's over-emphasis on "GDP growth" indicators with regard to measuring, and subsequently rewarding, the performance of local government officials. This sheer preference for the single dimension of GDP growth occurs at the expense of sacrificing other important yardsticks, such as protecting the property rights of local enterprises and establishing a healthy local credit environment. It is telling that the fastest growing local economy in China, the Guangdong province, is also the most affected "disaster area" for financial failures. Almost all of the recent high profile bank scandals happened in Guangdong and the province's average NPL ratio is one of the highest among China's localities.[9]

Other frequently cited causes of NPLs include the personnel and compensation mechanisms at China's state banks, which usually link the qualifications for senior management positions to political considerations and link lending decisions to the size, not the quality, of loans. For all these characteristics, the "big four" had acted more like government agencies, not commercial institutions.[10]

It is worth noting that examining the actual causes of NPLs has important implications for a better understanding of the "transition costs" in China's financial system. This issue is introduced in Section 6.3 where the debate over "who should bear the transition costs" in today's Chinese society is introduced.

6.1.3 **The urgency of banking reform**

Because banks are the weakest link in China's fast growing economy, success or failure of the reform of the banking sector could have broad international repercussions, given the fact that China has now become an important driver of global growth. Chinese state banks have traditionally measured success by the size of their loan portfolios, and the central task of banking reform is to change that to an operational culture based on profit.[11] In a widely shared opinion of many domestic and foreign experts, delayed banking reform could eventually

---

8. Yi Gang, "The NPL Ratio and the Measurements of Local Government Performance (yinhang buliangzichan lü yu defang zhengfu zhengji kaohe)," *Caijing*, September 20, 2002.

9. *Ibid.*

10. Ye, *supra* note 6.

11. Andrew Browne, "Maverick Plays Key Role in New Bank Post" *Asian Wall Street Journal,* January 4, 2005, M.1.

threaten a collapse of China's entire financial system and severely undermine the growth potential of China's economy.[12]

In this connection, it is worth reviewing the relationship between financial crises and economic growth. Recently, a new strand of the "finance and growth" theory has emerged to suggest a "re-evaluation" of financial crises and growth. According to this new study, cross-country empirical evidence indicates a robust link between occasional financial crises and faster GDP growth. The proponents of this "re-evaluation" of financial crises and growth argue that occasional crises can be welfare-improving when the benefits of higher growth outweigh the welfare costs of crises under some circumstances.[13] In theory, in an economy with severe credit market imperfections, the adoption of credit risk is a means to overcome the obstacles to growth by easing financing constraints. However, as a side effect finance fragility arises and thus crises occur from time to time. Therefore, there exists a trade-off between financial fragility and economic growth, i.e., "no fragility, no growth."[14]

However, this positive link between financial fragility and growth does not fit in well with China's situation. The potential systemic crisis of the entire financial system that a spectacular bank failure could engender is too devastating a scenario to imagine. It could severely impair the stability of China's economic structure and cause chain-reaction collapses in all sectors involved. Therefore, China's "big four" are in an urgent need of reform, before a systemic crisis erupts and dampens the growth prospects of China's economy in the future.

Moreover, China agreed as part of its WTO commitments to remove geographical and product restrictions on foreign banks and to allow the full opening of its banking sector in December 2006. This pressure of imminent financial liberalization adds even more urgency to the long delayed banking reform. There is also the looming challenge of a fast-forming "grey/aging population," to arrive in just 15 or 20 years.[15] The aging population problem would make China's future pension liabilities a formidable financial burden, and the banks' health is a crucial factor in meeting that challenge.

6.2   AMCs and NPL Disposal

Section 6.2 discusses the introduction of asset management companies (AMCs) by the Chinese government as a means to address the NPL problem.

---

12. "China's Banks: Beyond a Bail-out," *The Economist*, January 8, 2004, p. 13.
13. Romain Ranciere, Aaron Tornell & Frank Westermann, "Crises and Growth: A Re-evaluation" NBER Working Paper, No. 10073 (2003).
14. *Ibid.*
15. Francis Markus, "China's Greying Population," *BBC News*, January 18, 2005, online < http://news.bbc.co.uk/2/hi/asia-pacific/4184839.stm >.

6.2.1   The establishment of AMCs and the transfers of NPLs

During 1998, four AMCs were established by the Chinese government to help dispose of the estimated USD 500 billion in NPLs that had plagued China's banking system. The four AMCs are China Huarong Asset Management Corporation (Huarong), China Great Wall Asset Management Corporation (Great Wall), China Orient Asset Management Corporation (Orient) and China Cinda Asset Management Corporation (Cinda). At the time of their establishment, each AMC was responsible for dealing with NPLs of one of the "big four."

Over the following couple of years the government transferred, at face value, roughly USD 170 billion of bad loans from the "big four" to their respective AMCs, equivalent to more than one fifth of the banks' loan books. The loans were almost all made before 1996, and most of them were policy loans without collateral.[16] The Chinese government then warned the banks that the transfer of NPLs was their "last supper," which was later proven to be wishful thinking as the "big four" were to get more free meals in the ensuing several years, as Section 6.3 reports.

In June 2004, to help both CCB and BoC accelerate preparations for their overseas listings, the central bank and the Ministry of Finance organized another transfer of NPLs at the two banks, valued at RMB 278.7 billion yuan (USD 33.62 billion), to Cinda. The price paid by Cinda was a 50 percent discount of the book value. The purpose of this move was to make the books of both CCB and BoC look much healthier before they could invite external auditors to review their major financial indicators in order for the shareholding restructuring to take place, which was a necessary prior step to their overseas IPOs. As a result, both banks reportedly achieved a reduced NPL ratio of below 5 percent.[17]

6.2.2   The implementation of NPL disposal

Until recently, the disposal of NPLs had generally been a cumbersome process. First, the "big four" transferred the NPLs at face value to the AMCs because the banks themselves were prohibited by the China Banking Regulatory Commission (CBRC) to directly sell NPLs at below face value. The AMCs then recovered those bad loans or sold them to foreign bidders through auctions. In such auctions, the major buyers had been international investment banks. In order to participate in the NPL disposal process, it is usually necessary for these foreign banks to form asset management joint ventures with China's AMCs.

---

16.   "Casino Capital," *supra* note 4.
17.   Ling Huawei, "Before and After the Successful Bid of Cinda for NPLs at BoC and CCB (Cinda zhongbiao qianhou)," *Caijing,* July 5, 2004.

There had been several auctions of NPL portfolios to foreign banks. In 2001, a consortium of Wall Street firms led by three U.S. investment banks, of which Morgan Stanley was the largest shareholder, bought a portfolio of NPLs with a face value of USD1.3 billion from Huarong in China's first international NPL auction.[18] In February 2003, Goldman Sachs also sealed a joint venture purchase with Huarong for a package of NPLs valued at 1.9 billion yuan (USD 229 million).[19] In March 2003, after having established a similar asset management joint venture with Huarong, a Morgan Stanley-led consortium received final regulatory approval to buy 10.8 billion yuan (USD 1.3 billion) of Huarong's NPLs, which marked the largest such portfolio sale of NPLs in China's history.[20] More recently, as of January 2005 Great Wall was in the process of auctioning its remaining unrecovered NPLs, valued around RMB 150 billion yuan (USD 18 billion).[21]

To break the monopoly of AMCs in NPL disposal, the banks themselves have tried to enter this business by devising new methods that would circumvent the CBRC's prohibition on their selling NPLs at below face value. For example, in February 2004 CCB planned to pioneer a new type of distressed asset auction as it raced to become the first of the "big four" to launch an overseas listing. Instead of selling NPLs, CCB hoped to first separate the loan from its collateral and auction the collateral, in this case worth RMB 5 billion (USD 600 million). Meanwhile, BoC also planned an auction that would circumvent the AMCs and offer NPLs with a face value of about RMB 6 billion (USD 724 million) to foreign and domestic bidders directly. If permitted by the CBRC, these new approaches of the "big four" to splitting the market share of NPL disposal business would bring competitive pressure on the AMCs.[22]

6.2.3 The effect of NPL disposal

In general, the effect of NPL disposal has not been encouraging, at least seen from the quick accumulation of new NPLs at the "big four" after the 1999 bailout.

Officially, according to the CBRC, which oversees China's commercial banks and major financial institutions, the bad loans at the "big four" stood at a reduced total of 1.575 trillion yuan (USD 205 billion) and the banks' average

---

18.   Karen, Richardson, "China Company Sues U.S. Firms," *Asian Wall Street Journal*, February 5, 2004, M.1.
19.   Dow Jones Newswires, "China Approves Its Largest Sale of Bad Loans," *Asian Wall Street Journal*, March 14, 2003, A.4.
20.   *Ibid.*
21.   Owen Brown, "China Audit Identifies Firms' Illegal Practices," *Asian Wall Street Journal*, January 7, 2005, M.2.
22.   James Kynge, "CCB Pioneers Auction in Race to List Overseas," *Financial Times*, February 6, 2004.

NPL ratio dropped to 15.6 percent at the end of 2004.[23] The CBRC regarded this as a good sign and praised the banks for a "double reduction" in major NPL indicators.

However, while China's financial regulators may have stepped up their efforts to clean up the existing stock of NPLs, the country's banking system has yet to deal with another source of instability — new bad debt.[24] Moreover, the official figures may not be credible and the true level of NPLs may be much higher for reasons discussed below. Independent studies have found far more worrying results as compared to the government's statistics. For example, according to the estimate of UBS, even after the write-off of bad loans by the central bank and the transfer of bad assets or bad loans to AMCs, the average NPL ratio at the "big four" still stood at a stunning 40 percent at the end of 2003.[25] Besides, the AMCs were also criticized for their seemingly low recovery rates and for selling state assets at bargain prices, in particular to foreign buyers, as will be discussed shortly. The 2004 official figures showed the recovery rate of NPLs in cash terms was only 20.29 percent, meaning that the loss rate of uncovered loans was nearly 80 percent.[26]

6.2.4 The problems involved in the process of NPL disposal

Some serious problems have emerged in the NPL disposal process that expose the loopholes in the current institutional design and also signal the urgent need for further vigorous reform of China's banking sector.

The moral hazard of the "big four" and fraudulent transfers of NPLs

In the process of transferring their NPLs to the AMCs, the moral hazard of the "big four," as typically observed with every government bail-out measure, has led them to mis-categorize their problem loans and increase the bulk of NPLs transferred to the AMCs. In some cases, in order to disguise their business losses caused by poorly executed transactions or even financial crimes, some bank managers forged documents to make fraudulent NPL transfers.[27]

---

23. "China's Banks Cut Bad-Loan Ratio to 13.2 percent in 2004," *Asian Wall Street Journal*, January 14, 2005, A.3.
24. Matthias Bekier, "Drowned in A Sea of Debt," *Financial Times*, January 26, 2005, p. 9.
25. Anderson, *supra* note 2.
26. Xie Fenghua, "Have NPLs Really Realized a 'Double Reduction'? (buliang daikuan zhende shixian 'shuangjiang' le ma?)," *China Business Post* (*Caijing Shibao*), January 30, 2005, online < http://www.caijingshibao.com/Mag/preview.aspx?ArtID=10910 >.
27. Wu Chuanzhen & Su Yuan, "The Undisclosed Story about the 2 Trillion yuan NPL Disposal in China (zhongguo wanyi buliang zichan chuzhi neimu)," *Southern Weekend* (*Nanfang Zhoumo*), January 27, 2005, online < http://www.nanfangdaily.com.cn/southnews/zmzg/200501270977.asp >.

The lack of proper valuation and standardized procedural mechanisms in the process of NPL disposal

In the course of NPL disposal, there had been accusations by some domestic critics that in their disposal of NPLs, the AMCs had made "fire sales" to foreign investment banks at the expense of potential domestic buyers and China's "national economic security."[28] Such accusations intensified after an international auction held in 2003 by Huarong that resulted in more than 10 billion yuan (USD 1.3 billion) of assets being acquired by six foreign investment banks, the largest NPL portfolio auction in China's history.[29] Public criticisms have put Huarong and other AMCs under pressure to proceed with future NPL auctions to foreign buyers.

The real question to be asked is whether the prices paid by foreign buyers in previous NPL auctions were really "too cheap" and if so what had caused the under-pricing. The answer is that the difficulty in pricing China's NPLs properly was associated with the underdevelopment of market mechanisms for NPL disposal in China's transition economy. After all, China's AMCs only started the business of NPL disposal several years ago and there was no existing domestic experience from which to draw. Although NPL disposal in other countries, in particular some East Asian countries after the 1997-98 financial crisis, has provided some valuable lessons to China, its institutional environment and still-developing market mechanisms are not mature enough for efficiently implementing NPL disposal schemes. The first problem was that there were few domestic buyers interested in entering this market when the new business of NPL disposal first launched in China. At the beginning, few domestic institutions could imagine that NPL disposal would one day become an attractive business with potentially lucrative returns to the buyers of NPLs and simply shunned this market. Foreign banks, hoping to make inroads in China's financial industry, were the first active participants in NPL auctions at a time when the AMCs started to experiment with market-oriented schemes to dispose of the NPLs they had acquired from the "big four." Therefore, the initiating market players in China's NPL disposal, on the demand side, were international investment banks.[30]

The second problem was that while it seemed likely that the prices paid by foreign buyers were indeed "too cheap," the primary reason for the under-pricing was the lack of a proper valuation system and standardized auction

---

28. Wang Du, "China's NPL Disposal Needs to Be Vigilant of the Huge Trap Set up by Foreign Banks," 72 *The Economics Monthly (Jingji Yuekan)*, December 2004, online < http://www.jingji.com.cn/show.aspx?id=745 >.

29. The auction involved Switzerland-based UBS AG and Wall Street banks Citigroup Inc., Lehman Brothers Holdings Inc., J.P. Morgan Chase & Co. and Morgan Stanley. See Brown, *supra* note 21.

30. Wu & Su, *supra* note 27.

procedures for NPL disposal in China, such as information disclosure, property documents authentification and risk assessment. Besides, there were regulatory hurdles regarding government approval, which usually resulted in uncertainty and delay and this factor certainly had a negative impact on NPL pricing.

Aware of these institutional inadequacies, the CBRC has been stressing the need to both improve the capacity of China's AMCs in handling NPL auctions more effectively and to develop necessary market mechanisms to facilitate NPL auctions. As to the participation of foreign buyers, the CBRC is positive about the overall beneficial impact brought by their expertise and experience, and encourages the AMCs to continue to cooperate with foreign players.[31]

Irregular dealings and corruption at AMCs

Adding to the already discouraging problems of continuing formation of new NPLs at the "big four" and the low recovery rates at the AMCs, recently it was also discovered that in the process of NPL disposal, irregular dealings had occurred on a wide scale, some involving corruption and embezzlement by the personnel at both the AMCs and the "big four."[32] Specifically, in a 2005 work report of China's National Audit Office, 38 cases of illegal practices at the four AMCs, valued at 6.7 billion yuan (nearly USD 846 million), were identified.[33]

6.2.5 What Next

From the discussion of NPL disposal so far, it can be seen that the operational effect of AMCs is subject to both public criticism and government scrutiny, which will add more difficulties to redressing the alarming reality of newly created bad loans. Therefore, to effectively solve the existing NPL problem and slow the growth in new bad loans, further banking reform measures are needed, which must go beyond continuing write-offs of bad debt and capital injections. The key component of these measures is the creation of a modern banking industry based on a strong credit scoring and risk management culture, and at the heart of this effort is the need for better corporate governance.[34] This leads to the issue of shareholding reform and the preparations of the "big four" for overseas listings, which is discussed in Section 6.6.

---

31. Li Zhenhua, "Are AMCs Selling State Assets for Cheap? Foreign Investment Banks Elaborate the Chain of Profit Sharing in China's NPL Disposal (AMC shifou jianmai guozi? waizi touhang xishuo shiwulian)," *21ˢᵗ Century Business Herald* (*21 Shiji Jingji Baodao*), January 10, 2005, online < http://www.nanfangdaily.com.cn/jj/20050110/zh/200501100006.asp >.
32. Shen Jianli, "The National Audit Office Uncovered RMB 6.7 Billion of Irregular Dealings at Four AMCs," *Southern Daily* (*Nanfang Ribao*), January 21, 2005, online < http://www.nanfangdaily.com.cn/southnews/djjz/200501210283.asp >.
33. Brown, *supra* note 21.
34. Bekier, *supra* note 24.

6.3 Recapitalizing the "Big Four"

The government has over the past several years spent huge amounts of money to bolster the capital bases of the "big four," totaling USD 250 billion. The so-called "free supper" has been offered time and again despite the government's repeated warnings that every bail-out was the "last chance." While the latest effort of using China's abundant foreign exchange reserves to recapitalize BoC and CCB in December 2003 as well as ICBC in 2005 (and eventually ABC in the near future) may be an innovative method with relatively lower costs compared to other bail-out options, it also entails potential risk and indeed has increased the moral hazard of the "big four."

6.3.1 Capital injection by issuing special treasury bonds

In 1998, the government injected 270 billion yuan (USD 32.6 billion) into the "big four" by issuing special treasury bonds, and at the same time spun off 1,400 billion yuan (USD 169 billion) worth of their NPLs. As a direct result of this infusion, the capital adequacy ratio of each of the "big four" immediately reached 8 percent, the threshold required under the Basel Accord. However, the four banks had again accumulated 2,100 billion yuan (USD 254 billion) worth of new NPLs as of February 2004.[35] It seemed that the money injected failed to bring about expected performance improvement because the banks did not change their management systems and lending patterns after the recapitalization.

6.3.2 Capital injection by using foreign exchange reserves: an innovative bail-out method

China has a large build-up of foreign exchange reserves. In October 2004, these stood at more than USD 600 billion, about 60 percent of GDP, and were largely held in U.S. Treasury bills.[36] Making use of China's rich pool of foreign exchange reserves, the central bank in December 2003 provided BoC and CCB, the country's second and third largest lenders respectively, each with USD 22.5 billion. This move was aimed at increasing the capital adequacy of the two banks to pave the way for their subsequent shareholding restructuring and overseas listings.

---

35. Ye Weiqiang & Lu Lei, "Pros and Cons of US$45 Billion Re-capitalization," *Caijing English Newsletter*, February 10, 2004, online < http://www.caijing.com.cn/english >.
36. Lal, *supra* note 3.

According to some approving Chinese financial analysts, the government's decision to recapitalize BoC and CCB with foreign exchange reserves struck "a delicate balance between financial stability and monetary stability" because in this scheme the government provided the banks with capital without worsening its budget deficit.[37] At the same time, the money was injected through a newly created holding company, Central Huijin Investment (Huijin), which is wholly owned by the state, to allow the government to remove itself from direct ownership of the banks.[38] Huijin's role in the following shareholding restructuring of both BoC and CCB is discussed below in Section 6.4.

After the capital injections into BoC and CCB in 2003, China's largest lender, ICBC, also received a similar bail-out in 2005.[39] The capital injections paved the way for these banks' subsequent overseas listings. According to industry estimates, the amount of ICBC's capital injection could reach USD 45 billion (the actual amount later turned out to be USD 30 billion).[40] Because of its size, ICBC suffered more than any other state bank from years of policy lending. As of September 2004, its NPL ratio stood at 19.46 percent, which was described as "a scary figure for overseas investors" by Chinese bankers and was higher than China's official average NPL ratio of 13 percent at that time.[41]

As to ABC, the weakest and smallest of the "big four," it submitted its shareholding restructuring plan to the government for review in early 2005, in anticipation of a similar capital injection. Because of the heavy burden it has long assumed to provide rural policy loans, ABC is widely regarded as making the slowest progress in bank shareholding reform.[42] The method of capital injection, however, is still uncertain with regard to ABC, because the Ministry of Finance, as the owner of the "big four," recently expressed discontent about being overshadowed by other government agencies, primarily the central bank, in China's latest banking reform moves and hoped to regain a leading profile by orchestrating the next round of capital injections and providing the money itself. Regardless of the method of capital injection, however, it is the government — with taxpayers' money — which ultimately bears the cost.

---

37. "China's Biggest Lender," *supra* note 5.
38. Hu Shuli, "A Double-edged Sword: On Recapitalizing Banks with Foreign Exchange Reserves (waihui chubei zhuzi yinhang de liangren)", *Caijing*, January 20, 2004.
39. "China's Biggest Lender," *supra* note 5.
40. Bekier, *supra* note 24.
41. Wang Fang & Francesco Guerrera, "China Close to Approving Dollars 30bn Injection for ICBC," *Financial Times*, January 4, 2005, p. 17.
42 Sun Ming, "Agricultural Bank of China Re-submits Its Shareholding Reform Plan and the Method of Capital Injection is to be Determined (nonghang zaibao gugai fangan, waihui caizheng zhuzi moshi weiding)," *21st Century Business Herald* (*21 Shiji Jingji Baodao*), January 31, 2005, online < http://www.nanfangdaily.com.cn/jj/20050131/jr/200501310036.asp >.

6.3.3   Write-off of bad assets (the forgiveness of owner's equity claims of the Ministry of Finance)

After receiving the capital injection of foreign exchange reserves, BoC and CCB again were offered another free meal. In January 2004, the Ministry of Finance announced that it would use its owner's equity claims in the two banks, worth RMB 300 billion (USD 36.2 billion), to write off their bad assets.[43] This was viewed within Chinese financial industry as the government paying for the historical losses of the state banks out of its own coffers, for which Chinese taxpayers ultimately paid.

6.3.4 The problems associated with repeated bail-outs

The moral hazard of the "big four" and other financial institutions in anticipation of "free suppers"

For all its innovation, the approach of using foreign exchange reserves for bank capital injections has been criticized by some economists. The first problem is obvious: it could cause moral hazard not only at the "big four," but also at other financial institutions currently operating with dismal capital bases, especially when government bail-outs of troubled financial institutions seem to have become a repeated exercise.

In the latest round of bail-outs, it appeared to some that injecting foreign exchange reserves into state banks is a low-cost method in comparison with other options. As a result, not only the "big four," but also other troubled financial institutions, have come to believe that the government has found a new mechanism to save them. An appalling fact emerging from the lower levels of China's financial industry is that an army of 112 city commercial banks and 35,544 rural credit cooperatives is lining up for a "blood infusion" by the government, with their capital adequacy and NPL ratio even worse than that of the "big four." However, China's foreign exchange reserves, ample as they currently are, are not unlimited. With an illusion about a deep treasury box, the "big four" will not cherish the capital they have received as much as they should, and will expect more "free suppers" from the government as they proceed with further reforms.[44]

---

43. Zhang Xiaocai, "BoC and CCB Are Allowed to Write Off Bad Loans by Using RMB 300 Billion Yuan of Owner's Equity of the Treasury (zhonghang jianhang zaihuo zhongyang caizheng jū e touru chongxiao huaizhang)," *China Business Times* (*Caijing Shibao*), January 12, 2004, online < http://www.chinanews.com.cn/n/2004-01-12/26/390704.html >.

44. Hu, *supra* note 38.

Indeed, in analyzing the actual effect of repeated bail-outs, the unavoidable conclusion is that money spent on recapitalizing China's banks over recent years did not result in evident performance improvement. Since 1998, China has spent at least USD 200 billion in recapitalizing its banks and writing off bad loans, to little avail. Politically directed lending to favored enterprises, especially those in the "strategic sectors," has continued as before, and the previous write-off of bad assets was soon replaced by new ones. According to China's official statistics, at the end of 2004 NPLs still stood at USD 205 billion, or 13 percent of total banking assets. Some independent estimates put the level of NPLs at around USD 420 billion, or nearly 40 percent of GDP.[45]

The potential risks to the stability of the financial system

The second problem is the potential risks of using foreign exchange reserves to recapitalize the "big four" to the stability of China's financial system. Having sufficient foreign exchange reserves is usually an important indicator of a country's financial safety, and it is commonly understood that these funds should not be used on illiquid projects, such as strengthening the "core capital" base of state-owned commercial banks. Besides, some Chinese economists also believe that the capital injection with foreign exchange reserves will eventually harm the central bank's independence and regulatory credibility.[46]

In this regard, it is interesting to note that a veteran development economist and long time China observer, Deepak Lal, has sketched an ingenious scheme for better using China's vast foreign exchange reserves to help with the reform of both the country's banks and SOEs:

> ... There is a better way for China to use its reserves. At most, only a small proportion — say Dollars 100 billion — is needed to fend off any speculative attack in order to maintain the dollar peg. The rest - some Dollars 500bn, as well as any future accruals - could be put into a social reconstruction fund under the central bank. This would function like any other big pension fund, such as that for the World Bank, whose annual return, averaged over 10 years, has been about 8 percent. If the proposed fund for China could match this, it would yield an annual income of Dollars 40 billion, or 4 percent of GDP, which could be used gradually to cover the SOE's social burdens [now largely funded by the state banks]. The SOEs could then be treated as normal enterprises, to be privatised if viable and closed down if not... In time, as the SOE problem receded, the income from the fund could become the basis for a fully funded pensions system for China's ageing population...[47]

---

45. "Beyond a Bail-out," *supra* note 12.
46. Ye & Lu, *supra* note 35.
47. Lal, *supra* note 3.

This suggestion seems innovative and is tailored to the current situation of China's currency regime, financial development, pension liabilities and SOE reform. Therefore, this new idea warrants consideration in the next stage of China's banking and SOE reforms.

6.3.5   The debate over "transition costs" and "paying for a modern banking system"

In the process of recapitalizing the "big four," some controversies surrounding the merits of government bail-outs have been raised among the Chinese pubic, which are reflected in the debate over the "transaction costs" of banking reform during China's economic transition.

"Transition costs": Who should pay for them?

It is worth noting that in the process of China's banking reform, an intense debate has taken place among the banks, the government and the general public about the so-called "transition costs." Some Chinese bankers have suggested that it is the responsibility of the government to compensate the banks for accumulated losses caused by policy lending as well as lost profits due to policy restrictions on the scope of permitted banking business during China's economic transition.[48] In other words, in the view of the banks, the government should pay for the "transition costs."

However, recent public opinion, and indeed the position of China's banking regulators, has suggested that the banks' argument is unsettling because it sought to make the central bank the virtual ultimate guarantor of all troubled financial institutions. If the "big four" suffered their losses primarily from policy restrictions and state intervention, other domestic financial institutions, such as city commercial banks and numerous rural credit cooperatives, will apply the same argument to ask for government bail-outs. This would be a catastrophic scenario as the moral hazard could spread across-the-board within China's financial system.

Moreover, as to what constitutes real "transition costs," it is not up to the banks to properly define it since they tend to distort the cause-and-effect account and disguise the losses from stealing, embezzlement, expropriation and failed speculation in the stockmarket under the cover of "transition costs." In fact, from what is revealed in previous discussion of the causes of NPLs in Section 6.1, what constitutes the real "transition costs" seems to have some clear indications — the government, especially the local governments, which

---

48. Hu, *supra* note 38.

intervene in bank businesses, as well as bank staff who make blunders or cause losses in daily transactions due to incompetence, waste and corruption, both have their shares in contributing to the NPL problem, thus both playing a role in the accumulation of the "transition costs."

"Paying for a modern banking system"

The situation now is that the government is in a relatively weak bargaining position in negotiating reform measures with the banks while the general public, understandably, have little say in this interaction except expressing criticism in the media. The banks now hold all cards to exploit the government's concern about the danger of a systemic financial crisis caused by bank failures. In a sense, the moral hazard has led the banks to make a hostage of, or "hijack," the government's dilemma in fixing the financial system: it certainly cannot afford to let the banks collapse, but it also worries about the effect of money used. The result of this interaction, as judged from the current progress of banking reform, is that the government has been forced to take a position of "paying for a modern banking system," as professed by some policy makers.

However, the problem here is that this philosophy of banking reform is a misnomer, and would be more accurately understood as 'paying heftily for a uncertain prospect of a modern banking system," which implies a high risk of ultimate failure if it is not accompanied by a strategy of vigorous reform to turn around the corporate governance structure of the "big four." Failing that, regardless of how much has been paid, and certainly will be paid again, a healthy banking sector in China is only an illusion.

6.4 Shareholding Restructuring and Corporate Governance Improvements

After a series of measures to bolster the capital base of the state banks through both recapitalization and NPL transfer, the "big four" became ready for financial and shareholding restructuring, a necessary prior step toward launching overseas listings.

6.4.1 The old ownership and management system for the "big four" and the new changes

Formerly, the ownership and management system of the "big four" had suffered the same problem as China's SOEs had before the SASAC was established: the split of ownership and control rights between separate government departments. In the case of the "big four," until recently the Ministry of Finance had been the responsible agency to represent the state owner and to oversee the banks' incomes and expenses, while the CBRC had been in charge of personnel decisions as well as discipline and sanctions. To address the agency problem that this ownership and control structure has created, some Chinese economists have suggested establishing a "financial SASAC" to solely represent the state's ownership rights in the "big four." The reason why the SASAC itself is not suitable to play this role is that it would be a bad idea to have the same agency assume the ownership rights in both SOEs and their principal creditors, as it would certainly lead to conflicts of interest.[49]

Therefore, the shareholding restructuring at BoC and CCB, the two banks that had made most of the progress in the latest round of banking reform, would provide valuable lessons with regard to the reform of ownership and management systems in China's banking sector. In this new effort of the government to experiment with ownership reform at the "big four," the role of the Central Huijin Investment or Huijin, a newly created state holding investment company for the specific purpose of facilitating China's financial reform, is important. Under joint supervision of the Ministry of Finance, the central bank and the State Administration of Foreign Exchange, Huijin was set up after the foreign exchange reserve injection into BoC and CCB in December 2003 to represent the state shareholder in these two banks. Huijin is wholly owned by the state and has a clear mandate to represent the state owner in exercising its rights and responsibilities in the "big four" and other major financial institutions.

Although Huijin itself is still a 100 percent state-owned company, its new role in the shareholding restructuring at BoC and CCB as their founding shareholder at least allows the state to remove itself from direct ownership of the banks. In the meantime, new board structures were also created at the two banks, including seats for both domestic and foreign independent directors. When the banks' plan to introduce international strategic investors finally materialized, which further diversified their ownership structures before overseas listings, there emerged more meaningful results of the banking reform. Subsequently, both BoC and CCB entered the process of soliciting large international financial institutions for their interest in buying minority stakes in the banks.

As complementary measures to their shareholding restructuring, the "big four" have also reduced the size of their staff and reshaped their employment, compensation and welfare systems to allow market forces to play a bigger role in their daily operations.

---

49. Ling Huawei & Shi Chuan, "Huijin Corporation Taps Financial Assets Management," *Caijing*, October 4, 2004.

6.4.2 Shareholding restructuring and corporate governance improvements

Since 2004, except for Agricultural Bank of China or ABC, three of the "big four" banks started to embark on shareholding restructuring and corporate governance reform, in preparation for subsequent public listings in both domestic and overseas capital markets.

Bank of China

On August 26, 2004, BoC announced that it had completed its shareholding restructuring. Huijin became the sole shareholder in the restructured BoC. The new BoC inherited all of its predecessor's assets, liabilities and 188,700 staff. A board consisting of 11 directors, among them six from Huijin, was established and three supervisors were also appointed. In addition, Hong Kong's former Securities and Futures Commission chairman, Anthony Neoh, was appointed the first independent director of the restructured BoC. According to BoC, another foreign professional was soon to be invited to join the board some time later.[50] The bank also announced that as it proceeded further to invite new strategic investors, more directors would be appointed. In July 2004, a list of potential strategic investors was submitted to the State Council and Huijin for their review.[51]

In the shareholding structure of the new BoC, there appeared four foreign strategic investors, holding a combined 21.85 percent stake, which is considered by many as lack of effective control for each investor. An RBS-led consortium obtained 10 percent of ownership for which it paid USD 3.1 billion in investment; half the cash was put by RBS, the other half by the investment bank Merrill Lynch and the Hong Kong tycoon, Li Ka-Shing. Temasek, a Singaporean state investment company, was offered 10 percent of ownership for USD 3.1 billion in investment, plus an additional USD 500 million earmarked for IPO. The American express delivery company UBS received 1.61 percent of ownership for USD 500 million. Finally, the Asian Development Bank (ADB) was allotted less than 1 percent of shares by investing USD 75 million.

This relatively "loose" participation of foreign strategic investors has proven a controversial process among some critics, who doubt whether the strategic investors can have a large enough stake to exert real impact on the bank's business operations and corporate governance practices.

BoC also received RMB 10 billion (USD 1.25 billion) in investment from China's National Social Security Fund (NSSF) as its domestic strategic investor.

---

50. *Ibid.*
51. Bei Hu, "Neoh on Board at Bank of China," *South China Morning Post,* August 25, 2004, p.1.

China Construction Bank

On September 15 2004, CCB announced its completion of shareholding restructuring. The former state-owned bank was split into a holding group and a shareholding company. The shareholding company was devised to serve as a listing vehicle for its planned overseas IPO. The holding group, named China Construction Bank Group Co. Ltd (CCB Group), took over the bank's non-banking businesses, valued at around 1 percent of its total assets. As part of its restructuring plan, CCB also set up China Jianyin Investment Ltd. (Jianyin) to hold its stake in the new shareholding company, along with four founding stakeholders, including Huijin and another three SOEs as domestic strategic investors.[52]

In the shareholding structure of the new CCB, Huijin hold 85 percent of the shares of the shareholding company. In addition, Huijin controlled up to an additional 10 percent of shares through the holding group, which it owned exclusively. Therefore, Huijin in effect controlled 95.88 percent of the shares in the new CCB. Previous proposals from economists for Huijin to put together a professional management committee did not interest government's policy makers. Instead, Huijin's management team was staffed by officials from the government regulatory agencies, including the central bank, the State Administration of Foreign Exchange, and the Ministry of Finance.[53] Huijin initially appointed six directors to the board of the new CCB shareholding company.

Despite the setback at Huijin of not establishing a professional management team, the corporate governance structure of the new CCB seemed to be an improvement in some respects. On September 21, 2004, CCB appointed Masamoto Yashiro, chief executive of Japan's Shinsei Bank, as one of its two independent directors in a landmark step toward improved corporate governance.[54] This move made CCB the first of the "big four" to recruit a foreigner as an independent director as it prepared for an overseas IPO. The appointment of Mr. Yashiro and another independent director, who was a professor at Tsinghua University, was a breakthrough in China's banking sector, where appointments had generally been determined by Party and government

---

52. The remaining three major strategic investors in the new shareholding structure of CCB are all state-owned enterprises, including China Yangtze Power Company, Shanghai Baosteel Group, and State Power Grid Corporation.
53. Yu Ning, "China Construction Bank Nears IPO," *Caijing English Newsletter*, June 20, 2004, online < http://www.caijing.com.cn/english/2004/040620/040620ccb.htm >.
54. Zou Hua, "Masamoto Yashiro, the Independent Director of CCB, Hopes to Help the Bank with His Reform Experience (jianhang dudong Bacheng Zhengji: xiwang wode gaige jingyan youzhu jianhang)," *China News*, September 24, 2004, online < http://www. chinanews.com.cn/news/2004/2004-09-24/26/487656.shtml >.

affiliations. Some financial analysts believed that this move helped improve CCB's profile and was beneficial to the bank's overseas IPO.[55]

Meanwhile, CCB invited two foreign strategic investors to join its new shareholding structure. With USD 3 billion of investment, the Bank of America was granted 9 percent of ownership. It also promised an additional USD 500 million earmarked for IPO, which was later approved by the Stock Exchange of Hong Kong in CCB's Hong Kong IPO. Temasek again was successful in obtaining 5.1 percent of ownership at the price of USD 1.4 billion. This made Temasek a strategic investor of two Chinese state banks, which had also spurred controversy under current regulatory restrictions on foreign capital participation in state banks. Temasek was also offered the right to earmark additional USD 1 billion for IPO, but was subsequently refused by the Stock Exchange of Hong Kong due to concerns with fairness to retail investors.

Industrial and Commercial Bank of China

ICBC completed its shareholding restructuring on October 28, 2005. Huijin and the Ministry of Finance were the founding shareholders of the new ICBC. While Huijin contributed USD15 billion as equity, the Ministry of Finance retained RMB 124 billion of the existing capital. There were initially 14 directors sitting on the new ICBC's board, of them three were independent directors recruited from overseas: Antony Leung, the former financial secretary of the Hong Kong government, John Thornton, former president of the investment bank Goldman Sachs, and Qian Yingyi, a professor in economics at UC Berkeley. A supervisory board was also set up, with five supervisors starting to assume duty.

ICBC had attracted three foreign strategic investors to participate in its shareholding structure. It sold a combined 8.89 percent of shares to Goldman Sachs, Germany's Allianz AG, and American Express for a total of USD 3.78 billion. This marked the biggest ever single foreign investment in China's banking sector. Notably, all three strategic investors are not commercial banks themselves. In addition, ICBC also received another RMB 10 billion (USD 1.25 billion) in investment from the National Social Security Fund as its domestic strategic investor.

In general, foreign strategic investors of the three banks were subject to a "lock-up" period, usually three years, and agreements on long-term cooperation and training programmes.

---

55. Owen Brown & Phelim Kyne, "Chinese Lender Blazes a Trail; Construction Bank Names CEO of Japan's Shinsei As an Independent Director," *Asian Wall Street Journal*, September 23, 2004, A.3.

6.4.3 Reform of internal controls and risk management systems

Since early 2004, the China Banking Regulatory Commission or CBRC, the principal regulator of China's commercial banks, has been pushing measures to strengthen banks' internal risk controls and devised an "interim method," which took effect on February 1, 2005.[56] As a follow-up, in January 2005 the CBRC again issued a set of *Guidelines for Commercial Bank Market Risk Management* as well as the *Provisional Regulation on Assessment of Internal Controls of Commercial Banks*. In these documents, the CBRC urged China's commercial banks to improve their risk controls and internal monitoring as China's financial market opens to foreign competitors. The CBRC has indicated that it will tighten supervision over commercial banks where serious financial crimes have repeatedly occurred and pledged more inspections and punishment for wrongdoers. Meanwhile, because China's banking industry is poorly prepared to handle the new types of risk that are expected to multiply as the financial system is gradually liberalized, the CBRC also urged domestic banks to introduce risk control systems that would limit their exposure to financial market volatility.[57]

Other important regulatory initiatives taken by the CBRC in recent years to strengthen banks' internal controls and risk management include the following:

- Issued *Measures on Related Party Transactions* (May 1, 2004)
- Issued requirements for disclosure in *Circular on Annual Reports of Commercial Banks* (February 17, 2004)
- Issued *Provisional Guidelines on Due Diligence of the Board of Directors of Joint Stock Commercial Banks* (September 12, 2005)
- Issued *Guidelines on Corporate Governance of Joint Stock Commercial Banks* (June 4, 2002)
- Issued *Guidelines on Corporate Governance and other Regulatory Issues Regarding State-owned Commercial Banks* (effective April 24, 2006 and applicable to the "big four" and China's fifth largest bank, the Bank of Communications)
- Instructed commercial banks to increase reserve funds to cushion against possible losses caused by bad loans

In general, the promulgation of these regulations was largely spurred by the alarming fact that serious financial crimes happen too often in the banking industry because of lax internal controls. Corruption and embezzlement of funds at the "big four," sometimes involving stunning amounts, have been reported extensively by both domestic and international financial media in recent years. The most egregious bank scandals and corporate governance failures that have been recorded with the "big four" are discussed below

---

56. Duan Hongqing & Kang Weiping, "Financial Fraud Exposes Governance Weaknesses at the Bank of China," *Caijing English Newsletter*, January 24, 2005, online < http://www.caijing.com.cn/english/2005/05-1-24/05-1-24-4.htm >.
57. James T. Areddy, "China to Get Tougher On Crimes at Banks," *Asian Wall Street Journal*, January 10, 2005, M.2.

in Section 6.5. The most critical fact revealed by these cases is that China's banking reform not only faces the daunting task of reducing NPLs, but also the challenge of curbing corruption through tightened internal controls and improved corporate governance. However, because the legal and institutional environments during China's transition are still developing, these double tasks are not easy to achieve. This issue is revisited in Section 6.7, where the prospects for, and necessary future steps in, China's banking reform are reviewed.

6.4.4 Reform of personnel, compensation and employee welfare systems

In combination with shareholding restructuring, BoC, CCB and ICBC have also been active in promoting reform of their personnel, compensation and employee welfare systems. For example, they have moderately reduced the size of staff, set up requirements for re-applying for posts by existing staff, started to link compensation to performance, and engaged in recruiting talents from markets, including overseas markets. Most notably, BoC experimented with a global recruiting exercise in 2005 for 25 senior managerial and technical posts.

6.5 Egregious Corporate Governance Failures at the "Big Four" and Their Repercussions

Drawing on international experience in measuring corruption and governance quality, such as the Corruption Perceptions Index (CPI) tracked by Transparency International, two Chinese economists compiled an index of financial corruption in China (FCI). According to their estimates, for the year 2003, China's overall FCI stood at 5.42 on a scale of 0 to 10, with 0 as the best and 10 as the worst level of corruption. The banking sector recorded a medium score of 4.17, compared to the staggering figure of 7.26 for the securities industry.[58] These numbers are alarming, indicating the severity of financial corruption in both China's banking and securities industries. The cases reported below regarding China's banking sector are the most egregious ones and highly revealing of lax internal controls and other serious weaknesses in corporate governance of the "big four."

6.5.1 The BoC Heilongjiang sub-branch missing deposits case (2005)

A recent embezzlement case at a BoC sub-branch in China's northeast Heilongjiang province was revealed to the public in January 2005. This case

---

58. Xie Ping & Lu Lei, "A Study on Financial Corruption (jingrong fubai qiujie)," *Caijing*, January 10, 2005.

involved missing deposits of more than RMB 1 billion (USD 121 million). The missing funds were suspected to be stolen by the former manager of the sub-branch, Gao Shan, who fled overseas just days before the case was brought to light. Investigators from the police and BoC's headquarters launched a probe into the case, which uncovered serious internal control problems at the bank.[59] This was the latest in a series of scandals at the BoC in the past few years and was especially damaging when the bank was preparing for an overseas IPO. As a blow to investor confidence, Standard & Poor's noted that "the incident underlines weaknesses in the bank's relatively new internal control procedures."[60] This could delay the bank's much-anticipated domestic and overseas listings, because investment bankers had commented that unless BoC can show its risk control systems are capable of detecting problems in its sprawling branch network, investors would demand a discount on the offering price.[61]

6.5.2 The ICBC Nanhai branch loan fraud case (2004)

In June 2004, China's Auditor General released some shocking findings in his work report to the National People's Congress, indicating that a local private entrepreneur in Nanhai city, Guangdong province, Feng Mingchang, forged financial papers and conspired with bank executives to obtain fraudulent loans up to 7.4 billion yuan (USD 893.7 million) from the ICBC Nanhai branch. According to the audit report, a large portion of the loans was illegally transferred overseas. When the case was first revealed, it was reported that as much as 2 billion yuan (USD 233 million) had not been returned.[62]

In this episode, the delinquency on the part of the bank was outrageous: after being warned by risk-assessment officials from the upper branch that there were potential huge risks in lending to Feng, the Guangdong branch of ICBC continued to lend billions to his company and its subsidiaries. Some bank officials were arrested on corruption charges. The scope of wrongdoing was stunning: when the case was finally brought to trial in January 2005, some 80 government officials and bankers involved had been either detained by the police or reprimanded by the Communist Party.[63]

---

59. Duan & Kang, *supra* note 56.
60. "Foreign Listings in New York: Big Apple Blues," *The Economist,* January 27, 2005, p. 73.
61. James T. Areddy & Vivian Tse, "Millions Missing at Bank of China," *Asian Wall Street Journal,* February 1, 2005, A2.
62. Zhang Xiang, Chen Huiying & Pan Xiaohong, "Audit Report Lifts Veil on Corruption in Guangdong," *Caijing English Newsletter,* July 15, 2004.
63. Li Keyong & Zhang Xudong, "Xinhua Focus: The General Audit Office Reveals the Truth about RMB 7.4 Billion Loan Fraud in the Feng Mingchang Case (Xinhua shidian: shenjishu jiekai Feng Mingchang piandai 74 yiyuan neimu)," *Xinhua News,* July 6, 2004, online < http://news.sohu.com/2004/07/06/32/news220873232.shtml >.

According to the in-depth probe by China's financial media, the real mastermind of this loan fraud case was not Feng, but local officials in Nanhai city. They used Feng's company as a front to divert most of the loans overseas, in order to offset gigantic losses the local government incurred in capital and real estate speculations in Hong Kong years ago. Many facts pointed toward local government officials' manipulations behind the scenes.[64] For example, bank records showed that Feng's company and its affiliates obtained most of the loans by taking out mortgages on properties which they did not own or were grossly over-valued and the local land resource authorities provided Feng's company with a string of fake certificates for these properties.[65]

Therefore, compared with the outright corruption commonly exposed by Chinese media, the Nanhai loan fraud scandal posed much greater risks. It revealed deep-rooted problems in China's current political and economic systems during transition, calling for future reform measures to both combat corruption and clean up the banking sector.[66]

6.5.3 The BoC Shanghai and Hong Kong branches corruption case (2004)

On February 20, 2004, BoC announced that it had removed Liu Jinbao as the bank's vice chairman. Liu had been under investigation for suspected involvement in economic crimes since early 2002. In July 2004, government officials from the Ministry of Supervision confirmed that Liu was suspected of embezzlement, bribery, and illegally approving loans.[67]

The alleged primary wrongdoing was Liu's role as the head of BoC's Hong Kong branch in its problem loans totaling HKD 2.1 billion (USD 270 million) to a Shanghai-based private entrepreneur, Zhou Zhengyi, in early 2002.[68] However, the key factor in Liu's downfall was widely believed to be not the Zhou Zhengyi case, but another series of problem loans extended by BoC's Shanghai branch, when Liu was its general manager, to a local private enterprise group, Wantai.[69] The Wantai case was exposed in December 2003, when financial inspectors from the Communist Party's Central Committee discovered astonishing results in their probe into Liu's wrongdoing: Wantai had taken 28 loans, worth 1.48 billion yuan (USD 178 million), from BoC's Shanghai branch over four years. The total value of the loans plus interest was nearly RMB 1.6 billion yuan (USD 193 million). At the end of 2000, except for two loans that were not yet mature,

---

64. Hu Shuli, "Who's Behind Feng Mingchang? (shei kongzhi Feng Mingchang?)," *Caijing*, January 24, 2005.
65. *Ibid.*
66. *Ibid.*
67. Ling Huawei & Kang Weiping, "Embezzlement Woes Haunt BoC Hong Kong," *Caijing*, August 20, 2004.
68. Justin Lau, "Liu Sacked by Bank of China," *Financial Times*, February 21, 2004, p. 9.
69. Ling Huawei, "The Dangerous Triangle (weixian de sanjiao)," *Caijing*, March 5, 2004.

95 percent of these loans had become NPLs. What was more outrageous was that less than 25 percent of these NPLs were originally lent on collateral.[70]

As the probe into the Liu Jinbao case went deeper, more scandals erupted at the BoC's Hong Kong branch. In August 2004, the branch's vice chairman, Ding Yansheng, was taken in custody by mainland police for his involvement in alleged misappropriation of funds. Ding was suspected of embezzling funds owned by controlling shareholders of former BoC member banks before the Hong Kong branch's restructuring in 2001. Zhu Chi, another vice chairman of the branch, was later also under investigation for the same allegation. Specifically, Liu Jinbao was alleged of embezzling from the BoC's Hong Kong branch HKD 4 million (USD 513,000), while Ding and Zhu each took HKD 1.5 million (USD 192,000). After misappropriating the money, they destroyed original bank records. The sequential departure of these three people left only one senior executive remaining on the board since the branch's IPO on the Stock Exchange of Hong Kong in 2002. This scandal spurred growing investor concern over the bank's corporate governance and internal controls.[71]

6.5.4 The former BoC president corruption case (2003)

In December 2003, Wang Xuebing, a former BoC president, was sentenced to 12 years in prison for taking bribes worth RMB 1.15 million (USD 138,000) and numerous improper gifts.[72] Moreover, Wang was alleged to have overruled subordinates at the bank to make risky loans to favored clients and extend their credit terms during his tenure at the bank between 1991 and 1996.[73] His case came to light just months after a loan scandal erupted at BoC's New York branch. That scandal resulted in fines against the bank of USD 20 million by both U.S. and Chinese banking regulators.[74] The details of the BoC's New York branch case are provided below.

6.5.5 The BoC New York branch fines case (2003)

In January 2003, an investigation by the U.S. Office of Currency Comptroller (OCC) found BoC's New York branch guilty of misconduct, for which it was

---

70. Ling Huawei, "Top Bankers Brought Down by NPLs," *Caijing*, March 5, 2004.
71. Francesco Guerrera & Justin Lau, "Bosses Quit Bank over Scandal," *Financial Times*, August 17, 2004, p. 26.
72. "A List of Senior Bank Officials Implicated in Financial Crime Cases over Recent Years (jinnian yinhang gaoguan she an yilan)," *Caijing*, January 10, 2005, online < http://www. caijing.com.cn/coverstory/2005-01-10/2302.shtml >.
73. Richard McGregor, "Top Chinese Banker Jailed," *Financial Times*, December 11, 2003, p. 33.
74. Andrew Browne, "Bank of China Unit Faces Fresh Scandal," *Asian Wall Street Journal*, August 4, 2004, A1.

fined USD 10 million.[75] This incident was received by the Chinese government as a "welcome move" because the OCC's action would encourage reform in China's banking industry. Apart from the fine imposed by the U.S. regulator, as the parent company of its New York branch, BoC was also fined USD 10 million by China's central bank for failing to maintain proper supervision and internal controls.[76]

According to the investigators from the U.S. Treasury, the offences of the BoC New York branch took place in 1991–1999, including improper loans to people who had personal relationships with bank officials and fraudulent loan and letter-of-credit schemes.[77] These wrongdoings had resulted in a total loss of USD 34 million at this branch between 1992 and 2000.[78] In fact, such abuses were believed to be widespread in China's state banking industry, where influential borrowers often received special treatment and were frequently granted loans that eventually became NPLs.

6.5.6 The BoC Kaiping branch embezzlement case (2001)

By far, the largest case of spectacular embezzlement resulting from lax supervision and internal controls was the so-called "Kaiping Case" at BoC, which involved bank funds worth at least USD 483 million being stolen between 1992 and 2001 by three managers at a BoC local branch in Kaiping city, Guangdong province. The three managers in question, Xu Chaofan, Yu Zhendong and Xu Guojun, had absconded overseas with embezzled money days before an investigation by BoC's headquarters discovered their theft in October 2001.[79] Yu Zhendong fled to the U.S. but was returned by the FBI to Chinese authorities in April 2004, while the other two still remain at large.[80]

This theft was described as the biggest banking scandal in China since the establishment of the PRC government in 1949. Its scale was astonishing: the money stolen, USD 483 million, was more than the aggregate income of the city of Kaiping for the previous 10 years up to 2001, and the city had attracted just over USD 100 million in foreign investment by then.[81]

75. "Bank of China Theft Sets New Standards in Skullduggery," *South China Morning Post*, May 14, 2002, p. 3.
76. Hu Shuli & Gu Wei, "What Happened at the New York Branch of BoC? (zhonghang Niu Yue fenhang fasheng le shenme?)," *Caijing*, February 20, 2003.
77. Associated Press, "Beijing Says Bank Fine Serves As a Warning to the Industry," *Asian Wall Street Journal*, January 23, 2002, p. 4.
78. Hu & Gu, *supra* note 76.
79. Pan Xiaobing & Wang Feng, "The Kaiping Case Returns to the Spotlight (zaijie Kaiping an)," *Caijing*, May 5, 2004, online < http://www.caijing.com.cn/coverstory/2004-05-05/2510.shtml >.
80. Browne, *supra* note 74.
81. "Bank of China Theft," *supra* note 75.

This case exposed how weak the internal controls were at the bank. The three former managers at BoC's Kaiping branch were able to steal money from the bank for 8 years, and what is particularly appalling is that not only did the three go undetected but they were promoted during the time when the gross theft was taking place.[82] More importantly, theft on a grand scale like this could not possibly have been committed by only the three people that were identified as the chief culprits in the Kaiping case. Indeed, after Yu Zhendong was repatriated to the Chinese authorities by the U.S. government, new evidence emerged as the investigation continued, suggesting possible involvements of others at the bank. The complete version of the real story has yet to be revealed as the investigation proceeds further.[83]

6.5.7   The repercussions of bank failures and their solutions

The enormity of these most egregious banking scandals in China may cost the country much-needed investor confidence at a time when the state banks were preparing for overseas listings. The negative impact of these bank failures is particularly acute when China's transition has come to a critical point where the danger of an emerging "crony market economy" is looming large. In this context, banking reform, although primarily concerned with improving their corporate governance, especially with regard to the lax internal supervision and controls, requires complementary measures to be adopted in related areas, including, most importantly, anti-corruption and the transformation of the role of the government during transition.

This need for complementary reform is clearly demonstrated in those reported cases, whereby senior bank officials taking bribes and colluding with private businesspeople to approve problem loans appeared to be a common situation. The power to control and allocate economic resources has been frequently abused for rent-seeking purposes. This cannot be cured only through corporate governance reforms at the banks without also changing the institutional and legal environments that incubate or indulge these abuses.

Moreover, from what has been revealed, local governments have often played a large part in some of the most serious bank failures, and not accidentally, the province of Guangdong, China's fastest growing regional economy, has contributed largely to the spectacular bank scandals of recent years. There are two main reasons for this peculiarity. First, because the role of the government, especially at local levels, is not yet properly defined to accommodate the needs of a market economy, government officials often

---

82.   *Ibid.*
83.   Pan & Wang, *supra* note 79.

interfere with banks' lending decisions on behalf of their favored borrowers, which increases the likelihood of incurring NPLs. Second, because of the emphasis on single dimensional "GDP growth" indicators to evaluate government officials' performance, as has been insisted in recent years by the central government, local officials tend to disregard the need for nurturing a healthy credit culture and establishing effective property rights protection mechanisms in their jurisdictions, which is certainly not helpful in averting loan defaults or financial frauds.

Another problem associated with these bank scandals is that China's speculative stockmarket seems to have provided rent-seeking bankers with a strong incentive to illegally divert bank funds into the stockmarket for lucrative abnormal returns. This has had a negative impact on both the stockmarket and the banking sector, thus entailing the danger of threatening a systemic financial risk.[84]

Therefore, to effectively deal with bank failures and bring vigorous discipline and monitoring to the financial system, the following steps need to be taken at the next stage of China's financial reform:

(a) Strengthening internal controls and corporate governance in the banking sector, and establishing personal accountability, including criminal liability, of bank officials who fail to perform their duty diligently or conduct corruptive activities that cause questionable loans or NPLs.

(b) Further liberalizing the financial sector and introducing competition to the state monopoly in credit allocaion and share issuance, and bringing more market discipline into the financial system.

(c) Combating corruption in both the banking sector and the government to vigorously punish rent-seeking activities as well as outright fraud and theft.

(d) Implementing complementary measures to prevent the vicious interaction between illegally diverted bank funds and stockmarket speculation.

6.6 Overseas Listings of Chinese Banks

After all necessary preliminary steps had been taken (their actual effect is another matter and will only be judged fairly years later), the government started to sell minority stakes in the "big four" to international investors through their overseas listings. In this effort, CCB, BoC and ICBC made faster progress than ABC and their overseas IPOs took place in 2005 and 2006.

---

84. Hu Shuli, "What Crime Has Liu Jinbao Been Implicated with? (Liu Jinbao suoshe hezui?)," *Caijing*, March 5, 2004.

6.6.1 Reasons for overseas listings

As widely recognized, the most important reason for overseas listings is that forcing China's state banks to subject themselves to a much higher level of scrutiny by international market regulators, even at the cost of embarrassing exposures of scandals, may be an effective inducement to bring about systemic changes in the banking sector. The requirements of transparency, managerial performance and investor returns in overseas capital markets would be beneficial disciplines on China's banks and would compel them to meet the challenge from international competitors as China further liberalizes its financial sector.

According to expert opinions, the government's main goal in banks' overseas listings is not to raise cash. Compared to how much money the government has so far used to bail out the indebted "big four," which had reached a total of USD 260 billion in recent years, proceeds of overseas listings, not exceeding USD 19.1 billion for each bank, would be modest. Therefore, instead of more funds, the government hopes to introduce vigorous discipline and monitoring to banks' lending practices that must accompany China's transition to a market economy. For example, fixing lax lending standards that comes with inspection by international auditors and management consultants is critical if the "big four" were to compete effectively against foreign competitors when China's banking sector started to experience much greater liberalization since December 2006.[85]

6.6.2 The shadow surrounding banks' listing plans

One of the relevant issues concerning banks' overseas IPOs was the choice of listing location where the "big four" would launch their IPOs. The coming into force of the Sarbanes-Oxley Act had given China's banks second thoughts. Tightening securities market rules and ongoing investor litigation against listed companies, such as the class action brought by American investors against the insurer China Life, had deterred Chinese banks from listing on the New York Stock Exchange.[86] Instead, other less restrictive markets, such as Hong Kong and London, appeared to show stronger attraction to Chinese banks. Speaking on this international competition for large Chinese issuers, the SEC chairman Christopher Cox remarked in 2005 that Chinese banks opting out NYSE would be a sign of not meeting higher listing standards. This remark, however, was robustly rebutted by the Chinese government.

There were other difficult issues as well. For example, because some potential investors in ICBC, BoC and CCB were worried about the health of

---

85. "Casino Capital," *supra* note 4.
86. Bei Hu & Bloomberg, "Theft May Postpone BoC's Planned Flotation," *South China Morning Post,* January 25, 2005, p. 1.

the banks' balance sheets and questioned whether the banks' lending practices had improved enough to avoid a sharp rise in NPLs after their IPOs, they had pressured the Chinese government to pledge help to the banks as a condition for their overseas listings. International investors believed that a promise of financial support by the Chinese government was essential to mitigate fund managers' concerns about the first international IPOs from China's banking system. They demanded that the Chinese government make an open pledge to international investors because the market would not trust what the banks stated in their prospectuses.[87] These investors required the right to withdraw their investment if banks' books were worsen, or IPOs were not launched within certain time periods, or IPO prices were below their purchasing prices.

However, this demand for a government pledge from the international investors was not acceptable to the Chinese government. As just explained, the very reason of listing the state banks overseas is to introduce vigorous discipline and monitoring by both regulators and investors in mature capital markets, thus establishing effective corporate governance mechanisms to avoid further accumulation of NPLs. Therefore, an open pledge by the Chinese government that it will bail out the banks in times of financial debacles would actually work against the government's expectation of the banks' overseas listing — the removal of moral hazard from the "big four" and the installment of market discipline into their daily operations. Otherwise, the NPL problem would not diminish even after the banks went public on the overseas capital markets.

There were also controversies over the selling prices of ownership stakes. For all the three banks that had invited foreign strategic investors, the selling prices were just slightly above projected book value of bank assets (for example, CCB was priced at 1.98 price-to-book while BoC at 2.18). Some domestic critics had complained that these prices were "too cheap."

6.6.3 The launch of IPOs

Despite initial skepticism among many international investors, the speed of Chinese banks in pushing forward their IPO plans had been remarkable. Not long after their shareholding restructuring was completed, CCB, BoC and ICBC all had successfully launched their IPOs in Hong Kong; BoC and ICBC also conducted IPOs in the domestic A-share market.

CCB's Hong Kong IPO

CCB was the first of the "big four" to be listed overseas. It successfully launched an IPO in Hong Kong on October 27, 2005. It was the world's biggest IPO in

---

87. Francesco Guerrera, "Call for Beijing to Pledge CCB Aid," *Financial Times*, September 17, 2004, p. 28.

four years, raising USD 8 billion for selling 12 percent of shares. CCB's Hong Kong IPO was widely praised as a "landmark event" for China's banking reform.

CCB's Hong Kong IPO was well received by the local market: retail portion was more than 42 times over-subscribed; there was more than USD 60 billion of demand from institutions and corporations. CCB's post-IPO capitalization immediately reached more than USD 66 billion, making it one of the world's largest banks by capitalization. In CCB's prospectus, it disclosed incentive schemes and compensation arrangements for senior management, which indicated that the bank paid a total amount of RMB 12 million to five senior managers over 2002–04.

BoC's IPO in Hong Kong and subsequent listing in Shanghai

Following CCB's footsteps, BoC completed its H-share listing on June 1, 2006. It raised USD 11.2 billion for selling 15 percent of shares to public investors. BoC's shares were 76 times over-subscribed by retail investors and 12 times by institutions. Shortly after, BoC also launched its A-share listing on July 5, 2006 on the Shanghai Stock Exchange, raising another USD 2.5 billion. It made BoC the first state bank to have a non-simultaneous "H&A" dual listing.

ICBC dual listing in Hong Kong and Shanghai

On October 27, 2006, ICBC became the first Chinese issuer to launch a simultaneous "A&H" dual listing. Some commentators regarded this move as a "forced" action by the bank at the urge of the Chinese banking and securities regulators in response to domestic sentiment and political debate that had been centered on the near monopoly enjoyed by Hong Kong's stockmarket on China's highest profile listings.

Notably, ICBC was the first Chinese bank to launch road shows in Middle East, where state-owned investment firms of Kuwait and Qatar had been chosen as the bank's "cornerstone" investors. For international investors, ICBC's IPO in Hong Kong was launched in "near-perfect" market conditions: the Hong Kong's Hang Seng Index was then trading at six-year highs; Hong Kong's China Enterprises Index, which tracks the largest mainland companies traded in Hong Kong, was trading at nine-year highs. As a result, ICBC's IPO recorded an unprecedented demand for shares, raising USD 19.1 billion in total for selling 17 percent stake, making it the world's largest IPO ever. After IPO, ICBC immediately became the world's fifth biggest bank with a market value of about USD 148 billion.

6.6.4 After IPO, what next?

After the successful launch of IPOs of CCB, BoC and ICBC, for these banks the really difficult tasks are just ahead, even though their prospects remain largely positive given the resolve of the Chinese government to reform the banking sector. In particular, corporate governance reform is the "chemical change" of the banking sector which is difficult to take hold if not pressed with urgency and forcefulness. One question that needs to be asked is whether good corporate governance of banks is compatible with government control, which often raises the dilemma between banks' commercial objectives centered on profit making and political objectives centered on maintenance of "social stability."

Moreover, for Chinese banks it is still a long way to go before effective risk management and internal controls can be established. This challenge can be seen from their generally low levels of professionalism and lack of qualified personnel. Even as the banks were launching overseas IPOs, new cases of bank failure and corruption had been uncovered. One major cause for such malfeasance is that control of local braches still remains difficult due to banks' decentralized operational structures. Some commentators have also warned that the rising rates of profits and ROE (return on equity) at the state banks after their IPOs are exaggerated, that low rates of ROA (return on assets) actually reflect inadequate levels of equity and vulnerability to an economic slowdown.[88]

Therefore, the efforts of China's banking reform should not end at overseas IPOs, but should proceed to tackle politically more difficult aspects of reform, such as allowing wider participation of foreign and domestic private capital in banks' corporate governance structures, and making the board of directors more professional and its appointments independent of political considerations. Understandably, such tasks must be intertwined with complementary reforms in other aspects of Chinese economic and political systems, accompanied by the government's continuing retreat from the market.

6.7 **Summary**

According to recent progress reports by major international rating agencies such as Moody's and S&P, China's banking system is "in the midst of revolutionary change" and the outlook on China's banking system is "positive".[89] Even with these optimistic estimates, China's banking reform is by no means an easy task and is expected to be a gradual and highly challenging process in order to establish a modern banking sector operating on the basis of commercial lending and prudent credit scoring. Predictably, more resources and political determination are needed to push forward the banking reform. This is an overall assessment of the prospects of China's banking reform.

---

88. Weijian Shan, "Will China's Banking Reform Succeed?" , *Asian Wall Street Journal*, October 17, 2005, A.20.
89. Andrew Browne & Jane Lanhee Lee, "S&P 'Positive' on Two China Banks," *Asian Wall Street Journal*, December 1, 2004, M.3.

With respect to necessary future steps of reform, the following remarks are intended to provide some indications of reform direction and policy recommendations.

6.7.1 Two key issues in China's banking reform, both closely associated with reforming the legal and institutional environments

There are two key issues involved in China's banking reform: firstly, addressing the NPL problem; secondly, reforming the ownership structure of state banks and the poor corporate governance it produces. As earlier discussion suggests, the NPL problem is only partly attributable to state intervention, and a large portion of NPL creation has its causes in other aspects of China's transition economy that have been lagging behind market-oriented reforms. These other aspects are primarily related to legal and institutional underdevelopment during China's transition, such as the lack of effective bankruptcy rules to enforce lenders' claims, the weaknesses in local credit culture to honor loan repayments, and the single-dimensional role of local governments in promoting economic growth that has led to imprudent loan allocation. Therefore, in addition to reducing state intervention, the ultimate solution to the NPL problem would also require further progress being made in reforming China's legal and institutional environments.

Similarly, although reforming the ownership structure of the state banks is necessary, if without advances in transforming the role of the government to accomodate a market economy, a state owner with a controlling stake in shareholding banks would not essentially change its pattern of behaviour, leaving the removal of government intervention in banks' lending decisions an impossible task.

6.7.2 Devising mechanisms to contain rent-seeking activities is both a critical complement to banks' corporate governance reform aimed at strengthening internal controls, and a necessary condition for market mechanisms to develop in a benign environment

During China's transition, market-oriented reforms have come to a critical point where signs of administrative power entering into the market for rent-seeking opportunities are increasingly prevalent. In this sense, the danger of China moving toward a "bad market economy" is not an imaginary threat. In China's current institutional environment, where market mechanisms are being developed under a largely illiberal political regime, those with control over resource allocation, such as bank officials in charge of allocating credit, have a natural tendency to enter the rent-seeking process. This is among the primary causes for corporate governance failures at the state banks. Accordingly, devising mechanisms to contain rent-seeking activities, which in turn would lead to legal reform and government transformation, is a crucial complement to banks' corporate governance reform aimed at strengthening internal controls. In the meantime, the development of market mechanisms also needs to be free from the distortion brought by rent-seekers. In this connection, China's banking reform must proceed with the assistance of anti-corruption campaigns in the financial sector.

For example, in March 2005, the former chairman of CCB, Zhang Enzhao, abruptly resigned from the bank for "personal reasons," and had been under investigation by the anti-corruption department of the Communist Party. The real reason behind his departure from the bank, as widely speculated in China's financial industry, was not likely to be "personal" but possibly related to a lawsuit filed in the U.S., alleging that Zhang took a bribe of USD 1 million from an American firm for helping it secure a lucrative information-technology contract with the bank. The plaintiff in this case was a former business partner of CCB, Beijing-based Grace & Digital Information Technology, which claimed that it was deprived of business benefits under its previous contract with CCB. The principal defendant was Fidelity Information Services, an American financial services company, which was accused of bribing Zhang to sign a new contract that excluded the plaintiff. Accordingly, Fidelity Information Services was faced with the allegation that it violated America's Foreign Corrupt Practices Act, which prohibits American firms from bribing government officials in foreign countries in exchange for business opportunities.[90]

6.7.3   Fuller privatization of the "big four" is not a practical option for reform at current stage

China's banking reform, while closely associated with the SOE reform, is distinct from the latter in terms of viable ownership reform options. The shareholding restructuring and overseas listings of the "big four" are positive and necessary steps toward establishing a modern banking system in China, but further privatization would be extremely difficult for both economic and political reasons.

Under any potential privatization scheme for the "big four," who would be eligible for taking a controlling stake is a highly sensitive issue in a political sense, given the critical role of the banking system in China's economic

---

90. See "Personal Banking," *The Economist*, March 23, 2005. This latest bank scandal had spurred a new round of intense debates among both domestic and overseas commentators, over whether Chinese state banks were yet "ready" to go public overseas before "cleaning house" at home first.

structure. Economically, since the "big four" are all of gigantic size and in combination control 60 percent of China's total bank assets, to obtain a controlling stake would require capital investment worth up to 50 percent of China's GDP. This is in practice extremely difficult for any private or foreign equity investors to finance. Besides, foreign controlling stakes at the "big four" would result in billions of dollars pouring into China, thus putting the country's domestic monetary stability at tremendous risk and engendering an inflation crisis. [91]

Therefore, unlike China's SOEs, the "big four" are not suitable for privatization, at least at the current stage of banking reform. By comparison, a more viable option is to invite domestic and international strategic investors to hold minority stakes, which would be both politically realistic and commercially viable. Besides, overseas listings and even moderate reform of the ownership structure of the "big four" are likely to generate considerable corporate governance improvement, because disciplines in global equity markets can mitigate the agency problem much more effectively than could the domestic stockmarket, which is speculative and retail-oriented.

6.7.4   While shareholding restructuring and overseas listings would improve corporate governance of the "big four," to create further incentives to perform, the liberalization of China's financial sector also needs to be accelerated

Further opening up China's financial system under its WTO commitments would in general have a positive effect on its banking reform. As foreign and private competitors challenge the monopoly status of the state banks in providing financial services to the Chinese public, heavier pressure from the market could be imposed on the "big four" to perform and increase their operational efficiency and quality of service.

6.7.5   The complementary nature of structural reforms is a central theme of China's transition

The strong complementarity between structural reforms of China's banking system, SOEs, and stockmarket is not only implicated in the long existing lender-debtor relationship between the banks and SOEs, which has not been based on commercial terms for years, but is also evidenced by the risky pattern of bank funds illegally entering the stockmarket for lucrative returns on share

---

91. Zhong Jiayong, "The Implications of the Lowest Competitiveness of State-owned Banks in Beijing's Banking Circles," *Business Watch* (*Jingji Guancha*), December 2, 2004.

speculation, which creates more bubbles and increases the possibility of a systemic financial crisis. Therefore, China's banking reform cannot afford to be delayed further and must proceed decisively as an urgent priority. Failing that, the prospects of the privatization of SOEs and stockmarket reform could be severely compromised.

6.7.6 The proper sequencing of banking reform is that "cleaning house" and overseas listings should proceed simultaneously to create synergies

The specific issue of sequencing involved in the process of China's banking reform is highlighted in the ongoing debate in China's policy and academic circles over the appropriate approach toward reforming the "big four" state-owned commercial banks plagued by both NPLs and corruption.

On the one hand, some Chinese economists and foreign commentators argue that China's banking reform should adopt an approach of "cleaning house first, going public overseas second," which prioritizes corporate governance reform to strengthen internal controls and curb financial corruption over overseas listings. On the other hand, other economists advocate an alternative strategy, which sees overseas listings as an external lever to propel corporate governance reform and greater competition in the banking sector. The latter position on the sequencing of banking reform presents a rationale for accelerated financial reforms at later stages of China's transition, which is similar to China's primary motivation in joining the WTO in 2001, i.e., to obtain an external lever to precipitate deeper and broader structural reforms when domestic conditions have not been fully receptive to such advances.

In light of this controversy over the sequencing of China's banking reform, the basic judgment of this book is more in line with the latter position, i.e., pursuing overseas listings as a strategy for achieving external stimuli for otherwise reluctant or difficult reforms under existing political and institutional constraints. While it is uncertain how long and how much resource it will take to achieve meaningful results in domestic corporate governance reform and anti-corruption initiatives in China's banking sector (i.e., "cleaning house"), the urgency of preparing China's banks for greater competition from overseas financial institutions under the country's WTO commitments is clear. More critically, the complementary role of banking reform in helping achieve positive results in China's enterprise and stockmarket reforms provides an even stronger rationale for seeking overseas listings even if the banks are not yet independent commercial lenders and efficient resource allocators. It is widely held by many Chinese economists that external pressures from international investors and regulators could propel or force fundamental banking reforms at home, which might otherwise be off the government's reform agenda because these reforms will be painful and unavoidably bring about massive adjustments in the domestic economy.

Meanwhile, although overseas listings are *necessary* for creating incentives to perform and compete in China's banking sector, they are not *sufficient* to bring about good corporate governance, effective internal controls, and significant reduction of corruption. Rather, domestic reform initiatives to build good legal, financial and corporate governance institutions should go simultaneously with overseas listings to best utilize and capitalize on the benefits of good institutions available abroad and of the much tighter discipline provided by overseas markets.

7

The Chinese Experience in International Corporate Governance Debates

---

Chapter 7 explores both the potential of the Chinese experience to inform, or contribute to, major debates in contemporary comparative corporate governance, particularly in relation to transition economies, and the lessons that China should learn from international experience.

Section 7.1 examines alternative approaches to corporate governance that have been advanced by academics over the last two decades. Of these alternative approaches, an historical and political model, as opposed to a purely economic model, of countries' corporate governance regimes is emphasized in the Chinese context.

Section 7.2 depicts ongoing movements of international convergence of corporate governance, and also assesses the implications of the academic debate over which model should be, or already is, leading the direction of convergence for future corporate governance reforms in transition economies, especially in China.

Section 7.3 reviews empirical evidence on privatization and securities market failures in transition economies by closely analyzing the experience of Russian privatization and related capital market reforms. Section 7.3 also points out both the reasons behind the discontents underlying the Russian experience and the lessons China should learn from Russia.

Section 7.4 summarizes the lessons that China should learn from the international experience in corporate governance reforms.

7.1 **China and Alternative Approaches to Corporate Governance**

To present the conceptual basis of the global debate in comparative corporate governance research, Section 7.1 outlines several alternative approaches to the understanding of corporate governance that have been under contest over the last two decades. Of the alternative approaches, the historical and political model, as opposed to a purely economic model, of national corporate governance regimes receives special attention due to its particular relevance to the Chinese experience. In the meantime, the applicability of the legal and institutional perspectives on corporate governance to China is also discussed.

7.1.1 **The economic model of corporate governance**

The economic model of corporate governance, which was first developed by transaction cost economics within the law and economics disciplines, has primarily focused on advocating contractual solutions to the classical "agency problem" caused by the separation of ownership and control of modern public corporations.[1]

The primacy of contractual solutions to the agency problem

Despite the variety of opinions on the appropriate scope of constituencies to whom corporate managers should be accountable, the central idea under the economic model of corporate governance remains constant: the primacy of private and contractual solutions to reducing agency costs and maximizing shareholder value. Major private and contractual arrangements suggested by scholars to address the agency problem include managerial ownership, the separation of decision and risk bearing functions among corporate organs, and the presence of a large minority shareholder.[2]

Under the economic model of corporate governance, there is no room for government intervention in private transactions between firms and their

---

1.   The emergence of the "agency problem" was first pointed out in Adolf A. Berle and Gardiner C. Means, *The Modern Corporation and Private Property* (New York: Macmillan Co., 1933, c1932), who first noted the separation of ownership and control in public corporations. According to the authors, this separation dissolved the unity of private property, so no one "owned" the corporation anymore.

2.   See, for example, Michael C. Jensen & William H. Meckling, "Theory of the Firm: Managerial Behavior, Agency Costs and Ownership Structure," 3:4 *Journal of Financial Economics* 305 (1976); Eugene F. Fama & Michael J. Jensen, "Separation of Ownership and Control," 26 *Journal of Law and Economics* 301 (1983); Randall Morck, Andrei Shleifer & Robert W. Vishny, "Management Ownership and Market Valuation: An Empirical Analysis," 20 *Journal of Financial Economics* 293 (1988); Andrei Shleifer & Robert W. Vishny, "Large Shareholders and Corporate Control," 94:3 *The Journal of Political Economy* 461 (1986).

constituencies. It has been insisted by economists who follow the "Coase Theorem" that through the internal bonding and monitoring arrangements at the firm level (such as the board of directors, managerial incentive compensation and insider shareholdings) and the external control and discipline mechanisms at the market level (such as competition in product and capital markets, the managerial labor market and the market for corporate control), the agency problem can be effectively addressed.[3] In other words, a contractual rather than a mandatory model of corporate governance is the optimal model for achieving economic efficiency. Markets, not law, should prevail in shaping the structure of corporate governance.[4]

The marginal role of law

However, to insist on the primacy of contractual solutions to the agency problem does not mean that law's function should be ignored completely. Law still plays a marginal role where contracting parties fail to perceive all possible contingencies. According to the "corporation-as-contract" thesis proposed by some "Coasian" economists, while corporate governance arrangements are best left to private actors in corporate ventures to negotiate and select by contract, corporate law exists to "provide a set of terms available off-the-rack so that participants in corporate ventures can save the cost of contracting."[5]

In response to criticisms that managers can use their informational advantage to select unfair or exploitative contractual terms detrimental to investors, the "Coasian" economists contend that contractual corporate governance devices are unlikely candidates for challenge as mistakes if they have survived in many firms for extended periods. Markets, they claim, rather than regulation, should be the ultimate judge of the merits of specific corporate governance arrangements. Their message is clear:

> ...[U]nless there is a strong reason to believe that regulation has a "comparative advantage" over competition in markets in evaluating the effects of corporate contracts, there is no basis for displacing actual arrangements as "mistakes," "exploitation," and the like.[6]

Effectively, the economic model of corporate governance rejects corporate purposes other than maximizing shareholder value because the "Coasian"

3. Oliver Williamson, "Corporate Governance," 93 *Yale Law Journal* 1197 (1984), p. 1202; Anup Agrawal & Charles R. Knoeber, "Firm Performance and Mechanisms to Control Agency Problems between Managers and Shareholders," 31:3 *Journal of Financial and Quantitative Analysis* 377 (1996), p. 377; Frank H. Easterbrook & Daniel R. Fischel, *The Economic Structure of Corporate Law* (Cambridge, MA: Harvard University Press, 1991, 3rd Printing, 1996).
4. Frank H. Easterbrook, "International Corporate Differences: Markets or Law?", 9:4 *Journal of Applied Corporate Finance* 23 (1997).
5. Easterbrook & Fischel, *supra* note 3, p. 34.
6. *Ibid.*, pp. 31–32.

economists argue for an "enabling" corporate law which is designed out of economic consideration for corporate survival, not the objectives of "fairness" or paternalism.[7] Therefore, corporate law is regarded as having an "economic structure," that it increases the wealth of all corporate stakeholders by supplying the rules that investors would select if contracting were costless.[8]

The challenge from transition economies

While this "Coasian" approach has attracted much criticism in the ongoing corporate governance debate, the most difficult challenge that it has encountered comes from transition economies. The problem is evident: given the symptoms of underdevelopment in most post-communist states of legal and market institutions, such as the absence of an independent and non-corrupt judiciary, a sophisticated financial press, and effective mechanisms of contract enforcement and protection for property rights, the internal and external corporate governance mechanisms suggested by the "Coasian" economists are either weak or missing in these countries. Under such unfavorable circumstances, it is hard to reconcile the "Coasian" argument for an autonomous model of corporate governance with the reality of institutional deficits in most transition economies. Later discussion in setion 7.3 about privatization and corporate governance failures in transition economies, primarily Russia, will provide evidence of the difficulties of applying a purely economic model of corporate governance to underdeveloped institutional environments.

7.1.2 Political and historical determinants of corporate governance

Scholars critical of the purely economic model of corporate governance have suggested other determinants of corporate governance structures and corporate finance patterns.

The political model of corporate governance

A particularly influential opinion is provided by Mark Roe, who argues for a political model of corporate governance. In two important books, the first published in 1994 and the second in 2003, Roe has convincingly presented his case against the "Coasian" explanation for corporate governance. He argues that economic determinants are not primary in shaping corporate governance patterns; instead, "path dependence" can largely explain particular corporate governance models in different countries. He discovered that historical and political factors are important to the evolution of corporate governance practices in major industrialized countries, such as the U.S., the U.K., Germany

---

7. *Ibid.*, p. vii.
8. *Ibid.*

and Japan.[9] For example, the phenomenon of "strong managers, weak owners" observed in the U.S. corporate governance structure is not a result of economic efficiency, but a consequence of the American politics during the progressive periods, which was hostile to concentrated ownership by financial institutions and confined the terrain on which the large American enterprise could evolve.[10]

Other critics of the economic model of corporate governance have expressed similar views. Some argue that, as to the question of whether there is a link between corporate governance and economic efficiency, a firm conclusion is difficult to draw. In order to understand how existing corporate governance mechanisms come to respond to a changing array of problems in a given economy, one needs to study the impact of history and politics in particular countries.[11]

While some authors have looked at the political model of corporate governance at a systemic level and from an international perspective, other authors have offered specific examples at the firm level found in particular industries in individual economies. For example, empirical research on board size and composition in American firms has revealed that some outside directors play a "political role." A major finding in this aspect is that "politically experienced directors" are more prevalent in firms where politics matters more, such as firms that sell to government. In many cases, lawyer-directors are more prevalent in firms where costs of environmental regulation are higher.[12] These politically appointed outside directors are not necessarily associated with value maximization of firms because they tend to increase corporate operating costs (such as those related to meeting higher environmental standards), or put political constraints on firm activities. On the contrary, some researchers have discovered either a negative effect or little effect of more outsiders on the board of directors on firm performance.[13] The political reasons for adding politicians, environmental activists and consumer representatives to the board are considered to be a major contributor to this negative feedback.[14]

---

9. Mark J. Roe, *Strong Managers, Weak Owners: The Political Roots of American Corporate Finance* (Princeton University Press, 1994); Mark J. Roe, *Political Determinants of Corporate Governance: Political Context, Corporate Impact* (New York: Oxford University Press, 2003).
10. Roe 1994, *ibid.*, p. 283.
11. Ronald J. Gilson, "Corporate Governance and Economic Efficiency: When Do Institutions Matter?", 74 *Washington University Law Quarterly* 327 (1996), p. 345.
12. Anup Agrawal & Charles R. Knoeber, "Do Some Outside Directors Play a Political Role?", XLIV *Journal of Law and Economics* 179 (2001).
13. See, for example, Bernard Black, "The Non-Correlation between Board Independence and Long-Term Firm Performance," 27 *The Journal of Corporation Law* 231 (2002); Sanjai Bhagat & Bernard Black, "Board Composition and Firm Performance: The Uneasy Case for Majority-Independent Boards," 1053 *Practising Law Institute: Corporate Law and Practice Course Handbook Series* 95 (1998); Benjamin E. Hermalin & Michael S. Weisbach, "Boards of Directors as An Endogenously Determined Institution: A Survey of the Economic Literature," 9:1 FRBNY *Economic Policy Review* 20 (2003).
14. Agrawal & Knoeber 1996, *supra* note 3, p. 394.

The relevance of political determinants of corporate governance to China

The political explanation for corporate governance is very compelling in the context of China's enterprise and corporate governance reforms because it can help explain a number of phenomena in China's transition process that might be considered as having "Chinese characteristics." For instance, maintaining a large inefficient state sector that consumes more than half of state bank loans and receives heavy government subsidies is certainly not a good way of achieving economic efficiency. For the pure economic purpose of maximizing value, there should be no state control and ownership concentration in many of China's shareholding companies.

The government's insistence on continuing state ownership in ongoing enterprise and corporate governance reforms can only be explained by political reasons, such as retaining the ability of the state to impose on firms aims other than value maximization (employment maintenance, or provision of social safety net services, for example). In addition, the Chinese government is very keen on producing state-owned "national champions" that can have a strong international presence to show the advantages of "socialism with Chinese characteristics" (*zhongguo tese de shehuizhuyi*), which, if successful, would yield more ideological than economic premia. No doubt, the most important political reason for maintaining state ownership is to defend the Communist Party's ruling position under the current political regime. In giving up state ownership, the Party will virtually lose one of the most effective tools to control the process of resource allocation in Chinese society, which would pose serious challenges to the Chinese government whose authority and legitimacy increasingly rely on economic performance.

Another example of the political explanation for corporate governance patterns can be found in China's privatization experiment. One option for privatizing China's SOEs (including large ones) that has been studied by the Chinese government is to sell SOEs to both domestic and foreign private investors. The issue of who the preferred foreign private buyers would be is relevant to the discussion of political determinants of corporate governance. It is widely believed that wealthy ethnic Chinese in Hong Kong, Macau, Taiwan and other countries would make up a large portion of the potential "foreign" buyers. Because of these investors' Chinese origin, domestic opposition to the transfer of state assets (as compared to selling SOEs to westerners) is expected to be significantly reduced. This factor would certainly become a political (as well as cultural) facilitation for executing decentralized privatization at the next stage of China's enterprise reform because local governments usually welcome overseas ethnic Chinese businesspeople to participate in their local reform programs.

Finally, the argument for political determinants of corporate governance has one more supportive example: the bankruptcy regime in China. The logic under the economic model of corporate governance that markets automatically discipline inefficient firms does not apply to China's transition situation: inefficient firms do not exit the market as quickly as they should because pervasive local protectionism allows many of them to stay in business long after they would have died in mature market economies. Local protectionism in China is largely a product of political considerations as local governments are concerned more about social unrest caused by massive unemployment than they are about economic efficiency. Hence the negligible annual rate of bankruptcy cases in China, which was no more than 0.05 percent of all enterprises in the 1990s.[15]

7.1.3 Social and cultural factors that influence corporate governance

From another perspective, a "social norms matter" thesis has been proposed to further challenge the validity of the economic model of corporate governance. Some scholars regard social norms as an important factor that influences the patterns of corporate governance practices. They argue that social norms matter for corporate governance because they can significantly affect market value and increase the stock price of listed firms. Social norms matter most when law is the weakest in a given economy.[16] Strictly speaking, this emphasis on the role of social norms in shaping corporate governance structure does not closely follow the line of reasoning under the political model of corporate governance, but it nevertheless draws upon a country's history and politics when accounting for the formation and evolution of social norms. Social norms, such as "culture," can constrain certain corporate behavior to make firms respond to the prevailing public opinion in a given society. For example, widespread outrage in the U.S. over executive pay constrains it from going even higher.[17]

Peculiar social and cultural factors that influence the shaping and maintenance of business ethics and norms in a given country can sometimes be difficult for outsiders to digest or appreciate. For example, despite corporate governance reform in the aftermath of the East Asian crisis, in today's Korean corporate sector characterized by the dominance of family-controlled *chaebols*, there still exist some controversial, even irrational, corporate governance practices that are in stark conflict with generally accepted standards of corporate governance in the West, but deemed permissible by the domestic business community. This is acutely reflected in a protracted battle that had been unfolding dramatically between SK Corporation, South Korea's largest

---

15. Joe Studwell, *The China Dream: The Elusive Quest for the Greatest Untapped Market on Earth* (London: Profile Books Ltd. 2002).
16. John C. Coffee, Jr., "Do Norms Matter? A Cross-Country Evaluation," 149 *University of Pennsylvania Law Review* 2151 (2001) [Coffee 2001].
17. Mark J. Roe, "Can Culture Constrain the Economic Model of Corporate Law?", 69 *University of Chicago Law Review* 1251 (2002).

oil refiner, and Sovereign Asset Management, SK's largest shareholder, over SK's returning chairman who was found guilty of taking part in a USD 1.2 billion accounting fraud at one of SK's affiliates and spent seven months in jail, before returning to his previous post at SK. Since South Korean law does not ban persons convicted of fraud from holding corporate posts, Sovereign's attempts over the course of a 20-month battle to oust this individual were not very successful.[18]

7.1.4 Legal and institutional perspectives on corporate governance

In recent years, a new round of corporate governance debate has been increasingly engaged in exploring the relationships between the following variables: (a) countries' legal origins, (b) the quality of countries' institutions, (c) the effectiveness of countries' corporate governance measured by levels of investor protection, (c) countries' corporate finance patterns, (e) levels of countries' financial development, and (f) countries' economic growth. Specifically, two strands of literature on "law and finance" and "finance and growth" have developed a framework to analyze the complex nexus of correlations between these variables through cross-country empirical studies.

The "law and finance" theory

The "law and finance" theory employs legal and institutional perspectives on corporate governance. It predicts that historically determined differences in legal origins can explain cross-country differences in financial development observed today. Specifically, it is believed and supported by empirical evidence that countries with a common law tradition tend to provide stronger investor protection than countries with a French civil law tradition.

With respect to the relationship between law and finance, researchers have discovered the following nexus of causal links: (a) legal origins strongly determine levels of investor protection; (b) corporate ownership structure is primarily a result of different levels of investor protection; and (c) legal protection of investors, measured by both the character of legal rules and the quality of law enforcement, largely determines corporate finance patterns and levels of financial market development.[19] Consistently, scholars have found

18. See Francesco Guerrera & Song Jung-a, "Sovereign Moves to Oust SK Chairman," *Financial Times*, November 7, 2004.
19. Andrei Shleifer & Robert W. Vishny, "A Survey of Corporate Governance," 52:2 *The Journal of Finance* 737 (1997); Rafael La Porta, Florencio Lopez-De-Silanes, Andrei Shleifer & Robert W. Vishny, "Legal Determinants of External Finance," 52:3 *The Journal of Finance* 1131 (1997) [LLSV 1997]; Rafael La Porta, Florencio Lopez-De-Silanes, Andrei Shleifer & Robert W. Vishny, "Law and Finance," 106:6 *The Journal of Political Economy* 1113 (1998) [LLSV 1998]; Rafael La Porta, Florencio Lopez-De-Silanes, Andrei Shleifer & Robert W. Vishny, "Agency Problems and Dividend Policies around the World,"

that French civil law countries have both the weakest investor protection and the least developed capital markets, especially when compared to common law countries. The primary reason suggested by scholars that civil law countries have weaker investor protection is because they have less effective courts than common law countries.[20]

While it is widely recognized that financial markets appear to improve the allocation of capital, some scholars have studied the relationship between the efficiency of capital allocation and legal protection of investors. They have found that the efficiency of capital allocation is positively correlated with the legal protection of minority investors.[21]

In addition to legal institutions, including legal rules and law enforcement mechanisms such as courts, scholars have also suggested other institutions that are considered conducive to financial market development. For example, less corrupt governments and more informative accounting standards are regarded as important factors in promoting capital market development.[22]

The "finance and growth" theory

On the other hand, the "finance and growth" literature has sought to establish links between countries' financial development and economic growth. Cross-country studies have used various measures of the level of financial development to test its impact on economic growth. These measures include "financial depth" judged by the size of the formal financial intermediary sector, the relative importance of financial institutions, and financial asset distribution. Researchers have found that financial development is strongly associated with countries' economic performance as measured by several key indicators, such as per capita GDP growth, the rate of physical capital accumulation, and improvements in the efficiency of physical capital employment.[23]

55:1 *The Journal of Finance* 1 (2000) [LLSV 2000a]; Rafael La Porta, Florencio Lopez-De-Silanes, Andrei Shleifer & Robert W. Vishny, "Investor Protection and Corporate Governance," 58 *Journal of Financial Economics* 3 (2000) [LLSV 2000b]; Rafael La Porta, Florencio Lopez-De-Silanes, Andrei Shleifer & Robert W. Vishny, "Investor Protection and Corporate Valuation," LVII:3 *The Journal of Finance* 1147 (2002) [LLSV 2002]; Andrei Shleifer & Daniel Wolfenzon, "Investor Protection and Equity Markets," 66 *Journal of Financial Economics* 3 (2002); Thorsten Beck & Ross Levine, "Legal Institutions and Financial Development," NBER Working Paper, No. 10126 (2003).

20. O. Emre Ergungor, "Market- *vs*. Bank-Based Financial Systems: Do Rights and Regulations Really Matter?", 28 *Journal of Banking and Finance* 2869 (2004).

21. Jeffrey Wurgler, "Financial Markets and the Allocation of Capital," 58 *Journal of Financial Economics* 187 (2000).

22. LLSV 1998 and LLSV 1999, *supra* note 19; Simeon Djankov, Rafael La Porta, Florencio Lopez-de-Silanes & Andrei Shleifer, "Courts," 118:2 *Quarterly Journal of Economics* 453 (2003).

23. Robert G. King & Ross Levine, "Finance and Growth: Schumpeter Might be Right," 108:3 *Quarterly Journal of Economics* 717 (1993); Ross Levine, "Financial Development and Economic Growth: Views and Agenda," 35:2 *Journal of Economic Literature* 688 (1997).

In terms of the services provided by financial intermediaries for growth, it has been found that financial intermediaries exert a large, positive impact on total factor productivity (TFP) growth and therefore are conducive to overall GDP growth.[24] Comparing the different roles played by stockmarket and banks in fostering growth, evidence shows that stockmarket liquidity and banking development both positively predict growth, capital accumulation and productivity improvements, which is consistent with the assessment that financial markets provide important services for growth.[25]

The nexus of causal links

To summarize the "law and finance" and "finance and growth" theories, a nexus of causal links between several variables can be presented below:

> Legal origins → quality of law (including legal rules and enforcement) and institutions → levels of investor protection → corporate finance patterns and levels of financial development → outcomes of economic growth

Seen from the above illustration, corporate governance reform in countries with poorer investor protection should pay special attention to strengthening legal and institutional reforms that will afford investors stronger protection. For transition economies that have underdeveloped capital markets and weak legal and institutional environments, this task is not only urgent, but also difficult. As later discussion will indicate, there are many obstacles to legal reforms in developing and transition economies, with the most serious challenge posed by the "politics" of legal reforms. The "politics" of legal reforms in developing and transition economies is mainly reflected in the opposition to reforms from various interest groups who are concerned about losing their vested interests.[26]

7.1.5   Debates over the "law matters" thesis and the role of securities market regulation

The "law and finance" and "finance and growth" literature has resulted in an extended debate on the "law matters" thesis. The central issue of the debate is whether mandatory laws and regulations are superior to more autonomous solutions with respect to the functioning of corporate governance systems and

---

24. Thorsten Beck, Ross Levine & Norman Loayza, "Finance and the Sources of Growth," 58 *Journal of Financial Economics* 261 (2000).
25. Ross Levine & Sara Zervos, "Stockmarket, Banks, and Economic Growth," 88:3 *The American Economic Review* 537 (1998).
26. Florencio Lopez-de-Silanes, "The Politics of Legal Reform," Spring 2002 *Economia* 91 (2002).

capital markets. A considerable volume of research dissects, critiques, and debates the influence of investor protection laws, the efficiency of contract enforcement and private property rights protection on the effectiveness of corporate governance, the efficient allocation of capital, and the overall level of financial development.[27]

There are several representative opinions emerging from this contentious debate, which differ greatly. For example, while some scholars completely dismiss law's relevance for maintaining good corporate governance and capital market development, other scholars strongly advocate imposing strict laws and regulations to protect minority investors.

"Law is irrelevant or marginal" or "Alternative institutions can perform law's function"

As discussed earlier, some economists have developed a "Coasian argument" for an economic model of corporate governance. According to this view, compared to private and contractual arrangements of corporate governance, law is irrelevant or marginal to efficient transactions between firms and their investors and other constituencies.[28] Moreover, some scholars have suggested that in addition to private contracting, there exist other alternative institutions to perform the function that "law matters" advocates say the legal system needs to play, such as rules enacted by stock exchanges or self-regulation by corporate issuers for reputational purposes.[29]

Evidence from emerging markets shows that compared with legal institutions, firm-level corporate governance provisions matter more in countries with weak legal environments and firms can partially compensate for ineffective law and enforcement by establishing good corporate governance and providing credible investor protection.[30] Some legal academics also argue that social norms may play a bigger role than legal rules in shaping and determining corporate behavior. They suggest that there are areas of internal corporate behavior and decision-making that courts should monitor less rigorously because social norms adequately govern behavior.[31]

---

27. Beck & Levine, *supra* note 19.
28. Ronald Coase, "The Problem of Social Cost," 3 *Journal of Law and Economics* 1 (1960); Bernard S. Black, "Is Corporate Law Trivial: A Political and Economic Analysis," 84 *Northwestern University Law Review* 542 (1990); Easterbrook & Fischel, *supra* note 3; Easterbrook, *supra* note 4.
29. Brian R. Cheffins, "Does Law Matter? The Separation of Ownership and Control in the United Kingdom," XXX *The Journal of Legal Studies* 459 (2001).
30. Leora F. Klapper & Inessa Love, "Corporate Governance, Investor Protection, and Performance in Emerging Markets," World Bank Research Working Paper, No. WPS 2818 (2002).
31. Coffee 2001, *supra* note 16.

"Law matters; other institutions cannot substitute for law"

Regarding law's role in protecting investors, especially minority investors, there are also scholars who are "law optimists." They reject the "Coasian" argument for law's irrelevance and suggest that contrary to the "Coasian" argument, recent empirical research demonstrates that legal rules protecting investors matter in many ways and other institutions do not adapt sufficiently to substitute for law's function. In addition, it has been suggested that changing domestic legal rules — in particular through the reform of securities markets — can have a major impact on financial development.[32] To illustrate the point that law matters and legal reforms can have a large effect, evidence has been offered to compare the successful securities market reforms in Germany, the U.S., South Korea and Poland, and the negative example of the Czech Republic.[33]

"Written corporate law matters, but law enforcement and the effectiveness of securities regulation are more important than corporate legal rules"

John Coffee Jr. is a "corporate law skeptic" with respect to corporate law's function in promoting corporate governance and securities market development, and has expressed doubt, in the following terms, about a "paradigm shift" in financial economics from emphasizing the role of private contracting toward asserting the centrality of protecting minority investors by corporate law:

> ...A "paradigm shift" is now underway in the manner in which financial economics views corporate governance, with the new scholarship emphasizing both the centrality of legal protections for minority shareholders and the possibility that regulation can outperform private contracting... [However,] one possibility is that substantive differences in corporate law may matter far less than differences in enforcement practice. In turn, enforcement may depend more upon the strength of the incentives to assert legal remedies than upon the availability of legal remedies themselves... Another possibility is that differences in substantive corporate law are less important than the differences in the level of regulation that different nations impose on their securities markets...[34]

In his opinion, strong securities market regulation and strict enforcement of disclosure rules may be more important than corporate law. He argues that corporate law, which provides protection to minority shareholders against unfair self-dealing transactions at the firm level, may play only a secondary role

---

32. Simon Johnson, "Coase and the Reform of Securities Markets," Federal Reserve Bank of Boston Conference Series [Proceedings] 187 (2000), p. 188.
33. *Ibid.*
34. John J. Coffee Jr., "Privatization and Corporate Governance: The Lessons from Securities Market Failure," 25 *Journal of Corporate Law* 1 (1999), pp. 2–3.

in fostering good corporate governance and securities market development. What is of primary importance to strong securities markets and successful privatization, he suggests, is the level of regulation that different nations impose on their securities markets. Therefore, inadequate securities regulation plays the primary role in explaining privatization failures in transition economies.[35]

Though a "corporate law skeptic," Coffee does not dismiss corporate law's role as irrelevant, especially in the context of post-communist transition and privatization. According to him, corporate law, though of secondary significance, is still vital to good corporate governance and successful privatization in transition economies. For example, evidence reveals that deficiencies in Czech corporate law contributed to the systemic looting of Czech companies by their controlling shareholders.[36] The same was true with Russian corporate law, which was not effective in preventing self-dealing and expropriation of minority shareholders.[37]

The view that law enforcement and the effectiveness of securities regulation are more important than written rules in corporate law seems to have found supportive evidence not only in transition economies, but also at a world-wide level. A recent study on international differences in firms' cost of equity capital shows that countries with extensive securities regulation and strong enforcement mechanisms exhibit lower levels of cost of capital than countries with weak legal institutions. The effects are strongest for institutions that provide information to investors and enable them to privately enforce their contracts.[38]

"Law matters, but core institutions equally matter for strong securities markets": China's need for proper sequencing

Legal academics have studied the experience of transition economies in building functioning securities markets after privatization. They have come to realize that various corporate governance failures during and after privatization have much to do with the lack of institutions that control self-dealing and asset stripping. One of these missing institutions is strong securities markets that can discipline corporate behavior and afford investors effective protection. Therefore, establishing legal and institutional preconditions for strong securities markets is regarded as critical to successful transition. Among the core institutions suggested by scholars, the most needed are those that address information asymmetries and self-dealing.[39]

---

35. *Ibid.*, p. 3.
36. *Ibid.*
37. Bernard Black, Reinier Kraakman & Anna Tarassova, "Russian Privatization and Corporate Governance: what went wrong?", 52 Stanford Law Review 1780(2000), p.1780.
38. Luzi Hail & Christian Leuz, "International Differences in Cost of Equity Capital: Do Legal Institutions and Securities Regulation Matter?", ECGI Working Paper, No. 15/2003 (2003).
39. Bernard Black, "The Core Institutions that Support Strong Securities Markets," 55 *Business Law* 1565 (2000); Bernard S. Black, "The Legal and Institutional Preconditions for Strong Securities Markets," 48 *UCLA Law Review* 781 (2001).

The question as to which steps a developing country should take first to strengthen its securities markets — legal reform or building supporting market institutions — is a futile one, because a central characteristic of these institutions is that they interrelate and develop together and reinforce each other.[40] However, for transition economies, there does exist an issue of "sequencing," whereby caution is needed with respect to legal reform and transplantation: corporate governance reform in these economies should be much more basic and less "advanced." In other words, transition economies need "honest judges and regulators, good disclosure rules, and the beginnings of a culture of honesty," before it makes sense to worry about independent directors.[41] This point on sequencing is particularly relevant for the ongoing enterprise and corporate governance reforms in China, where calls for adding independent directors to corporate boards are very strong at present. Given the current underdevelopment of legal and institutional environments and inadequate pools of managerial talents in China, the applicability of this relatively "advanced" practice may need reconsideration.

"Laws and regulations matter, but their enforcement costs should not be excessive"

Some scholars hold a middle ground in the current debate on the role of mandatory legal rules and regulations in investor protection. In his study of the debate over regulation of financial markets, Luigi Zingales maintains that a strong case can be made in favor of more mandatory disclosure while it is unclear whether the benefits of other mandatory regulation exceed its costs.[42] He also analyzes the political barriers in the legislative process, which are largely erected by incumbent firms, to the emergence of an "ideal regulation model." Based on a careful calculation of potential costs and benefits of regulation, Zingales advocates a "skeptical middle ground" for financial market regulation, as compared to two opposite approaches taken respectively by the "extreme libertarians" who disapprove any type of regulation, and the "interventionists" who support massive intervention as remedies to market failures.[43]

"Law matters, but the causality between legal reforms and economic changes is backward": evidence from China

The issue of the causality between law and development outcomes has been extensively studied. Whether law is a "dependent variable" responsive to political

---

40. Black 2000, *ibid.*, pp. 1606–1607.
41. Black 2000, *ibid.*, p. 1607.
42. Luigi Zingales, "The Costs and Benefits of Financial Market Regulation," ECGI Working Paper, No. 21/2004 (2004), p. 53.
43. *Ibid.*, p. 54.

and economic changes, or an "active agent" that endogenously promotes political and economic outcomes has been subject to controversy. The New Institutional Economics school regards the causality as being from law and legal institutions to social and economic changes. This premise has been questioned by some scholars, who expressed criticisms of Douglas North's concept of path dependency, in terms such as the following:

> Path dependency is neither absolute nor timeless and leaves open the question of whether changes in formal law and legal institutions have been, or can be, an active agent in promoting socially beneficial change, or whether they are largely a dependent variable.[44]

Other scholars concur in such criticism and further offer alternative explanations for the causality debate. For example, John Coffee Jr. points out a backward sequence of legal reforms whereby legal developments have tended to follow, rather than precede, economic changes. The suggested reason for the backward causality between legal reforms and economic changes is that without a motivated constituency that will be protected (or at least perceives that it will be protected) by the proposed reforms, legal reforms are not likely to be initiated due to the lack of interested parties.[45]

One piece of empirical evidence of this backward causality can be found in China. According to some Western academics, China is an example that shows the possibility of economic liberalization without significant political and judicial reforms.[46] Law, on this view, is not an active agent in promoting economic growth, but a dependent variable in the development process that is responsive to economic changes. Specifically, China is an example to demonstrate the pattern of "crash-then-law" or "growth-then-law" of legal reforms.[47] The "crash-then-law" or "growth-then-law" thesis argues that the initial phrase of development is necessary both for a constituency to be formed and to set the stage for "crashes" or problems; legal change will then follow.[48] Legal reform is necessary in the second phase to prepare a country for further growth, or, conversely, to respond to the crash. Therefore, some scholars conclude that an efficient legal system may not be a precondition for initial market development, but a precondition for more mature, sustained development.[49]

---

44. Kevin E. Davis & Michael J. Trebilcock, "The Recent Intellectual History of Law and Development," Working paper at the University of Toronto Faculty of Law (2004) [unpublished], p. 26.

45. John J. Coffee Jr., "The Rise of Dispersed Ownership: the Roles of Law and the State in the Separation of Ownership and Control," 111 *Yale Law Journal* 1 (2001) [Coffee 2001b], p. 7.

46. Amy L. Freeman, "Review of *Bird in a Cage: Legal Reform in China after Mao*," 10:7 *The Law and Politics Book Review* 454 (2000).

47. Zhiwu Chen, "Capital Markets and Legal Development: The China Case," 14 *China Economic Review* 451 (2003).

48. Coffee 2001b, *supra* note 45, p. 7.

49 Chen, *supra* note 47, p. 470.

"Law matters, but the politics of legal reform matters more": evidence from China

Academic interest in the "politics" of legal reform has been on the rise in recent years. Empirical studies have revealed that despite heavy input from the movement of the "rule of law" reform in developing countries, the actual results have been limited. Judicial reform in particular has yielded little fruit.[50] It is a widely shared view that the primary obstacles are not technical or financial, but political and human.[51]

Evidence shows that there are strong opposition forces against legal reform in developing countries. With respect to legal reform in the financial area, the major blocking forces come from vested interest groups such as incumbent managers, workers, labor unions, and incompetent judges.[52] Given the considerable constraints, feasible legal reforms need to appease local opponents and be situated in a local enforcement context. In other words, "legal transplantation" may not be a workable strategy if local circumstances are not taken into consideration. Accordingly, blindly copying a list of investor rights or importing rules is not likely to succeed.[53]

Two primary lessons have been suggested by scholars regarding circumventing the "politics" of legal reform in developing countries. First, blindly transplanting the laws from developed countries and providing rights to investors will not necessarily work. Second, reform needs to be in accordance with the local legal system, however "backward" it might be. These lessons are of particular importance to China, where some western politicians, especially those from the U.S., have begun "pinning hope on the idea that promoting the rule of law will allow the U.S. to support positive economic and political change without taking a confrontational approach on human rights issues."[54] Predictably, this will not be an easy task. The "politics" of legal reform in China, while sharing many similarities with that of other developing countries, has some special features and may hinder the progress of reform.

In general, the politics of legal reform in China tends to be centered on forces that limit the development of legal institutions. For example, the Party-state pattern of governance and the Party dominance in national political and economic life are constraints on profound legal reform. Aside from the Party policies, other influencing forces include the state bureaucracy and the courts, the rise of the local party-state as a result of decentralization, the Chinese legal

---

50. Ronald Daniels & Michael Trebilcock, "The Political Economy of Rule of Law Reform in Developing Countries," 26 *Michigan Journal of International Law* 99 (2004).
51. Thomas Carothers, "The Rule of Law Revival," 77:2 *Foreign Affairs* 95 (1998) [Carothers 1998]; Thomas Carothers, *Aiding Democracy Abroad: The Learning Curve* (Washington, DC: Carnegie Endowment for International Peace, 1999).
52. Lopez-de-Silanes, *supra* note 26.
53. *Ibid.*, p. 92.
54. Carothers 1998, *supra* note 51.

culture (emphasizing the role of *guanxi* in social interactions) and overseas Chinese influence.[55] These factors are not necessarily fatal to advancing legal reform in China, but could constitute serious obstacles.

According to an American law professor who was among the persons mentioned earlier as having a strong interest in promoting rule of law in China, many of these constraints derive from basic political arrangements (such as the role of the Communist Party or the lack of a free press) or from deeply ingrained ideological and cultural beliefs (such as a belief that courts are like other administrative organs rather than a distinctive kind of institution or a view that law is basically an instrument of governing rather than a restraint on government).[56] Because of these constraints, an incremental and long-term approach to legal reform, instead of a rapid and wholesale style, is needed in the Chinese context of promoting the rule of law.[57]

Recently, there have been heated discussions about China's integration into the global community and the expected reform of its legal system, especially after China's accession to the WTO. Although a newly shared vocabulary about the notion of the "rule of law" has been emerging in China, it conceals, however, underlying differences in meanings that stem from profound contrasts between historical and current Chinese and Western notions about law and governance.[58]

Therefore, a cautious conclusion on the prospects and directions of China's legal reform is warranted. On the one hand, in adopting legal reform in relation to corporate governance rules, merely transplanting "law in the books" from western mature market economies without simultaneously developing the institutional foundations for these rules to function, is not likely to work. On the other hand, legal reform in the corporate governance area at the current stage of development should not give priority to the "advanced" mechanisms commonly found in developed countries (such as more independent directors), but needs to focus on strengthening some basic aspects of institutional capacity (such as an independent judiciary and competent securities market regulators).

7.2 China and the Debate on Global Convergence in Corporate Governance

Section 7.2 introduces the ongoing global debate on convergence or persistence in corporate governance around the world and assesses its implications for corporate governance reform in developing countries, especially China. At the

---

55. Stanley Lubman, *Bird in a Cage: Legal Reform in China After Mao* (Palo Alto, CA: Stanford University Press, 1999), pp. 299–306.
56. Paul Gewirtz, "The U.S.-China Rule of Law Initiative," 11 *William & Mary Bill of Rights Journal* 603 (2003), p. 618.
57. Lubman, *supra* note 55, p. 299.
58. *Ibid.*, p. 318.

centre of this debate is the following question: in an age of globalization and capital market integration, which model should be, or already is, leading the direction of global corporate governance on which different national systems will gradually converge? In answering this question, a general observation can be drawn that while it may be necessary to reach a certain level of global convergence on some fundamental principles of corporate governance, such as the accountability of the board of directors, investor protection and equal treatment of shareholders, it is still far from clear, however, whether there exists an "optimal model" of corporate governance that will dominate alternative national systems.

Therefore, the judgement of Section 7.2 regarding corporate governance convergence is two-fold. On the one hand, it may be necessary to reach a certain level of global convergence on widely accepted fundamental principles of corporate governance, such as the accountability of the board of directors, investor protection and equal treatment of shareholders. On the other hand, it is still far from clear whether there exists an "optimal model" of corporate governance, and there is hardly a "one-size-fits-all" solution to corporate governance reforms in transition economies.

Accordingly, Section 7.2 suggests that for an economy in transition, such as China, an appropriate approach toward corporate governance reform needs to avoid a tendency of "blind convergence" without first accommodating with distinctive domestic needs and conditions. Therefore, on the one hand, China should take into account internationally accepted standards and practices when undertaking corporate governance reform, in particular those spelled out in the *OECD Corporate Governance Principles*. On the other hand, local solutions that may not be in conformity with "global best practices," but nevertheless correspond to the existing economic, political and institutional environments during the transition, should be encouraged. By adopting such a gradualist strategy, China can avoid an "institutional vacuum" during transition, in which old institutions were completely destroyed or overhauled but new institutions have not yet been firmly established.

7.2.1 Efforts to promote convergence in corporate governance at the international level

On the practical side, there has been a visible trend of global convergence of corporate governance codes and guidelines to produce a set of "best practices" at regional and international levels. The first attempt of such sort was the OECD's *Principles of Corporate Governance* issued in April 1998, which sought to provide a set of corporate governance standards and guidelines for its member states to evaluate and improve their legal, institutional and regulatory framework for corporate governance. Another important multilateral development in this regard was the establishment of the Commonwealth Association for Corporate Governance (CACG) in April 1998 to promote excellence in corporate governance in the former British Commonwealth of Nations. Moreover, the establishment in 1999 of the Global Corporate Governance Forum via the World Bank and the OECD to create a formal program of governance assistance on a global basis marked another step toward convergence. An even broader project has been organized by the World Bank and the OECD to combine their efforts to promote policy dialogue on corporate governance issues through the Regional Corporate Governance Roundtables (RCGRs) covering Asia, Russia, Latin America, South-East Europe and Eurasia.[59]

7.2.2 The representative points of view in the debate on global convergence or persistence in corporate governance

Broadly speaking, there are five representative points of view on global convergence or persistence in corporate governance, as introduced in the following discussion. It can be seen that they present very different opinions. While the strong version of convergence optimism predicts systemic convergence, the strong version of convergence skepticism predicts systemic persistence in corporate governance.

Systemic convergence: formal and functional

In "The End of History for Corporate Law," Henry Hansmann and Reinier Kraakman propose a strong version of convergence optimism. They boldly argue not only that corporate governance convergence on a shareholder-oriented model adopted in the U.S. and the U.K., or the so-called "shareholder primacy" model, is both desirable and inevitable, but that corporate governance has already largely converged on that model.[60] The authors claim:

> The triumph of the shareholder-oriented model of the corporation over its principal competitors is now assured, even if it was problematic as recently as twenty-five years ago... [T]he standard model earned its position as the dominant model of the large corporation the hard way, by out-competing during the post-World War II period the three alternative models of corporate governance: the managerial model, the labor-oriented model, and the state-oriented model...

......

---

59. See Low Chee Keong (ed.), *Corporate Governance: An Asian-Pacific Critique* (Hong Kong: Sweet & Maxwell Asia, 2002), pp. 11-18; OECD, "White Paper on Corporate Governance in Asia," 2003, online < www.oecd.org >.

60. Jeffrey N. Gordon & Mark J. Roe (eds.), *Convergence and Persistence in Corporate Governance* (Cambridge: Cambridge University Press, 2004), pp. 6–7.

> We predict, therefore, that as equity markets evolve in Europe and throughout the developed world, the ideological and competitive attraction of the standard model will become indisputable, even among legal academics. And as the goal of shareholder primacy becomes second nature even to politicians, convergence in most aspects of the law and practice of corporate governance is sure to follow.[61]

The view of systemic convergence has drawn many criticisms, particularly from proponents of systemic persistence in corporate governance, as introduced later.

Formal convergence (*de jure* convergence)

In this debate, some researchers have advocated a "formal convergence" position that convergence in some important aspects of corporate governance (such as board composition) has occurred with respect to formal or written rules in countries' domestic corporate and securities law, without simultaneous convergence in the function that these rules are intended to play in their host jurisdictions.

For example, Ronald Gilson and Curtis Milhaupt take the example of Japan's recent corporate reform that allows large firms to abolish the board of statutory audit and adopt a U.S. style committee system for corporate governance, to illustrate the dynamics of the "formal convergence".[62] During this reform, Japan "transplanted some visible components of a U.S. style board committee structure, but without the complementary institutions that exponentially increase the functionality of the committee system in the host country," such as the judicial review of directorial independence that serves as a crucial complement to the committee structure in the U.S..[63] Therefore, the authors conclude, in order to utilize the new board option, Japan will need to create governance mechanisms that function quite similarly to those of U.S. firms.[64]

Formal persistence and functional convergence (*de facto* convergence)

In "Globalizing Corporate Governance: Convergence of Form or Function," Ronald Gilson argues for the possible emergence of a worldwide corporate

---

61. Henry Hansmann & Reinier Kraakman, "The End of History for Corporate Law," 89 *Georgetown Law Journal* 439 (2001), p. 468.
62. Ronald J. Gilson & Curtis J. Milhaupt, "Choice as Regulatory Reform: The Case of Japanese Corporate Governance," paper presented at the Law and Economics Workshop at the University of Toronto Faculty of Law, No. WS 2004-2005 (1) (2005) [unpublished, archived at the University of Toronto Faculty of Law Bora Laskin Library], p. 14.
63. *Ibid.*, p. 37.
64. *Ibid.*, p. 41.

governance system that is relatively uniform in functional terms, despite persisting formal differences.[65]

According to Gilson, functional convergence occurs when existing governance institutions are flexible enough to respond to the demands of changed circumstances without altering the institutions' formal characteristics.[66] The means of functional convergence include contracting and the so-called "piggy-backing" on the law of other jurisdictions, such as firms' decision to list on an overseas capital market with higher standards of corporate governance requirements than that of their home countries, as has been exemplified by some European firms listing in the U.S. capital markets. However, Gilson also points out that not every function can converge because of the difficulty in creating institutional complements that support the function. The difficulty in adopting a U.S. style venture capital system in Europe due to the lack of a highly liquid and dispersed market there is such an example.[67] Arguing along the same line, John Coffee Jr. also supports the functional convergence position by adding examples of convergence through corporate migration (primarily via cross-listing) and stock exchange harmonization.[68]

It seems that the functional convergence position is shared by some academics on both sides of the Atlantic. In a recent paper, several European economists review the history of the share price movements over the last two decades at Royal Ahold, a Dutch company that is cross-listed in Amsterdam and New York exchanges, to sketch some general observations on the trend of global convergence in corporate governance. The authors find that the co-existence of rather different regimes of corporate governance may be undercut by the reaction of institutional investors in the global financial markets to the actions of corporate management. Because poor corporate governance could lead to the destruction of firm value and the discounting in share prices by international institutional investors, cross-listing can be a strong driving force for global convergence of better corporate governance practices.[69] However, the authors also caution that convergence may have potentially disruptive effects on countries' existing corporate governance structures in the short run, as

---

65. Gordon & Roe, *supra* note 60, p. 18.
66. Ronald J. Gilson, "Globalizing Corporate Governance: Convergence of Form or Function," 49 *American Journal of Comparative Law* 329 (2001), p. 358.
67. *Ibid.*, pp. 344–345.
68. John C. Coffee Jr., "The Future as History: The Prospects for Global Convergence in Corporate Governance and Its Implications," 93 *Northwestern University Law Review* 641 (1999) [Coffee 1999], p. 653.
69. Gordon L. Clark, Dariusz Wójcik & Rob Bauer, "Corporate Governance, Cross-listing, and Managerial Response to Stock Price Discounting: Royal Ahold and Market Arbitrage — Amsterdam and New York, 1973–2004," paper presented to the 2004 Annual Conference of Canadian Law and Economics Association, October 12, 2004, Toronto [unpublished].

compared to a more beneficial impact on global financial markets in the long run.[70]

However, there have been counter-examples of functional convergence through "piggy-backing," i.e., firms going public in overseas capital markets with higher standards of securities regulation and corporate governance, thus voluntarily subjecting themselves to tighter market disciplines and requirements for investor protection. One example is from China, where some of its large and more competitive firms have started to accelerate overseas investment and expansion in recent years through cross-listing or mergers and acquisitions. After the coming into force of the Sarbanes-Oxley Act, some Chinese firms that originally had plans to launch a U.S. IPO had abandoned their plans, given the higher costs of an U.S. IPO embodied in the increased risks of shareholder class actions and the stringent disclosure and reporting requirements by both the SEC and the SOX. In searching for alternative channels, some of these firms have chosen to raise capital from U.S. institutional investors through rule 144A private placements which grant disclosure exemptions to foreign issuers, such as the filing of financial statements with the SEC, thus circumventing the SEC and the SOX altogether. Other Chinese firms, such as the big shipping company Sinotrans Ltd. and the carrier Air China, chose to open trading on the London Stock Exchange or launch a public listing in Hong Kong. [71]

Another recent example of the declining attraction of the U.S. capital markets to foreign companies comes from some European firms listed in the U.S.. After the coming into force of the SOX, European firms listed on NASDAQ or the NYSE have found themselves stuck in a dilemma of either remaining listed in the U.S. markets with higher compliance costs under the SOX requirements on disclosure and auditing, or exiting the U.S. market after taking pains to prove to the SEC that the number of their U.S. investors was less than 300 under SEC requirements, which is a time-consuming and expensive process. This difficulty in leaving the U.S. market is clearly demonstrated by the hard won victory of Last-minute.com, an U.K. internet operator, for its delisting from NASDAQ after winning a four-month court battle against the SEC over whether it had satisfied the conditions for exit and sending out hundreds of letters to its U.S. investors for their consent. As a consequence, some European firms had abandoned their plans to list in the U.S., including big names such as the car maker Porsche and the world's biggest re-insurance company Benfield.[72]

---

70. *Ibid.*, p. 19.
71. Laura Santini, "Chinese Firms Tap U.S. Market without IPOs," *Asian Wall Street Journal,* October 21. 2004, M.1.
72. Qi Hezhong, "European Firms Trapped in the U.S. Market: A Choice between Expensive Listing and Thorny Delisting (guapai taigui zhaipai tainan, ouzhou shangshi gongsi shoukun meiguo jiaoyisuo)," *International Finance News* (*Guoji Jinrong Bao*), October 25, 2004, online: < http://www.chinanews.com.cn/news/2004/2004-10-25/26 /498422.shtml >.

Despite the above counter-examples of functional convergence through piggy-backing, new evidence of functional convergence in other aspects of corporate governance seems to grow. According to Bernard Black, Brian Cheffins and Michael Klausner, there has been a trend of functional convergence in outcomes of corporate governance across countries in the specific aspect of out-of-pocket liability risk for outsider directors, despite large differences in law.[73] The bottom line of the authors' assessment is that outside directors of public companies in four common law countries (Australia, Canada, Britain and the U.S.) and three civil law countries (France, Germany and Japan) face only a tiny risk of out-of-pocket liability, as damages and legal fees incurred in director liability suits are paid by the company, directors' and officers' (D&O) insurance, or both.[74]

Systemic persistence: "path dependence"

In "The Theory of Path Dependence in Corporate Governance Ownership and Governance," Lucian Bebchuk and Mark Roe express skepticism that corporate governance and ownership structures have converged thus far and argue that structural imperatives help to explain why differences in corporate governance have persisted, despite convergence in many economic areas such as product standards.[75] The authors attribute this trend of systemic persistence to path dependence in the process of institutional development in a given country, which has a "lock-in" effect on the evolution of institutions once they are established under peculiar political, economic and social environments and constraints that may not long endure.[76]

Systemic complementarities

In "Path Dependence, Corporate Governance and Complementarity," Reinhard Schmidt and Gerald Spindler approach the issue of systemic persistence in corporate governance from the perspective of institutional complementarity.[77] In their view, the complementarity between the inherent components of corporate governance regime in a given country is the main reason why a rapid convergence toward a "universally best corporate governance system" is not likely to happen. However, according to the authors, there are possibilities of

---

73. Bernard Black, Brian Cheffins & Michael Klausner, "Liability Risk for Outside Directors: A Cross-Border Analysis," University of Texas Law School, Law and Economics Working Paper, No. 27.

74. *Ibid.*, p. 2.

75. Lucian Bebchuk & Mark Roe, "The Theory of Path Dependence in Corporate Ownership and Governance," 52 *Stanford Law Review* 127 (1999).

76. *Ibid.*

77. Reinhard H. Schmidt & Gerald Spindler, "Path Dependence, Corporate Governance and Complementarity," 5:3 *International Finance* 311 (2002).

convergence toward a common system that is economically inferior, such as the possibility of the "inefficient convergence" of corporate governance in Europe toward the Anglo-American model, in the sense that such convergence reduces total social welfare.[78]

7.2.3 Implications for China

The debate on convergence or persistence in corporate governance has deep implications for China as a developing and transition economy that has been undertaking corporate governance reform. While China should take into account internationally accepted rules and practices — particularly those spelled out in the *OECD Corporate Governance Principles* — in its corporate governance reform at the new stage of transition, local solutions that correspond to the existing legal and institutional environments should be accepted, even though these solutions are transitional and not perfect.

In fact, the *OECD Corporate Governance Principles* were the major reference when China was drafting its first *Code of Corporate Governance for Listed Companies*, which was jointly released by China Securities Regulatory Commission and State Economic and Trade Commission in January 2001.[79] However, the implementation of the Code has not been satisfactory because of the inexperience in competent regulation on the part of the CSRC and the lack of supporting or complementary mechanisms allowing the principles enshrined in the Code to function. For example, while the hiring of independent directors is required under the Code for Chinese listed companies, in reality it is very difficult to find enough qualified individuals to serve as independent directors, given the underdevelopment of human capital in China and the lack of an effective screening mechanism to select qualified candidates.

Therefore, proper sequencing and pacing should be the guiding principle in adopting global "best practices" in China where their institutional foundations – such as experienced and competent financial market regulators, sophisticated financial intermediaries, an independent and competent judiciary, an effective financial press, and a solid base of institutional investors — are still developing.

7.3 Corporate Governance Failures in Transition Economies: Lessons from Russian Privatization and Its Discontents

Taking Russia's mass and rapid privatization and its discontents as a major example, Section 7.3 addresses the issue of corporate governance failures

---

78. Gordon & Roe, *supra* note 60, p. 17.
79. The text of the Code can found at the CSRC website: < http://www.csrc.gov.cn/en/jsp/ detail.jsp?infoid=1061948026100&type=CMS.STD >.

in transition economies and the resulting consequences for economic development. As Section 7.3 shows, while there had been limited positive results such as those achieved in Poland, the primary lesson from privatization and corporate governance reforms in transition economies is generally unimpressive, which was exemplified by various privatization and securities market failures across the region of the former Soviet bloc, in particular Russia, where mass and rapid privatization had failed to bring prosperity.

7.3.1 The political reason for mass and rapid privatization

In Russia, "shock therapy" was adopted as the primary approach toward post-communist reform. It was a top-down reform package consisting of radical programs, aimed at swiftly destroying all existing economic structures at whatever cost and replacing them with a market system like that in West Europe. On the "shock therapy" list, the most difficult and complex was privatization. It was considered that the whole program of reform was contingent on the success of privatization.[80]

In the initial debate about how to privatize Russia's SOEs, the strategy of mass and rapid privatization finally prevailed as the primary vehicle to privatize medium size and large industrial enterprises. In fact, not only Russia, but most countries of the former Soviet bloc, had chosen mass and rapid privatization to privatize their medium size and large industrial enterprises, with the major exception of Hungary, which followed a slow and measured path of privatization.[81]

The gradual, firm-by-firm privatization approach was rejected for political reasons. The principal concern of radical reformers was to gain as broad support from the population as possible, in order to make privatization politically viable and to avoid a likely standstill of economic reforms that small-scale privatization may cause. As three key advisors on Russian privatization put it straightforwardly:

> The need to gain support for reform is the political argument for privatizing rapidly. If privatization is slow, the benefits to the population are by definition small, and hence the political capital they buy the reformers is small as well. Fast privatization is privatization that offers large political benefits from the start — exactly what a reformist government needs...Slowing it down further beyond what internal political forces accomplish will stop it altogether...[R]apid

---

80.   Peter Murrell, "What is Shock Therapy? What Did It Do in Poland and Russia?", 9:2 *Post-Soviet Affairs* 111 (1993).

81.   Ira W. Lieberman, Stilpon S. Nestor & Raj M. Desai (eds.), *Between State and Market: Mass Privatization in Transition Economies* (Washington: The World Bank, 1997), p. 1.

privatization buys enormous political benefits and thus allows reforms to deepen.[82]

7.3.2 The immediate outcome of privatization: the rapid rise of a new private sector

The shock therapists had boasted about the swift speed with which Russia's mass privatization had been conducted. For instance, one of the advisors on Russian privatization provided the following triumphant remark on its immediate outcome:

> ...[I]n a few short years, Russia managed to privatize more than 15,000 industrial firms — to turn over their ownership from the state to private investors. Together with more than a million new businesses and tens of thousands of newly privatized shops, over half the output of the Russian economy is now produced by the private sector — a higher fraction than in much of Western Europe. But privatization did a lot more than just reshuffle assets. It gave the declining state firms real owners, with real desires to assert their rights as investors, and hence gave Russian firms a hope of surviving in a market economy... As it destroyed central planning, it also destroyed the very roots of the Soviet state... Politically and economically, privatization truly transformed Russia.[83]

Although the shock therapists had expressed such elation, they had also voiced a moderate concern about the fact that a majority of privatized firms were transferred to "insiders." At the end of voucher privatization, managers and workers in combination controlled about two-thirds of the shares in the average privatized firm.[84] Also, they had conceded that corruption had been a serious problem throughout the program, especially in its second stage of implementation. The most egregious example of "illegitimate" privatization was the "loans-for-shares" (LFS) program in post-1994 privatization waves, whereby a few oligarchs became instant billionaires by taking over remaining state firms through fraudulent "auctions." The LFS program in 1995 was the most notorious scheme during the second phrase of Russian privatization. It was a quasi-privatization program designed to raise revenues for the Russian government. Unfortunately, this program was in no sense a "transparent" and

---

82.   Maxim Boycko, Andrei Shleifer & Robert W. Vishny, "Privatizing Russia," 2 Brookings Papers on Economic Activity 139 (1993), p. 148 [footnote omitted].

83.   Andrei Shleifer, Foreword to Joseph R. Blasi, Maya Kroumova & Douglas Kruse, *Kremlin Capitalism: The Privatization of Russian Economy* (Ithaca: Cornell University Press, 1997), pp. ix-x.

84.   John Nellis, "Time to Rethink Privatization in Transition Economies," IFC Discussion Paper No.38 (1999), p. 7.

"credible" process as originally intended. What actually happened was that, the Russian government put up shares of its own firms in private banks as collateral for needed funds; when the government defaulted on its loans, the private banks took over the firms in what might be viewed as a sham sale (i.e., a charade of collusive "auctions" in favor of friends of the government).[85]

Even the strongest supporters of the first phrase privatization, Ira Lieberman and Rogi Veimetra at the World Bank, regarded the LFS scheme as a "lose-lose" proposition for all of the stakeholders in Russia. They pointed out that it "...was non-transparent...involved clear conflicts of interest... created collusion... involved a nonlevel playing field, excluding foreign investors..."[86] In their opinion, the LFS scheme substantially discredited Russia's privatization efforts, causing the program to be widely viewed as "collusive and corrupt, failing to meet any of its stated objectives."[87] Yukos, until recently Russia's largest oil exporter, was transferred from the state to private hands exactly through the LFS insider deals. Its sale at a "ridiculously low price" — Mikhail Khodorkovsky bought a majority share stake for USD 170 million in a company approximately worth USD 180 billion — was labeled "the most scandalous offering" of the second phrase privatization.[88]

Despite all these negative factors mentioned above, in terms of speed and scale, Russian privatization was indeed unprecedented in history. Therefore, it is not surprising that some economists, mainly from the advisory teams for Russian privatization, have regarded it as a huge success. However, the line of reasoning, starting from the figures on speed and scale and directly arriving at the conclusion that firms were thus "depoliticized" and the job of privatization was done (and done brilliantly) is inadequate, to say the least. The fact that in Russia most business has been in private ownership since the mid-1990s does not necessarily mean that the private sector has become competitive and has been running efficiently. In fact, competition in post-privatization Russia generally does not function well, because entry of new firms has been very sluggish due to administrative barriers to small business, and this in turn has made it easier for existing firms to apply political pressure to secure their protection.[89]

Moreover, speed and scale have only a largely quantitative, rather than qualitative, explanatory function to highlight the significance of the huge

85. Joseph E. Stiglitz, *Globalization and Its Discontents* (New York: W. W. Norton & Company, 2002), p. 159.
86. Ira W. Lieberman & Rogi Veimetra, "The Rush for State Shares in the 'Klondyke' of Wild East Capitalism: Loans-for-Shares Transactions in Russia," 29:3 *George Washington Journal of International Law & Economics* 737 (1996), pp. 738, 758 and 759.
87. *Ibid.*
88. *Ibid.*
89. See Paul Hare & Alexander Muravyev, "Privatization in Russia," in David Parker & David Saal (eds.), *International Handbook on Privatization* (Cheltenham: Edward Elgar, 2003), Chapter 17.

transformation of the Russian economy. The transition process has been generally regarded as highly complex and involving the establishment of complementary institutions that can make the speed and scale of privatization substantively meaningful. One can imagine how this difficult task could invite serious problems if proper sequencing and pacing were not given sufficient consideration.

In addition, assessments based only on speed and scale have also neglected the "relativity test." Within a comprehensive review framework, the level of success of Russian privatization should not be measured in absolute and abstract terms, but needs to be balanced against costs and drawbacks. For an optimist reviewer, when calculating the benefits and achievements of Russian privatization, an important question to ask is "successful relative to what?" For example, one frequently visited issue in reviewing Russian privatization is the trade-off between efficiency gains for privatized firms (if there were any) and the distributional impact on the general Russian population. Therefore, the conclusion that Russian privatization was an "extraordinary success," or an "amazing achievement," or a "solid foundation" for recent growth of the Russian economy is not fully warranted without the support of empirical evidence on the financial performance of privatized firms and distributional effect of privatization within Russia's general population. As later discussion will reveal, the empirical evidence is largely unimpressive.

7.3.3   Insider control: the defining feature of corporate governance structure of privatized firms

The Russian privatization program offered generous benefits to enterprise insiders (both the workers and managers) in exchange for their support for reform. As a consequence, enterprise managers had gained a substantial amount of equity ownership and a very high degree of control.[90] This corporate governance structure did not move to incorporate more inputs from outside investors. The "powerless" shareholders have become a frequently cited pathology of corporate governance in Russian privatized firms. Such an ownership and control structure has proved inefficient, because it has created incentives for asset stripping and self-dealing, rather than for value maximization.

---

90. Andrei Shleifer & Dmitry Vasiliev, "Management Ownership and Russian Privatization," in Roman Frydman, Cheryl W. Gray & Andrzej Rapaczynski (eds.), *Corporate Governance in Central Europe and Russia* (Budapest: Central European University Press, 1996), p. 62.

7.3.4 General consequences of privatization for the Russian economy and society

Despite the original enthusiasm about the gains that mass and rapid privatization was anticipated to bring about, a decade later the well-intentioned, but arguably not equally well-conceived, program seemed to have frustrated the expectations of many. Mass privatization through voucher and the infamous loans-for-shares programs had devastating consequences for Russia. It did not succeed in bringing prosperity to the country. Instead, the reverse seemed to be true: Russia saw severe economic decline, intensified social and economic inequalities and increased poverty through the first decade of transition. As a consequence, growing domestic discontent had spread across the country, thus rendering the maintenance of social and political stability no easy task. The reformers who had actively pursued privatizing Russia "at all costs" were later showered with blame for selling state assets to crooks at ridiculously low prices, which had led to the rapid rise of a group of super-rich "oligarchs."

As an unintended consequence, Russia now often serves as a negative example to students of transition economics, showing how "shock therapy" failed to deliver promised prosperity, and how flawed transition policy could lead to disastrous outcomes. Russia certainly suffered: over the first decade of transition, it had experienced constant stagnation and its economy shrunk sharply. GDP in post-1989 Russia fell, year after year. The loss was even greater than Russia had suffered in World War II: in the period 1940–46 the Soviet Union industrial production fell by 24 percent; in the period 1990–99, Russian industrial production fell by almost 60 percent.[91]

Russia's economy has been showing some signs of strength for the past few years, largely due to the rise of oil prices in the international market, from which Russia gets much of its revenue. However, economists have warned that high oil prices make Russia's economy look much better than it really is and that the country is too dependent on commodity prices. These economists worry that when oil and metal prices fall, the country could be plunged back into darkness.[92]

It is also interesting to note that the defenders of "shock therapy" and of its positive effects in transition economies offered rebuttals to the criticism that Russia was "lost" as a result of flawed transition strategies. In particular, some of the original advocates for radical reform package offered their own version of interpreting the transition process, especially the controversial mass and rapid privatization in Russia, as opposed to the dark depiction presented by the critics. A recent interpretation of the Russian transition regards Russia as a "normal country" already. Its main arguments read as follows:

---

91. Stiglitz, *supra* note 86, p. 143.
92. "Lightbulbs," *The Economist*, February 8, 2002, p. 49.

(a) Contrary to what the critics had suggested, by the late 1990s Russia was not "a disastrous and threatening failure," but had become a typical middle-income, capitalist democracy.

(b) Russia's being a normal country (i.e., *only* a middle-income, not a developed capital state yet) is an amazing and admirable achievement, given its starting point as a "shortage-ridden, militarized, collapsing bureaucracy" of 1990, although to those who had hoped for more it is a disappointment.

(c) "Shock therapy" had worked in Russia, by transforming it into a marketplace of mostly private firms and an electoral democracy *irreversibly*.

(d) It is arbitrary to attribute all the flaws and problems in the transition process to the reform policies, especially to mass and rapid privatization, because a large part of the Russians' genuine suffering was caused by the unavoidable (therefore, unsurprising) costs of transition. Specifically, problems with income distribution should not be attributed to the *wisdom* of privatization strategy; rather, the blame should be laid on the ill-handled, corruption-ridden *implementation* of privatization.

(e) Russia's prospects in the immediate future are neither as bleak as the critics predict (i.e., Russia will stagnate,) nor as positive as the optimists think (i.e., Russia will soon become a developed capital state). Rather, Russia will remain a normal market economy and a capitalist democracy, albeit with flawed institutions and a great deal of state intervention.[93]

However, some Russian economists do not seem to agree with the conclusion that Russia today is a "normal country." For example, it has been suggested that such a positive statement is confusing, because Russia's genuine decline after privatization is an undeniable fact; and that if this could serve to prove that the country is "normal," the rhetorical device must have been faulty.[94]

7.3.5 **Firm-level economic consequences of Russian privatization**

As Thane Gustafson critically points out, there are three economic consequences of privatization for privatized firms: capital starvation, unstable ownership, and the continuation of soft budget constraints[95]. Also, by and large there had been no real restructuring, no substantial change of corporate culture, no effective corporate governance improvements, and no signs of effective use of scarce capital[96]. When capital infusions had become available in some rare cases,

---

93. Andrei Shleifer & Daniel Treisman, "A Normal Country," 83:2 *Foreign Affairs* 20 (2004).
94. See, for example, Matthew Maly, "My Comment on *A Normal Country* by Andrei Shleifer and Daniel Treisman," February 24, 2004, online < http://matthew-maly.ru/articles/eng25.shtml >.
95. Thane Gustafson, *Capitalism, Russian Style* (Cambridge University Press, 1999), p. 46.
96. *Ibid.*

managers had not directed the capital to new plant and new products, but to other purposes such as paying wage arrears, buying short-term treasury notes and other financial instruments in Russia's nascent capital markets, and repaying bank loans.[97]

Recent surveys on restructuring and corporate governance of Russian privatized firms provide no encouraging indications of significant improvements, but raise questions about the method, sequencing and pacing of privatization, as well as alternatives to privatization. For example, one recent survey paper by two leading experts in privatization finds that, although privatization is usually beneficial, and that it is often associated with general improvements in governance at all levels in a society, the positive results did not happen in Russia. The empirical evidence available so far indicates that insider privatization has been a failure throughout the former Soviet Union, especially in Russia, and that the concentrated managerial ownership structure that characterizes almost all privatized firms will likely hamper these economies for many years to come.[98]

On the dimension of efficiency gains and financial performance, Russian privatization did not deliver satisfactory results. The declining financial performance of firms in the post-privatization period is alarming. The available evidence offered in some empirical studies on Russian privatization suggests that privatized firms "merely don't perform much better than state-owned companies, if at all." The efficiency gains were so small that economists were debating whether they existed at all. This raises the question about the wisdom of having spent so much political energy in a program that turned out to be not very helpful for economic revival.[99]

7.3.6 The distributional impact of privatization

With regard to issues relating to efficiency and equality in post-communist transition and economic reform, there have been two unsettling questions. The first question is whether the goals of efficiency and equality are compatible at all. The second question is whether government actions are needed to overcome the distortion by the private actors and realize such compatibility in circumstances where it is indeed possible to make efficiency and equality compatible but private actors tend to prevent such compatibility. The Chinese experience in this aspect has not been positive, and has added more murkiness to debates over "efficiency *versus* equality" during the transition.

Since 1992, when the debate over whether markets should be officially endorsed in the Chinese "socialist system" was decisively resolved, China's

---

97. *Ibid.*
98. William Megginson & Jeffry Netter, "From State to Market: A Survey of Empirical Studies on Privatization," 39:2 *Journal of Economic Literature* 321 (2001).
99. Black, Kraakman & Tarassova, supra note 37, p.1780.

transition and economic reform have been overwhelmingly leaning toward the "efficiency" direction while sacrificing a considerable amount of "social equality," for which China has been criticized throughout the reform period. According to a survey on income disparity in China by the China Academy of Social Sciences (CASS), in 2002 urban residents earned three times more than their rural counterparts, a record high in the history of China's transition. The researchers in charge of this survey also claimed that even these figures did not paint a true picture of the disparity, which was commonly believed to be even wider. The primary causes for this astonishing income gap were the heavy tax burdens on rural population and the rampant corruption among local officials.[100] The survey also pointed out an alarming trend that the urban-rural income gap in China had become the widest in the world, taking into account non-monetary factors. An even more daunting prospect is that the gap will continue to grow in the coming years. The likely destabilizing impact of this increasing wealth gap on China's social and political structures cannot be underestimated. Now the Chinese government realizes that excessive distributional disparity not only creates huge challenges in maintaining social stability, but can also cost the now buoyant economy efficiency losses.[101]

However, as distinct from the Chinese story, Russian privatization was expected to bring about a positive distributional impact when the mass and rapid privatization strategy was selected. To begin with, carrying out a privatization program that was fair and equal to all participants had fundamental political economy implications when reform first started. The very reason for adopting the strategy of mass and rapid privatization was to gain popular support for reform before it could be completely blocked by opposition interests. Therefore, to "make every Russian an owner" was declared as the preliminary goal of Russian privatization. The political reason for radical reform was essentially a reflection of the need for a balanced distribution of benefits within the general population, if it was to proceed without serious political backlash. Logically, popular support could hardly be elicited unless the majority of Russian citizens could obtain a decent deal from the reshuffle of state assets. In this sense, the swift rise of a "Kleptocracy" class represented by the "oligarchs" in post-privatization Russia was certainly not a desirable outcome. In the meantime, the anticipated emergence of a new private sector run by honest business people hid not materialize.[102]

100. See Louisa Lim, "China's Wealth Gap Widens to Gulf," *BBC News*, February 26, 2004, online < http://news.bbc.co.uk/2/hi/asia-pacific/3488228.stm >.
101. Li Shi & Yue Ximing, "An Investigation of Urban-Rural Income Gap in China (zhongguo chengxiang shouru chajü diaocha)," *Caijing*, February 20, 2004, online < http://www.caijing.com.cn/coverstory/2004-02-20/2120.shtml >.
102. Black, Kraakman & Tarassova, *supra* note 37, p. 1746.

Broadly speaking, Russian privatization had failed on the dimension of "distributional equality." Evidence of severe social inequalities in post-privatization Russia abounds, including concessions from the shock therapists that Russia today is not a "just society." For example, in 2003, Russia's per capita GDP may lag behind Costa Rica's, but its headcount of billionaires was the fourth highest in the world, according to *Forbes Magazine*'s annual rating of the super rich.[103] Also, according to recent empirical studies, a new welfare pattern and a deep social stratification of society have evolved in post-privatization Russia, which are identified with large income differentiation and non-transparency of distributional relationships in society.[104] All these alarming trends reinforce a concern held by many international observers: in today's Russia, a potentially destabilizing factor is that wealth differences soar while the social pie shrinks.

7.3.7   Political consequences of privatization

It has been suggested that Russian privatization has left "a residue of popular distrust of privatization and market economy," which is exactly the opposite result to the original expectation that fast privatization would build popular support for reform.[105] In particular, the ill-handling of the "loans-for-shares" program, which was a corrupt and non-transparent transfer of state assets, precipitated widespread insider expropriation and thus contributed greatly to the political unpopularity of privatization.[106]

7.3.8   What went wrong?

In searching for reasons why the promises of Russian privatization were broken, a primary question to be asked is why performance of Russian privatized firms has lagged. Academics have extensively studied this issue, and have suggested a series of causal links.

The first suggested causal link is between the method of privatization ("insider privatization") and the prevailing feature of management control in Russia's privatized firms. Second, the insider control corporate governance structure has been found to create incentives to loot. Third, massive self-dealing and asset stripping resulting from distorted incentives of insiders ultimately led to the "fiascoes" of Russian firms.[107] These causal links can be illustrated as follows:

---

103. "Russia's Unpopular Billionaires on Forbes's List," 14:7-9 *Transition* 14 (2003).
104. Svetlana Glinkina, "Distributional Impact of Privatization in Russia," paper presented to the CGD (Centre for Global Development) Conference on Distributional Impact of Privatization, February 24–25, 2003, Washington, DC, pp. 53–54 [unpublished].
105. Black, Kraakman & Tarassova, *supra* note 37, pp. 1788–1789.
106. Megginson & Netter, *supra* note 98.
107. Merritt B. Fox & Michael A. Heller, "Corporate Governance Lessons from Russian Enterprise Fiascoes," 75 *New York University Law Review* 1720 (2000).

> Insider privatization → concentration of ownership and control in privatized firms → incentives for opportunism, asset stripping and self-dealing → the fiascoes of Russian firms

In the short period of time since privatization was completed, Russia had quickly earned a reputation for poor corporate governance.[108] In the absence of institutional constraints on insider opportunism, what had been induced was wealth destruction. Given the poor corporate governance of privatized firms, it is not surprising that short-term activities and asset stripping had become common practices for managers. The most serious problem of corporate governance failure in Russian firms was that rather than maximizing value, managers had turned to making personal profits from loss-making companies through "ingenious" techniques.[109] One popular device was to spin off private "daughter companies," owned by a narrow circle of managers and their allies, through which the output of the privatized firm was siphoned off. The "mother company" took the losses, accumulated debts, delayed wages and payments, and hold back taxes — while the profits went out the back door. Theft by "kleptocrats" had been rampant in privatized firms.[110] Performance of privatized firms, as a consequence, had lagged and had not been much better as compared with remaining state-owned firms.

Moreover, the proclaimed accomplishment of "depoliticization" of firms and private sector activities, which was regarded by the designers of Russian privatization as the first yardstick of good reform, also appeared hollow under close scrutiny. According to the designers, while the first yardstick of good reform is depoliticization, the second is corporate governance. The key objective of Russian privatization, however, should be the former, not the latter. This is because "controlling managers is not nearly as important as controlling politicians, since managers' interests are generally much closer to economic efficiency than those of the politicians."[111] This argument had been disputed by other scholars based on later research on corporate governance of privatized Russian firms that had led to a conclusion that "crooks are no better than politicians."[112]

Indeed, if the assertion that Russia today has achieved the goal of depoliticizing private businesses, one has to be very creative in explaining the following realities in post-privatization Russia, which are certainly not to be

---

108. Galina G. Preobragenskaya & Robert W. McGee, "Corporate Governance in a Transition Economy: A Case Study of Russia," paper presented at the Annual Conference of Academy of International Business, Clearwater, Florida, November 13–14, 2003 [unpublished].

109. See Gustafson, *supra* note 95, p. 50.

110. Black, Kraakman & Tarassova, *supra* note 37, p. 1750.

111. Boycko, Shleifer & Vishny, *supra* note 82, p. 121.

112. Black, Kraakman & Tarassova, *supra* note 37, p. 1789.

found in a better institutional environment conducive to genuine growth and prosperity: (a) the still pervasive intervention of politicians with privatized firms through various channels other than direct subsidies; (b) the still excessive administrative barriers and red tape that distort the incentives and activities of small business; and (c) the suspicious new alliance of oligarchs with politicians through controversial political finances.

To sum up, because by and large there had been no genuine restructuring taking place in Russian insider controlled firms, the proclaimed goals of privatization, including depoliticization of firms and creating a vibrant private sector, were not achieved. As is widely understood, the very purpose of privatization goes beyond the mere dismantling of state sector dominance in the economy (a "destructive" process); its essential task is to create a new form of competitive firm that can operate efficiently and make profits (a "creative" process). Viewing Russian privatization from this perspective, one can see that the impressive speed and scale with which firms were sold off did not guarantee the emergence of "real owners" with the incentives to monitor managers and the resource to enforce property rights. Given the regrettable results of too much "shock" and too little "therapy" in Russia's "big-bang" privatization, one would wonder if it turned out to have offered a modern vindication of Edmund Burke's judgment made two centuries ago: destructive revolutions often come to bad ends.[113]

7.3.9 **The primary lesson from Russian privatization**

The main result of Russia's mass and rapid privatization was to turn over mediocre assets to people lacking the incentives, skills and resources to manage them well, or to distribute high-quality assets to the resourceful and well-connected few who tended not to embark on restructuring of the acquired firms that might have justified their acquisition of the assets. Privatized firms typically performed not much better than the remaining state-owned enterprises. Thus, Kenneth Arrow called Russian privatization "a predictable economic disaster".[114]

Based on such grim results, the primary lesson from Russia's privatization is clear: in an institutional vacuum, privatization can lead and had led to stagnation and decapitalization rather than to better financial results and increased efficiency.[115] Some Russian economists concluded that "mass and rapid privatization approach was wrong," that it "should have been preceded (not accompanied) by institution-building," such as the eseablishment of an efficient

---

113. Edmund Burke, *Reflection on the Revolution in France* (Thomas H.D. Mahoney ed., Liberal Arts Press, 1955), cited in Black, Kraakman & Tarassova, *supra* note 37, p. 1803.

114. Nellis, *supra* note 84, p. 9.

115. *Ibid.*, p. 17.

corporate governance regime, prudential regulation for financial and capital markets, and effective insolvency or bankruptcy regimes. All were then too weak or simply lacking in Russia.[116]

As many scholars have pointed out, institution-building is an essential element in economic transformation. For example, an influential empirical study of Russian privatization concludes: "Economic revolutions that destroy existing institutions before new ones can be built are likely to founder, as those without scruples take advantage of the resulting institutional vacuum."[117] In post-privatization Russia, a self-enforcing model of corporate governance regime did not accomplish much, precisely because the institutional vacuum had rendered corporate law powerless in the face of massive self-dealing.[118] Therefore, multiple legal, institutional and microeconomic reforms are badly needed in Russia to improve corporate governance, such as effective mechanisms to control corruption, a strong securities market and independent courts.[119]

7.4 **Summary**

Section 7.4 summarizes both the lessons that China should learn from the international experience in corporate governance reforms and the possibility of the Chinese experience in informing ongoing debates in comparative corporate governance. Two points are of particular importance.

7.4.1 **Political determinants of corporate governance and legal and institutional perspectives on corporate governance are of particular significance to China**

China's enterprise and corporate governance reforms have followed a gradualist approach whereby mass privatization had not become a favorable policy option until recently, especially before China's accession to the WTO. This is primarily because when the transition was at an early stage, the political, economic and institutional environments posed huge challenges to radical and rapid reform.

---

116. *Ibid.*, p. 9 and pp. 16–17.
117. Black, Kraakman & Tarassova, *supra* note 37, p. 1803.
118. Bernard S. Black & Anna S. Tarassova, "Institutional Reform in Transition: A Case Study of Russia," 10 *Supreme Court Economic Review* 211 (2003). In this paper, the authors amended some of the early (positive) hypotheses about corporate governance in Russia made in 1996, when Bernard Black was advising Russia to draft a self-enforcing corporate law for Russian privatized firms. According to his later research, the law had been ineffective due to the lack of institutional constraints on massive self-dealing. See Bernard Black & Reinier Kraakman, "A Self-Enforcing Model of Corporate Law," 109 *Harvard Law Review* 1911 (1996).
119. Black & Tarassova, *ibid.*, p. 211.

The political considerations behind the continuing state ownership and control in China's partially privatized state sector, such as retaining an ability of the state to control employment and labor policies, should not be dismissed on the sole basis of economic efficiency. Over the course of seeking practical and workable initiatives under the existing political constraints, even after China's accession to the WTO, sequencing and pacing should continue to play a major role in implementing privatization and corporate governance reform. In the meantime, after China's accession to the WTO, more flexibility of transition strategies is also needed. This requires an accelerated speed of reform and complementary reform initiatives in related sectors, including the SOE, banking and securities sectors.

For China, legal and institutional reforms aimed at establishing market mechanisms and promoting a sound environment for the private sector to grow and compete on an equal footing with state enterprises are necessary conditions for successful corporate governance reform in both the SOE and banking sectors. Russia provided a negative example of rushed privatization in an institutional vacuum and this lesson should be learned by China. In addition, legal and institutional reforms need to address the "politics" behind them, which has a potentially blocking effect due to the attempt by vested interests to slow or hinder reforms for fear of losing their existing benefits and entrenched advantages. In many developing as well as transition economies, some incompetent judges and state monopolies in strategic industries are the most likely opponents to legal and institutional reforms. China should take the "politics" of reform seriously and address it sensitively during its legal and institutional reforms in order to establish sound foundations for the market. "Bribing/buying" the interest groups in exchange for their consent to reform through allocating more benefits of reform to them, or promoting competing forces in the national economic system that are supportive of reform, such as private entrepreneurs, are possible solutions.

7.4.2 A cautious note on the prospects of global convergence of corporate governance

As revealed by the experience of both Russia and China in their respective enterprise and corporate governance reforms, without establishing (if possible) complementary mechanisms, convergence of corporate governance systems in transition economies toward the U.S. model is not likely to succeed in bringing about the same effect which this model has had in its home market. Moreover, because it is very difficult for a reforming country to transplant from a host country systemic complementarities in corporate governance mechanisms and institutions without at the same time weakening or losing their original functions, the prospects for convergence, at least for transition economies, are still uncertain.

China has encountered this difficulty of convergence in experimenting with a hybrid corporate governance model that combines main features of both the U.S. model and the OECD *Priaciples of Corporate Governance.* China's *Code of Corporate Governance for Listed Companies* was intended to bring global best practices to its domestic firms. However, judged by empirical evidence of how Chinese firms have performed so far, this attempt at legal and institutional transplantation has only yielded limited results. This experience suggests that the convergence possibility may still be limited in the Chinese context of corporate governance reform, given the identified legal and institutional deficits (or a "governance gap") at the present stage of development. Therefore, while China needs to take into account internationally accepted standards and principles of corporate governance in its domestic reform, local solutions that may not be in conformity with international best practices, but which still serve as a second-best choice at a particular stage, should be accepted and adjusted later as the country's economic and institutional conditions both improve.

8

Conclusion

Chapter 8 concludes by reiterating the central argument of this book and the major findings in preceding chapters that support it. Chapter 8 also suggests the broad implications of China's experience for developing and transition economies in their pursuit of corporate governance reform and economic growth.

8.1 The Central Argument of This Book

This book proposes a dynamic theory of corporate governance which applies to transition economies — particularly, China — committed to a process of gradualism in legal and institutional reforms, as opposed to "big bang"-type reforms favoured by other commentators which have had mixed-to-poor results in Central and Eastern Europe. The proposed dynamic theory of corporate governance emphasizes the merits of sequencing, pacing, and complementarity of structural reforms in the SOE, banking, and securities sectors in an economy in transition from central planning to the market.

Specifically, the proposed dynamic theory of corporate governance sheds light on the merits, as well as limits, of "transitional" or "second-best" institutions adopted by China during its transition under a gradualist strategy. This gradualist strategy is in contrast to the "shock therapy" strategy for mass and rapid privatization undertaken in Russia, whereby necessary legal and institutional reforms that should have preceded or complemented privatization were missing, and the subsequent delinquencies in corporate governance of privatized firms and capital market regulation had resulted in widespread insider dealing, asset stripping and managerial abuses of shareholder rights.

In China's context, the "transitional institutions" are imperfect and not fully consistent with market basics, yet nevertheless efficiency-enhancing at the early stages of China's economic reform as stepping-stones toward the market under legal and institutional constraints. At later stages of the transition, these transitional institutions should be subject to adjustment or abandonment, such as government ownership and control of township and village enterprises or TVEs, which have been widely replaced by private ownership since the mid-1990s.

8.2   Re-interpreting "Gradualism" with Respect to Corporate Governance Reforms and Related Financial Reforms in a Transition Economy

There are three dimensions of the meaning and implications of "gradualism," the key concept discussed in this book. First, it refers to sequencing and pacing of reform initiatives under existing legal and institutional constraints in an economy in transition. Second, "gradualism" also requires complementarity and synergies between mutually supporting and contingent legal and institutional reforms. Third, "gradualism" is compatible with self-adaptability and self-adjustability in the process of corporate governance reforms and financial market development, which stresses the functions of "transitional" or "second-best" institutions designed to accommodate a country's existing legal and institutional environments in its early stages of transition, as opposed to a "convergence" approach which favors importing overseas experience or "international best practices" from mature market economies.

Measured against the three dimensions of "gradualism," one important clarification of the gradualist strategy adopted by China is that necessary structural reforms in China's enterprise, banking and securities sectors need not be "slow" or always subject to protracted delay regardless of changes in China's institutional environment as its transition proceeds. Rather, the sequencing and pacing of reforms can be self-adaptive by adopting an accelerating pace of reform at later stages of the country's transition, especially after China's accession to the WTO, which has made the need for deeper and broader structural reforms more urgent.

Another necessary clarification of "gradualism" discussed in this book is that in terms of appropriate approaches toward initiating and implementing reform schemes, developing and transition economies need to take into account the limits of legal and institutional transplantation. On the one hand, it might be tempting for these economies to import legal rules and institutional arrangements from advanced market economies in the process of their corporate governance reforms and financial market development. On the other hand, a critical constraint on such "convergence" approach is that without establishing necessary complementary institutions that support the proper functioning of the imported institutions in their home countries, any attempt at transplanting advanced experience from overseas is likely to produce limited results at best, and complete failure at worst, or even unintended consequences that may be the opposite of what was intended.

What is more, this constraint on convergence not only applies to developing economies trying to import "global best practices" from mature market economies, but can also be the case among developed economies as well. As illustrated in the controversy over Japan's recent effort to amend its corporate law to establish the Anglo-American type of rules on M&As (mergers and acquisitions), particularly on hostile takeovers, mature market economies cannot effectively transplant from each other otherwise workable corporate governance institutions without also establishing necessary complementary conditions. For example, Japan's latest attempt at importing the "poison pill" mechanism from the U.S. and U.K. capital markets without also importing necessary supporting institutions, such as judicial review of business judgments, the fiduciary duty of the boards of directors toward shareholders and shareholder litigation mechanisms, was harshly criticized by some economists as "imitating much of what is wrong with Anglo-American corporate governance."[1]

As to necessary legal and institutional reforms that should precede or complement privatization, they primarily relate to a country's reform efforts aimed at providing investors with strong protection and ensuring the proper functioning of basic market mechanisms, such as reforms in the banking sector and securities markets to introduce higher efficiency in resource allocation, to control financial fraud and corruption, and to curb insider dealings, asset stripping and managerial abuses.

Moreover, the "changing institutional environment" in an economy in transition refers primarily to situations where both market mechanisms and private ownership, which were underdeveloped or weak at early stages of reform, have evolved to the extent that continuing adoption of transitional or "second-best" institutions is no longer efficient, and more market-oriented institutions and an effective legal system based on an independent and competent judiciary are needed to replace the "stepping stones" toward a full market economy.

8.3   A Summary of Major Findings in This Book

The following text offers a brief summary of major findings in this book with regard to the experiences of both China and Russia in their respective

---

1. "Shaking Up Corporate Japan," *The Economist*, March 23, 2005.

enterprise, financial and corporate governance reforms during transition from a command economy to a market economy.

8.3.1 China

China's schemes of corporate governance reforms and related financial reforms have been implemented in three important sectors. Accordingly, this book presents these three major applications of the dynamic theory of corporate governance to China: (a) corporate governance reforms of China's state-owned enterprises or SOEs, township and village enterprises or TVEs and private enterprises; (b) reforms of the stockmarket and corporate governance of listed companies (including partially privatized SOEs and private enterprises); and (c) banking reform. The following summary is intended to highlight the respective effects of these reforms and lessons that should inform future reforms.

Corporate governance reforms of major types of China's enterprises, including SOEs, TVEs, and private enterprises

Corporate governance reforms of major types of Chinese enterprises, including SOEs, TVEs and private enterprises, have presented a unique perspective on the dynamics of transition under legal and institutional constraints. In general, the empirical review presented in this book offers a support for ownership reform aimed at expanding private ownership in the competitive sectors of the national economy. However, corporate governance reforms in China have also encountered a number of challenges, especially those attributable to legal and institutional constraints. This pattern of reform signals the need for a gradualist strategy. Some general conclusions can be drawn:

(a) The "politics" of economic reform and the underdevelopment of legal and institutional environments are the major determinants of a gradualist approach to corporate governance reforms in China.

(b) There has been a considerable distance between "design on paper" and "implementation on the ground" of corporate governance reforms in China. On the one hand, the deficiency or ineffectiveness in local enforcement of certain centrally mandated reform policies is both a reflection of the "central-local relationship" where interests at different levels of government diverge during the transition. On the other hand, local innovations and experiments with pilot programs are also an important source of new understanding of institutional development at the central level.

(c) Corporate governance reforms in China, in particular ownership transformation through privatization of SOEs, have produced positive results in terms of efficiency improvements, but also contributed to inequality between different social groups and regions. Therefore, the balance of "efficiency" and "equality" needs to be addressed to reduce social resistance and discontent that could hamper China's successful transition to the market.

(d) Transitional institutions can serve as "second-best" solutions to the building of efficient corporate governance structures at the early stages of reform. However, these transitional institutions needed to be promptly adjusted to meet new challenges when transition has proceeded to the next stages and the institutional environment has evolved.

(e) In reforming China's business sector, it is crucial to avoid the danger of falling into a "bad (crony) market economy." Some worrying signs of the state intervening in the business of the market during the process of corporate governance reforms in both the SOE and private sectors, such as using public power for private gains, must be taken seriously if China is to build a truly competitive enterprise sector and complete a successful transition to the market.

Stockmarket reform and corporate governance reform of listed companies

As to the reforms of China's stockmarket and corporate governance of Chinese companies listed on both domestic and overseas capital markets, the subjects of examination include partially privatized SOEs, particularly state monopolies, as well as private enterprises.

The sequencing of China's capital market reform and corporate governance reform of listed companies primarily concerns a policy shift from "borrowing" legal, financial, and corporate governance institutions from overseas (i.e., "piggy-backing" through overseas listings of Chinese firms), to "building" such institutions at home. While "borrowing" good institutions from overseas generated significant benefits at early stages of China's transition, this strategy had become no longer sustainable. At later stages of the transition, accelerated structural reforms are necessary for both China's own sake in building a full market economy, and for avoiding the "spill over" effect of China's poor domestic institutions across borders. The "spill over" effect is likely to be brought about by spectacular corporate governance failures of Chinese companies listed overseas, given the country's rapid integration into the world economy.

Another critical issue concerning sequencing in the reforms of China's stockmarket and corporate governance of Chinese listed companies is the challenge of searching for an effective solution to the problem of a split share structure identified with the division of tradable and non-tradable shares, which has been widely recognized among China's policy and academic circles as the most significant cause of the deficiencies in the institutional structure of China's stockmarket. The basic conclusion of this book on the solution to the split share structure is that making non-tradable shares tradable and therefore dismantling the inefficient share structure in the stockmarket, which usually results in poor corporate governance practices of listed companies, should be a top priority on the reform agenda of the government at the new stage of China's transition. The success of this critical task is a necessary precondition for other reform initiatives aimed at improving the operational quality of the stockmarket to generate real results.

By contrast, compared to the urgency of abolishing the split share structure, immediate removal of restrictions on foreign entry into China's stockmarket may not be considered a top priority in the sequencing of future reforms. While expanded entry of both foreign capital and financial institutions is necessary for enhancing competition in China's stockmarket, which should improve its operational quality, this assumed or asserted benefit of greater financial liberalization is subject to a critical limitation in the Chinese context — the slowness in the progress of reform of China's exchange rates and interest rates regimes. Specifically, the lagging progress in reforming or modernizing China's currency and interest rates regimes leaves much room for speculative foreign capital to bet on the re-evaluation of the yuan if free from entry restrictions, and therefore makes the full opening up of China's capital markets a much less urgent issue on the government's reform agenda. The primary concern of the government is that a systemic financial crisis could be engendered by abrupt capital inflows or outflows, when China's foreign exchange and interest rates regimes have yet to introduce higher levels of market-oriented reforms and liberalization.

Banking reform

The specific issue of sequencing involved in the process of China's banking reform is highlighted in the ongoing debate in China's policy and academic circles over the appropriate approach toward reforming the "big four" state-owned commercial banks plagued by both non-performing loans and corruption.

On the one hand, some Chinese economists and foreign commentators have argued that China's banking reform should adopt an approach of "cleaning house first, going public overseas second," which prioritizes corporate governance reform to strengthen internal controls and curb financial corruption over overseas listings. On the other hand, other economists have advocated an alternative strategy, which sees overseas listings as an external lever to propel corporate governance reform and greater competition in the banking sector. The latter position on the sequencing of banking reform presents a rationale for accelerated financial reforms at later stages of China's transition, which is similar to China's primary motivation in joining the WTO in 2001, i.e., to obtain an external lever to precipitate deeper and broader structural reforms when domestic conditions, especially the political will, were not fully receptive to such advances.

In light of this debate over the sequencing of China's banking reform, the basic judgment of this book is more in line with the latter position, i.e., pursuing overseas listings as a strategy for achieving external stimuli for otherwise reluctant or difficult reforms under existing political and institutional constraints. While it is uncertain how long and how much resource it will take to achieve meaningful results in domestic corporate governance reform and anti-corruption initiatives in China's banking sector (i.e., "cleaning house"), the urgency of preparing China's banks for greater competition from overseas financial institutions under the country's WTO commitments is clear. More critically, the complementary role of banking reform in helping achieve positive results in China's enterprise and stockmarket reforms provides an even stronger rationale for seeking overseas listings even if the banks are not yet independent commercial lenders and efficient resource allocators. It is widely held by many Chinese economists that external pressures from international investors and regulators could propel or force fundamental banking reforms at home, which may otherwise be off the government's reform agenda because these reforms will be painful and unavoidably bring about massive adjustments in the national economy.

Meanwhile, although overseas listings are *necessary* for creating incentives to perform and compete in China's banking sector, they are not *sufficient* to bring about good corporate governance, effective internal controls, and significant reduction of corruption. Rather, domestic reform initiatives to build good legal, financial and corporate governance institutions should proceed simultaneously with overseas listings to best utilize and capitalize on the benefits of good institutions and much tighter discipline provided by overseas markets, as indicated by the experience of Chinese companies listed overseas.

8.3.2 **Russia**

The spread of privatization programs around the world has been propelled by the inefficiency of state-owned firms and the resulting search for significant improvements in performance. However, there have been disappointments, particularly in the transition economies in Central and Eastern Europe. For example, "squandering and diversion of resources by political actors have often been replaced by squandering and diversion of resources by private actors," as Russia's experience with mass and rapid privatization demonstrated, whereby insider dealings, asset stripping and managerial abuses became rampant in an institutional vacuum due to the lack of legal and institutional arrangements to effectively protect shareholders.[2] Disappointments in these countries have raised a new question: how to ensure that privatization produces benefits.[3] As suggested by this book, pursuing necessary legal and institutional reforms that

---

2. World Bank, *World Development Report 2002: Building Institutions for Markets* (Oxford: Oxford University Press, 2002), p. 59.
3. *Ibid.*

should precede or complement privatization under a gradualist strategy is a better approach to the market, at least for some economies.

Most importantly, this book reviews existing evidence in academic research of the clear gap between the intended merits of a "big bang"-type transition as a "less reversible" approach to the market, and the mixed-to-poor results of mass and rapid privatization in Central and Eastern Europe, and in particular Russia's failure in implementing successful privatization under the "shock therapy" strategy.

On the one hand, the asserted benefits of "less reversible" reforms lacked convincing empirical evidence, as unsuccessful privatization may have actually generated added costs of redressing the missteps in previously implemented mass and rapid privatization schemes by "reversing" reform outcomes, such as the re-nationalization of previously privatized firms and state prosecution of private entrepreneurs on corruption and economic fraud grounds. The recent Yukos case was a dramatic example of how an ill-executed privatization scheme can cost both investors and the firm greatly if the government later pursued a "redress" policy. Yukos, a privatized oil company and formerly Russia's biggest oil exporter, was virtually re-nationalized in 2004 by the Russian government, and its former CEO and biggest shareholder, Mikhail Khodorkovsky, was facing criminal charges of theft of state assets, tax evasion and misappropriation.

On the other hand, "big bang"-type approaches are not the only alternative to achieve the goal of making market-oriented reforms less reversible. As China's experience in actively pursuing its membership in the WTO demonstrates, voluntarily opening up to greater liberalization of international trade in goods and services and actively participating in the world economy can produce similar incentives and stimuli for a transition economy to make commitments to "less reversible" market-oriented reforms.

8.4 The Broad Implications of China's Gradualist Strategy for Corporate Governance Reforms and Related Financial Reforms for Developing and Transition Economies

There are broader implications of China's experience in corporate governance reforms and related financial reforms for development, especially for developing and transition economies seeking to achieve economic growth under existing legal and institutional constraints. It is also important to note that there are both positive and negative lessons from China. These broader implications are summarized bellow.

8.4.1 Building market-supporting institutions is important for transition economies

During the transition from centrally planned economies to market economies, new market-supporting institutions must be created, which is a highly complex and unpredictable process.[4] In particular, if privatization precedes legal and institutional reforms, self-dealing and wealth destruction through asset stripping and stealing could lead to serious economic consequences in an institutional vacuum. This requires a sensible allocation of limited political capital in transition economies, which raises the challenge of sensible priority setting under information and political constraints.

8.4.2 Successful institutional development needs appropriate sequencing

During the process of transition, an institutional vacuum should be avoided. China's "dual-track" reforms have demonstrated the necessity of allowing the old or existing institutions continue to function, before new institutions can finally develop out of the transforming social, economic, and political settings.[5] The lack or mishandling of sequencing, as was the case in Russian privatization, could lead to disastrous social and economic consequences.

8.4.3 "Sensible, but imperfect" transitional institutions can promote economic growth

China's transition experience provides economists with a valuable source of information for new thinking on institutional changes that is different from neo-classical economics. One such example is the role of "sensible, but imperfect" transitional institutions in promoting economic growth.

As China's transition experience has shown, some transitional institutions can be more effective than best-practice institutions *for a period of time*. The need to adopt these institutions is determined by the fact that market-supporting institutions need adequate human capital that can enforce them, which will take years to develop in transition economies, at least at the early stage of their

---

4. John McMillan & Barry Naughton, "How to Reform a Planned Economy: Lessons from China," in Ross Garnaut & Yiping Huang (eds.), *Growth Without Miracles: Readings on the Chinese Economy in the Era of Reform* (New York: Oxford University Press, 2001), pp. 459-460.

5. Yingyi Qian, "The Institutional Foundation of China's Market Transition," in Boris Pleskovic & Joseph Stiglitz (eds.), *Annual World Bank Conference on Development Economics* (World Bank, 2000), p. 395.

reforms.[6] The role of transitional institutions, therefore, is best understood as the "stepping stones" toward a full market economy. When growth has been sustained and stabilized, it will generate sufficient economic and social resources to support more difficult reform programs, and also help strengthen the political will to pursue a more challenging and advanced reform agenda. At this stage, it is both desirable and necessary for a transition economy to move forward by adopting best-practice institutions, such as the rule of law and a well-defined property rights system, as the previously efficient transitional institutions become inefficient and eventually wither away or vanish.

8.4.4   China's gradualist approach to transition may not work, or work as well as with China, in other transition economies under different institutional conditions. In other words, there is no "one-size-fits-all" solution to successful transition and institutional development

As shown in its enterprise and corporate governance reforms, China's transition approach is characterized as "crossing the river by feeling for the stones" or "*mozhe shitou guohe*" and inherently rejects the "big bang" strategy that neo-classical economists regard as the only way to avoid the "partial reform trap" by rendering reforms "less reversible." The "partial reform trap" is a term used frequently by shock therapists, who had warned that if reform was not conducted in a swift and comprehensive manner, there will likely be a reversal of transition by the remnants of the old planning system.[7] Contrary to this prediction, China has not fallen into the "partial reform trap," and has also managed to make its reforms "less reversible" by actively participating in the global economy.

One crucial paradox of the "big bang"-type reforms has not received adequate attention: the impediments to planning a comprehensive reform strategy are similar to the impediments to planning the economy. The problem confronting designers of the "big-bang"-type reforms was the same information barrier faced by planners. Logically, designers of "big bang"-type reforms needed to know a great deal of information to decide on many specific schemes and initiatives, which was a very difficult task. Arguably, it would be easier to make such decisions on a piecemeal basis than to address them all at once.[8] Therefore, the case for gradualism seems to have another rationale from the perspective of informational constraints on reformers.

However, that gradualism has worked in China has largely depended upon the evolutionary and path-dependent nature of its institutional development,

---

6.   *Ibid.*, p. 394.
7.   See McMillan & Naughton, *supra* note 4, p. 459; Joel S. Hellman, "Winners Take All: The Politics of Partial Reform in Postcommunist Transitions," 50 *World Politics* 205 (1998).
8.   McMillan & Naughton, *supra* note 4, p. 469.

which means that other transition economies may not find the Chinese pattern of "piecemeal social engineering" suitable for their own institutional environments.[9] In this sense, the most important contribution of comparative research on transition economies may not be to inspire countries to *copy successful schemes*, but to *avoid mistakes* already made.

The major implication here is that the path toward a market economy is not a universal, "one-size-fits-all" set of prescriptions. Diverse approaches are possible. Therefore, policymakers must accommodate country-specific conditions, especially "initial conditions," in designing their countries' transition strategies.[10]

In summary, there are alternative paths to the market and transition, not necessarily all consistent with or similar to China's approach, which certainly has delayed some important reforms and policy changes, as reflected most notably in the slowness of China's political and government reforms. As this book suggests, the inherent contradiction between China's market-oriented economic reform and its still rigid political regime has contributed to some serious problems in its stockmarket and banking sector, such as the political logic of the stockmarket and the accumulation of non-performing loans at the "big four" state banks. This disparity in the progress of China's economic and political reforms has also heightened the risk of its falling into a track of a "bad (crony) market economy," if the state intervention in the economy does not withdraw or contract in the future and public powers continue to enter the market for rent-seeking opportunities and private profits.

---

9. The notion of "piecemeal social engineering" came from Karl Popper, which means that social evolution allows the designing of many *ad hoc* solutions for specific problems, and human ends can be achieved through small adjustments which can be continually improved upon. Karl Raimund Popper, *The Poverty of Historicism* (London: Routledge, 1957), p. 61.

10. Qian, *supra* note 5, p. 394.

Appendices

Appendix 1   Abbreviations

ABC	Agricultural Bank of China
ACFIC	All-China Federation of Industry & Commerce
ADB	Asian Development Bank
ALI	American Law Institute
AMC	asset management company
BoC	Bank of China
BoCom	Bank of Communications
BOT	build-operate-transfer
CACG	Commonwealth Association for Corporate Governance
CAO	China Aviation Oil
CAR	capital adequacy ratio
CASS	China Academy of Social Sciences
CBRC	China Banking Regulatory Commission
CCB	China Construction Bank
CEO	chief executive officer
CIA	Comparative Institutional Analysis
CIRC	China Insurance Regulatory Commission
CLSA	Credit Lyonnais Securities Asia
CPI	Corruption Perception Index
CSR	corporate social responsibility
CSRC	China Securities Regulatory Commission
EMBA	Executive Master of Business Administration
EPS	earnings per share
ESA	employee shareholders association
FBI	Federal Bureau of Investigation
FCI	Financial Corruption Index

FDI	foreign direct investment
FIE	foreign-invested enterprise
GDP	gross domestic product
GEM	Growth Enterprise Market
HKD	Hong Kong Dollar
ICAC	Independent Commission Against Corruption
ICBC	Industrial and Commercial Bank of China
IIF	Institute of International Finance
ILO	International Labor Organization
IMF	International Monetary Fund
IPO	Initial Public Offering
IRRC	Institutional Investors Research Centre (of the United States)
LFS	loan-for-shares
LSE	London Stock Exchange
M&A	mergers and acquisitions
MBA	Master of Business Administration
MOF	Ministry of Finance
MBO	management buyout
NASDAQ	National Association of Securities Dealers' Automated Quotations
NCE	New Comparative Economics
NPC	National People's Congress
NPL	non-performing loan
NSSF	National Social Security Fund
NYSE	New York Stock Exchange
OCC	Office of Currency Comptroller
OECD	Organization for Economic Cooperation and Development
OTC	over-the-counter
PBOC	People's Bank of China
P/E	price-earnings ratio
PORC	Public Offering Review Committee (of the CSRC)
PWC	PricewaterhouseCoopers
QDII	qualified domestic institutional investor
QFII	qualified foreign institutional investor
RBS	Royal Bank of Scotland
R&D	research and development
RMB	Renminbi
ROA	return on assets
ROE	return on equity
SAFE	State Administration of Foreign Exchange
SASAC	State-owned Assets Management and Administration Commission
SEHK	Stock Exchange of Hong Kong
SETC	State Economic and Trade Commission
SFC	Securities and Futures Commission (of Hong Kong)

SME	small and medium-sized enterprise
SOE	state-owned enterprise
SOX	Sarbanes-Oxley Act
S&P	Standard & Poor's
SPC	Supreme People's Court
TFP	total factor productivity
TVE	township and village enterprise
UK	United Kingdoms
UN	United Nations
U.S.	United States
USD	American Dollar
WHO	World Health Organization
WTO	World Trade Organization

Appendix 2   Chinese Government and Regulatory Agencies

China Banking Regulatory Commission (CBRC)
中國銀行業監督管理委員會；中國銀監會

China Insurance Regulatory Commission (CIRC)
中國保險監督管理委員會；中國保監會

China Securities Regulatory Commission (CSRC)
中國證券監督管理委員會；中國證監會

Central Huijin Investment Company Limited (Huijin)
中央匯金投資有限責任公司；匯金公司

Ministry of Finance (MOF)
財政部

Ministry of Supervision
監察部

National Audit Office
審計署

National People's Congress (NPC)
全國人民代表大會

People's Bank of China (PBOC)
中國人民銀行

Public Offering Review Committee (PORC of the CSRC)
股票發行審核委員會；發審委

State Administration of Foreign Exchange (SAFE)
國家外匯管理局

State Council
國務院

State-owned Assets Management and Administration Commission (SASAC)
國務院國有資產監督管理委員會;國資委

State Economic and Trade Commission (SETC)
國家經濟貿易委員會;經貿委

Supreme People's Court (SPC)
最高人民法院

Appendix 3   Chinese Terms

baozhuang shangshi (包裝上市)   going public through packaging less rotten assets

bo sha (搏傻)   to believe that there is someone more foolish than yourself in stock trading

chengbao jingying zerenzhi (承包經營責任制)   responsibility contract system

faren gu (法人股)   legal-person shares

fuye (輔業)   ancillary business(es)

ganqing (感情)   personal bonds

geren gu (個人股)   individual shares

guanxi (關係)   social connections, social relations

gugai (股改)   shareholding structure reform

guojia gu (國家股)   state shares

guojiutiao (國九條)   nine-point policy guideline released by the State Council on developing China's capital markets

hongding shangren (紅頂商人)   businesspeople wearing "red hats" (describing Chinese government officials or Communist Party cadres who hold corporate posts)

jianjinshi minyinghua (漸進式民營化)   gradual, step-by-step privatization

jiushi (救市)   to bail out stockmarket

lihao (利好)   positive news in stockmarket

likong (利空)   negative news in stockmarket

mianzi (面子)   sense of shame

minyinghua (民營化)   privatization

minying qiye (民營企業)   private enterprise

quan liutong (全流通)   full floatation of shares

quanqian (圈錢)   predatory, free-lunch style fund-raising

mozhe shitou guohe (摸著石頭過河)   crossing the river by feeling the stones

shuanggui zhi (雙軌制)   dual-track system; dual-track approach

wei guoqi jiekun (為國企解困)   save state-owned enterprises from financial difficulties

wenti fuhao (問題富豪)   tycoons with questionable origins of wealth

wulong zhishui (五龍治水)   five dragons fighting the flood (describing multiple government agencies splitting ownership and control rights in state-owned enterprises)

xiandai qiye zhidu (現代企業製度)   modern enterprise system

yigu duda (一股獨大)   dictatorship of one shareholder

yuanzui (原罪)   original sin

yuanzui fuhao (原罪富豪)   tycoons with original sin (describing Chinese rich businesspeople with questionable origins of wealth)

zhongguo tese de shehuizhuyi (中國特色的社會主義)   Socialism with Chinese characteristics

zhuada fangxiao (抓大放小)   grasp the large, release the small

zhuangjia (莊家)   sophisticated manipulators of share prices

zhuye (主業)   core business(es)

Appendix 4   Chinese Language Financial Newspapers and Journals

Caijing *(Caijing)*   財經

Caijing shibao *(China Business Post)*   財經時報

Diyi caijing ribao *(China Business News)*   第一財經日報

Er shi yi shiji jingji baodao *(21st Century Business Herald)*   21世紀經濟報導

Guoji jinrong bao *(International Finance News)*   國際金融報

Jingji guancha bao *(Business Watch)*   經濟觀察報

Jingji yuekan *(The Economics Monthly)*   經濟月刊

Liaowang dongfang zhoukan *(Oriental Outlook Weekly)*   瞭望東方週刊

Nanfang zhoumo (South Weekend) 南方週末

Nanfang ribao (South Daily) 南方日報

Renmin ribao (People's Daily) 人民日報

Shanghai zhengquan bao (Shanghai Securities News) 上海證券報

Shangwu zhoukan (Business Watch) 商務週刊

Souhu caijing (Sohu Caijing) 搜狐財經

Xinlang caijing (Sina Caijing) 新浪財經

Yazhou shibao zaixian (Asia Times Online) 亞洲時報在線

Yazhou zhoukan (Asia Weekly) 亞洲週刊

Zhengquan ribao (Securities Daily) 證券日報

Zhengquan shibao (Securities Times) 證券時報

Zhengquan shichang zhoukan (Securities Market Weekly) 證券市場週刊

Zhongguo jingji zhoukan (China Economic Weekly) 中國經濟週刊

Zhongguo xinwen zhoukan (China Newsweek) 中國新聞週刊

Zhongguo zhengquan bao (China Securities Journal) 中國證券報

Zhujiang shibao (Pearl River Times) 珠江時報

Appendix 5   Glossary

Agency problem   Also referred to as the principal-agent problem. In economics, agency problem points to the difficulties that arise from a conflict of interest under conditions of incomplete and asymmetric information when a principal hires an agent. The principal-agent problem is found in most employer/ employee relationships, for example, when shareholders hire top managers of corporations.

A-shares   Shares issued by listed companies on China's mainland stock exchanges in Shanghai and Shenzhen, which are denominated in Chinese currency *yuan* (RMB) and until November 2002 had been restricted to domestic investors. Since November 2002, foreign institutional investors that have obtained the joint approval by China Securities Regulatory Commission (CSRC), the People's Bank of China (PBOC) and the State Administration of Foreign Exchange (SAFE) can also trade A-shares with an allotted quota of funds. This is called the "qualified foreign institutional investors" (QFII) scheme.

Asian financial crisis   A period of financial crisis that erupted in East Asia during 1997-98, and raised fears of a worldwide economic meltdown. The crisis started in Thailand in July 1997 with the financial collapse of the local currency, Thai baht, caused by the decision of the Thai government to float the baht, cutting its peg to the USD. As the crisis spread, most of Southeast Asia and Japan experienced attacks on their currencies, devalued stockmarket and other assets prices, as well as a steep rise in private debt. Indonesia, South Korea and Thailand were most affected by the crisis. Hong Kong, Malaysia, Laos and the Philippines were also hurt by the devaluation of local currencies and assets. China, India, Taiwan, Singapore and Vietnam were less affected. It has been suggested that multiple factors were responsible for the eruption of the crisis. It is widely believed that the crisis was chiefly caused by financial market liberalization combined with a weak financial infrastructure and poor institutional foundations for investor protection, particularly poor corporate governance. By 1999, however, the economies in East Asia were beginning to recover.

Asset management company (AMC)   A company that invests its clients' pooled fund into securities that match its declared financial objectives. These companies earn income by charging service fees to their clients. Due to their larger pool of resources, asset management companies provide investors with more diversification and investing options than investors would have by themselves. Mutual funds, hedge funds and pension plans are all run by asset management companies.

Asset stripping   Selling the assets of a business individually at a profit. The term is generally used in a negative sense as such activity is not considered productive to the economy. Asset stripping is considered to be a problem in economies such as Russian or China that are making a transition to the market, where managers of a state-owned enterprise have been known to sell the assets which they control, leaving behind nothing but debts to the state.

Basel Accords   Refers to the banking supervision Accords (recommendations on banking laws and regulations), Basel I and Basel II issued by the Basel Committee on Banking Supervision (BCBS). They are called the Basel Accords as the BCBS maintains its secretariat at the Bank of International Settlements in Basel, Switzerland and the committee normally meets there.
Basel I refers to a round of deliberations by central bankers from around the world, which resulted in a set of minimal capital requirements for banks published in 1988 by the BCBS. Basel I is now widely viewed as outmoded, and a more comprehensive set of guidelines, known as Basel II are in the process of implementation by several countries. Basel II was initially published in June 2004. It aims at creating an international standard that banking regulators can use when creating regulations about how much capital banks need to put aside

to guard against the types of financial and operational risks banks face. Basel II sets up rigorous risk and capital management requirements designed to ensure that a bank holds capital reserves appropriate to the risk the bank exposes itself to through its lending and investment practices. Generally speaking, these rules mean that the greater risk to which the bank is exposed, the greater the amount of capital the bank needs to hold to safeguard its solvency and overall economic stability.

"Big four"   China's four state-owned commercial banks. They are Industrial and Commercial Bank of China (ICBC), China Construction Bank (CCB), Bank of China (BoC) and Agricultural Bank of China (ABC).

Blue chips   High-quality stocks of well-established companies which have stable earnings and no extensive liabilities. The term derives from casinos, where blue chips stand for counters of the highest value. Most blue chip stocks pay regular dividends, even when business is faring worse than usual.

Brokerage   A firm that acts as an intermediary between a purchaser and a seller. A brokerage is also referred to as a *brokerage firm*. A brokerage firm completes any necessary legal paperwork, obtains the appropriate signatures, and collects money from the purchaser to give to the seller. Since the buyer and seller are employing the brokerage to complete the deal, the brokerage may collect a portion of the money obtained. In some cases, a brokerage receives money from both parties. In others, the brokerage receives a commission only from the seller. Brokerage firms are most commonly thought of in relationship to the sale and purchase of stock shares.

B-shares   Hard currency-denominated shares in China's securities markets that are sold to foreigners — and since February 2001 also to domestic investors — but are mostly worthless. For some investors in the B-share market, a main reason for buying the "worthless shares" at all is their speculation that the now separate A-share and B-share markets will eventually converge, and when this finally happens they will make huge gains by selling these shares at much higher prices.

Buyer beware   Also referred to as *Caveat emptor.* This is a principle in commerce, meaning that without a warranty the buyer takes the risk and could not recover from the seller for defects on the property that rendered the property unfit for ordinary purposes. The only common exception is if the seller actively concealed latent defects.

Capital adequacy ratio (CAR)   The ratio which determines the capacity of a bank to meet its time liabilities and other risks such as credit risk and operational risk. It is expressed as a percentage of a bank's risk weighted credit exposures. This ratio is used to protect depositors and promote the stability and efficiency of financial systems around the world. Two types of capital are measured: tier one capital, which can absorb losses without a bank being required to cease trading, and tier two capital, which can absorb losses in the event of a winding-up and so provides a lesser degree of protection to depositors.

Capital structure   A mix of a company's long-term debt, specific short-term debt, common equity and preferred equity. A company's capital structure reflects how it finances its overall operations and growth by using different sources of funds. Debt takes the form of bond issues or long-term notes payable while equity is classified as common stock, preferred stock or retained earnings. Short-term debt, such as working capital requirements, is also considered to be part of the capital structure. When people refer to capital structure they are most likely referring to a company's debt-to-equity ratio, which provides insight into how risky a company is. Usually a company more heavily financed by debt poses greater risk, as this company is relatively highly leveraged.

Central state-owned enterprises (Central SOEs)   The largest SOEs in China under central government control, with the State-owned Assets Supervision and Administration Commission (SASAC) as their custodian. There were 155 of such enterprises as of July 2007. These enterprises are the subject of the "grasp the large" (*zhuada*) scheme whereby they are not subject to full privatization and the state owner retains control of these firms.

Chaebols   A Korean word which refers to a specific form of family-controlled business conglomerate in South Korea. It means "business group" or "trust." *Chaebols* maintained close connections with the government. *Chaebols* formed the core of South Korean economy in the 1960s and the success of the economy before the 1990s was largely dependent on the stability and prosperity of *Chaebols*. *Chaebols* started to decline in the mid-1990s when the Asian financial crisis erupted. The crisis exposed the weaknesses in South Korea's economy and the mismanagement within the *Chaebols*.

Coase Theorem   A concept used in law and economics discipline which is attributed to British economist Ronald Coase. This theorem states that when trade in an externality is possible and there are zero transaction costs, bargaining between parties will lead to an efficient outcome regardless of the initial allocation of property rights by law. This theorem, along with his 1937 paper on the nature of the firm (which also emphasizes the role of transaction costs), earned Coase the 1991 Nobel Prize in Economics.

Comparative Institutional Analysis (CIA)   A branch of scholarship in institutional economics. The CIA scholarship endorses the merits of institutional diversity and complementarities. It also suggests a path-dependent and evolutionary pattern of institutional development in a particular country. The CIA scholarship has made a salient contribution to inter-disciplinary research on development through its attempt at theorizing about the likely interactions between different patterns of institutional development in individual countries through regional and global economic integration. The CIA scholarship has been advanced largely by Masahiko Aoki, and is well theorized in his book, *Toward a Comparative Institutional Analysis* (MIT Press, 2001).

Corporate bond   A type of bond issued by a corporation. The term is usually applied to longer-term debt instruments, generally with a maturity date falling at least a year after their issue date. Corporate bonds are often listed on major exchanges and electronic communication networks (ECNs); the coupon (i.e., interest payments) is usually taxable. Despite being listed on exchanges, the vast majority of trading volume in corporate bonds in most developed markets takes place in decentralized, dealer-based, over-the-counter (OTC) markets.

Corporate social responsibility (CSR)   Also known as "corporate responsibility" or "corporate citizenship." A concept whereby corporations consider the interests of society by taking responsibility for the impact of their activities on customers, suppliers, employees, shareholders, communities and other stakeholders, as well as the environment.

Crony capitalism   A term describing an allegedly capitalist economy in which success in business depends on close relationships between businesspeople and government officials and those close to political policymakers receive favors allowing them to earn returns far above market value. It may be exhibited by favoritism in the distribution of legal permits, government grants, special tax breaks, and so forth. Crony capitalism is believed to arise when political cronyism (partiality to friends, especially by appointing them to positions of authority, regardless of their qualifications) spills over into the business world. Crony capitalism is widely considered as a fundamental feature of some economies in Latin America and East Asia.

Cross listing   A practice whereby a company lists its shares on one or more foreign stock exchange, in addition to its domestic exchange.

Curb credit market   Informal financing channels outside the formal banking system.

Delisting   The practice of removing the stock of a listed company from a stock exchange so that investors can no longer trade shares of the stock on that exchange. This typically occurs when a company goes out of business, declares bankruptcy, no longer satisfies the listing rules of a stock exchange, or has become a privately-held company after a merger or acquisition.

Directors and Officers (D&O) liability insurance   Insurance payable to the directors and officers of a company, or to the company itself, to cover damages or defense costs in the event they are sued for wrongful acts while they were with that company. Typical sources of claims include shareholders, shareholder-derivative actions, customers, regulators, and competitors (for anti-trust or unfair trade practice allegations). D&O insurance is usually purchased by the company itself, even when it is for the sole benefit of directors and officers, primarily for attracting and retaining senior management.

Dual listing   A practice whereby a company's securities are listed on more than one exchange for the purpose of adding liquidity to the securities (usually shares) and allowing investors a greater choice in where they can trade their shares.

Dual-track system   An approach of China's economic reform at early stages of transition in which the non-state sector gradually developed alongside the state sector. China began its reforms by permitting entry of non-state firms and state firms to sell outside the plan, while the old planning system was not immediately abolished but only vanished gradually. Markets then spread and gradually revealed inadequate institutional arrangements, thus pushing forward the process of marketization and institutional changes.

Emerging markets   A term coined in the 1980s by World Bank economist Antoine van Agtmael. It is sometimes loosely used as a replacement for *emerging economies*, which are considered to be in a transitional phase between developing and developed status. Examples of emerging markets include China, India, Pakistan, Mexico, Brazil, Chile, Colombia, Argentina, Peru, much of Southeast Asia, countries in Eastern Europe, the Middle East, parts of Africa and Latin America.

Financial depth   A measure of the quality of a country's financial infrastructure by the size of the formal financial intermediary sector, the relative importance of financial institutions and financial asset distribution.

Financial liberalization   A term that describes a process of legislative and regulatory procedures aimed at curbing the administrative constraints on the activities of banks and other financial institutions. It is an integrated part of a country's overall economic liberalization, with a specific objective to promote the role of the market and to minimize the role of the state in determining credit allocation. Proponents for financial liberalization in developing economies in an age of globalization emphasize the ultimate objective to accelerate the integration of a developing economy into the global market economy based on capitalism. The key components of financial liberalization include deregulation of interest rates, removal of credit control, privatization of government banks and financial institutions, relaxation of restrictions on the entry of private sector and/or foreign banks and financial institutions into domestic financial markets, introduction of market-based instruments of monetary control, and capital account liberalization.

Foreign direct investment (FDI)   The practice of a company from one country making a physical investment into building a factory in another country.

Golden parachute   A clause in an executive's employment contract specifying that he/she will receive large benefits in the event that the company is acquired and the executive's employment is terminated. These benefits can take the form of severance pay, a bonus, stock options, or a combination thereof.

Growth Enterprise Market (GEM)   An alternative stockmarket in Hong Kong established to provide growth enterprises to raise capital to develop and expand their businesses. Companies listed on the GEM do not have to fulfill the tighter requirements of profitability or track record imposed on issuers of the Main Board of the Stock Exchange of Hong Kong (SEHK).

Hang Seng China Enterprises Index   A freefloat capitalization-weighted index comprised of H-Shares listed on the Stock Exchange of Hong Kong and included in the Hang Seng Mainland Composite Index.

Hang Seng Index   A barometer of the Hong Kong stockmarket. The constituent stocks are grouped under Finance, Utilities, Properties and Commerce and Industry sub-indexes.

Hang Seng Composite Index   Aims to cover 90% of the market capitalization of stocks listed on the Main Board of the Stock Exchange of Hong Kong.

Hang Seng Mainland Composite Index   Constituents of the Hang Seng Composite Index which derive at least 50% of their sales revenue from mainland China.

"Helping hand" versus "grabbing hand"   The terms "grabbing hand" and "helping hand" refer to two different models of government in transition. These terms were first coined in Timothy Frye & Andrei Shleifer, "The Invisible Hand and the Grabbing Hand", 87:2 The American Economic Review 354 (1997), pp. 354-55. According to the authors, under the "helping hand" model, bureaucrats, though subjected to limited and organized corruption, are intimately involved in promoting private economic activity, while law plays a limited role. Under the "grabbing hand" model, government is not just as interventionist, but much less organized and more corrupt, than in the "helping hand" model, while predatory regulations are usually adopted to extract rents from private businesses. Russia is regarded as a typical example of the "grabbing hand" model, while Poland is considered in conformity with the "helping hand" model.

H-shares   Shares issued by companies incorporated in mainland China and approved by the CSRC for a listing in Hong Kong. The par value of the shares of these enterprises is denominated in RMB, and the shares are subscribed for and traded in HKD or other currencies. H-share companies are usually state-controlled entities, and many of them are state monopolies in strategic industries such as oil, telecommunications, steel, aviation, highway transportation, banking and insurance, even though competition is eroding their franchise.

Information asymmetry   A condition in which at least some relevant information is known to some but not all parties involved. Information asymmetry causes markets to become inefficient, since all the market participants do not have access to the information they need for their decision making. In economics and contract theory, information asymmetry deals with the study of decisions in transactions where one party has more or better information than the other. This creates an imbalance of power in transactions which can sometimes cause the transactions to go distorted. Typical consequences of information asymmetry are adverse selection and moral hazard.

Insider privatization   A method of privatizing state-owned enterprises through selling ownership stakes to enterprise insiders, including former managers and employees. In Russia, insider privatization was the primary means of transferring state assets to private hands during the transition process. Insider shareholding, particularly the controlling shareholding by managers, has become the dominant ownership structure of privatized firms in Russia.

Insider trading   The trading of a company's shares or other securities by individuals with potential access to non-public information about the company. In most countries, trading by corporate insiders, such as officers, employees, directors, and large shareholders, may be legal, if this trading is done in a way that does not take advantage of non-public information. However, the term is frequently used to refer to a practice in which an insider or a related party trades based on material non-public information obtained during the performance of the insider's duties at the company, or otherwise in breach of a fiduciary duty or other relationship of trust and confidence or where the non-public information was misappropriated from the company.

Internal control   A process designed to help an organization accomplish specific goals or objectives. At the organizational level, internal control objectives relate to the reliability of financial reporting, timely feedback on the achievement of operational or strategic goals, and compliance with laws and regulations.

Investment bank   A type of financial intermediaries that helps companies and governments raise money by issuing and selling securities in the capital markets (both equity and debt), as well as providing advice on transactions such as mergers and acquisitions.

Kleptocracy   A term applied to a government that extends the personal wealth and political power of government officials and the ruling class at the expense of the general public. A kleptocratic government not only often awards the prime contracts and civil service posts to relatives or personal friends of government officials rather than the most competent applicants, but also creates projects and programs at a policy level which serve the primary purpose of funneling money out of the treasury and into the pockets of the executive. Post-privatization Russia is regarded by analysts to have shown signs of a kleptocratic government.

Leverage　The amount of debt used to finance a firm's assets. A firm with significantly more debt than equity is considered to be highly leveraged.

Local state-owned enterprises (Local SOEs)　Chinese state-owned enterprises under local government control which are usually of small or medium size. These enterprises are the major concern under the "release the small" (*fangxiao*) scheme, which is aimed at introducing foreign and private capital into the ownership structures of these firms, which usually involves deeper ownership diversification or fuller privatization.

Lock-up period　A predetermined amount of time following an initial public offering (IPO) during which employees and close associates of the company who are given shares are not allowed to sell those shares.

Market capitalization　The total dollar market value of all of a company's outstanding shares. Market capitalization is calculated by multiplying a company's shares outstanding by the current market price of one share. Investors use this figure to assess a company's size and value. Also frequently referred to as "market cap."

Turnover rate　The volume of shares traded in a year as a percentage of total shares listed on a stock exchange, outstanding for an individual issue or held in an institutional portfolio.

Moral hazard　The risk that a party to a transaction has not entered into the contract in good faith, has provided misleading information about its assets, liabilities or credit capacity, or has an incentive to take unusual risks in a desperate attempt to earn a profit before the contract settles.

New Comparative Economics (NCE)　A branch of scholarship in institutional economics which argues for the centrality of institutional reforms to national economic performance. It also endorses institutional diversity within capitalist economies, with an emphasis on the "politics" of countries' institutional choices. The NCE is systematically articulated in Simeon Djankov *et al.,* "The New Comparative Economics", 31 Journal of Comparative Economics 595 (2003).

Non-performing loan (NPL)　A loan that is in default or close to being in default. According to the standard set by the IMF, a loan is non-performing when payments of interest and principal are past due by 90 days or more, or at least 90 days of interest payments have been capitalized, refinanced or delayed by agreement, or payments are less than 90 days overdue, but there are other good reasons to doubt that payments will be made in full.

Oligarch   A word which originally denotes the significant influence wealthy individuals may have on the life of a nation. In post-privatization Russia, it is very common to apply this term to any business tycoon, regardless of whether or not he or she has real political power. The term came into wide circulation after the collapse of the former Soviet Union, in reference to a small group of individuals who acquired tremendous wealth, significant political influence and often even have controlled mass media in some post-Soviet republics.

Over-the-counter (OTC) trading   Trading of financial instruments such as stocks, bonds, commodities or derivatives directly between two parties, as contrasted with trading on a formal exchange.

Path dependence   A phrase frequently used in institutional economics to explain how the set of decisions one faces for any given circumstance is limited by the decisions one has made in the past, even though past circumstances may no longer be relevant.

P-chips   Shares issued by Chinese private enterprises in overseas capital markets, especially in Hong Kong.

Piggy-backing   In connection with something larger or more important; a ride on the back and shoulders of another person. Used in this book to describe a pattern of practice by companies from one jurisdiction to list in an overseas jurisdiction with stricter securities regulation and better investor protection than in their home market.

Poison pills   A term originally referring to any strategy, generally in business or politics, to increase the likelihood of negative results over positive ones for a party that attempts any kind of takeover. In capital markets, this term specifically means a strategy used by a company to discourage a hostile takeover by another company through making its stock less attractive to the acquirer.

Price-earnings (P/E) ratio   A valuation ratio of a company's current share price compared to its per-share earnings. Calculated as: Market Value per Share/ Earnings per Share (EPS). For example, if stock A is trading at RMB24 and the earnings per share for the most recent 12 month period is RMB3, then stock A has a P/E ratio of 24/3 or 8.

Primary market   The market for new securities issues. In the primary market, the security is purchased directly from the issuer.

Qualified domestic institutional investor (QDII)   A scheme used in capital markets to allow financial institutions to have access to investments in offshore markets such as securities and bonds. Similar to QFII (Qualified Foreign Institutional Investor), it is a transitional arrangement which provides limited opportunities for domestic investors to access foreign markets at a stage where a country's or territory's currency is not traded or floated completely freely and where capital is not able to move completely freely in and out of the jurisdiction.

Qualified foreign institutional investor (QFII)   A scheme used in an economy which is at an early stage of financial liberalization to allow limited foreign participation in the holding and trading of stocks on domestic exchanges. In China, since November 2002, foreign institutional investors that have obtained the joint approval by the CSRC, the People's Bank of China and the State Administration of Foreign Exchange can also trade A-shares with an allotted quota of funds.

Quota system (of share offering)   A share issuing system used in China until 2001, which was first introduced when China's two stock exchanges were established in the early 1990s. One of the main purposes of the quota system was to limit the number of companies to be listed and the amount of shares to be issued. Under the quota system, local governments were responsible for the primary review of the qualifications of local firms for IPOs before they submitted their decisions to the CSRC for final approval. The central feature of the quota system was that it was driven by administrative considerations.

Red-chip companies   Companies with the following characteristics: (a) the companies have at least 30 percent shareholding held in aggregate by mainland China entities, and/or indirectly through companies controlled by them, with the mainland China entities being the single largest shareholders in aggregate terms, or (b) the shareholding of the company held in aggregate directly and/ or indirectly by mainland China entities is below 30 percent but is 20 percent or above and there is a strong influential presence, on a judgmental basis, of mainland China-linked individuals on the company's board of directors. Red-chip companies are largely controlled by private companies which registered parts of their businesses overseas (e.g., in the Virgin Islands) as listing vehicles to circumvent domestic regulatory approval requirements for overseas public listings, which apply to all H-share companies.

"Red hat" enterprises   A metaphor referring to a popular practice among Chinese private entrepreneurs in early years of reform, whereby private businesses were registered as rural collective enterprises or township and village enterprises (TVEs), with the consent of local governments (i.e., putting a "red hat" on the firm as a cover). The purpose of doing so was twofold. On the one hand, the entrepreneurs could avoid breaking the ideological taboo on overtly promoting private business and become qualified for business facilitations controlled by local governments, such as bank loans and technological support. On the other hand, by offering a "red hat," local governments could share a considerable portion of profits. A major drawback is that controversies over whether the "red hat" should amount to an "ownership investment" by the local governments have frequently arisen.

Registration system (of share offering)   A share issuing mechanism used in China that was introduced in 2001 to replace the quota system. The registration system was aimed at liberalizing the processes of IPO pricing and the review of listing qualifications previously controlled by regulators and administrative agencies, by introducing a more market-oriented screening system whereby the role of the CSRC was expected to be less substantive in judging firms' listing qualifications.

Related-party transaction   A business deal or arrangement between two parties who are joined by a special relationship prior to the deal. For example, a business transaction between a major shareholder and the corporation, such as a contract for the shareholder's company to perform renovations to the corporation's offices, would be deemed a related-party transaction.

Return on assets (ROA)   An indicator of how profitable a company is relative to its total assets. ROA gives an idea as to how efficient management is at using the company's assets to generate earnings. Calculated by dividing a company's annual earnings by its total assets, ROA is displayed as a percentage. Sometimes this is referred to as "return on investment."

Return on equity (ROE)   One of the most important financial ratios which measures a firm's efficiency at generating profits from every dollar of net assets (assets minus liabilities) and shows how well a company uses investment dollars to generate earnings growth. ROE is equal to a fiscal year's net income (after preferred stock dividends but before common stock dividends) divided by total equity (excluding preferred shares), expressed as a percentage and calculated as: Net Income/Total Equity.

Sarbanes-Oxley Act (SOX)   Also known as the ***Public Company Accounting Reform and Investor Protection Act of 2002***. It is a U.S. federal law, enacted on July 30, 2002 in response to a number of major corporate and accounting scandals, including those affecting Enron, Tyco International, Adelphia and WorldCom. SOX was named after sponsors Senator Paul Sarbanes and Representative Michel G. Oxley and signed into law by President George W. Bush, stating it included "the most far-reaching reforms of American business practices since the time of Franklin D. Roosevelt."

SOX establishes new or enhanced standards for all U.S. public company boards, management, and public accounting firms. SOX also establishes a new quasi-public agency, the Public Company Accounting Oversight Board (PCAOB), which is charged with overseeing, regulating, inspecting, and disciplining accounting firms in their roles as auditors of public companies. SOX also covers issues such as auditor independence, corporate governance, internal control assessment, and enhanced financial disclosure.

Secondary market   A market in which an investor purchases a security from another investor rather than the issuer, subsequent to the original issuance in the primary market.

Shareholder primacy   The notion that the interests of shareholders should come first in corporate decision making, putting aside or in a secondary order considerations for the interests of other stakeholders such as creditors and employees.

Share structure reform   A scheme of reform in China's stockmarket, starting in 2005, to make formerly non-tradable shares tradable. Under this reform, the minority shareholders holding tradable shares are paid a "consideration," in the form of cash or warrants, by controlling shareholders for the latter to obtain convertibility of their non-tradable shares.

Shock therapy   A term used in economics to refer to the sudden release of price and currency controls, withdrawal of state subsidies, and immediate trade liberalization within an economy, usually also including large scale privatization of previously public owned assets. Russia adopted a "shock therapy" strategy to implement its post-communist transition, particularly in pursuing mass and rapid privatization, which had resulted in some unfavorable social and economic consequences.

Sponsorship system (of share offering)   A share issuing system introduced to China's capital markets in February 2004. It was aimed at bringing in more market forces into the share issuing process, whereby a "sponsor," usually a brokerage firm, was to be responsible for supervising an IPO applicant for one year before making a listing recommendation to the CSRC. The sponsor must undertake certain monitoring responsibilities after it submits recommendation documents to the CSRC.

Strategic investor   An individual or institutional investor that adds value to the money being invested with the investor's contacts, experience, and knowledge of market.

Total factor productivity (TFP)   Addresses any effects in total output not caused by inputs or economies of scale. For example, a year with unusually good weather will tend to have higher output, because bad weather hinders agricultural output. A variable like weather does not directly relate to unit inputs, so weather is considered a total-factor productivity variable.

Transition economies   Economies which are changing from a centrally planned economy to a market economy. Transition economies undergo economic liberalization by letting market forces set prices and lowering trade barriers, macroeconomic stabilization where immediate high inflation is brought under control, and restructuring and privatization in order to create a financial sector and move from public to private ownership of resources.

Treasury bond (T-bond)   A marketable, fixed-interest U.S. government debt security with a maturity of more than 10 years. Treasury bonds make interest payments semi-annually and the income that holders receive is only taxed at the federal level.

Tobin's Q (or Tobin's q)   A measure of a firm's financial performance named after James Tobin, Yale University economist. It refers to the ratio of the market value of the firm's assets (as measured by the market value of its outstanding stock and debt) to the replacement cost of the firm's assets. A Tobin's Q ratio greater than 1 indicates that the firm has done well with its investment decisions.

Tradable shares/non-tradable shares   China's stockmarket has long been plagued by the problem of a split share structure whereby shares issued by listed companies were divided into tradable and non-tradable categories. The tradable shares were generally held by public investors, which accounted for about one-third of the outstanding shares. The non-tradable shares, which accounted for about two-thirds of the outstanding shares, were primarily held by the state and legal persons. Since 2005, a share structure reform (*gu gai*) started to make non-tradable shares tradable.

Underwriter   A type of financial intermediaries that administers the public issuance and distribution of securities from a company or other issuing body. An underwriter works closely with the issuing body to determine the offering price of the securities, buys them from the issuer and sells them to investors via the underwriter's distribution network. Underwriters generally receive underwriting fees from their issuing clients, but they also usually earn profits when selling the underwritten shares to investors. However, underwriters assume the responsibility of distributing a securities issue to the public. If they fail to sell all of the securities at the specified offering price, they may be forced to sell the securities for less than they paid for them, or retain the securities themselves.

Valuation   A term used in finance, meaning the process of estimating the market value of a financial asset or liability. Valuations are required in many contexts, including investment analysis, merger and acquisition transactions, financial reporting, taxable events to determine the proper tax liability, and in litigation.

"Wenzhou model"   A prize model of market-driven local growth at early stages of China's economic reform, identified with the experience of Wenzhou city, Zhejiang province. Under this growth model, the private sector was allowed to release its productivity and competitiveness, while subject to few policy and regulatory constraints by the local government during the early years of China's reform. The local government was very supportive in aiding the growth of private enterprises with regard to allocating factors of production, removing local red-tape and facilitating the cooperation between local businesses and external as well as foreign partners. In other words, the workings of the market were relatively undistorted and the private sector was left relatively autonomous to pursue business opportunities. This model has shown signs of decline in recent years as China's transition has progressed to an advanced stage.

Write-off (of bad debt)   A term used in banking to describe the accounting practice of removing from banks' balance sheets non-collectable debt, such as a loan on a defunct business or a credit card due that is now in default.

Index